The American Poet

Weedpatch Gazette

For 1993-1994

Samuel D. G. Heath, Ph. D.

iUniverse, Inc.
New York Bloomington

The American Poet
Weedpatch Gazette For 1993-1994

iUniverse books may be ordered through booksellers or by contacting:

iUniverse
1663 Liberty Drive
Bloomington, IN 47403
www.iuniverse.com
1-800-Authors (1-800-288-4677)

ISBN: 978-1-4401-5791-2 (sc)
ISBN: 978-1-4401-5792-9 (ebook)

Printed in the United States of America

iUniverse rev. date: 06/30/2009

Contents

Chapter one	1
Chapter two	27
Chapter three	52
Chapter four	77
Chapter five	120
Chapter six	169
Chapter seven	218
Chapter eight	243
Chapter nine	266
Chapter ten	291
Chapter eleven	316
Chapter twelve	340
About the Author	365

Chapter One

January

Matthew 19:13-15
Jeremiah 9:23,24

Well it seems I am either Right Wing or Conservative depending on which media source writes or talks about me. Media people and others who would like to be thought of as "liberal" know very well how the game is played and use adjectives accordingly.

I can only hope that I can focus attention on the primary reason for my campaign for the State Senate: saving our children and schools. I am acutely aware of the fact that this is a most difficult issue upon which you can try to get people to focus their attention. The Lord knows it has been proven to me time after time, that people or the leadership does not take such an issue seriously. The proof of this statement can be found by the very condition of the schools together with the apathetic response of the majority of the electorate. Friends have tried to dissuade me of making this my primary concern but I am adamant about it. My only hope is that people will begin to understand the principle of what is really at stake and that is nothing less than the very hope, soul and character of America!

I am not running against the other candidates. I assume they are capable and concerned men. Some, like Phil Wyman, I have met personally and he and Jim Costa have been on my mailing list for some time; they know my views very well. I am not running against these men; I am running for the sake of our children and grandchildren. Good as these other men may be, I suspect they will try to dodge the issue of the schools because of their own ignorance of what is to be done about it and no one wants to display their ignorance on such a vital issue.

This is not meant to be derogatory; we are all ignorant, just about different things. My main area of practical expertise is education. It happens that I believe this to be the most vital issue we must face in America. But I have to say that it would be patently dishonest if these other men, in an attempt to hide their ignorance, should try to make the campaign about the economy, for example, when the most obvious fact of all is that unless we turn education around there can be no hope whatsoever for the economy, let alone hope of a future for our nation and our young people.

It is my further hope that the media will help in making this a vital issue of the campaign. I have yet to see this happen but I know it can. If it does, and if the other candidates will enter a discussion of it, much good can be accomplished in bringing things into proper focus and priority. But, regarding the media, it is obvious that I will have to keep my wits about me.

For example, I am "racist," according to some when I discuss the problems of multiculturalism. Oddly, the "ethnic cleansing" by Jews, which is their history and present activity in Israel, is not labeled for the actual racism it represents by these same "some." And these same Jews have the gall to set up a howl in this nation at the slightest thing they can construe or distort as anti-Semitism? But if they are to play this dirty game of racism in their own nation, people like myself are not going to let their Xenophobia (their word) go unchallenged! Do they practice a double standard? Of course! Who said this battle for the Soul of America was anything but a dirty war?

In respect to the flap over the KKK putting up a cross in public in Cincinnati after Jews had put up a Menorah, where were the churches? Conspicuous by their absence! And who were those "Americans" who were "protecting" the symbol of Israel's racist Judaism and attempting to prevent the, legally sanctioned, setting up of America's non-racist Christian symbol? The whole thing makes as much sense as the recent attempt in San Francisco (where else?) by "good liberals" to overturn the conviction of a proven murderer, a Mr. Sandoval, on the grounds that the prosecutor had cited the Bible's injunction about capital punishment!

It makes me wonder; if Jews had attended the recent rededication of the Capitol in Alabama waving Israeli flags, whether those would have been confiscated as the police did of Confederate flags? I wonder, further, when the Gestapo will find the possession or display of the American flag by private citizens "unacceptable" because of its being "offensive" to "certain minorities!"

I'm glad I took the time and trouble to visit the Aryan Nations compound in Idaho and was able to sit down and talk with Richard Butler and Carl Franklin otherwise I wouldn't have the necessary background to read the recent article about Randy Weaver in The New American. The writer, a Mr. Fotheringham of the John Birch Society, contends that Richard Butler is playing a role in which an attempt is being made to discredit Idaho's conservatism to further his own agenda. But even the best of conservative information can be distorted and I have to wonder if Mr. Fotheringham's isn't a case in point.

While he doesn't say, I doubt if the writer had ever met Mr. Butler or talked to him personally as I took the trouble to do. I won't go so far as to say there is no truth in the writer's conclusions but I somehow doubt them. You don't really know a man unless you take the time to sit down with him eye-to-eye, each able to look into those "wells of the soul," and listen to what he has to say.

The quite lengthy article accuses Mr. Butler of "using" Randy Weaver. As we witness the "using" of those dispossessed Palestinians by both Israel and Lebanon, further, knowing the history of how Zionists sacrificed European Jews to their purpose, it makes for a plausible scenario. The weakness of such a scheme is the failure to consider the actual person accused: Mr. Butler.

Thus the truth of all history, of all understanding, is only derived from primary sources. So it is that accusations without such sources has to be suspect and might very well fail of their purpose when that is lacking. This is the reason that I have been adamant in my contention that even such disparate ideologies as those of Louis Farrakhan and me might find much common ground by frank and open, face-to-face discourse. But agreement on courses of action toward solutions which would avoid those Hitlerian ones could only be accomplished when the goals are set by Truth, Reason and Facts, not peculiar biases and prejudices. We are becoming an angry and frustrated nation and unless Reason, Truth and Facts are dealt with in the most candid and ruthless manner, we will fail of civilized solutions and our children and grandchildren will bear the tragic consequences of our failure.

The Battle of the Scrolls is heating up. You will remember my comments on this subject. Another case of "Who do you believe when interested parties are set on a course of hiding the truth?" I have to warn my readers once again, keep your eyes on this matter; the consequences of the outcome are incalculable. When you witness the Vatican and Zionists working in collusion, all kinds of red flags begin waving.

Speaking of which, the U.N. plans another "master-stroke" under the guise of "protecting" indigenous, minority peoples throughout the world. Seems, according to Worldwatch Institute, the assimilation of minority groups such as the Aborigines in Australia, etc. is a threat to the flora and fauna where these groups have lived. The fact that the U.N. is interested in such a thing is cause for alarm but the further fact that this proposed "universal declaration" has the support of the World Bank should an unmistakable red flag! The World Bank and the UN, like the Vatican and Zionists, the Supreme Court and Masons, make for a most dangerous combination.

People like Isaac Fulwood, past D.C. police chief, represent a few brilliant points of light. When asked the underlying problem of crime in our nation's capitol he replied: "The destruction of the schools, family and family values!"

He applied this to the nation as a whole as well. As the Murder Capitol of the nation, D.C. represents very well the problem this man, having the facts and experience to know what he was talking about, illustrates so pragmatically.

This came up as a result of a TV special about violence in America, a pretext to make our right to bear arms, as usual, the scapegoat for the liberal agenda's fight against the Second Amendment. I'm sure the interviewer was somewhat disappointed by Mr. Fulwood's assessment. He and many other Black leaders know that guns are not the problem. The wholesale destruction of anything approximating family values is under attack in this nation but you won't find that the subject of the media's attention. The enemies of America's families and children are working on a well-proven premise; the fact that the "average" citizen won't bother to attempt to do anything about it until, they hope, it is too late!

As a case in point, my campaign addresses the concerns so well expressed by Mr. Fulwood, particularly his concerns about education. In spite of the Members of the National Commission on Excellence in Education report; A Nation At Risk back in 1981, in spite of all I personally have written and made speeches about, not one single legislator over these many years has even bothered to ask me for suggestions concerning the problem. Perhaps Mr. Grace was correct: "Get rid of 535 scoundrels in Congress and start all over!" Certainly this is Damerell's conclusion in regard to teacher's colleges. Of course, one look at the membership of the Commission that produced A Nation At Risk told me it would be a useless report.

Now you wouldn't believe all these legislators, over 60 on my mailing list, could be so obtuse concerning the facts about the problems in education. But as I said for years of education: It's not as bad as you think, it's far worse! These men simply aren't qualified to do anything constructive about the problem and, continuing to ask the "experts" who made the mess for solutions, they further doom anything constructive being accomplished.

For example, you would think that the leadership would recognize the fact that if the Big Bug of our educational system, Mr. Honig, is stealing what he can from the taxpayers, that message is being sent loud and clear to young people. The subterfuge of his wife's "business," QEP being used to rip off the people only makes it more onerous. Imagine the effrontery of openly stealing almost a million dollars of grant monies to feather their own nests not to mention those "special people" that were on QEP's payroll! Then try to tell me or anyone else such people give a damn about our children and "values!" Such is the level of "expertise and concern" of our educational "leadership." And it doesn't' speak very well for those that are supposed to be guarding the hen house either. In my opinion, more of these educational "leaders" should be following the example of ex-superintendent Lee Burns of Wauchula, Florida and become janitors!

Seems Stephen Wagner the former chief financial officer for Newport Beach schools got caught with his hand in the till. He embezzled more than 3 million dollars from the school district. The fact that he was doing this over a period of years proves my contention that virtually no school district can afford to have a proper audit of its books; one of the primary reasons that such theft is commonplace. Again: No Accountability; the money is "just there!" He had accumulated five homes, two Mercedes cars, gems and his-and-hers fur coats while doing his bit to "further the cause" of California education. Mr. Wagner was also found guilty, not surprisingly, of four counts of filing false tax returns. Seems he wanted to make "restitution" rather than go to trial.

I'm left wondering if he planned to make restitution with the money he stole? The way the schools keep records, they could have done the usual thing and given him a glowing recommendation, the usual device used to get rid of a bad administrator or doctor, to another school district. I'm personally well acquainted with this procedure of the schools. Then, in a short time, he could have stolen enough from the new district to pay off the old one!

This reminds me of the incident of one of my past principals, one Perry Fuller. An ugly condition existed that required me to go to his office once only to be told by him: "We do our own dirty laundry; we don't hang it out for the people to see!" Later, this same principal was caught shoplifting and, unhappily for the educational establishment's philosophy so well described by this principal, the local paper, The Valley Press, got hold of the story and printed it. How did the district resolve the problem? It allowed him to move up to the district office for the rest of the school year and gave him a glowing recommendation on the condition that he would seek employment elsewhere. Must have worked because I learned he became an administrator for another school district from which he retired a short time ago. I'm not sure why this reminds me of the high school teacher I knew who divorced his wife and married one of his students. The district didn't even blink. I may yet have to write the book I have threatened in order to tell all I personally know of such things.

I have said repeatedly, there is no accountability in education and, as long as the money is "just there," people are going to keep stealing it. And please, don't go "anecdotal" on me, telling me about all those "good" teachers and administrators that truly care and are trying to do the job. I met a goodly number of them personally in the over two decades I worked in the schools; people like Karina O'Malley who knows the "praxis" concept of education.

My criticism stands in spite of the anecdotal exceptions simply because they are just that: Exceptions!

More common is the nauseating story in Newsweek of one Joseph Fernandez. Have you heard of "Daddy's Roommate" and "Heather Has Two Mommies?" Mr. Fernandez is using all the usual sodomite clichés and distortions, name-calling in order to get these abominations that glorify perversion accepted by the schools in Queens, N.Y. Using the usual propaganda of the sodomites, he is trying to force the schools to use a curriculum called "Children of the Rainbow," a 443 page multicultural propaganda tool. Quote: "It includes a section called: 'Fostering Positive Attitudes Toward Sexuality' in which first-grade teachers are urged to 'include references to lesbians/gay people in all curricular areas.'" Tragically for young people and children, most of the New York districts have already accepted this depraved sodomite and child-destroying curriculum.

Here in California, the "leadership" has approved textbook guidelines that include curricula "discussing" perversion in "non-judgmental" (read: approve perversion) terms! Where is the "leadership" for our own schools? Mr. Honig and our legislators are "too busy doing business as usual!" Consequently, unless we do something about it quickly, Daddy's Roommate and Heather's Two Mommies are going to hit our schools! As with those that are so quick to label people like myself as Discriminatory and Racist, I ask you to look at the "pedigrees" of those same who are trying to tell us that teaching the acceptance of perversion to our children is "good" for them! One more time: What is the pedigree and agenda of such people?

Minneapolis: "The first trial of a former Roman Catholic priest accused of sexually abusing dozens of children in three states ended Friday in his conviction...." And will any of these children die of AIDS? You have to wonder. Speaking of the dread disease, the cost of treatment is now anticipated to rise 48%, to $15.2 billion a year, by 1995! And most of us cannot even afford a doctor or dentist for ourselves! No wonder health costs are becoming prohibitive for the majority of average citizens! Bad enough that our faucets are leaching lead into our drinking water causing incalculable damage to both children and adults. We can take common sense action against the manufacturers of these devices. But in respect to the much more devastating problems of perversion and AIDS? Who in the "leadership" has the guts to face this with such common sense?

Can anyone with an ounce of common sense entertain the notion that such perversion is going to contribute to anything but more destruction of the already miserably failing condition of education in our schools? Will Mr. Clinton sacrifice Chelsea to the violent and ignorant D.C. school system to make a "political statement?" I think not! Nor would I!

Winners, not losers, write history. Only now are we able to deal with many of the unpalatable facts of our own history as a nation, with the histories of WWI and WWII. Granting that our present level of communications technology makes hiding the facts more difficult, atrocities still are committed by the "good guys." In cases like Randy Weaver and Manfred Roeder's, evil men and systems can still, like bad doctors, "bury" their victims and "mistakes."

Mr. Stephen Fahsbender, of radio station KNZR, makes an excellent point in his paraphrase of Jesus' statement: "What does it profit a nation to gain the whole world and loose its soul, or what will a nation give in exchange for its soul?" Perhaps the recent switch of radio station KIWI from easy listening and classical music to "either Spanish or Adult-oriented rock" speaks to the point.

But, the leadership today is woefully ignorant of the wisdom of the past. One of America's earliest writers, C. B. Brown wrote: "How little cognizance have men over the actions and motives of each other! How total is our blindness with regard to our own performances! I have erred, not through sinister nor malignant intentions, but from the impulse of misguided, indeed, but powerful, benevolence." So it is that I have come to pray; Lord, protect me from well-intentioned men, men who mean well but have neither the experience nor qualifications to actually do well!

People have an itch they can't scratch. Since they don't generally know what is best, or even, for that matter, what they want, they look to leaders. God help them when such leaders are no better than "well-intentioned!"

I agree with Abel's assessment that Cooper wrote the American Epic in his Leather-Stocking tales because "...they are an implicit idealization of our national adventure." Cooper's theme of the victory of love over lust is lost to this generation. Curiously, men of different races and cultures learned to love one another during the Viet Nam war. The "good" part of war is the emotional high, the camaraderie, and the dependence on others to do their part when your life is at stake, the pulling together in common cause and, the dark side of love, the common hatred of a common enemy.

Cooper was one of our foremost social commentators. He, as so many other thinking men, came to the inescapable conclusion that class distinctions were impossible to avoid. Too bad Marx, Engles and others couldn't see the truth of this maxim. According to Cooper: "Classes do, and will, exist in this country, as an incident of civilization; a truth every one can see as respects those below, though his vision may be less perfect as respects those above him."

Cooper, because of his privileged status, earned the enmity of those that, because of their own lack of either genius or privilege, understandably tried to pull him down to their level by the very same name-calling and subterfuges in the guise of "democracy and fairness" practiced today. Say what you will, Carnegie, for example, had a valid point in this regard. But Cooper recognized the common greed inherent in men and, like Jesus Christ, "knowing their hearts, did not commit himself unto them." Cooper fought the good fight and, regardless your opinion of whether a "landed aristocracy" is more productive of Enlightened Self-interest as opposed to that of Manufacturers one must admit of the fact that a ruling class has always prevailed in government.

Our so-called "public" schools are dedicated to producing an underclass of thoroughly ignorant future citizens which will be easily led, not by Enlightened Self-interest, but by an equally thoroughly unscrupulous and greedy, well educated, upper class. As I warned years ago, the schools are in the business of producing a "Slave Generation," not educated men and women who will accept responsibility and be productive either to posterity or to the general welfare.

Contributing to the agenda of our ruling class, "Economies have always been subject to bouts of the flu, but what we have now is not just a bout of the flu but an underlying cancer." Isabel Sawhill of Washington's Urban Institute, "Economists are using, more and more, the big "D" word of the world economy."

Recently, in Germany, three neo-Nazis were sentenced to prison for the beating death of a "Leftist" and injury to eight others. In this country, we have a "letter to Santa" asking for a job for the writer's dad, food for his mother and help in "getting to Heaven" for himself. The genuineness of the letter has been called into question but the sentiment of it cannot be.

I have installed in my "data base" the following: Duke University recently named Nannerl Overholser Keohane, a woman, as the University's president. Clinton is busy naming women to important government posts, and a woman, Clarissa Pinkola Estes, billing herself as a Jungian analyst has a best seller titled: "Women Who Run With the Wolves." The only thing that saves this book from falling into the relative merits and interest level of such works as "Great Moments In Ping-pong" is its unashamedly anti-man phraseology. Couched in the usual language and phrases of Jewish and pseudo-intellectualism, the Man-bashing book rides the crest of the waves of the media propagandized frustration of all those women with that itch they can't scratch; somehow, some way, it is all a conspiratorial conceit of men that makes any distinction of any real differences between men and women. I may have to go back and re-read my own book on the subject. I had come to the conclusion that there were some real differences! But I had come to the conclusion that the differences were created of God to be compatible, not competitive or combative. I did not accept Sam's conclusion that "Men and women are natural born enemies."

If all factors such as housing, welfare, schooling, loss of jobs for legal citizens, etc., etc. are considered, illegal aliens cost the California taxpayers about $30,000 a head per year. It takes the taxes of about thirty-five honest, working, California citizens to support each illegal. This is money lost to the citizen's own children and family, the California economy, etc. Now you don't have to have the wisdom or loquaciousness of a tree full of owls to see where this leads- just where we are! When is the leadership going to wise up to this fact and say and do the hard things which must be said and done? And when is my generation going to accept its responsibility for allowing such a destructive travesty to come into being and flourish instead of passing the buck on to young people? We made the mess, not our children! It is this abysmal failure to accept our responsibility for the mess that has led us into Cooper's "Institutionalized Iniquity!"

"I pick up the telephone and call the local garage. I can't understand the person on the other side of the line. I'm not sure he can understand me. They're all over the place, and they don't speak English. Do we want more of this?" Senator Robert Byrd from the Senate floor last June.

I thank the Senator for voicing my own comments on the subject over the past few years. He could have included doctors, lawyers, government employees and a host of others in his complaint concerning foreigners. He could also have mentioned the fact that while white population remains constant, Non-white population triples from births and immigration, largely illegal. And citizens get to foot the bill for this travesty! And, to add insult to injury, the courts are encouraging more of the same from illegal Haitians, Cubans, Mexicans, etc.? What is the agenda of those that are decimating America through such obviously overt acts of destruction which can only lead to further, racial, ideological and cultural alienation, the continued hurt, anger, distrust and frustration of our own citizenry?

There hasn't been much on the news about Wallace Tope. "Who," you ask? Right! Seems Wallace, a white man who was caught in the madness of the recent L.A. riot got his head kicked in by two Mexicans, Fidel Ortiz and Leonard Sosa because he blocked their paths to a drug store they were trying to loot. Wallace further "invited" the attack by trying to give these thugs Gospel tracts. Wallace lies in a coma now, his last words to his attackers, according to a witness, Jesus Ortiz, were: "Believe in Jesus."

Having lost my own brother, Ronnie, not long ago, my heart went out to Wallace's brother, Dennis, a vice-principle at Mojave High School. I called him and let him know that I shared his grief. A brother is someone very special and, as with the loss of my daughter, Diana, not something you ever get over; it stays with you constantly. You learn to deal with the grief and you go on with life but it is different. You no longer have the visits and sharing, the phone calls, notes and letters. There was someone there you could count on that understood you and now they are gone.

Dennis didn't express much hope that Wallace would survive or, even, come out of his coma. I faced the same situation with Diana. But she died of a motorcycle accident. Ronnie died of a heart condition. But Wallace; what will he have died of? Trying to speak up for Jesus Christ. A Martyr? What else could you call him?

The article in front of me as I write is from the Bakersfield Californian. The headline: "Faith Destroyed: Savage beating of his evangelical brother during the L.A. riots fills man with 'hate.'"

As we talked, Dennis didn't express the hatred of the headline. His grief for his brother was too real for that. But his question, "What I'd like to know is why weren't all the other preachers out there, and why was Wally all alone?" hit a very responsive chord in my own heart. My years-long criticism of the "business of the churches" came full force upon me.

There is a warfare going on in respect to the Truth. The Truth of the Gospel is a thing that is hated by all evil men and women. They love their sin and hate anyone who would confront them in their sin. Jesus made it unmistakably plain that those that would stand up for Him were at risk. As in any war, people get hurt, maimed, killed.

The biggest mistake in Wally's case would be for those whose own agendas demand it to succeed in making his tragic confrontation of evil a "racial incident." It wasn't! It would be foolish to deny that Wally's being white worked against him, but the larger factor was still his confronting these evil men and standing in the way of their wicked purpose. I didn't know Wally; I wish I had. But I knew what he was trying to do. I tried to do the same thing when I used to teach in the very area where he was beaten and kicked into a coma.

If those of the Klan had tried to erect a cross in Cincinnati while the Jews and their puppets were picketing, the Klan members, greatly outnumbered, would have been at grave risk even as Wally was. Every one of us that tries to take a stand for the Gospel, for the Truth, is at risk. Granted, you would never know this from the attitude of modern "saints" as they "struggle against the powers of darkness" in the comfort and sanctimonious safety of their pews; the "service" oh so carefully choreographed with the "proper, spiritually uplifting hymnody" and listening to comfortable sermons. Perhaps the New Systematic Theology that is so badly needed will have a section covering "The Gospel as a comfortable, non-controversial, non-confrontational 'message'!" Most present day "spiritual leaders" like Schuller certainly subscribe to this "gospel." As a friend keeps telling me, "We all have our own pilgrimage." Isn't a marvelous thing when that "pilgrimage" allows the modern "saint" to sit back comfortably and let the Devil win by default?

The Christian is required to take his stand for the Truth of the Gospel. It is a Truth that confronts the evil that men do. But Jesus did not command us to bear any sword but the Sword of the Spirit in proclaiming that Truth: The Word of God! The Gospel is not like the ideologies of Muslimism or Judaism, Conversion by the sword! It is, preeminently, a message of God's love. The rejection of that love carries its own penalty, a penalty for which God alone is the Judge (Hebrews 9:27). But the proclamation of that message, The Truth, requires Christians to be in harm's way. But as long as we do what is right, the consequences, even to our hurt, are in God's hands.

I wish everyone would read M.E. Bradford's book: "Against the Barbarians and Other Reflections on Familiar Themes." The New American, December 14, has an excellent review of the book. The author, as I have done, points out the fact that the educational leadership and their "sheep" in American schools have, too successfully, supplanted the literary and historical truths and traditions of our nation by the writings of Marxists, feminists, primitivists and degenerates. But our schools, suffering this very kind of "leadership" in our universities, plagued with Jewish, Leftist, Multi-cultural intellectualism, are at the mercy of an agenda which is set on destroying any vestige of pride in our national origins and Christian beliefs. My thanks to Bradford for his noble work and The New American for providing the review.

I recently watched a great "show;" Rush Limbaugh on Donahue. What a treat to watch the sparring between these two. Since Rush is on my mailing list, he knows of my criticism of him. Rush, you didn't have to go so far in justifying such criticism by playing Donahue's game in regard to the question of accepting perverts in the military. You tried to wiggle your way out just as you did on the question of abortion. I am left wondering, now, about your own "conservative" agenda? You acted so much the "politician" that I do have to wonder? A man of real convictions on these issues would have answered in an unmistakable fashion and not, as you did, equivocate. Unless he has other aspirations in which case true convictions are generally subordinated to "let's make a deal?"

As in the case of Gonzo TV shows like Montel Williams', you only make a bad situation worse. The rampant ignorance and race hatreds put on display as per the recent airing of Williams and John Metzger serve no purpose other than making Mr. Williams richer at a cost to Negroes. Metzger is unabashedly racist by his own definition. But Mr. Metzger's racism is not nearly as deadly a force as shows like Mr. Williams' which most certainly do nothing to promote understanding but, on the contrary, put the most hurtful kind of ignorance on open display to the entire nation.

Now I am not accusing either Williams or Metzger of ignorance. Both know what they want and each has his agenda of getting what he wants. In Metzger's case, his historical points are accurate and viable; his "wants" patently obvious regardless one's acceptance or rejection of the point of view. But, due to the very format and time constraints, he is easily made to look the fool. Mr. Williams, however, practices the hypocrisy of all Gonzo TV personalities where the cause of "liberalism" is touted all the while knowing that such "shows" can contribute nothing of value because of the very constraints of time, etc. that objectively prohibit any real understanding of the hugely complex issues involved.

The best approach to an understanding of the issues is the printed word together with lengthy seminars of men of good will and understanding meeting in concert. I do my "bit" by producing the equivalent of a 400 to 500-page book each year through my essays and meeting with groups and individuals as time allows. My recent travels throughout the nation took a large amount of time. And, in answer to some of you who have asked, all my travel is at my own expense; no one contributes anything to this and, as a result, I owe no "favors."

While the puppet-masters attempt to focus attention on the "terrible white man's abuses," Black Moslems butcher and sell Black non-Moslems into slavery in Africa and, at the same time, try in every way possible to destroy the only successful entity in Africa: South Africa! Insane! While I'm about it, why don't we consider the interesting "contradiction" of white devils trying to save Blacks as per Somalia? You want to make sense of this? Why aren't those "noble Africans" helping their "own people?" The honest black people I know in this nation agree with me on what the result will be of turning South Africa over to black rule: Khartoum and Watts!

In respect to Somalia, I'm hearing, more and more, the question: "Why are we over there when the needs of our own people are not being met?" Fair question; don't expect a satisfactory answer from the "leadership." I won't leave you hanging on this one. But I'm going to come the long way round it.

A new child support law is in effect which is getting a lot of publicity in California. In 60% of the 43,000 child support cases in the hands of the Kern County D.A.'s office the custodial parent is on welfare. Now I have been a single parent. I know how hard it is to provide food, shelter and clothing as a single parent. The single hardest thing is to attempt the impossible, to be both father and mother to children who will always need both. And, like most, I failed miserably in the attempt. We never outgrow the need for the love of parents and others in our lives.

I didn't have a father. He left my brother and me when I was only three years old and I never saw him again. The "grandparents" on his side of the family never cared enough for my brother or me to even keep in touch. I guess my mother didn't care about what this loss meant for the future. Though her youth might excuse her selfishness in this case, she didn't exhibit much more concern for my brother or me in her future choices. Her own parents, our grandparents, proved too easy to take advantage of and left her to follow her own agenda the rest of her life without her children being a burden to her. Consequently, I know virtually nothing about my father's side of the family.

Nor were my brother or I ever to inherit anything but memories from any family members. Thank God we had a Grandfather (maternal) who cared enough to take over the responsibility from which our father ran away. From that experience, if nothing else, I knew I would never do that to any of my children. And I didn't, even though it meant child-support payments from my first marriage for eighteen years due to that "itch" women can't seem to scratch.

It should be obvious to all that court-ordered child support seldom covers the actual expenses of caring for children. In my case, due to that "itch" of another faithless woman, the priorities had to be the essentials of food and shelter for my youngest son and daughter. Since I had custody of the children, (hard to believe their mother didn't want them), it was all I could do to provide the bare essentials for them. This never left enough for the nice things I wanted to do for my children. Don't expect children to understand this; they can't! They are too often wondering what they did to make "Mommy or Daddy" leave them. They cannot understand why they can't have that new dress or toy or even a trip to McDonald's. And quality time; where does that come from when, as I did, you have to hold down a job just to provide the necessities?

No, I didn't get welfare or child support from the missing parent. The courts don't exactly favor single men parents. As one man in similar circumstances told me, if he had known how the court was going to deal with him, even though he had, as I did, child custody, "he would have left the country." Many do.

I did, at a later date, more out of anger that their "mother" wanted nothing to do with her own children, go to District Attorney, Ed Jagel's office, to file papers in an attempt to force her to contribute something for the sake of the children. I was also somewhat curious about what the "system" would do when the shoe was on the other foot. Imagine a man trying to get the system to make a woman contribute to child support?

In spite of the fact that she was earning almost $50,000 per year, more than twice my income at the time, and was "free" of her children (and me), it seems the system couldn't deal with my case. After about six months and hearing nothing from Jagels, I called and was informed that his office didn't know anything about my claim or me! Was this because a woman assistant D.A. had "handled" the paperwork? I had to wonder. Jagels' office wanted me to fill out all that voluminous paperwork and start over again from scratch. I declined. I had learned what I suspected all along; the system is based on ruining men, not helping children.

But the most salient point is the fact that the curses of divorce, favored by women by a factor of better than two to one, and adultery most often leave the "other" parent, usually a man, in such desperate circumstances that it is often impossible to meet the actual expenses of both the needs of children and a "second" household. The fact is that both parents are in a no-win situation financially. But the damage to the children and society is incalculable, far beyond any dollars-and-cents figure.

As I just told a reporter for a local TV station, I plan to see this campaign through regardless of the worthiness of the other candidates because I don't see or hear anyone speaking for children! I hear about some of the very real problems that California and the nation are facing. But neither in this campaign nor in the national elections just past did anyone really address the concerns for children and particularly not in that one area that impacts the whole society: the schools!

Oh they paid the usual lip service they have been giving it for years, but it is painfully obvious that no one intends to really give it the priority it desperately needs. Who really speaks for the children, those little ones who have no voice or choice? I don't wonder at the rebuke of Jesus when the "grown-ups" attempted to keep those little ones from "bothering" him. What bothered him and me is the way those little ones have been shut out by the overweening self-interest of those that obviously don't give a damn for children, particularly in the schools! Christian or not, my mind reels with the "judgment" I would meet out to those that betray and abuse these little ones! And nowhere have I witnessed such abuse of the magnitude I have seen in the schools!

I worked in conditions where I was far more acquainted with probation officers and Child Protective Services than any "parents." I have seen unspeakable abuse perpetrated on children by every segment of society. But the main abuser has become the school system.

A child readily overcomes dad taking his belt to him for the sake of discipline. But how does that same child overcome an institution where he is a virtual prisoner to the whims of the "system?" And if that system, from the likes of a "Honig" on down is teaching that all morality is "relative," that mom and dad can't really make the child do anything he does not want to do, that mom and dad don't know what is best but the system does, that the school knows God doesn't really matter, that parents have no voice in the decisions of young people but the school will dictate the "correctness" of those decisions.

Who, do you suppose, has the best interests of the child at heart- the system, an amoral system at best without any absolute values, or the parents? The tragedy of our present condition is the fact of so many "throw-away" children, the result of broken homes, teen births, a runaway welfare system that actually rewards the indiscriminate breeding which leads to illegitimate babies and an evil system which robs men and women of the integrity of doing honorable work, that has forced the need of two paychecks and the resulting latchkey kids. How did it happen that a woman staying at home and nurturing children somehow became "second class status" for women? Just who started preaching this doctrine of women should find "fulfillment" outside of the historically honored and successful framework of a home and children? Look to our laws for a great part of the answer.

Another part of the answer was the insanity of those of my generation, during the sixties particularly, suddenly preaching a doctrine of "children know better than adults what is best!" A brief review of the psychobabble of the "experts" in the courts, government, psychology and education of the period is enough to make you throw up! And who sold this abortion to the schools in the name of what was "best" for children? If there were ever grounds for a conspiracy theory directed to the destruction of our nation, the evidence for it exists during this time frame if nowhere else.

This is one of the reasons that, as per the Bible, I consider divorce and adultery "perversions," and nowhere is such perversion so clearly discernible as in the impact on children! I think Reason dictates that, in most cases, notwithstanding the Biblical injunctions, divorce and adultery, as with homosexuality, are the acts of utterly selfish, irresponsible people. As a result of the harm done to children, such behavior should be held, and, in general, has always been, contemptible by the moral standards of any society.

In the commonest language possible, no one has anything but contempt for any "man" who has to sneak in the back door to another man's wife! And what, do you suppose, do people think of the woman, especially the "mother," who lends herself to such a "man?"

As hypocritical as cultures may be in actual practice of their distinctively public mores, those mores still stand along with the condemnation of those that fail to adhere to them. Such is the equally common condition of human nature for which laws and rulers are needed.

Now, as with the situation in Somalia, if the laws and mores of a society are going to be at cross-purposes, if we are going to condone the forsaking of children for the sake of some "itch" to have it "our way" by fiat of the courts, the innocent, the children, and the future of a nation, are going to be the sacrificial cost of such selfish behavior.

In Somalia, you wind up with a "dysfunctional nation." In America, you wind up with "dysfunctional" families and children. And how long, you must ask yourself, can such destructive conditions go on in America without its becoming a dysfunctional nation?

My years of working with young people in the schools, my personal experience as a child and a father, my study of history and literature lead to inescapable, immutable conclusions. Unless the laws and values of a nation reflect the sanctity of family, unless they reflect the need to prepare the future generation for responsibility to its families, there can be no "future" worthy of the name.

And how are the schools reflecting the help and support of homes and families? The situation demands cooperation and, though it is obvious that the schools and parents must work together, we find only growing enmity between them, adversarial positions where the children get lost in the shuffle. In this insane condition, the parents are suing at the drop of a hat and the schools, knowing they are failing across the board, resort to all kinds of subterfuges to escape accountability.

As to values men like Benjamin Franklin counseled the need for moral absolutes. And they gave full recognition to the need of God as the basis for those absolutes. It is patently insane to attempt any teaching of values without a Righteous Judge by whatever definition and men like Franklin owned that historically immutable fact of human nature.

As a Christian, it grieves me to see the churches dispensing the "consolations of religion" while ignoring the Great Commission. When it comes to outright theft, it pays to steal Big if you are going to steal and few exemplify this better than those like Jim and Tammy Baker. But what is the excuse for those who support these charlatans? To watch the "churches in action," it appears God was wrong! Men are called to build empires that allow them to live in luxury and stroke their overweening egos at the cost of shaming Jesus Christ. The same rule applies in government and education.

The L.A. City Schools have "lost" $73,000,000! No accountability; the money is "just there." How many "educators" have profited from the utter lack of accountability at the cost to the children in this district? Now I know where the "lost" money went. But don't count on any among the leadership in either the schools or the legislature asking me where the money went, they won't! I'm going to share a secret with you: They Don't Want To Know! If this arouses your curiosity, and it should, drop me a line and I'll elaborate. But

I'll give you a hint; the same rule applies in this case that applies in adultery; "Everybody does it!"

I love a mystery. I revel in the anomalies of science and astronomy. As a lover of good literature, I am entranced by the mystery of Shakespeare. Recent research into the authorship of the plays and sonnets has opened new doors of possibility leading to a greater understanding of the peoples and times of the Victorian Era. Edward Vere, 17th earl of Oxford is the latest and, to me, most logical contender for authorship. It was a most fortuitous time that led to the translation of that greatest masterpiece of the English language, the King James Bible. Those that love language will understand what I mean.

Hermeneutics is the science of interpretations from writing. As scholars pour over the works of other writers contemporary with the Bard, the way things are said, the descriptive phraseology and knowledge of the events described are the keys to authorship together with the witness of contemporary writers and history. The actual value of the work, not the workman, is the essential. History is filled with dubious "authorships" but the works remain to speak for themselves. One aspect of genius is to speak or write those old truths in new ways; just as a new coat of paint makes the old bright and fresh once more.

It is not genius to think of the world a stage and all are players upon that stage. Such a thought is a commonplace. But, Tomorrow, tomorrow, tomorrow...life, a tale told by an idiot strutting that stage, full of sound and fury signifying nothing.... Ah, that is something else again! And if our lives have plumbed the dark, forbidding depths of inconsolable grief and the choice to live when to depart would be far better is made on the basis that: "Tired with all these, from these would I be gone. Save that, to die, I leave my love alone."? So it is that the genius of language, regardless the author, speaks. Whether for that One who makes the sun rise in our souls or for the children, as in my own case, the choice is made to live for the sake of that love which, alone, stills the siren voice of that "beyond" and you become grateful for the fact that you are not unique in either the beckoning or the choice. Tragically, when you have attained any number of years, it is likely you will know someone who lacked the love to see them through the midnight of the soul. So it is that, lacking hope of a future, confused by the utter lack of moral absolutes and caring love, the poor, shabby, depraved and pauperized substitute of lust failing miserably, suicide becomes the second, leading cause of death among our teenagers.

No one would accuse me of falling into the camp of a transcendentalist. But, as I have often said, the appreciation of the genius of men does not depend on the character of such. So it is that I often find things of great value in the works of men while decrying their philosophies or persons. Emerson is one such man. He wrote: "It is the best part of a man . . . that revolts against his being a minister . . . We fall into institutions already made, and have to accommodate ourselves to them to be useful at all, and this accommodation is . . . a loss of so much integrity and . . . power . . . in order to be a good minister, it is necessary to leave the ministry." But, "Without accommodation society is impracticable . . . Society everywhere is in conspiracy against the manhood of every one of its members . . . whoso would be a man must be a non-conformist." So it is that the fields of politics, religion and education are filled with "conformists," those "amiable men" without any real convictions worthy of the name.

It is easy enough to understand the thinking of men like Emerson and Thoreau; I spent enough time in pulpits and the churches and education to do so. My "failure" to become an "amiable" man in these institutions proved my undoing. It is easy enough to understand the disillusionment of Emerson and Thoreau, as with that of Franklin, Jefferson, Hamilton, Adams, with their "species." Even as I have witnessed over the past decades, the betrayal of our children and our nation through the selfish disinterest and apathy of "amiable" men and women working in unconscious collusion with the wicked enemies set on our destruction and enslavement to Caesar. And I cry out, once more: Who speaks for the children!

I do pity Emerson and those of genius who, forsaking the ancient landmarks, "grieve that grief teaches them nothing." No matter the common stirrings in the souls of people as they look out at the stars or the beauties of God's creation all around, if the lessons of grief are lost to a man or woman, they have little to offer of any practical value to others, particularly to children. It is the manner in which I have dealt with the grief in my own life that I know will be of incalculable worth to my own children as they continue to meet their own exigencies and opportunities.

Speaking of the ancient landmarks, I hope no one will construe my comments as a seeking to put Humpty Dumpty back together again. I was watching the news when the ugly story of a Negro child on "Santa's" lap being asked if he "had ever seen a Monkey?" was aired. The child told the white Santa "No." The Santa then told him to "look in a mirror and he would see one!" This dreadful, for so it is to me, incident perfectly describes my inability to be a "good racist." I will continue to do all in my power to return us to Constitutional government, to the ideals of those good men and women who paid the price for our liberty; in short, I am an American with a precious birthright and the responsibility to confront and contend with the evil that threatens to enslave us! But children should never have to suffer discrimination; they have enough to suffer in this society without having to face the ugliness of destructive ignorance and prejudice. And I will say, without qualification, that anyone who doesn't feel the pain of that Negro child has no genuine love for children regardless their color! But no amount of "laws" will make people like this "Santa" care!

No one of any humanity can look at what is happening in Somalia to those starving children without it tearing at their hearts. I don't care what color those children are, I know that the whole world has a terrible judgment to come for such conditions being allowed. I also know it is the evil of the "leadership" of those in Africa that should be held to account. I found the same anger at the injustice of such a thing stirring my soul as I witnessed the incident of that "Santa." I find the same anger when I think of the children suffering in this nation due to the evil of men and women in our society.

"Take our lands and make us your slaves but give us bread for why should we die?" Thus those ancient Egyptians cried out to Pharaoh to save them during the severe famine that ravaged the land. Joseph had "saved" the people at the cost of enslaving them. During the decades I worked with thousands of children in the schools, I was forced to watch the "enslavement" of our young people just as surely as what happened to those Egyptians. No, I didn't see hoards of emaciated bodies; I witnessed the starvation of their souls, of their hopes of a future, the destruction of their families through the evils of a society that no longer cherished its children, and denying God, had no answers for the geometrically mounting problems of that society. And, denying God, only "Pharaoh" remains to "save" us!

Will men and women of Reason come together for the sake of the children? I hope so. I live in such hope. I don't require such people to subscribe to my belief system. It is only required that they be reasonable and have a genuine, caring concern for children and families. They must, of course, in order to be able to offer practical solutions, be qualified and experienced to do so. Good intentions, as with the "stroking of egos," alone, will never suffice. If it were not for my years of experience of working in the schools, it would be the height of presumption, obviously, for me to put myself forth as being a candidate with something of value to offer.

"A new broom may sweep clean but an old broom knows where the dirt is!" When it comes to the sins and ills of education, this "old broom" knows where the dirt is. You can only gain limited input by bringing someone from the educational establishment into converse with someone from industry, for example. Both may be knowledgeable of their own areas of expertise, it takes someone with experience in education to know its problems and someone with experience in industry to understand its needs. But the happiest confluence of conditions that would promote reasonable solutions would be for people like me with experience in both areas to have the authority to address the situation.

Is there hope for cooperation between Clinton and me? Yes. I like cats, cigars and saxophones. While he plays Alto and I, Tenor, it's essentially the same instrument; with all that going for us, why shouldn't there be hope?

A recent request and survey form I received from The Heritage Foundation prompts me to make a comment in its regard. Those of you who are acquainted with the organization know of its reputation for "conservatism." But it, like William Buckley and Rush Limbaugh's "conservatism" is tinged with a large amount of suspicion by conservatives like me.

A primary ingredient of my own suspicion is the overweening concern of such for Israel as a "friend" to the U.S. Nothing could be further from the truth, a point I made in responding to Ed. Fuelner, the president of The Heritage Foundation. For example, no nation is so guilty of the Xenophobia of which Jews accuse the U.S. No nation is so opposed to "Democracy" or a truly Republican form of government as per the ideals of our founding fathers than Israel.

Were it not for the poor dupes like Pat Robertson and Jerry Falwell who continue to propagandize the truly moronic oxymoron "Judeo-Christian" lie, the U.S. might have a better chance to examine the "ethnically-cleansed" nation of Israel for the patently racist, bigoted and prejudiced nation it really is. But, to accept the hypocrisy of Israel and Jews in this nation for what it really is, the U.S. would have to apologize to South Africa, Germany, etc.

So, in view of the real facts of Israel, I accept the further fact that the relationship to Israel is for the continued "benefit" of our having a door to the Middle East and a staging area for anticipated "need." Also, in view of the fact of such a disparity between Israel and the U.S. in regard to cultures and ideals, one is left asking how Jews have such an utterly disproportionate voice in the affairs of our own nation? Just read my books and essays and you will know. It's a dirty picture of special agendas, intrigues and, the ultimate goal, of the destruction of all the ideals of our founding fathers and hope of a future for our children.

If the onus of Anti-Semite is to be applied to me because of confronting the ugliness and hypocrisy of those that would destroy my country, I wear the label proudly when such an appellation is earned by my standing up for those ideals and the work that needs to be done to give my children and grand-children hope of a future.

My warning to those Judeo-Zionists who would try to force their truly racist, prejudiced, bigoted religion on my country; I am your bitter enemy and will fight you with all the means at my disposal including your agenda of trying to force the teaching of perversion as "acceptable" through the auspices of your ACLU in our schools! And your name-calling won't avail with me; I know my enemy too well to be afraid of your brand of propaganda and I am well equipped to deal with it, including your pervading Jewish Intellectualism which threatens the destruction of our schools, families and culture! If the churches and politicians are afraid to confront the evil that Jesus Christ commands as the duty of all Christians, I am not! And not because I am courageous but because of the overriding love I have for God's Word and all children beginning with my own. I know their only real hope of a future and a future for my country is to confront such evil and fight against it.

"What can the righteous do if the foundations be destroyed? Help, Lord, for the Godly man ceaseth!" Where are the "Godly" men who should be speaking out for historical, American ideals, who should cherish children? They, apparently, don't exist! Could such an all-pervading system of evil exist throughout the leadership of our nation if they did?

In my travels and reading I have become well acquainted with the mind-set of those, like the Masons, Zionists, JWs., etc. that want anarchy in our nation because they believe they will inherit a nation of slaves out of the ashes who will do their bidding, who see themselves the Darwinian choice, the rightful "inheritors" of the earth.

As the use of such words like Xenophobic, Racist, Bigot, Intolerant are successfully applied to those like myself who would stand up for the children and American ideals, political correctness gains the ascendancy. Who would have ever thought that anyone who has the common sense disgust and revulsion toward perversion in America would be successfully labeled "Intolerant?" It makes me want to vomit when I see the likes of Barbara Streisand and John Denver given a world forum to shove perversion down the throats of Americans! And what is the agenda of those wicked enemies of decent Americans who are making sure that decent values are labeled "Intolerant" when the lovers of perversion are given such a forum? See how the twisting and distorting of healthy common sense attitudes are labeled by the enemies of America and its children? Remember the warning of God about a generation that calls evil, good and good, evil?

There can be no doubt whatsoever that there is a conspiracy of evil that is set on the destruction of America, that is set on the destruction of everything of real and lasting value and morality which is common to all human beings who love children and have any concern for their future.

But is such concern being given a voice in our elected leadership? NO! What do we hear and see instead? Politically Correct speeches and laws which will further the destruction of every noble ideal of those that paid the price of our betrayed liberty to do and be a good nation which cherished its posterity!

And where are the voices in the pulpits that would obey God and confront and contend with such evil? Silent! Sure there are some men who will preach sermons about these evils which are destroying our nation but are such "preachers" encouraging the "flocks" to actually get their hands dirty in the work? NO! And the reason is simple; they are paid hirelings who exist at Caesar's pleasure, spiritual eunuchs who have no stomach for the fight! These "leaders" will let those that pay their salaries sit in the comfort and safety of their pews and ease their unholy consciences with pious platitudes and the hateful "hymns of hypocrisy" which vilify and profane God, which God most surely despises from the unholy lips of these wicked and false servants!

In trying to get these false prophets and servants involved in the real work God has called us to, I have had to recognize the thinking of those men like Franklin, Jefferson and Thoreau that the "species is not worth saving!" But it took some years for Emerson to come to the conclusion that: "The mass are animal, in state of pupilage, and nearer the chimpanzee." Emerson gave in to the ease of a respected old age, accepting his conclusion and obituary of humanity in general. Thoreau was honest in his appraisal: "The audiences do not want to hear any prophets. ... They ... go to the Lyceum to suck a sugar-plum." And so the churches today, so it is that the churches and government become the domains of those very persons the churches and government were invented to prevent in their evil purposes!

We are forced to accept, in all honesty, the hugely, unpalatable truth of such raw and harsh conclusions by the very conditions of this age. And, unless good men and women stand up to confront it, we are doomed and we have doomed our children! But when such "good" people cannot even be bothered to write a letter to their congressman, cannot even be bothered to attend a school board meeting, cannot even be bothered to give a word of encouragement to those that are trying to do battle against the powers of darkness, can such people even be considered "good" by any sensible definition? I think not!

In regard to elected representatives in government, if the obvious priorities and concerns are not children, families and schools, proven moral values, of what benefit are any of the other "concerns?" There is no future for any nation that does not, first and foremost, concern itself with the welfare of its posterity. Any other course of leadership is either insane or so utterly selfish as to defy definition short of such an overwhelming conspiracy of evil that one is forced to grant it credence! And if the "best" of conservative voices are the likes of Robertson, Limbaugh and Buckley- God help us!

Recently, armed robbers in Germany stole an arsenal of explosives, machine guns, rifles, pistols and bazookas from an army base. There are a large number of such caches in this country and a number of groups who, like those Germans, intend to enforce their ideologies. I suggest we pay attention to the fact that Germans form the single, largest ethnic group in the U.S., 57.9

million strong! This might help to understand the ideologies of Tom Metzger and Robert Butler. These are not stupid men!

Of course it helps foment the anger and frustration of American citizens when blatant law-breakers like the illegal aliens, Mexicans, Haitians, Chinese, Cubans, etc. are allowed to remain and our "leadership" and courts actually sanction the breaking of our laws by such criminals! Once more, we have to ask, "What is the agenda of such wicked leaders?"

Britain is doing the sensible thing by legalizing drugs and in doing so, has brought drug use under proper, medical control. But, as I have said so many times, when such a common sense approach to the problem is not followed in our own nation, we have to consider the "conspiracy" element: Just who is profiting by allowing the insane policies of illegal drugs and immigration to continue?

Studies project that Mexican and Asian populations will grow by 48 per cent in America, the Negro population by 28 per cent and the white, by 5.6. Social Services, aware of this, recently sent out a memo that states: "One language is not necessarily more appropriate than another and acceptance of this is critical to working together effectively and harmoniously. The department has a responsibility to provide services in the language of the applicant/recipient when necessary for the delivery of services."

This angers me. It angers all sensible Americans. I know Negro and white "recipients of services" don't have a problem with English. Then why is the State so anxious to give away taxpayer money to those that don't speak our language and are, in all probability, illegals as well? More of the conspiracy of evil to engender hatred and anarchy!

Why should congressmen get retirements? I am opposed to any retirement pay for all elected officials from the president on down. I would also set the salaries of elected persons to the median wage of those represented. This common sense approach to electing real citizen representatives and bringing the cost of government under control has about as much chance as accountability in the schools until good leaders are elected!

Will we ever see some leader in Congress or Sacramento stand up and say: "Perversion is good for children!"? Of course not! Why, that would be insane! But when these same "leaders" pass laws forcing the teaching of perversion as "good" in the schools, aren't they saying exactly that! Of course they are! But when Cranston called the entire Senate a "bunch of crooks," the most they could offer in retaliation was a flimsy "censure" of his conduct. The best Bush could do to cover his backside is sign pardons.

Now I am going to call the entire legislature and the governor a bunch of "Child Destroying, Sodomite Supporters!" Didn't you know that our "leaders" have passed legislation allowing the Sodomites to sue the schools and churches if they are denied employment because of "sexual orientation?" You do now! Watch the Sodomites with their natural ally, the ACLU, get on the bandwagon of attacking the schools and churches aided by "cooperative courts!" As with Ms. O'Hare, where were the churches when the enemy came in and planted this field of tares?

I compare this with the looming apocalypse of our inability to clean up nuclear waste. Seems the "leadership" has grossly underestimated the problem. As with the schools, accountability is non-existent. From Congress to Westinghouse, NASA, the Department of Energy to you name them, "No one is responsible!" But an astronomical amount of graft and corruption money went into some people's pockets leaving a problem of catastrophically, cataclysmic proportions!

The POWs from the Korean "Conflict" that were sent to China? Our own Kern County is "host" to that boatload of illegal Chinese. A federal judge blocks the common sense welfare cuts for new, state "residents?" AIDS is making orphans of children at a rising rate, Russia releases secret papers on Americans downed by USSR, Harry Blackmun of Roe v. Wade infamy tells a graduating class they are entering a world "without strong leadership and deteriorating moral values!" The sheer hypocrisy of the man leaves one speechless! Negroes and Mexicans accuse each other of "hate crime" in a recent altercation leaving the courts an interesting (insane) conundrum of their own making. Steven Ross, chairman of Time Warner dies of cancer; wonder how he is explaining his part in the destruction of family and children to God? His millions of blood money won't buy off the worms of Hades or quench its fire.

A couple of young thugs went on a rampage with pellet rifles shooting out the windows of about thirty cars. Police can't call this a racist attack because they are prohibited from asking the race of the victims! Insane! Two Filipinos are arrested for preaching Christianity in Arabia. Doesn't matter; Jew or Muslim, neither know anything of genuine tolerance. But they will sure heap abuse on America for "failing" in regard to what they, themselves, will not stand for!

As we face the new year will anything change in regard to things like H. H. Brackenridge's observation of "...avarice hiding behind the grimace of religious appearances."? Emerson was a genius in originality and his sympathy and sincerity were rare talents. In his sincerity, he wrote: "Men are conservative when they are least vigorous, or when they are most luxurious. They are conservatives after dinner, or before taking their rest; when they are sick or aged: in the morning, or when their intellect or conscience has been aroused, when they hear music, or when they read poetry, they are radicals." How very perceptive.

I admire A. B. Alcott in his sincere love of children but despise his destructive concepts of their education. I love Mozart but despise his vulgar profanities and refuse to accept the diagnosis of Tourette's Syndrome. The man himself was obscene. When only generalities will serve, it fails to use specifics. No matter the genius we admire, if the persons are less than honorable, the best they can offer is work that is better than they. If we exercise wisdom, we will take of the work and apply it to more noble purpose irrespective the giver.

There is no lack of knowing what to do; we lack the leadership that will stand up and confront an evil system and its practitioners. Reader's Digest is replete with denunciations of the rape and pillage in government and other institutions of society but where are the leaders to give voice to undeniable evidence of such selfish wickedness?

A high school student wrote a letter to the editor of the Bakersfield Californian decrying the dismal state of education in Kern schools. His last words: "Education is one of the most important things in my life and I hope it can be improved." My heart goes out to this young person because I know there is little chance of that happening unless the evil people who have the rule are cast out of government and the educational leadership.

Algebra will continue to be a "mystery" to pupils, not because of its inherent complexity, but because those that teach the subject, together with those that dictate how it and a host of other subjects is to be taught, have no real knowledge of the real world or genuine love and concern for young people. This is only one small part of the component whole that has doomed education.

My point is that unless we do something about the present conditions in our society, and immediately, this generation will be defined as the one that destroyed America! And as with the "tinkerers" in education, if those same tinkerers are allowed to continue to rule us, we are doomed! Will God bless those that refuse to do battle? I think not!

I expect to "hit the airwaves" these next two months of campaigning. There isn't much time due to the limits of this special election and I hope you will do more than "pray" for me. Without the practical help James warned of, "praying" is an insult to both God and me!

If elected, I promise you a senator who will stand up against the evil of an evil system. If I can do no more than make the wicked attack me, at least we will succeed in flushing out those that are afraid to take such a stand. Then it will be obvious who the real enemies of America are and be able to deal with them. Let's make our "leaders" confront the truth for a change and force them to deal with it! Let's flush them out of hiding behind special interests and make them give an account of their stewardship! If we work together, it can be done!

I'll leave it to my old friend, Gary North, together with Buckley and Limbaugh and so many other "conservatives," to stomp ants while the elephants are rampaging through the village. As for me, I'm grabbing my Elephant Gun and going hunting! Are you with me?

Chapter Two

The Okie Intellectual

February

Galatians 5:6

The storms moving through this country the past few days have given us an abundance of much needed rain and snow. The trees, vegetation and the critters must be especially grateful. As I write, the sky is overcast with low clouds hanging mistily about the mountains. The air is clean and deliciously scented with the aroma of the grasses, pine and oak. There is an emerald greening of the hills and the lake, river and streams are promising a good fishing season to come.

Speaking of fishing reminds me of the time I was wading in a small stream coming off the old Kern River, fishing pole in hand, before the lake covered the spot. A warm weather system had been moving through the valley and there were clouds about and occasional thunder. Some of you may remember the old, steel, telescoping rods; these were the predecessors of fiberglass rods. So there I am, wading in the middle of a stream, steel fishing pole in hand. Suddenly, a brilliant, blue flash cracked along the bank of the stream less than ten-feet away from me to my right, breaking off the branches of shrubs and trees like pistol shots. I was enshrouded with the acrid smell of ozone.

Why the stroke of lightning didn't choose that long, steel pole in my hand I will never know. But, like the time I tried to dig a Mojave Green out of a collapsed burrow with a two-inch stick, it didn't take much time to realize the stupidity of my actions after the fact. One of several times the Grim Reaper has been cheated of my life through no cooperation of mine; quite the contrary.

It's warm in my "shanty" house and I'm grateful for the view of snow-capped mountains out the windows while KVLI plays the songs of yesteryear in the background; I wish my children and grandchildren could enjoy all this with me. But I must be constantly on guard against living in memory and wishing at the risk of losing the ability to dream. "There I can walk, and recover the lost child that I am without any ringing of a bell." But, "If I have no friend, what is Nature to me?" And there is nothing like the kind of writing

I am compelled to do to leave me friendless. People have never wanted to hear the Truth when it applies to their own evil and apathy. They still prefer Thoreau's sugarplum to the words of the prophets.

As long as I am still living in the area, I take advantage of this to make more frequent trips to the places I knew and loved as a boy. The recent rain has the little stream flowing at the old mining claim. It still enchants as it did those long, decades ago. The mica on the sandy bottom reflects its shimmering golden color through the clear, sparkling water, so much so that I recall first seeing it and thinking the riches of Croesus were at hand.

I walk up the stream, its tinkling chuckle as it burbles over the granite rocks keeping up a lively conversation as entrancing now as then. I'm heading up to the Indian campground I discovered as a boy. The haunting melancholies of the place, the remembrance of such a simple time of simple joys among kind, honest and loving people, my grandparents pervading my memory.

As I approach the campground, my eye picks up the telltale glint of obsidian, the volcanic glass betraying its presence by reflecting the sun. I pick up the chip and peer, once more, through the marvelous, smoky, volcanic piece of glass and feel the presence of the Indians who worked this wonderful material with such consummate skill.

My roots are common with the red-skinned natives of this area. Like them, I hunted the quail, squirrels, rabbits and deer that supplied the family pot. As I stand in this sacred spot, a crow is circling, his caw and cackle mixing with the laughing stream that seems to contribute rather than subtract from the solitude of the place.

A rather stiff, cold breeze is blowing. There is snow on the mountains but the sun is shining brightly in the crystal clear air and the sky is azure with a few, small, brilliantly white clouds dotting the heavens as they move briskly along to some unknown appointment in the East. As I stand in the cold, brilliant sunlight looking into the crystal clear waters of the stream, I think that there is no like cleansing agent in Pilate's Laver which will remove the bloody stain from the hands of the betrayers of my children and my America. How much rather would I give myself over to the memories of the happiness and joy of boyhood in this spot rather than such ugly thoughts incessantly intruding. But when the older man fronts a fact; the boy and the young man recede and take their memories with them.

I've already served my apprenticeship as "Elder Statesman" through life's experiences and the reading, writing and teaching of our national history and literature. All that is left is confronting the evil system and its adherents that are enslaving my children and grandchildren.

The times require no less than what those noble men and women of our revolution gave for our liberty, may, in fact, require even more of us because the evil of our time seems worse than what they faced. For example, they never had to face the government, schools and media-enforced acceptance of perversion on either side of the ocean!

Our present system of government reminds me of a dying animal which, as long as it can crawl, snap, growl or moan, denies with all its draining resources of strength and breath, the encroaching death-throes stealing over its body and senses. Much as the trapped coyote or wolf may even gnaw through its own leg to be rid of the source of its agony and humiliation, government which has lost and forsaken the moorings and direction of morality, may, in mindless retaliation, chew up those that would bring it into the captivity of servitude to the people it is supposed to serve and represent.

The neo-Nazis in Germany have drawn a lot of attention but what of Alessandra Mussolini, granddaughter of Il Duce and niece of Sophia Loren, who, elected to Italy's parliament, is leading many people in the country, replete with Nazi salutes, swastikas and black shirts? Will Italy's recession and corruption in government provide, once more, the opportunity for the ghost of Il Duce to resurrect? One thing is immutable: History and human nature will not be denied regardless of the tenets of humanism!

The media-hyped, revisionist "history" of the holocaust continues to get broad play as per the recent article by one James Rudin. Using the usual "labeling" of "Anyone who doesn't agree with us is stoking the ovens of Auschwitz and loves Nazis," the propagandists of Jewish Intellectualism would destroy honest attempts by honest scholars in search of truth. At the same time we read of an 11-year-old girl shot and killed by Israeli troops! Rabbi Rudin, I have a bulletin for you: Until Israel gives up its own bigotry and prejudicial hatred for anyone who is not Jewish your protestations of Anti-Semitism will continue to fall on deaf ears! The Jew, Howard Singer, "strikes a blow for religious freedom" by winning a ruling from the federal Equal Employment Commission for the right to wear a skullcap on his job as a postal worker but I have to wonder if Christian workers would fare as well if they tried to wear a shirt with a cross or the name Jesus on it?

As for the churches, why is it that organizations such as the KKK and Aryan Nations continue to try to do the job that you should be doing? It ought to shame the churches but, knowing churchgoers and "leaders" as I do, I expect they will continue to avoid battle and leave it to others to do the dirty work for them.

My grass-roots campaign has had many advantages. TV, radio and newspapers have treated me kindly; my not having any political machinery and a lack of "labels" has the media intrigued. "Just who the heck is this guy anyhow?" seems to get their attention. We all love a mystery and the fact that someone can mount a campaign without any "special interest crowd" is such a novelty to everyone that it has a natural attraction of interest.

I enjoyed circulating my own nomination papers. I met so many new folks that I would never have known had I followed the usual route of politicians and had a paid circulator do the job. It was also an invaluable mechanism by which I could listen to what people had to say about politics in general. Sadly, most don't have much hope of anything getting any better. While agreeing that people like me, if elected, could change things, folks don't really believe it can happen; and I fully understand their pessimism.

The mass of men live lives of quiet desperation. It is a curious fact that while Marx and Engles were writing the Communist Manifesto, Thoreau was writing Walden. But Thoreau was laying the groundwork for personal accountability, not as Marx and Engles, the repudiation of the value and responsibility of the individual. Thoreau made the obvious point that a far more subtle and keener slave-master was at work in Massachusetts than that of any Southern one. He repudiated the "liberalism" of the Governor of Massachusetts who would enslave by laws of men, laws that served to deny the Higher Law of God.

I recently received a note from a man whom I respect very much, an M. D., Dr. "Joe." His note reminded me, once more, of the difficulty of finding men of sound mind who are not so immersed in themselves that they can find time to think and discuss the issues of thinking and concerned, responsible men. Of such men like Dr. Joe, Thoreau and myself: "There is the instinct for society, but no society. The society that I was made for is not here. ... If life is a waiting, so be it." So it is that many times I feel I have either lived too long or born to the wrong generation, one that can never accept the truth that "a true account of the actual is the rarest poetry." For example, one would think that a fact so easily discernible as Thoreau's complaint of the churches would be sufficient vindication and cry for reform: "The religion I love is very laic. The clergy are as diseased, and as much possessed with a devil, as the reformers... The church is a sort of hospital for men's souls, and as full of quackery as the hospital for their bodies...One is sick of this pagoda worship." Thoreau's remarks are "dittoed" in regard to government as well.

My problem, as my detractors rightly point out, is my propensity to postpone all "practicalities" in favor of a singing cricket or calling quail. What they fail to realize is the necessity of the cricket or quail (and the feeding of the squirrels, D.R.) in order to properly ascertain the truth of: "The frontiers are not east or west, north or south; but wherever a man fronts a fact!" And only then do the "practicalities" of life come into proper focus.

Our only Native American criminal class, government in general, continues, like the pulpits of America, to engage in verbal flatulence, failing miserably to address the hard issues of our nation. Where is the "leadership" while perverts gain the ascendancy? Why aren't they honest enough to stand up and say: "Perversion is good for our nation and its children!" Why do they let judges do their dirty work for them as per New York, Florida, Colorado and California?

It doesn't take much insight to clearly perceive the leadership as insanely perverted, greedy and egotistical, not just "crazy" as per Perot. That old political maxim holds sway in congress and pulpit: "You don't have to explain what you don't say!" In the meantime, those honest, hard-working people who want something better for their children are stymied by having to offer their children as sacrifices to Caesar on the altar of state schools, courts and legislatures which are dedicated to their further betrayal, the glorification of evil and providing the "underclass" Caesar requires of an ignorant, slave generation.

I am trying to make the obvious point that where there is no true accountability, there is no responsibility. The failure of our "leadership" lay in the fact that the "Buck" never finds a place to stop! The conditions in our government, churches and schools don't seem to be anybody's fault! I'm trying to get the message out to the people that we can't afford to get bogged down in history; our generation must confront the evil mess we allowed and deal with it pragmatically without blaming our ancestors and making excuses. You all know that I'm a pretty fair historian; and while that helps to understand the problems and the required mechanisms of solutions, it doesn't serve as an "escape hatch." ACCOUNTABILITY is still the single fact alone that can deliver us!

The power to tax is the power to corrupt and destroy; and without concomitant accountability! No wonder the L.A. City Schools can "lose" 73 million dollars and no one, not even the teacher unions or the state legislature, wants to know where the money went!

As I wrote before the national election, Clinton is proving his hypocrisy of winning on promises that were, as should have been so patently obvious, impossible of keeping. But his appeal was to those drones that still want a free ride on the backs of workers. Unhappily, it would appear that Bush had orders to "throw the election." He couldn't have behaved so stupidly otherwise.

Enlightened Self-interest demands we follow Franklin, Paine, Adams, and Jefferson. Diverse as their views on some particulars, they freely admitted to realities of greed and morality; such has always been the case with those who are ready and willing to deal with pragmatic and empirical truth, the backbone of Enlightened Self-interest.

There are no answers in the religious right, the moderate or liberal positions. The only workable path is that of those absolutes which are common to humanity. America's unique character was based on those absolutes and unique opportunities. We would never have achieved greatness by following a too-narrow path.

Bill Bennett with his Empower America, Ross Perot, Rush Limbaugh and Pat Robertson all make the proper "noise" but fall short of the mark due to their own, personal agendas. I applaud these men in their efforts to keep the pot boiling, but the really hard issues still fail of a concerted voice due to the personalities involved.

The New American of January 25 has an outstanding article regarding the agenda of perverts, Normalizing Perversion, which I wish every American would read. The "grand design" of the sodomites has been to make divorce easy and divorce laws punitive to men (they have succeeded), to make adultery a joke (they have succeeded), to subvert the family through such laws which would advance their cause under the guise of Civil Rights (they are succeeding), and, through such mechanisms, make our children sacrificial slaves to the State.

An incredible scenario is unfolding before our very eyes. The perverts are, with media cooperation, making such inroads in every segment of society that I have to wonder if God's judgment on America can be delayed much longer. I have written much about this pervasive evil but nothing I have said compares with the present course of Mr. Clinton actually proposing to force the military to openly invite the sodomites into the ranks. As I have said before, I can think of nothing else that would be so demoralizingly destructive to our armed forces and put our whole nation at such risk as this caving in to these perverts.

It has been pointed out that one out of every seven votes cast for Clinton came from perverts. And our president seems to be actually proud of this! If Mr. Clinton is a Southern Baptist, it leaves me wondering just what kind of Baptist Church finds him welcome in its ranks?

Since such a thing as attempting to force the military to openly accept perverts into its ranks is so insane on the face of it, I do have to wonder: Is it just possible that this is Clinton's way of trying to "get even" with a military which, justly, despises the draft-dodging president? Does he think that he can "punish" the military by such a mechanism and get away with it? It's too bad Mr. Clinton has never read that Bible he ostentatiously carries into church. And, if he has read it, it's too bad he doesn't believe it! I would settle for his believing the immutable dictates of history that prove that no nation can survive the acceptance of perversion in its society notwithstanding any religious connotations.

Regardless of religion or the lack of religion, no society, Hindu, Moslem, Jewish, Buddhist, Arab, African, etc. countenances perversion in its society.

And if Mr. Clinton, Barbara Streisand, John Denver et al. think they can force it on American society by fiat of law, by the propagandizing of an evil media, they are inviting a disaster, civil and military, of incalculable proportions! Even apart from God's clear warnings on the subject, my own confidential sources of information make this a given. Regardless of Mr. Clinton's "debt" to perverts, no nation survives the lack of moral absolutes and there can be no moral absolutes without confronting perversion as the thoroughly repulsive and destructive thing it is!

Tom Paine's "Common Sense" brought about the Revolution. Harriet Stowe's "Uncle Tom's Cabin" brought on the Civil War. No literary historian will argue these facts. When people think the Power of the Pen belongs to the mass media they are badly mistaken. The Power of the Pen belongs to people like me who will never cease to speak out about the evil that is threatening our nation. And we number in the many of thousands! Desk Top Publishing has put enormous power in the hands of people like me, and no power on earth can shut us all up! Caesar cannot remove this threat to his evil agenda any more than he can confiscate all of our guns. An armed and vocal populace remains to confront him and confront him we will!

Further, if Mr. Clinton and his cohorts continue to tell us, hypocritically, that the "fix" for our economic woes will mean some "pain" and we, the great unwashed know he is exempting all those fat cats, including himself, from that "pain," he further invites the coalescence of all patriotic factions to confront Caesar's evil purpose.

My friend in Atlanta supplied me clippings concerning the recent attempt by Governor Zell Miller to have the Stars and Bars removed from the state flag. According to the Atlanta Journal and the Atlanta Constitution his audience openly booed the governor. It may have had something to do with his threat that many of Georgia's congressmen would lose "black votes" if they didn't agree with him!

The governor, apparently, doesn't know much about the history of the South. I can't understand his self-serving comments concerning an appeal to the "Party of Lincoln" otherwise. Even given his obvious ignorance of history, one finds it hard to excuse, as with Mr. Clinton, his ignoring the common sense threat that real patriots like The Sons of Confederate Veterans hold politically. Founded in 1896 in Richmond Virginia, the organization's first leader was J.E.B. Stuart Jr., son of the Southern general. Some of the better known "sons": Patrick Buchanan, Sen. Strom Thurmond, Sen. Jesse Helms, Sen. Trent Lott, retired Gen. William Westmoreland and three former Georgia governors: Lester Maddox, Ernest Vandiver and Herman Talmadge. The organization has chapters in 38 states together with chapters in France, England, Belgium, Switzerland and the Mariana Islands. One quote from spokesman Charles Lunsford should suffice: "We're fighting against censorship in the Stalinist mold...We're an oppressed minority." Folks, the battle is really heating up!

I find myself, more and more, having to find common cause with vile men of genius who, at least, have the courage of their convictions. Such a man is Gore Vidal. Quote: "...the United States is the master of the earth and anyone who defies us will be napalmed or blockaded or covertly overthrown. We are beyond law, which is not unusual for an empire; unfortunately, we are also beyond common sense." Are you listening Mr. Clinton?

David Halberstam rubs our noses in the fact that the leadership cannot talk candidly about China, Kenneth Clark makes the appropriate "noise" about the dismal condition of our schools, Arthur Schlesinger Jr. does a good job of presenting FDR's agenda of socialism and National Review tries to tell us Mexicans really want to "acculturate!" A thoroughly mixed bag of signals.

The genius of Mark Russell: "The Clintons are not abandoning public education. Some of Chelsea's classmates will be the children of public school teachers (I could have told Mark that such children make up a majority of private school children). She will be attending the Sidwell Friends School in Washington, originally founded as a Quaker institution. A coincidence, inasmuch as her father became a Quaker during the Viet Nam War."

One of the nastier replies to one of my articles that appeared in the Bakersfield Californian was by, whom else, a public school Spanish teacher, one Mr. Munro. He tried to make "cultural diversity" the object of my opposition to bilingualism, the old "Have you stopped beating your wife" ploy. Now who is going to say that cultural diversity is bad? I have long made the point that when cultural "diversity" becomes divisive by accentuating an alien culture, such as that of the Mexican, it becomes a bad thing. When I had to circulate my nomination papers in both English and Spanish, I resented it. When I have to listen through pre-recorded messages in both Spanish and English when I call a utility company, I resent it. When I have to choose between Spanish and English at my bank, I resent it. My tax dollars are squandered foolishly enough as it is; to further acerbate a bad situation by providing "interpreters" at the Welfare Office and Post Office adds to the resentment. And this is a common sense resentment against an insane policy that does nothing but cause natural resentment! It has nothing of racism about it!

Of course, my rebuttal letter to Mr. Munro's asinine and self-serving attempt to make my opposition to forced bilingualism something racist was refused publication. A very "nice" letter from Dianne Hardisty of the Californian "explained" the paper's refusal to print my letter. "I was a candidate for public office and enough had been said on the subject to provide balance." But a few days later, yet another attack on me by one Sophia Trueluck, a young Negro woman who is a sophomore at California State University, was prominently displayed in the paper. Obviously lacking any maturity of reason or knowledge of the real history of slavery, and not likely to have the real history taught in such a school, she was permitted to vent her ignorant and bigoted views on my position and, like those of Mr. Munro's, given the blessing of the press without my being able to refute her. So much for the Californian's "fairness" and Dianne Hardisty's "enough being said for balance." What the paper doesn't seem to understand is that, as a publisher myself, I am not without the resources to make this hypocrisy known to a great many people, including a large number of our state legislators and national organizations without their "help" and am doing so. But I have to give them credit for continuing to carry Dan Walter's column. And they did print Senator Byrd's remarks dittoing my concerns over so-called bilingualism.

Bottom line: The voice of Truth, Fact and Reason does not have many supporters in the media. As a result, more graffiti covering cities like Bakersfield and freeway signs that are rendered illegible by the gangs. Mr. Munro, Ms. Trueluck and Ms. Hardisty, would of course, refuse any responsibility for the part they play in contributing to this destructive insanity.

Maybe FBI Director, William Sessions, would agree with people like these? After all, if the head of the FBI can lie and steal, why should anyone take Fact, Truth and Reason seriously?

Maybe a few more counties like Catron and five others in New Mexico, all the counties in Utah, Clark County in Nevada and Siskiyou in California will get the attention of the Feds. Seems these counties have adopted the Constitution as their county constitutions. This provides a mechanism of making their county law superior to that of the state and equal to that of the Federal Government and restoring Proper Self-Government to the people! Fascinating! I'm sure I'll be reporting more on this curious action on the part of some Fed-up folks who have tossed a real bombshell at the Bureaucracy.

Some of you have expressed an interest in how I come up with such interesting information that you are not likely to find in the popular media. My readers of a long while know the answer to this question. For some of you newer readers, you would do well to contact the Freedom Foundation at 1438 N. Hollenbeck, Covina, CA. 91722. Also: Aid and Abet Newsletter. P.O. Box 8787, Phoenix, AZ. 85066. In fact, I receive information from approximately 50 such organizations that are dedicated to personal liberty and responsibility. Locally, newspapers like the Liberty Bell and the Enterprise News cover much of this material.

In fact, there are so many organizations dedicated to reclaiming our historic freedoms that most politicians would shudder if they knew and the Feds are actually paranoid, as per the Randy Weaver debacle. The Feds, as I have pointed out, are working in the dark because they can't trust their 12,000 plus, paid "informants" and they can't recruit real patriots to infiltrate and pimp for them.

The courts do the best they can by beating up on such patriots. But my warning of long time still stands; when the people have had enough and are hurting badly enough, judges and politicians had better start cashing in their foreign bank accounts and start looking for a hole to hide in! The new "Minutemen" are all out there and they still have their guns; all that is lacking is that "Leader" who will cause them to coalesce.

I warned during Desert Storm that it was only the "opening gun" to a permanent U.S. "presence" in the Middle East. I also pointed out the "need" for the U.S. to establish itself in Africa. Seems Somalia is the staging area for this "need." In spite of Congress being Israeli Occupied Territory, the need for a gateway to the Arab oil fields has always been a given. Somehow, I don't think it takes that much perspicaciousness or suprasensibility to figure all this out- certainly I don't think Arab nations are having any difficulty doing so.

Americans used to be able to face elemental realities; they no longer do so. We have been cheated of the inalienable rights to do so. For example, why shouldn't a man be able to have a couple of acres and build a cabin on it for his family at a total cost of about $10,000? Get rid of the unconstitutional "building codes" and a family, once more, could actually own their own home rather than renting from the bank! Common sense alone dictates that a family would far rather reap the benefits of their own labor than be slaves to the state and its banks. And, again, common sense dictates that children are far better off being raised in an environment of family and family labor for family benefit than the drug and crime infested cities. Who stole this natural right and personal liberty from families?

The "Land" is still there. But who stole the opportunity for men to be men, women to be women and children to be children? By all means, read Cooper, Thoreau, Hawthorne, Melville, Poe and a host of others to get at the bitter root of the problem. Of America Theodore Parker wrote: "There is always a conservative element in society...which resists the further application of Christianity to public affairs...Here I think it is represented by the merchants.... Here trade takes the place of the army, navy, and court in other lands.... It takes the place in great measure of science, art and literature.... All is the reflection of this most powerful class. The truths that are told are for them, and the lies."

We do not lack for Savonarola's in our own history. But where are they now? Were it not for my being the beneficiary of Hawthorne's "cursed habits of solitude," I would have been far more outspoken in time past. Maybe my campaign for state senate will rectify this. Since I have long agreed with Brownson that "...no reforming leadership could come from 'priests and pedagogues' ...They always league with the people's masters," I have found myself the recipient of a far deeper orthodoxy, that of Truth, Fact and Reason.

I admit to the "frailty" of hearkening more to the cricket's song and the call of the quail than to the staccato yammering of commerce but: "Let men, true to their natures...lead manly and independent lives; let them make riches the means and not the end of existence.... This curious world which we inhabit is more wonderful than it is convenient; more beautiful than it is useful; it is more to be admired and enjoyed than used." And, please, don't mistake either Thoreau or myself for those that would abuse men at the cost of saving an owl or tree! If Truth, Fact and Reason held sway, such a "choice" would be neither "convenient nor necessary" because of the truth of the fact that: "I would rather suffer evil the natural way.... The only good one can do another is to give him an example of a true life.... and to maintain one's self on this earth is not a hardship, but a pastime, if we will live simply and wisely."

In Thoreau's attack on the laws and Governor of Massachusetts in which he correctly, and prophetically, labeled such laws as enslaving by keen and subtle masters worse than Southern overseers, he called to the higher law of God as evidence of the chicanery of politics. "What signifies the beauty of nature when men are base? ... Who can be serene in a country where both the rulers and the ruled are without principle? The remembrance of my country spoils my walk. My thoughts are murder to the State, and involuntarily go plotting against her."

Without ignoring the fact that "getting a living" and caring for a family is of the greatest importance, acknowledging that Plato might have found the society of philosophers "comfortable" because his aunt remembered him in her will, there is still the essential need for the philosopher and poet. I could wish that the necessary poetry and prose for our time could be read with such purity by men and women that they could do so without harm and still understand. But such is not the case. Fact, Reason and Truth dictate that the issues have become such that nothing but a candid ruthlessness offers a way out of the present chaos.

One such truth is the fact that the opportunity for necessary, menial tasks that provide learning and independence are denied our young people. Just what "learning" and "opportunity" are there in "flipping hamburgers?" There is far more of building character in digging holes, weeding gardens, caring for livestock and making the earth yield her increase, of framing your own cabin on your own land, than anything our young people presently learn in our schools.

If young people could learn these tasks, and they would, given a wiser and more responsible and caring, elder generation, in the hope of maintaining their own independence and liberty, we would restore their hope of a future. Given the proper parameters of responsibility and liberty, given the proper role of the schools to advance technology by relying on aptitude and propensity rather than a dilution of the lowest, common denominator, the future could be restored to our children. Reading, writing and ciphering to the extent of necessity is learnable by the end of the fourth grade. The complexities of literature and history, of higher mathematics and science, are the purview of a society that both cherishes its young and, at the same time, acknowledges the necessity of providing those practical skills that enable young people to "do for themselves."

Obviously having lost our moral moorings and being without a moral compass, the young bear the brunt of a careless generation that has betrayed their hope of a future, and without moral absolutes how could it be otherwise? If I'm to be labeled "Intolerant" of the agenda of sodomites, of that kind of "cultural diversity" which is engendering racial strife, destroying any hope of reclaiming the birthright of my children, if I am to be called "bigoted and prejudiced" by the enemies of my America, so be it! Let the battle lines be unmistakably drawn and take a careful look at who is doing the name-calling!

If there is to be abuse heaped, let it come on my generation that betrayed our children! Would young people be drawn to rock stars and pornography, drugs and violence if we hadn't countenanced the evil, from the beginning, rather than taken a stand against it? Maybe it will have to come to the point that good men and women must serve their time in prison as a testimony against such an evil system that is destroying and enslaving our children. If such is the case, it would be ignoble for us to be outside of prison! Maybe the time has come to trade the Caesar-created class of "drug criminals" for those, like myself, who harbor Thoreau's brand of "murder of the State" in our hearts! I will take my stand with Patrick Henry who, under better circumstances than those patriots face today said: "If this be treason, make the most of it!" Far better to be adjudged of such "treason" than supporting and enabling, especially by silent acquiescence, the real treason that is presently cloaked by the infamous laws and distortions of reasonable laws, that have stolen our liberty and promises to enslave our children!

As for the churches, may God do what is necessary to bring them to their knees; this is the only position from which they have any righteous appeal to Heaven! But God has given fair warning of His judgment beginning with His Own House!

(I wrote the following before learning of Ms. Baird's failure to be accepted as Attorney General but felt the comments should be shared with my readers. The point is the continued protestations of Baird and her continued attempts to justify her criminal actions in spite of the fact that We the People could never hope to get away with her flaunting of the law. This attitude hasn't changed on the part of those who feel they are above the law, law that is meant to "control the little people!" We are still left with Mr. Clinton's "not considering such a thing a problem!").

The inauguration ceremonies: Just how much hypocritical hype are we to endure? And, Mr. Clinton, just what do you intend to do about your new, attorney general, Zoe Baird, knowingly hiring illegal aliens (not "immigrants")? Is it, as per your press secretary, Dee Dee Myers, "Not a problem" with you? I think you better reevaluate your position on this one. If Ms. Baird's newly discovered "concerns" for "motherhood" is to serve as an excuse, how are you going to prevent any among us, the great unwashed, from using like excuses for criminal actions?

Isn't it bad enough to find excuses for criminal actions on the part of the nation's most highly placed "cop" and expect us to take such a miserably lame excuse seriously and then expect us to abide by the very same laws you and your ilk openly flaunt? You've bitten off more than you can ever possibly digest on this one. This is your choice for the person who will, among other things, "supervise" the Immigration and Naturalization Service? You just gotta be kidding? And just for the chance to show us all how "very, very concerned" you are for placing women in the highest offices of the land? Forget it! I'm not impressed by anything but the extreme contempt you yourself show for our laws! But, then, you have already expressed your contempt for law so eloquently that nothing you do should surprise us. You say you "Desperately want to make a difference." How about starting with dealing honestly with this charade? If you don't, I shudder to think of what other "differences" you have in mind for the American people!

Now that "motherhood" ala Ms. Baird serves as an excuse for flaunting the law alongside Neil Bush's "stupidity" plea for his part in the S&L thievery, I suppose we can expect an escalation of "patriotism" being the excuse, as per ex-president Bush's pardons, for flaunting any number of other crimes. Tragically, I expect our new "leader" to fully implement the hedonist dogma of the "boomers" that "children know best." But this is one "gray head" that is going to do his utmost to confront your silly, corrupt, hypocritical, selfish and, even stupid agenda of furthering the betrayal of our nation and our children!

As the new "Rehoboam" of our nation, you would do better to listen to the wise counsel of us gray hairs than the silliness of your young friends. Otherwise, you will repeat the mistakes of that other young man who destroyed the kingdom. If you don't, you will deserve no more pity than Rehoboam.

Thinking of Mr. Clinton's choice of Attorney General reminds me of the tragic story of Sodom and Gomorrah. It was a bright and sunny morning when the inhabitants of these two, great cities awakened and said to themselves: "Boy, it sure is a good day to become perverts!" So it was that all the inhabitants of these cities got together with the city fathers that same day and said: "Honorable Fathers, we have all decided to become perverts. We ask your blessing on our noble enterprise."

The honorable fathers, not to be outdone by such a courageous stand by their citizens took an immediate vote, it was unanimous of course, and replied: "Go to it!"

Thus it was that in just one day, Sodomy became the law of the land. There were the usual celebratory activities like bashing straights and tossing them out of the city, confiscating their homes and busily designing curriculum to teach children how good perversion was for their mental health and well being.

All might have gone well for the Sodomites except for one niggling detail; The Lord didn't quite agree. In fact, you could say He was genuinely ticked off. The historical end of these cities is supposed to acquaint us with just how ticked The Lord, in fact, was.

Now I don't really believe the Sodomites really achieved their exalted status of infamy and perversion in a single day no matter how bright and sunny it was. But I do feel they had, eventually, the blessing and approval of the "city fathers." Further, it must have "seemed like a good idea at the time!" The brimstone that covered their infamy and perversion was supposed to disabuse of such a notion and to be a lesson for all time. Unhappily for America and Mr. Clinton, the message seems, once more, to be lost. But God hasn't, at last report, changed His mind about perversion. And as long as children remain the "natural prey" of perverts, neither will I!

I've taken a break to clean out my soul with "Rose-Marie" starring two of my favorites: Nelson Eddy and Jeanette MacDonald followed by a Randolph Scott Western and "Sergeant York" with Gary Cooper; just a reminder that people of my generation knew a kinder, gentler America where romance and justice, verities of morality, were still recognizable ideals. But I still enjoy the music of Jolson also. Incurably romantic!

But, faced with judge Jeffrey Bayless and lesbian activist, Nancy Bailey, telling the people of Colorado to go to hell, what they want doesn't count, I have to seek relief from the insanity all about in those simpler and kinder times of long ago and I try to find a balance with "sauntering," art, literature, music and classic films. Funny, it really wasn't that long ago come to think about it. I have to wonder if Ms. Bailey knows the two teen-age girls who tortured and burned to death a 12-year-old girl for "wrecking" their homosexual affair? I wonder if Mr. Clinton is fully aware of what he is inviting into the military if he forces it to accept sodomites into the ranks? Probably no more than the Jews who have made 415 "swastikas" of those 415 Palestinians.

Seems the schools are going to try, again, to "teach values" without mentioning God! Since the Supreme Court kicked God out of the schools, they have been trying, vainly, ever since, to find a suitable replacement. Maybe Aaron's Golden Calf might be worth a try? The equivalent is already in place via evolution and the World Bank so why not?

Have you heard of the two school districts in California (where else?) that are suing each other? The lawyers have already made over $3.3 million off this "sweet deal" of taxpayer money! Bottom line: Take the money out of the classrooms and taxpayer's pockets and put it in the lawyers'! Makes as much sense as teaching "values" without God! I recall, in the 60s, when the L.A. City Schools spent multiplied thousands of the taxpayer's dollars producing a silly book which went out to all the teachers in the district entitled: Teaching Values. Not one mention of God, of course, and the teachers, understandably laughed at the thing and we all wondered who was trying to make a reputation for themselves at our expense?

At the same time teachers are seeking protection from gun-toting pupils threatening violence and math scores no better now than in the '80s, I can't seem to get people's attention on the need to take our schools back from those that are destroying them! And some of these "destroyers" are in the ranks of "teachers!"

My good, Christian friend, Paul Durbin, made it to Arkansas with his "message" for Mr. Clinton. It turned out to be a real exercise in frustration, but as I shared with Paul: The work fails when God's people fail!

You will remember me writing of Paul when, some time before the election, he set up "shop" at the intersection of highway 178 and 99 with his prominent display of signs asking Mr. Clinton to acknowledge the destruction to our nation of people like Jane Fonda and the perversion which threatens our children. I was honored to be #4 in signing his petition.

Well, as I said, Paul made it to Arkansas but he met with the most frustrating scenario imaginable. He wanted to make sure the message got to the president-elect and tried to locate someone with property proximate to the governor's mansion where he could set up his display. No one would allow the signs on their property. Curiously, he said the best location belonged to someone who thoroughly agreed with him but, in fear of the neighbors, couldn't allow him to use their property for his signs.

Paul called me upon his return to California and I shared his grief and great disappointment that even those who claimed to be Christian were "afraid" to stand up and be counted. I hope the videotape, at least, will make it to our, now, President. Men with the courage of Paul Durbin deserve to be heard but they are too easily dismissed as one of the "little people," part of the "great unwashed," of whom the "leadership" is so disdainful and find so distasteful.

RANDY WEAVER: The continuing tragedy!

Ever since my trip to Idaho last summer and the resulting essays my readers received, it has been a personal responsibility of mine to do all in my power to make sure the Feds do not get away with these murders, the murders of Randy's wife, son and, to a great extent, our personal liberty as Americans.

I am most gratified and hopeful to learn that one of the most successful trial attorneys in the nation, Gerry Spence, will defend Randy. Mr. Spence has a well-deserved reputation for defending the cause of liberty against an unscrupulous Big Brother. Another prominent and successful attorney, David Nevin, will also be involved. As a defense team for Randy and Kevin Harris, these attorneys have submitted an eight-inch stack of grand jury transcripts, autopsy reports, etc. the result of which should, under ordinary circumstances, require the dismissal of all charges.

But Caesar cannot afford to have his Gestapo made to look bad. Least of all can he afford to be proven to have murdered innocent people and then try to "bury" the bodies without giving an account of his actions. I would refer my readers to my earlier essays on this subject to get a fuller understanding of what happened and just how much is at stake for all Americans in this tragedy.

One prominent fact should be kept before everybody; Randy Weaver belonged to no White-Supremacist organization. He did, in fact, accept the history of America, a predominantly White history, he did, in fact, recognize the insanity of the laws that have stolen our birthright as Americans and the attempts of "interested parties and organizations" to make white people ashamed of their history and those Sons of Liberty who gave us the freest nation in the history of the world!

Further, Randy Weaver believed he had a right to go off into a wilderness and carve out a future for himself and his family without Caesar coming after him. Altruistic? Many would say so. But, just what was wrong with Randy's hopes and dreams for his family and, most importantly, what made such a thing "altruistic?"

Certainly such a thing was not altruistic in the historical framework of our founding fathers, our Constitution and Bill of Rights. In fact, it was the Randy Weaver's that made this nation the most powerful in the history of the world, men who willingly forwent the "comfort" of riches and, cherishing their children, would, by their own honest industry and sweat, build, with their own hands, a better inheritance and future for them.

Now the betrayers of our nation and our children have murdered Randy's wife and son, now they are trying to cover their backsides by "burying" Randy and Kevin so Caesar and his henchmen's own dark purposes won't be exposed. If speaking Truth, Fact and Reason be Treason, let Caesar make the most of it! "Give me liberty or give me death!" is not a tired cliché with me; it is not a dusty and musty outmoded concept of heretics but the cry of any man worthy of being called such!

Those that know me know of my own affinity for wilderness places, the mountains and desert, the rocks, trees, streams and critters. I draw strength and hope from the environs of solitary places where men have not corrupted the environment with concrete and asphalt. But neither do I deny the necessity of "manufactures" for the well being of our nation and our posterity. However, the soul of a nation resides in that better part of men who recognize the necessity of the lessons that can only be learned in an environment untainted by commerce.

And, for those who are of such independence that they are willing to forego the comforts and technological conveniences of the cities, they should be allowed the freedom to do so without Caesar's intervention, let alone his punishing them for such independence of character, a character without which America would never have achieved its prominent status among nations.

But, in Randy Weaver and Kevin Harris' case, Caesar is that wounded animal I just wrote of. Caesar is turning, snapping his teeth, growling and threatening all who would oppose him in his unholy cause of enslavement and forced worship of the "State!" The cause of hope among real patriots is Caesar's obvious fear that his dark purpose is not only in jeopardy, but that he is in danger of being exposed for the unholy thing he, in reality, is! I write and speak in such hope. When Caesar and his Gestapo have to act in such a murderous fashion against women and children, I know they are scared and, rightfully so!

Some, even I, have wondered about Randy leading his family in harm's way. Upon reconsidering the criticism I have asked myself the question: Was there any justification for Randy's thinking he might be doing so? I don't believe so. I think he had every right to believe that he was actually leading them into a place where they could live with their values intact and removed from the very dangers which threatened their way of life. I seriously doubt

Randy thought there was any chance that Caesar and his agents would come after them in their solitary, mountain retreat. I certainly don't fault him for not comprehending the extreme paranoia of Caesar and his Gestapo or the extremes they are capable of in trying to extirpate those they consider a threat to their evil agenda.

For those of you who are not yet aware of Randy's real "crimes" they were his refusal to pimp for Caesar and his belief in racial separation. He is not a white supremacist nor did he belong to any white supremacist organization. He is accused of having white supremacist "literature." God help me when the Feds decide to search my place of business. Their only problem would be deciding which body of literature to choose from. They would discover an embarrassing wealth of riches from every organization imaginable including the Masons, ADL and Nation of Islam's. Quite a conundrum for the poor suckers; what they would never find is my list of paid subscribers for my treasonously inflammatory publications.

Now, faced with the motion of dismissal on the grounds of extreme prejudice against Constitutional Rights by U.S. Attorney's Office and the FBI, the "wounded animal" has dug a pit for itself from which it cannot extricate itself without heralding its trampling of every human, decent, Constitutional right of Randy Weaver, his family and Kevin Harris. A most unenviable, and dangerous, position. Hopefully, if the Feds don't get in the way, I'll get Randy, Kevin and Gerry Spence's view on this and be able to share it with you in the near future.

Among the political prisoners of Caesar, there are few more pitiable than Yorie Kahl. Seems just as he would have been eligible for parole, a knife was planted in his prison cell in order to thwart his possible release. He was convicted of this crime on the sole word of a guard. The system refused to even check for fingerprints on the weapon knowing Yorie's would not be found.

The FBI has involved itself (sound familiar?) in the matter and is planning to move Yorie to a prison in Colorado where he would be in 24-hour lockdown for the rest of his life!

I would urge all of you to contact Yorie's mother, Joan Kahl by calling Karen Meyer-Pro American Press - (701) 544-3511 and asking what you can do to help. I would further urge you to send a strong letter to the Attorney General's office, Room 5119, Tenth and Constitution Ave., N.W., Washington D.C. 20530 and another letter to Gov. Robert P. Casey. State Capitol, Harrisburg, PA. 15343. If enough concerned patriots contact these people, they will not be able to "bury" people like Yorie and Lyndon LaRouche and so many others.

I, personally, intend to try to "piggy-back" the cases of Randy Weaver, Kevin Harris and Yorie Kahl. They are prisoners of conscience whose real crimes had to do with personal liberty and Constitutional Rights. The claim and exercise of a Constitutional right cannot be converted into a crime. Miller v. U.S. 230 F2d 486 at 489. But Caesar is converting such exercises of our Constitutional rights and liberties into "crimes" on a wholesale basis. And he will continue to do so as long as the "sheep" remain silent!

One interesting avenue of confronting some of Caesar's minions, judges, lay in the fact that: A judge loses all immunity when he acts in absence of jurisdiction. Lucarell v. McNair. Under such circumstances, and they are far more common than most would suspect, "No immunity exists for any person, Administrative, Executive, Legislative, Judicial or otherwise. No claim of 'Good Faith' or ' Discretion' can prevail." In other words, for example, judges may be punished criminally for willful deprivations of Constitutional rights. 18 usc sec.242 Imbler v. Pachtman. So much ignorance of our rights under the Constitution such as Constructive Notice with Demand, Reservation of Rights and Forced Testimony leaves Caesar carte blanche to act in violation of those rights.

As I write, the hills are silhouetting themselves in the dusk of twilight. The stars will soon appear; the one unchanging source of beauty and promise that never fails. It's hard to deal with such harsh and diabolical machinations of corrupt leaders and still maintain a balance of hope and beauty; particularly when your own heart is drawn to the call of quail and the bark of squirrels, the whispered song of wind soughing through the pines, the murmur and splashing play of a clear and unspoiled trout stream and the fragrant aroma of the trees and grass washed clean by the recent rains.

Far off, and faint as echoes of a dream,
The songs of boyhood seem...
Yet here at least an earnest sense
Of human right and weal is shown;
A hate of tyranny intense,
And hearty in its vehemence,
As if my brother's pain and sorrow were my own. Whittier.

Like my friend, Paul Durbin, the "leadership" found Randy Weaver "distasteful." The fact that Randy considered himself an American with certain inalienable rights in spite of the lack of a "proper pedigree" except for serving his country as a Green Beret, together with his refusal to pimp for Caesar made him not only abhorrent to the Gestapo but an actual threat to national security!

If Caesar were really interested in "national security" he should look into things like the ADL's "A World of Difference." This propaganda "curriculum" is being foisted off on the Kern Schools and others in an attempt to eliminate all references to "color" even to the extreme of doing away with phrases like "black reputation" and "yellow coward." With money provided, ostensibly, by the Irvine Foundation, the ADL has the support of over 200 civil rights organizations in disseminating this propaganda. Call (213) 446-8000 for more information on this material. The Teacher self-assessment questionnaire A questionnaire "For Your Eyes Only!" section alone is enough to warn the careful reader of just what this propaganda hopes to accomplish in fanning the fires of prejudice and bigotry in the Jewish/Marxist Intellectual mold. Any teacher who actually tries to fill out this questionnaire does so at great risk. Tyrants and despots have always used such mechanisms to ferret out the "Enemies of the State." The ADL, as usual, is into extreme "sensitivity training" and organizations like the KKK are provided as the time-honored "bogeymen" to force the "correct-speak" of the infamous ADL and its only "worthy" Jewish Intellectualism.

It's interesting to note that California State Schools Superintendent Bill Honig, you know, the indicted "educator," says he can keep up with his "duties" by putting in one afternoon's work a week. This is supposed to keep taxpayers from worrying about who is keeping the store while he faces criminal charges; pretty fancy salary for someone who can keep up with the work by putting in one afternoon a week at it.

Brings to mind the exorbitantly expensive and cushy offices and staff all our politicians seem to require to do their "duty." Quite a number of their staff is exceptionally attractive as well, I have noted. Maybe if I'm elected I'll find a pretty secretary. Almost makes it worth the trouble don't you think?

But apart from the advantages of surrounding yourself with a bevy of attractive ladies, $800 chairs and $2,000 desks, offices which rival a sheik's harem room and burgeoning Taj Mahal's which the taxpayers obviously feel these politicians need, we, the great unwashed, get to visit our money on rare occasions where the atmosphere is designed to keep us in our place, hat in hand and heads bowed (cowed) by the exquisite finery of it all and secretaries who view us as some unmentionable material on the end of a stick. How dare one of us have the temerity to even request an audience with such powerful people so above our own humble stations? Talk about not knowing your place! If you haven't yet submitted to this valuable learning experience of being properly humbled, try visiting your local congressman, let alone a federal senator or representative. You really owe it to yourself to personally view the trappings of power.

Among the Boston Brahmins, exemplified by Dr. Oliver Wendell Holmes, as intelligent and erudite as they were, they, like so many others, failed to understand Thoreau's "...it is bad to have a southern overseer, but worse to have a northern one!" In short, the Brahmins could work up a great deal of righteous indignation concerning the Negro slavery of the cotton fields, of the

South's peculiar institution, and conveniently ignore the far worse conditions of the wage-slaves of the cotton mills on the Merrimack for twenty-five cents a day who kept the Northern Brahmins rich, not comfortably warm, but unnaturally hot.

The result of all the chaotic insanity of Caesar's laws and minions leads to things like Thomas Fleming, the editor of Chronicles (Feb. '93) writing about the Italian crisis and concluding his excellent article with this sober pronouncement: "The revolution cannot be made overnight, and the first step would be the creation of a movement devoted to the long-range goals of political devolution, privatization (ours is not a free enterprise system), protection of the national interest in matters of immigration, trade, and foreign policy, and the reassertion of our old cultural identities as a European and - dare we echo the Governor of Mississippi? - a Christian nation. If there is no movement or party willing to embrace a Leghist program, then one needs to be formed, and if that is impossible, my advice is to stockpile ammunition and invest in bulletproof doors and shutters."

When, as a result of having to confront the evils of wicked and greedy masters, I feel so alone, it is comforting to find men like Mr. Fleming so likewise knowledgeable of these same things reaching the same conclusions and not afraid to call a spade a spade. May his tribe increase.

Seems the Kern Board of Supervisors adopted a resolution honoring Rabbi Menachem Mendel Schneerson, the Lubavitcher Hasidic Jew who is believed by some to be the Messiah. I haven't heard of the Rabbi denying this accusation. Notwithstanding the many good works of the rabbi, I do find it curious that the Board of Supervisors chose to do such a thing. Did they purposely choose to ignore the prominently avowed racism of the "good" rabbi and his Kabalistic agenda of the subjugation of all sub-humans (all those who are non-Jewish)? I do indeed wonder? After all, the thinking of the Zionists goes hand-in-glove with those Serbs who have engaged in the atrocities and rapes in Bosnia. But that's different?

In speaking to various groups during this campaign for State Senate, it becomes increasingly evident that the "movers and shakers" are not really interested in the schools or the future of young people. A meeting of the Republican Elite in Tehachapi recently made this point indelibly clear. The questions were directed at the economy, as usual, and showed no concern for the schools whatsoever. This in the face of the conviction of the State Superintendent of Schools, as of the 28th, and the message this is sending our young people.

When people who are supposed to be concerned leaders evidence such an apathetic attitude to the future of our children, I well understand their hurt and hopelessness. On the most pragmatic level, you would think these leaders would at least pay attention to the enormous cost of the failure of our schools. It would be a major step toward healing the state's economy if just this one issue were given its needed priority. Even those politicians, well-meaning, who refer to their own children in their concern for the schools are only well-intentioned, not qualified to address those concerns and will, as usual, continue asking the same people who made the mess for answers. Insane!

I found much more genuine interest and concern, in spite of the obvious self-concerns, on the part of the California Teacher's Association in my speaking to them. Even folks with the Kern Labor Board were more in tune with the need to save our schools. But with CTA, at least these people are knowledgeable of the problems unlike the group in Tehachapi and I could converse knowledgeably with them about what should be the several states and the nation's primary concern, our children and their education!

In spite of the beating-up I do on the failure of the schools, I have never lost sight of the fact that one cannot blame school personnel for feeling that the leadership and society as a whole, has deserted them and they see little hope of that situation being reversed. At least these people can relate to me knowing that I do, in fact, understand the problems they face. Unhappily, without proper leadership in their own ranks, they can do little to effect needed changes and are further alienated from those that might be willing to help.

There are some good people, friends that talk about "Choice" as per a voucher system of some kind as an alternative to public schools. I have tried to explain my position of opposing this to these folks. The Parental Choice In Education Initiative presently being circulated in the state, for example, is so full of loopholes for political chicanery that I shake my head that otherwise reasonable people are giving it any credence. But such emotional issues cloud the minds of many otherwise reasonable people.

Pragmatically, historically, Educational Choice is the purview of those who can afford it or are willing to make the necessary sacrifices. Bear in mind that I started three private schools myself. To try to make such "choice" available on a wholesale basis as per vouchers of some kind is utopian dreaming. It not only won't happen, economic realities preclude any such thing. There is just no way to afford such a thing on anything like the scale envisioned. More importantly, to sacrifice the public schools and a multi-billion investment of taxpayer money to such unrealistic dreaming is to give the Devil the game by default. We need to save our schools, not abandon them!

If the schools get the proper leadership, unlike the "Honigs," and the "Willie Browns," and they get the support they need, and I mean real support, not throwing money down a rat hole, they will do better. I know this. But can they presently hope that this is going to happen?

Our new President campaigned successfully (and fraudulently) on the stump of the economy. Now elected, he has spent his time in office playing to the perverts (And I'm sure you have noticed that neither he nor the media has said anything about the very real threat of AIDS in such a scenario). What happened to all his rhetoric about the economy? In fact, what was his emphasis in his very first address to the nation? The perverts! We do have to ask ourselves how his priorities got shifted in such a dramatic fashion? But we are getting nothing better in relation to our children and the schools. The rhetoric is there, as usual, but where are the qualified and responsible leaders? They are playing to the "economy." And we are going to keep electing the same people who not only have no solutions, which they have already proven in the offices they have held, but are more interested in political "careers," their own egos and greed?

I was meeting with a group in Bakersfield the other day. An Egyptian businessman (Islam Auto Sales) was in attendance. In private conversation I asked him about his concerns in America. Bottom line: His concern was making money and helping "his people." He said he had no interest or concern about the history of America or our founding fathers, just making money. Now that was honest. At least he didn't fall into that propagandized, multicultural claptrap that is being sold by the enemies of America. Don't think for a moment that illegal aliens and immigrants have any interest in anything but money. America is still the "land of opportunity" to these people but the opportunity is "get the money" not "acculturation!"

In spite of the enemies of America attempting to, at every turn, make me ashamed of being WASP, that is still what made America great; that is the heritage of the freest, most powerful and prosperous nation in history and far from apologizing for my belief in those Ancient Landmarks, in the Biblical Principles which forged this nation, I will continue to stand for them and my birthright and duty of pronouncing them and denouncing their betrayers!

I confront the leadership of the churches for eating at Caesar's Table but credit to who credit is due. I applaud Jerry Falwell, James Dobson, Pat Robertson and others who, at least, speak out about the perversion that threatens America. The battle for the Soul of America needs all the help it can get and these men, in spite of not being able to do battle with the needed candor and vigor due to their tax-exempt status, are being faithful in what they can do and I am grateful for that.

My new book, "The Lord and the Weedpatcher", is being received well. The pictures of Dust Bowl South-east Bakersfield (Little Oklahoma), the mining claim before the lake went in, the old SouthBay life in the magnificent 50s are worth the price of the book. The text is filled with stories from life in these areas in the early 40s and through the 50s. Anecdotal, because both young and old like stories, I'm sure most people will enjoy it.

I am also going to try to help my friend, the Cowboy Poet, Vern Burandt, publish a book of his poetry. Some of it is really outrageous but Vern calls a spade a spade and really gets under the skin of politicians. His colorful career in dealing with the bureaucracy gives him a lot of insight and I'm sure many readers will delight in his unique way of telling it like it is!

My schedule for February, due to the election of March 2nd, is getting full. I will be speaking to groups like the Christian Coalition of California, California Citizens Committee For Responsible Government, various social service and patriot groups and clubs and school board associations, etc. I'll be busy but am grateful for the chance to make the needs of our children and young people known in a way that only people like me are aware. After all, win or lose, that is why I'm in the race to begin with.

All of this together with a full publishing schedule makes for little time to get out among the trees and critters. But what's a poor, simple Okie to do? Like you, I'll do the best I can and trust The Lord for His part in it all. Who knows, I may meet that companion I seek who can put up with an Okie Intellectual and Poet?

It's unfortunate that I have to wade through such material as AB 3825 in order to understand just what the risks to our liberty are, to understand the evil agenda of those, like Willie Brown, who are attempting to undermine every vestige of personal liberty and commit us, further, to economic suicide in California. This is hard, and, usually, thankless work. But it is a part of my job and contributes to my credibility as someone who understands the problems. This is one of the reasons I get so many requests to quote my material in other publications.

It would be well, however, for those that think the solutions to our state and national woes are so simple, to read some of the legislation with which we must contend before they go off half-cocked and engage in useless rhetoric regardless of how well-intentioned. Again, qualifications, not good intentions, are what matters and gets the job done. There is a need for patriots to speak their minds, but leadership requires more; leadership requires people who know the whole picture and are qualified to supply answers.

Among the other interests and likes I share with our new President such as cats, cigars and saxophones is Gone With the Wind and Southern writers in general. It's that Southern gentility that gives me some hope that the new President may be open to reason once all the dust has settled. I was right there with him, in spirit, when he let that frog go in the river rather than taking the poor critter with him to froggy bottom. I don't really believe he wants to be the American Pharaoh of the Exodus and the destruction of Egypt or the Rehoboam of ancient Israel's final apostasy and destruction, of our own nation's demise. For the sake of our children and young people, I will continue to pray that God will get hold of his heart and lead him in the path of Truth, the Gospel of The Lord Jesus Christ which he professes to believe. After all, he has the same Bible I have; all he has to do is determine to believe it! That, together with the factual history of our national origins as a nation and adherence to those principles of our founding fathers would give him the answers he needs to set us, once again, on the path of those ancient landmarks from which we should have never removed.

As I was returning to Lake Isabella from Ridgecrest the other day, the sun was glancing through broken clouds with a brilliant array of glorious colors. The rugged mountains, resplendent with their magnificent granite formations, spoke to me in the familiar language I came to understand as a child. As long as my own heart is open to such beauty and communication, I can maintain hope that all is not lost; that Truth, Fact and Reason may yet prevail. After all, the only thing necessary is for men like President Clinton and others to acknowledge the truth of our own history and heed those ancient landmarks, those absolutes of truth and morality with which all human beings give acquiescence and which, our founding fathers, more than any others in history, worked into those documents of government which were to lead us for the sake of our posterity, documents which owned our allegiance to, and dependence upon, God, His Word and His Son.

While politicians worry, like a dog with his bone, the issues of abortion, perversion, etc., I will pray that God will lead them to consider the things that promote the General Welfare, the national good and contribute to the hope of our young people rather than the "special interests" of the enemies of God and our nation. Satan and his "ministers" still do business as "angels of light" but those who genuinely care for others can still "discern the spirits" and act accordingly.

But the "leadership" should pay close heed to the maxim: It doesn't take great writers to write with great effect; witness Paine, Stowe, and Hitler. Be warned!

Chapter Three

Christian Perspective

March

Titus 2:1-8

There has been another death out at the old mining claim.

My son, Michael, has re-joined me here in the Lake Isabella area. It was tough on him trying to make it on his own up north. So he called me and I cranked up the old Dodge and drove up to Stockton and picked him up; gave me a chance to see my "little Angel," his sister Karen, and my little grandson James, in Merced.

As long as I have Michael's strong back, I decided to get a chore out of the way that I had been putting off for some time. There was an old refrigerator and some trash to be hauled off from the backyard of one of my rental houses here in the Valley. So, firing up the '64 Chevy pickup, we went out to the house, loaded the old truck and headed out to the local dump.

It was a beautiful day and the work went quickly. We stopped off in Wofford Heights for a cup of coffee and chatted with a couple of friends. As we drank our coffee, the local radio station, KVLI, had an announcement concerning a wreck on the road we had to take going back to Bodfish. But, not willing to backtrack 22 miles, I decided to risk it and take the direct route toward the accident.

As we approached the accident site, it became evident that it was a really bad one. Not only that, it was on a part of the road that ran directly through our old mining claim of Boulder Gulch (Now Boulder Gulch Campground). There have been a number of accidents here over the years due to the steep grade of the highway and the fact that Sawmill and Hungry Gulch roads both come out on the highway at this point and unless one is very careful, vehicles can pull out in front of fast (often too fast) moving traffic.

CHP had the road blocked, so, knowing the area as well as I do I pulled off on a dirt track that would take me around the campground and back on the highway. Accidents are a magnet of curiosity so when I found a convenient spot at the campground to park, we stopped and got out and walked toward the crash site.

It was a bad one, one of the worst I have seen around the Valley. Six vehicles were involved, a couple so badly mangled the makes and models couldn't be discerned, hardly recognizable as vehicles. Two were over the bank of the road on the West, two were over the bank on the East and two were still on the roadway.

A large number of emergency vehicles were at the scene; fire, ambulance, tow trucks, CHP and Sheriff vehicles. A body lay on the ground in front of us, covered with a thin blanket. It turned out to be that of Patricia Montgomery, the manager of my local bank. Now, the tragedy became personal.

The vehicles were a really mixed bag- an open Jeep, a Ford Bronco, a large Milk truck, a pickup, and a couple of passenger cars. The way the vehicles were tossed about and crushed, it seemed a wonder that only one person had been killed though a number had been seriously hurt.

Before too long, a CHP helicopter had landed and news media people began to arrive. Michael and I watched as an ambulance crew came over and picked up Patricia's body which had been lying in front of us and loaded her in an ambulance, a final rite of passage that this poor woman could never have anticipated as she had gone about her normal business of the day just a short time ago. I had to once again consider what I have experienced so many times in the past, how in an instant our lives can be irrevocably altered, even snuffed out.

Standing on this site where my grandmother and great-grandmother had both passed away quietly in one of the old tarpaper cabins we had lived in so long ago, I thought of the tragic consequences that another death here would bring. People's lives had just been changed forever in the blink of an eye. Death and torn, twisted bodies. People at Patricia's bank will be in shock over the fact that they will no longer see her at her normal work station, an abrupt and terminal vacancy; the person is irrevocably gone!

When you view such a scene, you notice the debris; not only the various parts of the vehicles strewn about, some recognizable, some not, but the things of most tragic interest are the personal articles that, only moments before, had such relevance to normal life, things like shoes, torn articles of clothing, the Burger King toy; that and a small, stuffed animal jars you with the chilling thought that a child may have been hurt. A bottle of Jean Nate. Had that belonged to the dead woman? Broken glass everywhere.

I walk over to the little stream I mentioned in my last essay and let reverie wash out the tragic spectacle of the accident and that poor, unfortunate woman's body being loaded for transport, the toys and personal effects which had been savagely thrown about my old "home." The carnage of the highways has become such a commonplace that we hardly give it a thought- until it happens in our own lives! None of these people had started their day with such a thought of this ever happening to them. That is the nature of "accidents." They always happen to someone else.

I survived my worst accident, on a motorcycle, many years ago. My eldest daughter, Diana, did not. But such things change your life and, if you are the survivor and a loved one is lost, it affects the way you think forever after.

As I drive around the Valley, I know it well enough to beware the potential hazard areas. As I drive the Canyon Road to Bakersfield, I know every turn of the highway intimately. I have traveled this road since 1940 and have been driving it since 1952. I know I am driving it safely but, invariably, there will be some idiot roaring up on my bumper so very anxious to kill himself or someone else just to "save" five minutes. It was undoubtedly just such an idiot that caused the carnage I viewed at the campground.

Accidents don't happen; they are caused! is a familiar phrase. Is it any "accident" that our schools have become the only avowedly "Atheistic" institution in America?" No, you don't have anyone admitting this or even mentioning it but it is the truth nevertheless.

There is only a handful of professing atheistic organizations in the entire world. Many are agnostic but extremely few are atheistic. Yet, here in America, the single government institution, the only one that has such an impact on our future as a nation, is exactly that: Atheist! Certainly, when pressed on the matter, our elected officials will admit that prayer, the Bible, any mention of God or Jesus Christ by a teacher is anathema in our schools. But Atheist? Heavens NO! Further, the schools will enforce the Big Lie of evolution as fact rather than "theory" but to even mention Special Creation? Again: Heavens NO!

But Truth, Fact and Reason plainly declare our schools to be Atheistic to the core. Our founding fathers would never have believed such a thing possible or, I am sure, they would have, without dissent, made provision in our Constitution to include God as the only motive force for moral behavior and values in any educational system. They easily owned their reliance and allegiance to Divine Providence and the need for The Lord's guidance and protection in every other way. Who dares to say they wouldn't have done so in this most important instance?

As for those, primarily my brethren of the religious right, who insist on claiming that the schools have a religion, secular humanism, and, therefore are not "godless," hence, not "atheist," I call their attention to the fact that atheism is, by strict definition "godless." In spite of the fact that secular humanism follows the "god of this world," the Devil, its proponents, like those Jewish leaders of old who were condemned of Jesus for having the Devil as their father, know nothing of God or the Truth of God. Hence, by definition, the schools are godless institutions (the Devil not being God), because of the very fact that there is only one True God and He is the God and Father of the only begotten Son, Jesus Christ. Trying to define the schools as anything but atheistic flies in the face of both the legal and religious definitions under which the schools operate.

I asked the question some time back: If this is not to be a Christian Nation, then what is it to be? It was, fundamentally, a Christian Nation in the philosophy of the founding fathers as is easily evidenced by the historical facts and documents including our Declaration of Independence, Constitution and Bill of Rights together with the earliest literature of the nation.

On the most pragmatic and empirical level imaginable, it is patently obvious that the schools cannot do the job of teaching morality and values without a guiding principle of acknowledging God! It wasn't long ago that the Ten Commandments were displayed on classroom walls. Whose idea was it that this was "bad?" Who decided the Pledge of Allegiance, including the phrase Under God was bad for our children? Just whose idea was it anyhow, that kicking God out of the schools was in the "best interests" of our children and nation? Probably the same people who decided to gut our steel and auto industries and made it more "profitable" to move our jobs and factories to foreign countries, the same people who decided perversion is good for our society and children, the same people who decided illegal aliens "contribute" to our nation's well being!

It should be obvious that no matter how much constructive work is done in reclaiming our schools, none of it will avail if the single most important thing, the motive force for moral relevance and behavior, God, is missing; but if He is not the God of Christ and the Bible, then whose?

If the strictest Platonic reasoning is applied to the case, we will either have the indiscriminate anarchy I have long warned of, with ethnic cleansing in our own nation, blood in the streets, or good men will come together to confront Caesar and his minions with an ultimatum: Either shape up in the traditions of those ancient landmarks that made us a great nation, blessed of God, or face the consequences of rebellion by those that will fight to reclaim them! And I repeat: If this be treason, make the most of it!

I, like many of you, am growing weary of taking my walks with murder of the State in my heart, spoiling my days and wreaking havoc of my dreams for my children and in no other institution of government is such villainy and tyranny as obvious as it is in our atheistic school systems. But what we live with, which is so destructive of our nation and young people, has been no "accident." It has been carefully contrived by the betrayers of God and our nation. Many are shaking their heads over the "carnage" and wondering: "What happened? How could such a thing happen?"

I knew, going in, that the subject of education would be a difficult one on which to campaign and so it proved to be. I have had decades of experience in trying to save our schools. So it is that after doing so much campaigning on the issue, I realized that I would never be elected on this basis; it is just not a priority with people or the legislature. In spite of the conviction of Honig on such an obvious ploy of using his office for personal profit, he still, like most politicians, Clinton included, "doesn't see it as a problem!"- The obvious conflict of interest and his threat to subordinates if they didn't use his wife's "service," QEP.

In speaking with senator Don Rogers, I came to the conclusion that I should withdraw from the state senate race and give my support to Mr. Phil Wyman. The problem we faced in this election was that, apart from myself, there were no other genuinely conservative choices. Phil was well known to me and I knew that, while he lacked my experience in the field of education, he was genuinely concerned with the condition of our schools and would accept my input. Further, Phil, with his considerable experience in the state legislature and his promise to give me an active voice in school reform, would be able to "hit the ground running" while it would take a great deal of time, time we don't have, for me to gain such experience in Sacramento before I could have any hope of being effective.

So, with the wise counsel of my friend, Don Rogers, and in consultation with Phil, I made the decision to withdraw in the hope that these men will accept what I have to offer from my own expertise in education. With this hope in mind, I called for a press conference on February 11 where I made the following statement to the media:

DONALD HEATH for STATE SENATE

February 5, 1993

In view of what is at stake in the forthcoming election for State Senate, I have, after consultation with Senator Don Rogers and Phil Wyman, decided to withdraw and give my support to Mr. Wyman.

I entered this race because of my conviction that someone had to draw the attention of people to the need of our young people and our schools and there were no qualified people in the state legislature to address these needs.

My deep respect for the counsel of Senator Rogers, his proven record and the qualifications of Mr. Wyman with his considerable experience in government led me to believe, that, my best course of action in gaining a continued voice for the needs of the schools and our young people could best be served by my withdrawing and giving my assistance to Mr. Wyman as the only other candidate who could serve with hope of success in this area.

It is my hope that men like Senator Rogers and Mr. Wyman will accept my continued input concerning education for the sake of our schools and relevant education for our children as I will continue to maintain my position that unless we solve the problems of education, we will not be able to offer our children hope of a meaningful future.

I would urge all those that have supported me in this campaign to give their help to Mr. Wyman knowing that we will have, as with Senator Rogers, a good man and another strong, conservative voice in the state legislature.

My deepest thanks to those of you who have offered me such help and encouragement in this campaign; if we succeed in getting Mr. Wyman elected our labors will not have been in vain. (End)

All three local television stations were represented at the press conference together with radio and newspaper media and it went very well. Phil and his campaign manager, Dan Dillenger, were there with me as well. Phil was very gracious in his remarks concerning my qualifications and particularly my experience in the schools and his genuine gratitude for my endorsement of his candidacy.

Unhappily, the TV stations, while doing a satisfactory job of covering my remarks, aired none of Phil's. I have to attribute this to the media's agenda of denigrating a solid, conservative such as Mr. Wyman and, since I was withdrawing, focus on me rather than giving him airtime. If they only knew the continued and mounting danger I represent to their own agenda I'm sure they wouldn't have given me such good coverage!

Further, I am still scheduled to make appearances to various organizations and I will keep beating the drum for taking back our schools from the grip of the Enemy. I will continue on radio with the help of good men like Richard Palmquist and Bill Lucas and, of course, I will continue to wield my most powerful weapon, my writing, in spite of: "Sometimes one must fight for what one believes in. Other times it's best to skip the country." This from National Review. Another one, the title of a book in another of NR's cartoons, the media's concept of me: "The Joy of being a Bastard!"

And so, I will hope for your prayers and continued support for me as I try to do the job that must be done for our schools and young people knowing that we have some good, truly conservative men in the legislature. To this end, I ask your prayers and support for Mr. Wyman. He is most deserving of such or I wouldn't have given him my endorsement and withdrawn my own candidacy. The biggest problem remains in California: that of the conflict between the welfare mentality of the Democrats ala Willie Brown and those like Wilson, Rogers and Wyman who are trying to do something constructive about the situation.

A glaring, recent example of the problem is Governor Wilson's attempt to prohibit the use of taxpayer's money going to educate illegal aliens. You would think such an affront to common sense wouldn't encounter any resistance. But there stands Willie and company, the Democrats, refusing to allow the governor to eliminate this expensive insult to the schools and us. I applaud the governor and Assemblyman Richard Mountjoy, the sponsor of the bill that would prohibit the use of tax money to educate undocumented aliens (one of my campaign issues), for, at least, trying. But how can we expect common sense answers to our economic suicide as a state when the Democrats, those who hold office on the basis of the continued betrayal of our state by selling out to the welfare crowd and others who want a free ride on the backs of taxpayers, continue to have us by the throat?

Perhaps some of my writing got into the hands of Rep. Toby Roth, R-Wisconsin. He has introduced legislation that would make English the official language of the U.S. This common sense legislation, as per my own views, would cut off Federal funding for so-called "bilingual education," and bilingual ballots, government forms, etc. He also, apparently, shares my view that if you can't read and write in English you shouldn't be able to vote or get a driver's license. I hope all of you will support Mr. Roth in this. It will be interesting to see who in congress will attack this much-needed and long overdue legislation.

At the same time, our Governor will ask the Fed to pay up for California's continuing to have to cover the mess created by congress in having to pay for the illegals in our own state. Wilson has asked $1.45 billion but this is only a fraction of the real cost as per crime, etc. with which the state has to contend because of these criminals who are only after the money, free medical, dental and welfare and could care less about our country otherwise.

I continue to monitor the "race" problems overseas. It is interesting to watch police in Europe and England gaining notoriety as they are accused, more and more, of becoming "racist." Only a devout fool would not realize that police are human beings, family men, who recognize the threat of alien, and, too often, racial ideologies to their own nations and the future of their children. If "ethnic cleansing" becomes the rallying cry in our own nation, the "grunts" in our police departments will play a prominent role. The "enemy" will come from those on the Federal payroll. Just as the repulsive facts of J. Edgar Hoover become more and more obvious, perverted "leadership" at the Federal level will mitigate in fomenting anarchy in this nation.

Personally, I would love to see a few of these Spanish radio stations blown up. I get so angry at turning the radio dial and encountering this alien language cluttering up more and more of the airwaves. This is nothing but propaganda for the multicultural enemies of America and I want to see it stopped! You find the bleeding hearts crying out against the "outrage" of a John Varela wanting to march for the KKK in Bakersfield but never a word in the media about the obvious subversion of a foreign language being given such prominence. I know, personally, of two good men on our Board of Supervisors but they are so intimidated by the media propaganda of "prejudice" that they don't dare speak to this situation, and, in fact, go along with the decision to urge a boycott of the proposed KKK's demonstration against immigration. But if perverts wanted a parade, I'm sure the Supervisors would go along with that. And, of course, they would have the blessing of the Kern Human Relations Commission. The insanity of it all!

A Negro woman is given prominence in speaking in our local college concerning her role in the Civil Rights movement of the 60s but no Caucasian person dares encourage pride of white achievement. Compare the work of an Angela Davis with someone like Thomas Jefferson and you will have the sodomites, the NAACP, the ACLU etc. screaming "Prejudice!"

Side-by-side are two stories in the local paper: "L.A. Protects Gay Workers" and "Accused Priest Resigns." Seems the "Rev." Richard T. Coughlin, founder of the All-American Boys Chorus was doing more than leading the singing. Odd that no connection is made by the leadership or the media between these two things or the Chicago Police using street blockades to control crime. No society can hope to make sense of insanity and the court's attempts to do so only obfuscate and acerbate the situation further. As a result, Posse Comitatus and Vigilante Police groups grow correspondingly. Recently, a cop who blew away a shotgun-wielding criminal was reported to have engaged in "High-fives" with his fellow officers after the incident. This, together with the shooting and killing of two lawyers by another lawyer in Texas, might offer hope to some.

As comic relief to all the madness, I hear from informed sources that the book, "Why The Clinton Administration Failed," is already being readied for the presses. Nepotism (The Iron-busted Maiden otherwise known as the power behind the throne) together with the wet-behind-the-ears, snot-nosed kids he chose as "counselors" and playing footsy with the sodomites are the primary reasons for his failure to lead or keep his word, which, everyone quickly learned, he wasn't sure of in any event.

I present the following for your consideration, particularly all you "professional politicians." If, in a "hypothetical conversation," a man offers to blow away Willie Brown (or, increasingly, Mr. Clinton), and I encourage him to do so, I am guilty of conspiracy to murder. But if I engage in a legitimate act of warfare, I cannot be tried for a crime.

I submit, further, particularly for those of you who claim the name of Jesus Christ that if America was founded as a Christian Nation, the act of rebellion against the tyranny of the King and his minions, our Revolutionary War, was done by claiming the approval of God and repeated requests for His help in the rebellion. The seeming incongruity of this action can only be accepted as proper under the following conditions:

First: the cause must have been righteous by God's definition of righteousness. Second; the courses of action including that of war must have delegated, proper authority and leadership to be lawful. If these two conditions were not met, the rebellion would be without the approval of God, history, or civilized men.

If there is to be a confrontation of Caesar in a contemporary context, the same conditions must be met. Bearing in mind that the Crown treated our founding fathers as "rebels" and "traitors" we must accept this possibility as a result of our own confrontation with the tyranny that we must now face. This confrontation was not for the faint-hearted then and it will not be for the faint-hearted now!

We have just celebrated Whiskey Flat Day in Kernville. I drove a float (quite a grandiose appellation for my '64 Chevy pickup) in the parade to represent Phil Wyman. My son, Michael, sat in the back holding a sign for Phil. Sorry about that Phil, Po folks got po ways. It was a lot of fun except for the interminable shoving up and down on the clutch in the old truck for about an hour.

As I later sat in the park by the river, a young fellow walked over pushing his bicycle and sat down and we struck up a conversation. Seems he was a ferrier down on his luck. He was presently residing in a tent down river somewhere until he could collect his welfare and food stamps. I shared some of my woodsman lore with him, particularly how to keep coals alive so he could easily get a fire going early the next morning. The nights are cold right now and this would help him considerably.

I mentioned the fact that it really wasn't that many years ago that people lived without electricity and indoor plumbing. I was raised in such a fashion myself. A few years ago, I was living in similar circumstances. I lived like an animal, as I felt then, homeless and not knowing where my next meal was going to come from. No money, no job, no family due to a betraying, adulterous wife, no place to live, a situation where just to be able to close a door and have some privacy was a pure luxury. Therefore, I could easily commiserate with this young fellow's situation. And, thanks to my experience in Little Oklahoma and the mining claim days, could offer him practical advice on survival skills.

It was when the conversation turned political that the going got heavy. Here was another example of many I have met of a man who was more than willing to become a "soldier" to "do some killin' of those that need killin'." All these desperate people need in order to start shooting is the leader they can trust and follow in blind obedience. It reminded me of a recent conversation with an old friend, "J," who said if someone offered him $300,000 he would be more than willing to "take out" an unnamed "leader." I thought his price a rather unusual one and pointed out to him the fact that there were too many people who would do the same thing for the smallest fraction of his price. I'm sure this dampened his entrepreneurial enthusiasm somewhat. The actual threat, however, of this approach to the solutions for our national insanity of enslaving by laws and taxes, of economic suicide by penalizing individual rights to life, liberty and the pursuit of happiness predicated on the individual's personal liberty and responsibility, of the sanctity of family and personal property, is reaching a boiling point. When life becomes irrelevant and hopeless, too many "soldiers" are simply a waiting army, waiting for that "leader" who will cause them to coalesce.

Too many people are raising the question of whether it wouldn't be more productive of needed changes in government to engage in "lawful warfare?" The documentation, the very wording, of our righteous grievances against Caesar is already written as per the founding fathers. It would be difficult, even presumptuous, to attempt to improve on the words of men like Paine and Jefferson and, later, Thoreau.

So it is that the very same conditions (even worse, in my opinion) prevail which led to our Revolution. The documents of rebellion against tyranny are already written. All that seems to be lacking is the virtuous, righteous leadership that would pledge its life, honor and worldly goods to the cause of freedom and liberty.

It is interesting to note what South Africa is going through at this point in time. Seems F.W. de Klerk's government is proposing a bill of rights aimed at forcing future black governments to honor human liberties and property rights, free speech and political freedom, freedom of religion, etc. very similar to our own Bill of Rights. Of greatest interest is the attitude of the media that is accusing de Klerk of hypocrisy in insisting on these rights.

What the liberal media refuses to confront is the fact that South Africa had no need of such a "bill of rights" as long as it was under white control. The white government had those safeguards in regard to its citizens but de Klerk knows, even as I have written, that once a black government is in control, there will be chaos without such a bill of rights being legislated to protect all citizens without regard to color or "tribal affiliation." There is evidence aplenty in Africa of what the results will be otherwise when "Sons of Ham" are in control. I am sure that de Klerk also knows that even such "guarantees" guarantee nothing if black leadership continues its historic pattern in Africa and there is no evidence that this will change; quite the contrary.

A not inconsiderable subject that is fomenting rebellion in the hearts of real patriots is the issue of perversion. The perverts are upset about a recent study which only emphasizes the fact that AIDS is, predominantly, a homosexual disease. But the sodomites will continue to try, with ACLU help, to make us all afraid of the disease and make it a "common" concern. This isn't the flu folks; and ignoring morality and common sense does put heterosexuals at risk. But the disease is, just as its first name called it: Gay-related!

I'm sure that another study which shows lesbians have a far greater incidence of things like breast cancer, two to three times greater, in fact, will be attacked as well as "discriminatory" and further evidence of "intolerance." But, as with the issue of pornography, will women pay attention to their responsibility in such things or will they continue to make such things the "fault" of normal people? Not as long as women of the type Clinton keeps pushing are the best they can do for "leadership."

As to the leadership of a new Boston Tea-party and revolution, I am most certainly one such in my heart. How, as a Christian, can I think otherwise against such evil and injustice?

Willie Brown "blasts" the prosecution of Honig. He continues to defend a man who is guilty as sin at the same time such a "leader" led more than half of California's school districts into deficit spending, districts which, at this time, will require "bail-out" monies to continue to operate without any accountability. At the same time we are being told that unless the Republican Party "moderates" its stance on issues such as abortion and "improves" its image of "intolerance" Rich Bond says the party is on a "sure path to disaster." So it is, as I explained to the leader of CTA, I may be a "poor" Republican but I would make a worse Democrat!

Just exactly who is doing the name-calling? Who is saying that I am "intolerant" for confronting the evils of abortion and perversion? Just who, exactly, is supporting the tax-and-spend Capets of our national disasters of moral and fiscal suicide?

Perot makes the point of Clinton's choices for Attorney General that the latest one, Kimba Wood, "...trained as a Playboy Bunny but never worked as one...That's like 'I smoked but I didn't inhale.'" Perot is certainly right in pointing out the fact that people like Clinton have an arrogance that they and those they approve, people of their "station in life," are above the laws that constrain the great unwashed. But when it comes to arrogance...? Ah, Mr. Perot.

But when I get into such a mind-set, in order to escape the ugliness of it all, even temporarily, I hark back to those simpler times in which I would far rather lose myself in the reverie of those things that are pure, joyful, of good report. And I admit to, among other things, approving Clinton's restoring the good music of those 2,000 albums that have been gathering dust in the White House since 1981, at least the ones that pre-date rock. I would even rather involve myself in the interesting things like Faulkner's niece, Dean Faulkner Wells, meeting with Jack Hemingway in order to bury the hatchet over the remarks made by Faulkner of Hemingway as a writer.

South Pacific is one of our all-time great musicals. Richard Rogers and Oscar Hammerstein II really outdid themselves on this one. With a cast led by Ezio Pinza and Mary Martin, the play and movie, the unsurpassed music lives in the hearts of multiplied millions. Michener would never have believed his "Tales of the South Pacific" could have resulted in such a romance of brilliance.

The great musicals of American art still speak to all those who refuse to give up the dream that men and women can still find love; those who don't seek it out or give up are the much poorer for it. Such people cheat themselves of the haunting truth of Some Enchanted Evening and Bali Ha'i for fear, perhaps, of not being able to endure the pain of This Nearly Was Mine. Such cowards will never understand Carefully Taught.

I was only beginning to learn to play the clarinet and saxophone from the great music teacher of old Kernville, Williard Swadburg, when the music of South Pacific came onto the airwaves in the late 40s. But I added the songs as quickly as possible to my, then, slim repertoire. Music became such a passion of mine in high school that I joined with another boy, Russell, as the only two boys in a class of girls for Music Appreciation. Now that was truly "heroic!"

As a man, I still hold on to the dream of finding the warmth and love that only a woman can provide. I am still that Cock-eyed Optimist:

I hear the human race, is falling on its face, and hasn't very far to go. But every Whippoorwill, is selling me a bill and telling me it just ain't so!

But I'm stuck like a dope, with a thing called hope and I can't get it out of my heart!

One of the nicest compliments I have received recently was from a woman who said she enjoyed reading my writing because it was "down to earth." I even explain things like *chiliest* when writing about theology rather than trying to dazzle and impress with linguistic footwork. I will forego the high-sounding rhetoric, no matter how erudite, and the jarring of literary critics that the lyrics of such music as that of South Pacific don't qualify as poetic "art." Let me bear the brunt of those who are so callous as to not recognize the merits of such things while I pity them as they remain outside the pale of romance.

If a man or woman can relate to This Nearly Was Mine, who has felt the pain of Paradise Lost without it destroying them, without making them give up the dream of Paradise Regained, they are really alive. Those of us whose hearts are moved to look into the distance and give ourselves to the haunting melancholy of Bali Ha'i are not without hope of that love that will fulfill our purpose and destiny as human beings. Such people never give themselves to the "lessons" of hatred (Carefully Taught) simply because other people are "different."

In spite of the pain of the continual betrayal of love, the music remains in my own heart but I have been robbed of the memories. I can recall the warmth and softness of the women I have known, but their betrayal of love by their infidelity has stolen their faces from memory, stolen the secrets of lovers, stolen the special, precious memories of the sharing of lives, the meeting of the challenges of life together for the benefit of one another, of family; so much loss, huge chunks of life itself buried deeply in the subconscious as callous protection from the pain and grief of tragedy. It's not unlike my delight in placing a fresh flower on the nightstand of my "Lady." She is gone now, betraying my love for her for the cares and concerns of this world, the easy seduction by so-called "men" who prey on silly women who are easily flattered and go for the "better deal," betraying the flowers and the things of real value for those things that will only perish in the using and the sins of the flesh.

I can't help but wonder if the churches will ever get beyond the dusty, musty stories of past glories and battles won; the rudimentary fundamentals of the faith and recognize the longing of hearts, the need for the gentle strength of faith that builds on the present rather than the constant recitation of the past. A far more powerful sermon could be preached on the themes of South Pacific than the tired clichés of Moses in the bulrushes, the dusty tales re-hashed endlessly. To teach the young the grand, old stories is necessary. But when the pabulum is simply supplied a garnish and expected to sustain the adult, something is missing- the meat! But the churches are no more heedful of this missing ingredient, confusing it with "theology," than they are of the necessity of hearts which seek meaning in meaningless ceremonies and, consequently, find those needs only hollowly met.

If I were back in the pulpit, I would preach on South Pacific. I would quote Corny as Kansas in August and ask the relevant question: Who made such feelings "corny?" I would reach out to hearts with God's own love in Some Enchanted Evening and Bali Ha'i. I would address the reasonable questions of Carefully Taught and ask, further, what happened to our music which used to be fun (Phil Harris and Spike Jones), romantic (Rudolf Friml, Rogers and Hammerstein) inspiring (Sousa), lilting, spirited and just plain good to listen to (the Big Bands)? And the same could be said of our literature.

You can't have loving mothers and fathers when you have faithless husbands and wives. So it is that in too many cases today, children are a curse rather than a blessing. Invariably, when a nation loses its moral compass and forsakes its moral absolutes we discover too late that true love and romance, together with family and children, are the victims. Sadly, the churches don't seem to be able to deal with the fact that only real men are able to do the job God requires for the success of family and real men don't cave in to the whims of women but "rule" as God says they must. But the churches are to blame, more than any other institutions, for the lie of "equality." And, as a result, women and children suffer the corresponding loss of true romance and proper leadership.

Once in a while, I have to mention my old friend since high school days, Gary North. Since I was the human instrument of his becoming a Christian so many years ago, I continue to feel a responsibility for him in spite of the way he steadfastly refuses to acknowledge my own ministry; I am, he says, "Doomed by my refusal to see things his way!" By that, he means, my mule-headedness in not subscribing to many of his schemes and doctrines. There is the fact that I am his "elder" in the Gospel in spite of his chaffing under such a thing. But "children" continue to go through that rite of passage during which they think they know better than their parents. Gary is no different in this respect.

But Gary, as president of ICE, does put out some good material. So good, in fact, that the Wallstreet Journal, for which he once worked, once accused him of fomenting anarchy. I have always applauded Gary's own stubbornness in this regard. I particularly liked Ken Gentry's recent treatment (Ken is a contributing member of ICE) of: "Orthodox Christianity is Anti-Semitic?" Dr. Gentry does an outstanding job of confronting the hypocrisy of the oxymoronic Judeo/Christian pap that so many ignorant people have been sucked into. But, as with the clear and, you would think, unmistakable Word of God Himself on the subject, so-called Christian leaders still perpetuate this abortion of a lie and call all those who don't agree Anti-Semitic. To quote Gentry's conclusion:

"In Ice's book (Thomas Ice) 'Ready to Rebuild' there is a picture of him, with delight in his eyes, sitting down with Gershon Salomon, the Jewish founder and head of the Temple Mount Faithful. Now as a good Christian, I am sure Tommy warned Salomon of the soon coming holocaustic judgment on Israel. And I am sure as a Christian pastor he presented Salomon the Gospel of Jesus Christ, pointing out that He and He alone is 'the way, the truth, and the life.' Of course, I just recently purchased some ocean front property in Arizona, too." Gentry also deals with Hal Lindsey's theological abortion of Christian Zionism.

I bring Gary up at this time because of a recent article of his in The Freeman magazine. The subject, the public schools, is, of course, close to my own heart. Although Gary lacks my qualifications and experience in the area of education, this deficiency often leading even good men awry, we couldn't be more in agreement on the facts he faces in this excellent article.

Before going any further, however, it would be a good thing to give credit where credit is due. I am always careful to encourage men who are doing battle by citing them where I use their material. How about it Gary? Aren't you using my material in regard to your articles, among others, in your series concerning Leadership and Discipleship? After all, we are supposed to be on the same side, aren't we?

Since I am opposed to voucher systems, I have suffered some antagonism by the religious right. I am grateful for the fact that Gary agrees with my point of view on this subject. Gary's bottom line is what I am leading to, quote, re: school administrators: "They only want to discover a new source of tax money that will be acceptable to the voters, or better yet, that will not be subject to public elections at all."

As I have said myself, repeatedly, and Gary concurs, the Feds will make sure that any so-called "choice" as per a voucher system will only come, if at all, with enough strings attached to make sure that any school which accepts a "scrap from Caesar's table" will make that school Caesar's dog!

Gary's economic analysis is superb in regard to so-called "choice" in regard to vouchers. He follows my own reasoning in such to the logical conclusion that it will not only fail to do what its supporters claim and think; it will be only one more bureaucratic, tax and spend, socialistic nail in our economic coffin allowing even more tax-fattened hyenas to gorge themselves. This would be a "victory" for the religious right?

Gary also deserves credit for publicizing the economic disaster of Jerry Falwell's empire. Falwell's Liberty University was valued at $55 million in 1990. Today, it is valued at $5.2 million. Why? Because Falwell's "University" is estimated at net value and that dropped a whopping 90% in just two years!

As Gary says: "In the blink of an eye, Mr. Falwell went from a central figure in the nation's stage to a bit player, burdened by enormous problems." Poor Jerry is $73 million in debt with assets of just $5.2 million and his Old Time Gospel Hour is $16 million in debt.

I warned Jerry some few years ago of two things: One; God does not call men to build empires for themselves in His name. Two; you can't do business for The Lord on the Devil's terms. This point in particular regard to the subjects of Jerry's "deal" for accreditation for his "university" and becoming Caesar's dog through tax-exempt status. This is not an attempt to vilify Jerry Falwell but to point out the danger that lurks for all of us who get our eyes off God's Word and priorities. "Take heed, lest, when you think you stand, you fall!"

Delusions of grandeur are not the sole purview of the wicked. God's people are also susceptible to the "cares of this world and the deceitfulness of riches." It takes real spiritual discernment to avoid the Enemy's traps. You are bound to fall into the pit if you get your eyes off the priorities of humility and concern for others. Becoming a victim of your own press is the downfall of many, otherwise, good men and women. And, if you surround yourself with nothing but "yes men" who are telling you how great you are all the time, this egotistical monster will turn and rend you in time.

In this regard, I know too many people personally who are at risk and, where possible, I have, as a friend, warned them. I wish Mr. Clinton would take this advice and get some elder counselors who won't just shake their heads in agreement when he makes decisions.

I give publications like National Review and people like Bill Buckley a hard time of it but still keep in touch. NR is still a media source of value to me. For example, in the February edition there is a most interesting letter from Oklahoma state representative, Bill Graves, who echoes my own writing on the subject:

"...the record demonstrates that America's foundations were and are Christian sociologically, historically, and constitutionally. In 1892 the U.S. Supreme Court expressly held in Church of the Holy Trinity v. U.S. that America is a Christian nation. Upon the nation's founding, virtually every state required public office holders to believe in God, Jesus Christ, and the Bible (see some of my earlier essays on this very point).

"Justice Joseph Story wrote: 'The real object of the [First] Amendment was not to countenance, much less to advance Mahometanism or Judaism or infidelity by prostrating Christianity, but to exclude all rivalry among Christian sects, and to prevent any national ecclesiastical establishment. Probably at the time of adoption...of the First Amendment...the general if not the universal sentiment in America was, that Christianity ought to receive encouragement from the State.'

"You (NR) say that 'nations simply do not belong to an order of things that can be said to follow Christ, or partake of His nature.' Yet, Psalm 2 states that the Lord holds those rulers in derision who take counsel against Him and His anointed. The kings and judges of the earth are instructed to 'serve the Lord with fear' and to 'Kiss the Son.' Jesus Christ is the 'ruler of the kings of the earth.' Governor Fordice was correct." Of course, this statement by the honorable Bill Graves calls attention to the fact that unless one accepts the integrity and veracity of God's Word, the honorable Representative's quote from Psalm 2 falls on deaf ears."

I'm also indebted to NR for the excellent review of Thomas Sowell's book: "Inside American Education." The omission of a reference to Damerell's

"Education's Smoking Gun" is, however, a gross oversight. Also, some reference to Copperman and, even, to myself and a few others like-minded would have been helpful as well. But I have long since given up working myself into a high dudgeon over things like this. As to his position on vouchers, that is understandable from the Roman Catholic bias. But Sowell, here as elsewhere, is not expected, sadly for a scholar, to exercise objectivity.

Sowell dwells at some length on the role of the NCAA that brings up an interesting, sociological point in regard to the media's inordinate coverage of sports in general. It was interesting, for example, that important as the state Senate race is here in California, the same stations that covered my press conference gave a few, scant minutes to this, virtually cutting out comments by Phil Wyman, but spent about a third of the broadcast time on sports. Even the weather was a more prominent subject. In fact, a single segment of the sports coverage, a fight on a basketball court, had more airtime than the press conference! I wonder that this doesn't say more to our "leadership?"

"The University of California at Berkeley has found a Berkelyesque way of handling its most prickly problem: Andrew Martinez, the student who has achieved national notoriety by coming to class buck naked. It has suspended him for sexual harassment. We knew he was doing something wrong, but we couldn't put our finger on it." N. R.

"The lecturer at a formal lunch gave the source of the word politics as being poli=many and tics=ugly, blood-sucking parasites." Daniel Tausig, M. D. Richmond, VA in N. R.

It was some time ago that I called attention to the fact that only one member of the U.S. Congress had a voting record of a net cut in spending. I mention this to call the Birch Society's very valuable publication, TRIM, to your attention. Virtually every citizen of the U.S. should receive this most important pamphlet. Simply write to: TRIM, P.O. Box 8040, Appleton, WI 54913 or contact your local JBS representative. If you were receiving the TRIM bulletin, you would know that the staggering $4 trillion national debt is a most rosy figure. The actual debt, because of obscene "retirements" of Feds, etc. is actually an insanely impossible $15 TRILLION!!! The DAILY interest on the $4 trillion is $800 million. "Thanks to 'cost of living adjustments,' hundreds of thousands of retirees make more poolside than when they were working!" Young people don't call them the "Greedy Geezers" without justification.

GM losses are expected to exceed $23 billion, IBM, Sears, and other major companies are in deep trouble. The primary reason? Health care and other related costs for retirees! Far too many people, largely employees of government institutions like the FED and the Military are able to put in as little as 20 years and "retire!" And just look at the retirement benefits for politicians! It's positively, obscenely sickening!

Without fear of contradiction the situation is not going to improve for taxpayers until we have an informed and responsible electorate. The "democratic" rabble will continue to do us in until we have real reform in voter eligibility, a sacred cow of monstrous proportions.

Our own "conservative" representative in California, Bill Thomas, actually voted for legislation which would increase the cost to individual families $3,589! Just who is able to afford this kind of tax increase? Small wonder Thomas is endorsing McDermott in the senate race instead of Phil Wyman. You would have to flip a coin to tell the difference between the phony Republican, McDermott, and the other tax-and-spend Democrat contender, Jim Costa! Don't take my word for it, just "follow the money" and see where the support for these politicians comes from! Folks, I can't afford the taxes I'm paying now; and to take another $300 a month out of my budget instead of cutting government spending? Mr. Thomas, we can't afford your brand of "conservatism" and this kind of thievery! You, like so many others, are just a wolf in sheep's clothing masquerading as a conservative!

I wonder if Mr. Thomas has a comment on the recent legislation which would require manufacturers of plastic pails to put "Child Drowning Warning" labels, in both English and Spanish no less, on their products? Federal law requires the use of specific colors for the labels and the ubiquitous Orange encircled slash and all will conform to ANSI standards. As with the onerous seatbelt and helmet legislation, Caesar shows his "concern" for all the poor sheep that simply must be "protected" by him and his Gestapo agents. In addition to school handouts of condoms, will Caesar begin to demonstrate "safe sex" on prime time and follow us into the bedroom to make sure we are "doing it right?"

As Mr. Clinton tells us we are going to have to make "sacrifices" to deal with the budget deficit, doesn't it ever occur to any of these tax-fattened hyenas, these ignoble liars and cheats, that only by cutting government spending will we ever be able to approach a solution to our economic woes? Mr. Clinton, even though you succeeded in lying yours and your wife's way into the White House, don't think the American people are going to be seduced by your chicanery. Go ahead and continue your seduction of silly women, that's your forte, but don't think it's going to bail you out of the mess you created for yourself by your lies.

While I'm about it and since it concerns Caesar's plans for us sheep, I must mention a most valuable book, "Global Tyranny...Step By Step" by William F. Jasper. This epic coverage of the history and agenda of the U.N. for the New World Order can be ordered through your local JBS representative. Please get a copy. You will be glad you did.

Kevin Phillips in his new book, Boiling Point, helps to cut through the insanity and chaos of our present "leadership." As an economist he writes of the obviously chaotic dichotomy of Clinton and Perot's appeal; two different people with two entirely different messages; and both with large followings. Phillips' main question at the end, "If inequality is growing, what can elected officials do about it?" remains unanswered. It would have served Phillips well if he had read my essay concerning the scientific study of "chaos" or seeming "randomness."

Any attempt at "definitions" or "answers" which include such disparate sociological factors like populism, elected leadership and government intrusion into cultural mores and taboos is bound to find itself stymied if not, in fact, contradictory unless the mechanisms of chaos are thoroughly understood. It's most unfortunate that the majority of those that try to deal with economics are not good scientists and mathematicians, that they have such an abysmal ignorance of the physics of their subject.

It is difficult, as a professional writer, to get all the conversation with others I desire. To quote Oliver W. Holmes:

"Conversation must have its partial truths, its embellished truths, its exaggerated truths. It is in its higher forms an artistic product. ...Conversation which is suggestive rather than argumentative, which lets out the most of each talker's results of thought, is commonly the pleasantest and the most profitable." And so I have found it to be at its best among those who think and care for others.

Among those thinking Brahmins, Francis Parkman said, apropos of our present circumstances:

"What can a handful do against a host in a country where the bought vote of the unlettered boor can neutralize the vote of the wisest and the best?" Yet Parkman would be consigned to the Fascist camp by today's liberals for stating such an obvious truth. Particularly in views of his position concerning things like universal suffrage and women's "rights." But no analytical and unprejudiced review of the facts can lead anyone to any other conclusion that such "great levelers of society" have done anything but reduce us to the tyranny of the mob who chant for a free ride on the backs of the workers and responsible people, those like the Clintons and Willie Browns, that have cheated us of personal liberty and would take from those that have earned and give to those that would rob, cheat and steal. And how much "tidier" to do it with Caesar's sanction and coercion!

It is just such things that led one great thinker, Herman Melville, to suspect that the cosmos were rather unsympathetic to the dreams and hopes of mankind. But, of course, Melville knew his Bible and was conversant with the thinking of Ecclesiastes 9:11. Too bad more of his "professional" critics are so woefully ignorant. And just how uncommon is it anyway that, as a romantic, he should experience the familiar of "...the romantic writer whose splendid early vision of the beauteous forms of nature fade into the light of common day...Though with rapt sight, in childhood, we behold many strange things beneath the moon, and all like Mardi looks like a tented fair - how soon every thing fades. All of us, in our very bodies, outlive our own selves."

As one of those rare men of genius who articulates the voice of "Everyman" Melville wrote to his "shipmates and world-mates: 'The Articles of War form our domineering code, and the worst abuses we suffer are those we inflict upon ourselves and there is no effective appeal to official justice to remedy them, Each man must be his own savior.' "

So it is that Emerson, Melville, Cooper, Hawthorne, Thoreau and those like myself who are like-minded together with our founding fathers know that the "salvation" we speak of in respect to our nation can only come by men who will stand up to confront the evil which has always, historically, sought to destroy those of us who believe in personal liberty and responsibility and are willing to pay the price.

And, if, as Melville said: "Failure is the true test of greatness," I have proven to be successful beyond my wildest dreams! Many are the times I ask myself the question: "How could one man in just one lifetime make as many mistakes as I have?" My mind boggles at the thought! But, unlike Melville, it has not been "...my earnest desire to write those sort of books that are said to 'fail,'" it just seems to have worked out that way because, like Melville, "To write entirely other, I cannot!" But as with Melville, Hawthorne and Poe, I must write in such a fashion that the very blackness proves the appropriate and needed backdrop and contrast for light that the light itself may be clearly seen as such.

It is presently estimated that 99% of the universe is invisible. ROSAT, weighing only dark matter, gives us this estimate. David Davis of Maryland University and NASA "suggests that the universe may one day halt its expansion." The theory is that an expansion to some 10 trillion trillion times its original size in about a sextillionth of a picosecond left a precisely balanced cosmos which will eventuate in perfect equilibrium after which the stars will burn out and matter will evaporate into a whisper of pure energy (Newsweek). I do wonder, when I read of such things, if the astronomers are conversant with God's description of this scenario? Probably not.

So it is in our own lives that too often the light becomes darkness because of the evil men do. As a consequence of such evil, the "light that lightens every man born into the world" is not seen as such, is, in fact, most often despised and the prophets and preachers of the Light are ridiculed and persecuted. As a result, 99% of what might be seen if the love of the Truth held sway in men's and women's hearts remains "invisible."

You can't dance with the Devil and appreciate the wonders of God's creation or really love anyone beside yourself. So it is that the purest poetry is, in fact, a true account of what is real, what is actual. The ugliness of insane, demon possessed chasing after the psychotic fantasies of "equality" between the sexes, of "equality" of perverts, of "equality" of ideologies and races dooms the work of common sense approaches to civilized answers by reasonable men to our problems as human beings. One example: which is the more honorable, to rob by a gun or to rob by discriminate taxing?

I dearly love the singing of George Beverly Shea. One of my favorites is: If I Could Pray as a Child Again. There are so many good things I wish I could re-capture of my own childhood. I wish I could kneel, once more, in the warm alkali dust of Little Oklahoma and shoot marbles with my little friends. I wish I could hear, once more, the singing of the faithful and simple Okies and Arkies of Faith Tabernacle, of Grandad's booming voice and the lilting music of Grandma's piano. I would far rather be the victim of this kind of fine madness than the ugly realities of what children face today.

I do wonder, on occasion, how many great men of power and authority have come to the end of their years with the thoughts of *Rosebud* becoming their preoccupation and the last, whispered word from their dying lips. I will not have it so because I will always find the poetry of the true and actual the purest form of expression and though the heart has its reasons of which Reason knows nothing, as long as I keep the barking of squirrels, the call of quail, the melody and message of Bali Ha'i in their true perspective and never betray them by selling out to the common brass of this world's tawdry "treasures," all will come right.

How many men of power and influence do I know and have known who would gladly pay a king's ransom to just be able to get one night's undisturbed sleep! How many of them know they need that visit to my trout stream and, yet, with all their "success" can't seem to find the time to do so? The words of that old Justice come often to mind. When asked why he spent so much time fishing, he said: "Because it reminds me of how very unimportant those things are which consume my time otherwise." How very much better off we would all be if more of our leaders would spend more time fishing than doing the mischief they feel is their "occupation."

I do apologize. Writing is a very solitary occupation and I occasionally would do better to go fishing myself. Physician heal thyself! Yet, as the shades of that night seem to be falling wherein no man may work, I seem to be driven to say so much with so little time in which to say it. I really would avoid Martha's trap of being cumbered about many things and losing the better which no man can take away. So it is that I take the time, make the time, to "saunter," to visit the squirrels and quail, the streams, mountains, rocks and trees and hold my conversations with the Lord and loved ones in His marvelous, yet often inconvenient, creation which gives me the solitary courage and strength to face the solitary task of the writing.

There are hard things that need doing and hard things that need saying but I am left, often, telling The Lord: This way is too hard and the gate too narrow! Honestly, don't you, at times, feel the same way? How very susceptible of human frailty we all are in the final analysis. The Glory of Evil beckons and, like moths to the flames, we too often respond to that rather than the hard and narrow path of Truth and Righteousness. Fortunately, The Lord knows our weaknesses and made provision for them with that One who really understands; who went through it all and experienced it all, without failing, for our sakes.

Sword of the Lord (January 29) has an interesting article: Will the SBC be intimidated by the Masons? The primary point of contention is whether Masons can make a choice for their church if that choice comes into conflict with their Masonic vows? Real Christians who are members of Real Churches have never had this conundrum and, considering the power the Masonic Order wields, it would be foolish of anyone who is not a real Christian to find themselves facing such a choice.

I just received No. 70 of the Aryan Nation's publication, "Calling Our Nation," in which some of my criticism, expressing disappointment of the New American's handling of the Randy Weaver persecution, appeared. I appreciated the use of my comments and hope many will read them who would not hear of them otherwise. My thanks to Richard Butler and Carl Franklin. Of great interest in this edition of Calling Our Nation was the fact that Carl Franklin had appeared on the Montel Williams show and had been given an opportunity afterwards to address a largely Negro audience. I'm sure they heard things from an entirely different view than the media propagandized one they are accustomed to.

Included in this edition was also an enclosure, "The Balance," a newsletter of Civil Rights and Current Events published by the Cause Foundation of Houston Texas and edited by D.M.A. Hollaway. I mention this because of the excellent treatment by this publication of the Randy Weaver/Kevin Harris case. I wish everyone could read this publication. But you would also have to receive Calling Our Nation in order to get the whole truth of the matter. If you are interested, and you should be, write: Aryan Nations P.O. Box 362 Hayden Lake, Idaho 83835. If you ask for No. 70, you will also read a very interesting article about the discovery by researchers in the Belfast Library of Maine of a "missing" 13th Amendment of our Constitution! Why was this Amendment missing? Seems it Prohibited Lawyers from serving in government! Even further, it would have prevented government from granting any special privileges to itself, its members, or specific groups or individuals of the public. My Lord! Where is this Amendment when we so badly need it! "So began a seven-year nationwide search for the truth surrounding the most bizarre Constitutional puzzle in American history - The unlawful removal of a ratified amendment from the Constitution of the United States."

That should certainly whet your appetite to learn more. Order a copy of No. 70 and read the whole, most certainly, bizarre, story. You'll not only find your gorge rising, you will want to hang the perpetrators of this outright betrayal of the American People! You will also get an update on someone I mentioned some while back, the pitiful case of General Otto Ernst Remer, an 80 year-old German man who had the guts to come forward to confront the media propagandized holocaust hoax. It seems the German High Court has given him a virtual death sentence for doing so. It has sentenced him to 22 months in prison that, according to physicians, he cannot possibly survive. The German patriot's answer to his sentence: "I have no fear of death. I do that which I have always done: I fight!" What do you suppose will galvanize American patriots to come to this increasingly necessary point in our own battle against the powers of darkness?

"My great objection to government is, that it does not leave us the means of defending our right; or, of waging war against tyrants...I am not well versed in history; but I will submit to your recollection, whether liberty has been destroyed most often by the licentiousness of the people, or by the tyranny of rulers? I imagine, Sir, you will find the balance on the side of tyranny." Patrick Henry as quoted in TK.

All of us need the encouragement of learning of the wisdom of the past. We need the wisdom, warning and encouragement of The Lord. In Psalm 36 we read: Concerning the sinfulness of the wicked: There is no fear of God before his eyes. For in his own eyes he flatters himself too much to detect or hate his sin. The words of his mouth are wicked and deceitful; he has ceased to be wise and to do good. Even on his bed he plots evil; he commits himself to a sinful course and does not reject what is wrong.

I would entertain more hope for our nation if our leaders in government would heed the wisdom of our founding fathers, of our early Statesmen, of God Himself; but I don't see this happening. And when I consider the Heavens, the stars and that incomprehensible vastness, when I think of the possibility that our planet and we are made of exotic matter which astronomical physicists conjecture is uncommon in that vastness, like the Psalmist I wonder at God's special purpose in creating Man in His image. The stars alone make any sense of immortality or eternity and that yearning in our own hearts that tells us there has to be a purpose in it all that will make it all worth while, that there is indeed a reward for the righteous and work to be done for which this life and world is the proving ground.

The passing of Audrey Hepburn and Thomas Dorsey saddens me. Audrey gave us music and romance of the classic stature; Thomas gave us Precious Lord, Take My Hand and, to confound those of my brethren, I find the love of God in both. Buried on the same day as Dorsey was Thurgood Marshall. As they stand before the Righteous Judge of the Universe, which is more likely to hear: "Well done, thou good and faithful servant?" How will God judge between Precious Lord, Take My Hand and Plessy v. Ferguson? I know the one will continue to bring comfort and hope to people but the other opened a door to continuing evil in the guise of Civil Rights.

20/20 hindsight is only of use when the lessons are learned and put into practice. Isn't it interesting that sociologists are just now discovering that romance is not the sole purview of European cultures? Granted the fact that European cultures gave the Art and Voice to such in an unparalleled fashion, it's quite incomprehensible that only now have the "experts" found romance in all, widely diverse, cultures. And, sure enough, this "new" discovery had resulted in the usual *book of discovery*, "Anatomy of Love: The Natural History of Monogamy, Adultery and Divorce" by Helen Fisher. Apparently she has just discovered Cole Porter and Ertha Kitt as well. Now why didn't she save a lot of time and unnecessary verbiage by just asking me? Oh well. Perhaps she knew I love opera but don't care for ballet. I do not mourn the passing of Nureyev. While appreciating the art of vile men and women of genius, being perverts is not a criterion for such no matter how the media and revisionist "histories" portray it.

Melville, Cooper and Hawthorne would, I'm sure, be the first to tell real patriots of the need to use the gifts of writing and speaking to do much more than tell the facts. Jefferson was not only great Statesmen; he knew how to put the facts into epic prose. If the common people are to hear us gladly, we must use such gifts to articulate our cause in a similar, inspiring fashion. Unhappily, much of what I read and hear which is intended for good fails, just like most sermons, because of this pronounced lack to meet the heart's needs. Heart and Mind must work together to get the job done and move people to proper action. Here, as in most instances, good intentions will not suffice; only real qualifications count.

Among such qualifications must be the understanding of the Glory of Evil as so well portrayed in Ahab's hunt and the dark power that haunted Poe. That dark side is common to the human condition but the appeal to the epic overcoming of evil must be both intelligible and emotionally satisfying. The failure of the churches is in their not recognizing, standing for and teaching this imperative of humanity, trying, instead, to make it "religious" and consign it to the dusty repository of "theology."

There is always the danger that the indiscriminate reader may draw wrong conclusions from bare facts. But when those facts are couched in language that draws both heart and mind, only then is the proper message received and a proper course of action decided. Truth, Fact and Reason are never to be divorced from the heart's needs otherwise failure is guaranteed.

In the meantime, I'm overdue to take a walk among the pines and rocks. I need to commune with loved ones and consider the days of Iron Men and Wooden Ships, of a childhood that was filled with such promise of a future that held such wonders and opportunity. And, of course, it will be a solitary occupation. I wish you could join me.

Chapter Four

Christian Perspective

April

II Samuel 12:1-14

Fathers and Daughters

It has been many years since I have written a love letter but I wrote one just recently and sent it to a very beautiful young lady. She is Kellie Martin, one of the stars of Life Goes On. This is going to take some explaining, of course, for those that know me and, most importantly, to not embarrass Kellie and my children.

I don't believe there is in the whole of Scripture a more heart-rending story than that of Nathan's confrontation of David's sin as described in the 12th chapter of II Samuel. It is made all the more significant because of the issues involved, love and romance versus lust. It is the significance of that poor man's little ewe lamb that is either pure or vile depending on the heart condition of those that read the story. If you are not familiar with the story, I hope you will read it; only then will you know what I mean as you read this essay.

I have been a TV-basher for decades. I have not recanted my position but, thanks to Kellie, I have another perspective that was misplaced until I considered her and the show in which she stars.

You all know I am not given to "mindless entertainment" vis-à-vis TV. When it comes to TV series, I never got much beyond The Waltons and Little House. I read, travel and write; I don't watch TV. But, by chance, I was switching channels one evening and a young lady's eyes stopped me in my tracks. I found myself riveted to the screen in a way I have never before experienced. It was crazy!

Discovering that the show was a series called "Life Goes On," I recalled skipping past the thing on a number of occasions without bothering to stop and check it out. That was before I saw Kellie's eyes. It happened that this occurred on the Family Channel and the segment I was watching was a re-run. I watched till the show was over, the uneasiest feeling clouding my mind.

That little lady's eyes were haunting me and I didn't really know why? What was wrong with me?

I'm not usually so slow on the up-take. Finding out that the show, in re-runs, aired at 6PM weekdays, I tuned in again the following evening and watched the entire thing. I did this all week. Those eyes bewitched, enchanted and haunted me together with the growing realization that this young lady was not just "playing a part," she genuinely cared about people.

Maybe, I told myself, my love of young people, the thousands of teenagers I have worked with in the schools; maybe the answer to my uneasiness lay in that? No, that wasn't it. I know the tenderness evoked by the eyes of a baby, but it wasn't that either although it was somehow vaguely close.

I didn't realize it at the time, but I had seen those eyes before and had succeeded in burying the memory so deeply that the pain of recalling them was more than I felt I could endure. It had taken years to overcome the pain of seeing the light of those eyes snuffed out and I struggled desperately, unconsciously, to keep the memory of them buried along with my eldest daughter, Diana.

Because of the inherent selfishness of adultery and divorce and the cruelties of judicial systems, I didn't have much of a chance to know Diana as a father longs to know a daughter. Before I realized it, she was a young woman and I hadn't even gotten to really know her as a child.

This was a painful thing for me. I don't know why I thought it would make any difference but I decided, one evening, to take Diana and her brother Daniel, my oldest son, to dinner in Redondo Beach, my old "turf." I would risk telling them a story that, I hoped, might make a difference.

It went this way:

Not so very long after the divorce, I met a girl; nothing unusual in that, particularly not in the Camelot days of The South Bay of the late 50s. I was young and handsome, had a Cadillac convertible and a good job, loved music and knew a lot of people, had a lot of friends, especially in the theater arts. We were the young and beautiful people of the 50s South Bay, living the lives others could only dream of or see in movies.

Life was gay and carefree, we were the true Immortals of the age and the world was our oyster. Then I met the girl who was to shape my life and destiny; irrevocably. Stunningly beautiful, even by extravagantly high South Bay standards, red hair, green eyes, slightly short of five-foot tall and a figure that defies description. But it was her voice, more than anything else that was the epitome of femininity. Her voice was that of a choir of angels, a divine music unparalleled in the universe.

Here, at last, was the very physical personification of all that the poets and artists had tried in vain to capture, the reason for slaying dragons and hewing out wilderness places, a reason to cheerfully face any obstacle, any danger, the reason which gave reason to the sun's rising and setting, gave intelligibility to life itself, definition to soul, to heart, to being! Here was love to exhaust the Poet's Thesaurus of words and phrases in its most raw and profoundly jealous and unforgiving essence, demanding virtually everything! This Pearl of Great Price! Only one thing was lacking, a lack for which I had no experiential frame of reference, a lack which was to doom my own heart's best efforts; she didn't have Kellie's eyes.

I gave it everything I had to offer. I lived, really lived, for months, in that heavenly aerie where only those that really love ever dwell. But I was the "innocent" in such affairs of the heart. I didn't know how to guard against the enemies of such a thing, I didn't know the hatred such beauty could engender in the hearts of others. Tragically, my love for this beautiful girl was betrayed and I nearly died for the loss. I drank heavily for a while but found no relief from the pain and grief in that and soon gave it up. And though I wouldn't die, neither was I ever to fully recover. While her eyes had not been Kellie's and I had not, at the time, any basis of comparison, when I last saw her as a woman fully grown and having gone through several men, her eyes had become hard and brittle, cynical and suspicious. I grieved more for that than almost anything else. It was then that I learned what was to become too common in my experience over the years. This beautiful girl had an ugly father, but as with many such "fathers," he had been able to hide his ugliness.

Redondo, Hermosa, Manhattan Beach, Malibu and Venice of the 50s were a fairyland, filled with magic and beauty. The Albatross in Malibu, with its dining area built out over the surf, the quaint, picturesque little place up Trancas Canyon and the beautiful drive up to it, clean, uncrowded beaches. My friends in the various theater groups and the music, oh, the music! I still played clarinet and sax. There was more than enough magic in which to seek the love I had found and lost but I was never to find it again, not even in such a rare environment.

A most peculiar thing; none of my friends and acquaintances of the time seemed to understand what it was, exactly, I was looking for? They didn't even understand just exactly what it was I thought I had lost; as one girl told me at the time: "You don't have any trouble getting any girl you want. What's the problem?" I couldn't seem to give her a satisfactory answer.

There have been a number of women since the "girl," their warmth and softness filling the needed role that exists in all men's lives. But never again was I to find that real romance that I had once known.

As we sat there, the father telling his teenage children that he had once known what real love was, had, in fact, experienced it in all its grand and bitter facets, had drunk its cup from brim to lees, and had never betrayed its memory, a hush, almost church-like in its reverential aura, seemed to surround us. I realized that I had, after the years had done their task of giving me the words, been able to make what I had, and had lost, real to my daughter. I had emptied my very soul to her in the hope of giving her something of real value. I had been able, after all these years, to tell her that her father had experienced the very thing that the poets and great artists, the composers and their music try to explain. I was trying to tell her not to ever lose hope of real love, never to settle for second best but to find that man to whom she would be the poetry of being of his very existence; she was of far too great value to settle for less and would spend her life feeling cheated if she settled for anything less, that it would be a constant empty, aching yearning until it was satisfied.

Almost as though it were cued, we got up silently from our table. I paid our check and we walked out into the summer evening. I drove the children back in silence. I had to return to Lancaster but it was hard to tell them goodbye. As we got out of my car, Diana walked around to me and, putting her arms around my neck and looking directly into my face said: "Daddy, I really do love you!" Then she kissed me. She was crying softly but I could see Kellie's eyes through the tears for the first time in my life and my very heart and soul melted within me. There would be no turning back from this, the most profound truth in the universe, the purest expression of love between a man and a woman that can possibly exist! And it was the look in a daughter's eyes for her father! Far beyond any physical thing, far beyond any attempt at definition, Pure beyond any understanding this side of eternity. Innocent beyond innocence, Trust beyond trust, a totality of the giving, in sacredness far beyond anything the churches claim knowledge of, the utterly selfless giving of the very being of the person in absolute trust and understanding, Deathless, Immortal!

For many years, I have tried, vainly, to find that look in the eyes of other women. Invariably, it has worked out in continued betrayal of love where those eyes didn't exist and, through loneliness and desperation, I took the risk anyhow.

TV Guide lists Life Goes On as #1 among the 10 top shows recommended for Teens. Quote: Parents who struggle, kids who cope, and believable love. And it is Kellie, largely, who makes it believable. But such "believability" is only achieved through the vulnerability of genuinely caring about others; no matter how masterful the actor or actress, this is not something that can be learned as a "craft," it is either there or it is not. And, so, I fear for Kellie, as I do for Karrie, as someone who has that rare and precious gift of really caring and because of this, they are vulnerable to the evil that men do and those eyes betray their love to those who would take advantage as well as to those who would return that love in kind.

People have often asked why I don't write fiction rather than the hard and thankless task of history, philosophy and politics. It wasn't until, after all these years of keeping the memory buried, only to have it reawakened by Kellie, that I have a proper answer.

No man, knowing what I do, can deal with a fictitious romance. Oh, I tried a few, only to cheat others as well as myself in the process; I have "conned" myself into believing many things which were not so in order to assuage the pain of loneliness, who of us has not?

But to attempt to describe the indescribable; I cannot. I can place flowers on the nightstand of my "Lady," I can try, with all my powers, to describe my feelings to her, I can do the thankless and grimy tasks of day-to-day living and "punching a clock" as expressions of my love, but if those eyes of innocent trust and wonder and unreserved giving are missing, I soon realize, as it continues to play itself out, it is all in vain.

Damned by an age which despises Cooper and Thoreau, the art of language, hopes, dreams and ideals of true love, of true romance, our young people have been cheated of the most precious thing of all; the ability to give and receive pure, unselfish love, this having been betrayed and traded for unbridled lust where our young girls are the predominant victims, an age where we are learning, more and more, that our young girls are preyed upon by even those of their own families! How willing I would be to put the rope around the neck of any who would betray the trust of a child in such a fashion! These maimers and cripplers of innocence cannot be human beings! They are beasts; devouring, unclean, predatory, destroying animals and should be treated as such!

As I began to face up to what Kellie had opened in my own soul that I thought had been successfully buried, the question was what to do about it? For several days I struggled with the question. So it was that I determined to write the "love letter."

I know nothing and everything about Kellie Martin. It's what I know of genuine love and romance, what I know from her eyes that truly counts about Kellie, that makes me fearful for her and all the "Kellie's" she represents. So it was that the letter was one I might very well have written to one of my own daughters or a thousand Kellie's. Certainly my girls have been the recipients of the thoughts of their father. But, how many times did I fail to warn those thousands of teenagers I was entrusted with in the schools? Now, having seen Diana's eyes once again in Kellie, I had to at least try to do something about it.

Not long after the incident I have described my little girl was killed in a motorcycle accident after having been married just less than a year. She lay in a coma for several days. Danny and I would sit by her side, reading and praying, hoping against hope that she would come out of it. But it wasn't to be. She slipped quietly away from us without ever regaining consciousness.

Would telling any of this to Kellie be of any meaning or help to her? The heart continues to have its reasons of which Reason knows nothing so I felt I had to make the attempt. Those eyes are far too rare and precious not to try!

Sure, I can tell myself that true love and romance were not in the curriculum guide when I was a teacher. And, to be fair to myself, I did my utmost to make my young charges aware of my own feelings in such matters. But I could, should, have done more!

Kellie's eyes are those of my daughter Karen's as well. But Karen has been hurt and betrayed so much in her young life, seeking love and fulfillment that she is beginning to lose the open, wonder-filled, pure, honest, trusting elements of these wells and windows of the soul. People who care as much as Karen and Kellie can never hide what they really feel, their eyes betray them. I grieve to see in Karen's eyes the increasing knowledge of an evil world of selfish, using and abusing, people.

Are we now a society for which genuine love and romance are anachronistic, a harking back to simpler times where the search for such a Holy Grail was not an exercise in quixotic futility? I will not have it so! Not as long as there are girls like Kellie, not as long as there are daughters who can truly love their fathers like Diana and Karen and evoke the purest love in the universe in those father's hearts!

I'll never forget the time I took Karen out for our very first "grown-up" dinner together. She was only seventeen but she was breathtakingly beautiful. I had difficulty believing that this beautiful little "woman" was my own daughter, the little girl I use to tumble with, cuddle, tease and tickle.

I had made reservations for the dinner at one of the finest restaurants in the area. Every eye in the place was on us. I was bursting with pride that my little girl was pleased to let her daddy show her off and show her off I did. Now you just can't do this with your sons. A father has an altogether different relationship with sons. As they grow up, they become men in their own right; but those little angels? Never! They will never become women; they will always be Daddy's Little Girl!

Karrie (she will never be Karen to her dad) couldn't possibly have known the turmoil of my own thoughts as we sat in this fashionable restaurant and I savored every moment of this precious time together. I wanted to capture it forever, indelibly, on my heart and soul, to have it there for recall when the shadows of life began to lengthen, when she would move into her own sphere of living her own life and dad would recede.

What kind of men are the "Daddies" of all these girls who sell out their dreams of a good man so cheaply? Just what are the fathers of all these young men who treat girls so shabbily teaching them? What redeeming note can be sounded for a culture that treats its children in such a fashion, leaving them without their right to dream and hope?

You may be wondering about Laura (always Laurie to me), my other daughter. Laurie inherited the worst of the betrayal of love and family. I am forced to wait, hoping and praying that she will recover the dream that was wrenched so violently away from her. Until that day, the subject is too painful to write about. Also, I have a hard-earned reputation for never betraying a confidence. Powerful men and women have chosen me as a confidante on this basis because, curiously, they find it very difficult to find people they can trust and, yet, this doesn't lessen their need, as human beings, for someone they can talk to.

About a year ago, a CEO who heads a large organization covering 22 states called me about a personal problem he was having. In the course of the conversation I asked him: "J... don't you have anybody you can trust?" His reply stunned me: "No one!" At the most human level imaginable, here was a man who "commanded legions" whose most basic need, someone he could simply talk to and share with was denied him.

It's a pity I haven't been in closer contact with those in show business, especially young people. I have been remiss in not keeping in touch with so many over the years. There is probably no other business where loneliness is so rampant. Being by its very nature so fiercely competitive, as I well know, betrayal is a commonplace. There are two, broad classes of people who never know who their real friends are: One; the wealthy and powerful. And two: beautiful women.

But now, thanks in large part to a little lady with wondrous eyes, Kellie, I am going to try to reach out to a group of people who, while as actors and actresses, attempt to portray love, find themselves, too often, failing to find even one person they can trust, let alone, love without reservation.

It is a truism that it is, indeed, lonely at the top. Too many times, in seeking gratification of the ego in reaching "success," the things of real value fall victim. Hence, too many times, as I last wrote, "Rosebud" becomes the preoccupation of later life and the dying word on the lips of the powerful.

It was the greatest expert on love who ever lived who said that even though love were betrayed seventy times seven, the heart of the real lover never stops forgiving and seeking, never fails of the hope that "next time" it will be found.

My critical remarks concerning "women in general" over the past, few years have led some to the distortion that I don't like women. Nothing could be further from the truth. I candidly admit that I'm not sure that I will ever be able to trust another one but I'm more than willing to try.

Further, these "critical" comments have most often been directed at a system which has victimized both men and women, too often casting them in an adversarial and competitive relationship rather than one in which each looks and works for the best for the other. Perhaps it is the purview of a man who still finds meaning in the music of the great musicals of the theater, who still finds the barking squirrel and the call of a quail or the singing of a cricket more important than so many other things which demand of our time, to find some sense in all the madness of this age. I do admit saying, at one time, that I had discovered that while women loved poetry, I hadn't found one yet who could live with the poet. But I haven't given up hope of finding such a one.

Because of Kellie, I have opened a host of old wounds that might defy healing otherwise. As I draw them into the light, I see more closely the stars, the trees, rocks, mountains and streams of my sauntering, the things I have sought refuge in so that I might have the courage of my convictions and write and speak as I have these past years.

When I have written of the evil that men do, nowhere is such evil more apparent than in its destructiveness in the lives of our young people. When I speak out about the abuses of children in our schools and society, when I agonize at the loss of their hopes and dreams of a future and my anger flames against their betrayers, I realize that the righteous wrath that inflames my soul has its source in what I, personally, know of real hopes, dreams, love and romance because of the fact that I have never given up, never betrayed, the best part of the child within myself.

Maybe this is because my great-grandmother and my grandparents who were so very transparent in their love for my brother and me and for one another taught my earliest lessons in the subject. Maybe it's because I was raised reading Cooper, Hawthorne, Thackeray and so many others who held on to the dream. Maybe it was my earliest experiences as a child in the wilderness of the forest fastness where I could actually live the romance and adventure of which men like Cooper wrote.

Or, maybe, it really took hold when I moved to Redondo Beach and discovered girls at Mira Costa High school. The tragedy of my life seems to have been my unwillingness to compromise the ideals of real love and romance as so eloquently expressed in our best literature, our best music and art. I could never involve myself with one of these beautiful girls with the thought of ever betraying them by unfaithfulness and, unreasonably as it seemed to turn out, I actually believed that my own faithfulness would be returned in kind, thinking they felt as I did about the matter. To me, it was a simple, basic thing: One man, one woman. If you had one, you had your limit!

I have been born to the wrong generation. That's not to tell God His business but as some of my detractors have pointed out, any man who says that God has made mistakes must surely endure the mark of Ichabod over his brow mustn't he?

As I got on in the business of making a living over the years, particularly in the schools, I came into increasing contact with the government agencies like CPS and the Juvenile Justice System. I began to know the probation officer better than the parent. The horror of what was happening to our children and young people became a living nightmare for me. I witnessed the loss of moral absolutes and moral leadership for the children. The decimation of the 60s continues to do its dirty work in the schools and homes of America.

As I would, increasingly, become exposed to the burgeoning Social Service "answer" to our betrayal of our children, my heart would sicken at the growing number of "children having babies," the increasing number of such very young girls, children themselves, actually, with one or more babies, sitting in welfare offices waiting to go on the dole or trying to find a sympathetic ear for their hopelessness. I would wonder where the men were? Where were the fathers of these babies, the husbands of these child-brides?

I was born to the wrong generation- obviously. Imagine having the mind-set that no real man worthy of the name would be able to bear the shame of abandoning his responsibility to these girls and these children!

And so it was that a litany of sorrows was beginning to be formulated in my mind and would lead to my work of the last, few years. A challenge to the evil that men do, a challenge to the tyranny of Caesar and his minions who would lead the betrayal of our young people and their hopes and dreams.

I have written so much on this theme in the political context that it would be unfair to my readers to rehash it here. What I have failed to do until now is to give vent to my own heart's anguish as I watch these girls with babies trying to cope with a system of evil not of their making. Sure I blame women for not leading where they are the most effective; I blame them for their part in allowing their sex to become a commercial commodity to be bartered, for lending themselves to the system of pornography to satisfy the unholy lust of evil men. But they can never be blamed for the evil that so-called men do, the evil of the "double standard" where the girl was to be pure and chaste but it was acceptable for the boy to be "experienced!" Just who, exactly, were the purveyors of this invidious, twisted, distorted lie from the very bottom of the pit of Hades!

It will take a book of many pages, a huge data base, to make sense of the immensely complex issues, twists and turns of history, that have led to what children and young people face today. Evil men and seducers have a long and black history. But there was a time in this nation when we cherished our young, when we planned for our posterity, when we knew and practiced the truth of that implacable and immutable imperative of history: A nation which does not cherish its young has no future as a nation.

It's cold now here in the mountains. We're expecting a snowstorm. We have a new, county complex in our small community. It will facilitate dealing with the increased welfare cases which are, more and more, being referred from Bakersfield because the cost of housing is cheaper here than there. I see, more and more, young girls, often pushing a stroller with a baby and a toddler at their side, heading up the road to the welfare office in the cold.

I'm reminded of the young lady who told me things were better for her now compared to when she was in Flagstaff and had to pull her little girl in a wagon through the deep snow to go to the store a great distance away. The "husband" was in jail. Things were much better for her now.

The curse of beauty; so many of these girls are pretty but their attractiveness proves to be their tragedy when they are led to believe that "boys" will commit and provide for them. Where is the mature leadership of family, of a society, which should be able to teach them better, should set the examples of morality and good judgment which these girls so desperately need? Who is going to tell them the truth of the fact that boys only want one thing from them and when that is given so freely, it has little value! Why aren't they being taught to wait for a real man in their lives, why are they being encouraged to squander the preciousness of their youth on snot-nosed brats who have neither the ability or intention of providing for them as a real man would? So it is that I was either born to the wrong generation or I have simply lived too long. I am an anachronistic dinosaur who refuses to accept the bludgeoning of such evils as terminal. I don't seem to be able to accept my fate and just let go.

Hollywood, as well as the schools, churches and families, must give an account; and our leaders in government? Dear God in Heaven, what they have to account for!

There is a man, Mr. Jim Costa, who is running for state Senate. In 1986, while a member of the state Assembly, he was arrested for soliciting sex from an undercover police officer. He had a 19 year-old girl with him and wanted the decoy officer to join them for a "threesome." He agreed on a fee of $50.00 and was promptly arrested. He was fined $255 and placed on three years probation. Mr. Costa was never reprimanded by the state Assembly and, in fact, continues in that position while he tries to win a place in the state Senate. Quite obviously he is not the man of character I once judged him to be.

I was having a cup of coffee, recently, with an acquaintance and I mentioned this to him. His reply startled me: "What's wrong with that?" he said. I started to argue with him but stopped when I suddenly realized he was actually attempting to excuse his own immoral behavior by defending it through a surrogate: Mr. Costa! The evil in men's hearts.

What does this tell anyone, especially our young people, about the "leadership" of our nation? When it comes to the sins of the flesh, we are drowning in a sea of sickness with no land in sight and no spiritual beacon of hope.

I'm too good a psychologist to not recognize the symptoms of hopelessness and self-destructive behavior and be able to predict the results; the rising tide of suicide among our young people, the joining of gangs, the high crime rates and drug use, the immature seeking of love and meaning in destructive sexual activity which results in disease, unwanted babies and children on welfare, young girls without any hope of anything better. My generation has a lot to answer for!

It was in another life that I sat with my arm about a beautiful girl in my convertible by the beach in Palos Verdes and watched the sun set; the waves wash the shore and listened to Ebb Tide on the car radio. With that beautiful, warm, soft girl in my arms in such a setting, the world was a kind place and understood the needs of lovers. But a beach apartment was $35.00 a month, gas was 15 cents a gallon, homes were $3,000 at 3% and one paycheck easily supported a family. Oh yes, a dozen roses cost $2.50 and an Orchid corsage was $2.75.

I could spend an evening at the old Ambassador Hotel's Coconut Grove with my girl for a total cost of $25.00; dinner, dancing and live entertainment all included. We could cruise Sunset with the top down and never worry about other people; just as we could do going to Malibu or driving Pacific Coast Highway from Manhattan Beach to San Diego. We did indeed live the lives of Lotus Eaters.

Beauty is always in danger and at the risk of envy. That is the reason for so much that is ugly being whitewashed and thereby "christened" equal to beauty. When I visit the scenes of my youthful Camelot, it is hard to believe the devastation, the wholesale destruction of so much that was once a source of such beauty and joy of living.

I don't know, yet, how long Life Goes On has been airing. The new episodes have Kellie caring for a boy with AIDS. With the objectivity of a new viewer, I look at Kellie in the old re-runs and Kellie in the new episodes. She is growing up. I'm watching her with a father's compassion. It might be Karrie or Laurie on the screen and I find myself wishing I could offer her my own counsel, could help her through the pain of growing up and deal with the unfairness and injustice all about. A flashback to Marilyn Monroe reminds me of the desperate loneliness of so many show business personalities and the Manson's and their type who through their own ugliness would try to destroy beauty. There are a lot of sick and evil people out there who would hurt those who they envy.

There are a few who remind me, occasionally, to take a look over my shoulder once in a while; this primarily because of my political essays. But I doubt that there are any in our society who have more legitimate fear of Kooks and Cranks than those who are in show business. This has to, together with the multitude of those who would try to "use" successful people, make for limited friendships.

Curious, isn't it, that the industry, Hollywood in particular, which gives us the illusion of love would be so desperate for it itself? Notwithstanding all the sex and violence, this is an industry filled with lonely people who are largely trying to find the very things, love and trust, commitment and fidelity that they "sell" so effectively as fairytales, playing the parts that elude them in real life.

Are the majority of us any different? I think not. The only real difference is that most of us aren't making our living by acting out our fantasies. We will accept the placebos and do our vicarious "living" through the personalities we view on screen. It wouldn't help our own fantasies much to wonder about the loneliness, hurt and disappointments of our "beautiful people." It wouldn't help us to know the tragedies of their own lives in their failures to find the things of real value we all need and seek.

As I watch Kellie in her role of Rebecca dealing with the boy with AIDS, as I compare her eyes with the early episodes of her girlhood, I find a change, the change I watched in my own daughters' eyes as they became young women. And I hurt. Do they have to grow up in such a fashion that what was so sweet and innocent has to change to suspicion and distrust through having to face too many hard choices while they are children? What can we say of a society that no longer encourages innocence and wonder, a society that steals our children's rights to a childhood?

I have told my girls that no matter what they do in their lives, they will always be my little angels; they will never become "women" but will always be my daughters. But not the most loving father will ever be able to protect his little girls from discovering, for themselves, the tragic fact that the majority of boys and men will take advantage of them if they allow it.

More and more, I am hearing girls of the age of Karrie and Kellie telling me there are no good men their own age. There is too much truth in what they are saying. The welfare offices testify to the ugly truth of their condemnation.

Would it do any good to point to the high divorce rate and call attention to the fact that so many girls are molested by a stepfather or one of his relatives? And, further, that this is because the mother usually has the custody of the children and doesn't usually waste much time filling in the missing father's side of the bed?

Would it do any good to point out the fact that our schools, entertainment media and society seems to shove our boys and girls together in relationships for which neither are prepared? Would it help to call attention to the fact that young people, especially our girls, are so desperate for someone to love them that they are easy prey to anyone who shows them a little kindness and consideration, someone who seems to have some time for them and cares for them?

I can't see the world from Karrie and Kellie's eyes but I can see their eyes as only a father can. Regardless of their experiences with other men in their lives, Karrie and Kellie will always be the kind of girls who will need their fathers. A father should be the man who never fails them. If they should find good husbands, these men should never fail them either.

I mentioned in my last essay that if I were to ever get behind another pulpit, I would preach on South Pacific. But that is because I know the Bible and the heart of God well enough to do so. For example, This Nearly Was Mine is not a romantic cliché in my life; I lived it.

Among my theological writings, there is my treatment of the loss of innocence in The Garden. As long as Adam and Eve were true to love, they shared each other's innocence; when a third party, Satan, was allowed to intrude, innocence was blasted. When a young man and woman come together, each for the first time, there is the sharing of innocence all over again, "The two become one." Allow a third party to intrude, and innocence is blasted once again. As with virginity, once betrayed it is never to be regained. It is a tragedy of monstrous proportions that purity and chastity is treated of such slight value in our contemporary society.

We have invited the wholesale blasting of purity, chastity and innocence in our society and are reaping a whirlwind of hopelessness. We now live in an age where the things I have boldly put into print regarding my daughters and Kellie call up the most vicious thoughts of things like "Something About Amelia", and, most recently, "Not In My Family," of the perversions of bestial men who prey upon the innocents.

It was still possible, when I was a freshman teacher, to give a girl or boy in one of my classes an encouraging hug of genuine affection. No longer; we now live with an evil connotation attaching to virtually all male/female relationships.

I think Marilyn vos Savant is a remarkably clear-thinking woman. When asked which she considered the most powerful, love or reason, she replied: "I think love is more important, but human reason is more powerful. Love may give us some great intentions, but reason is what actually gets the job done." Not the most romantic phraseology but she is certainly accurate in her assessment.

If that girl thinks that boy really "loves" her, why won't she give "reason" a chance? Reason dictates that real love seeks to please the object of that love, not make demands to satisfy itself.

Having sons as well as daughters, I have much to say on that subject as well but the message, while the same in its most profound similarities, is different in many respects. It is essentially different in respect to the responsibilities that attach to the relationships between fathers and daughters as opposed to fathers and sons.

As a man, I want my sons to be able to meet certain demands as men that I do not expect of my daughters. Not that I don't have high expectations for the girls, but I know men have the ultimate responsibility for leadership. No man can ever blame a woman for his failure as a man. I want them to be the kind of men that deserve the respect of women like Karrie and Kellie. This is not easy in our society.

Cheating has become a commonplace in our schools. But when leaders themselves cheat, why be surprised that the people follow? If we have a system that seems to reward those without ideals of morality and integrity, why should we be surprised that our children respond to it in such a self-destructive fashion?

The lesson of the 60s was that without moral restraints a society is bound to drift into moral anarchy. But I have learned the lessons of a tender heart because of my daughters and girls like Kellie. I have learned that they need the genuine love of a man, they need the music, poetry and flowers and unfailing, gentle strength.

I remember a time when it was enough to sit by the hour and listen to Nat King Cole with that soft, warm girl in my arms. Now our young people seem to think sex is the most significant expression of love and lose that which is of far greater value in the process.

In my solitude as I walk among the pines, rocks and hills of the forest, my attention is drawn ever more to the plight of our young people. Who really speaks for them? What is my generation really doing of any consequence that offers them hope of anything changing for the better?

Long after my years at Cal State Long Beach, after teaching in Watts and East San Jose, I realize that things have not gotten better for those whose frustrations led to the '65 riots, Woodstock, Selma and Kent State. I know the answers are in my clear, mountain stream and the call of the quail. I know they are in those classrooms where teachers have a chance to make a difference to those young people if teachers really care. I know the answers are in the way parents respond in love to the needs of their children.

But we now have a society that does not love children, that warehouses them and expects them to by-pass childhood and punishes them for having dreams and hopes of a future. The problems and answers are national in scope and require a hugely complex database. An understanding of the function of chaos is essential to coming up with solutions. Human behavior is complex in the extreme. We don't even understand the mechanisms of the relationship between the father and the daughter and the husband and the wife. I do know there is a difference in the innocence and purity of each, a difference in what would be evil in the one case and holy in the other. But how that distinction is made without any effort of will or mind in some and not in others I don't know. I just know it is the basest, most destructive evil imaginable where the distinction fails.

Because of the evil that men do, we seem not to be able to deal with the questions with the required honesty. Not a few will censure me for being so forthright in my own comments and will say: "How can you put your very soul on the line so openly when you know you are going to get hammered in the process?" I don't have an answer for you; I only know I'm compelled to try no matter how badly I may fail in the attempt.

In its own way, it doesn't place me at any more hazard than my speaking the truth in regard to the other evils with which our young people have to contend. But in the case of real love and romance, if men like me are to spare our own feelings, if we are more concerned with embarrassing ourselves than trying to reach out to our young people with hope and understanding, they will continue to be left with the purveyors of lust as their teachers.

I am known as a right wing, religious and political conservative. It will seem strange to many of my readers to see me seeming to defend anything in regard to the entertainment industry. But if you can relate to my own heart's concern for young people, you will understand my trying to bring the issue of the exploitation of young girls and women, especially, by this industry out into the open. I am gratified to see people like Shelly Winters finally speaking openly about it.

No other industry has been so deadly in regard to the exploitation of women, especially the attractive ones. I know how odd it seems to the general readership that I would be defending those who seem to "have it made." But, in my own experience, this is not the case. Very few of even the most beautiful girls and women make it successfully in this industry. It doesn't help their cause that so many willingly give themselves to exploitation.

In my case, I know that if I didn't have beautiful daughters who I love more than my own life, I probably wouldn't give it much thought. But it takes fathers worthy of the name to concern them in this matter. Further, we all know the impact the industry has on our young people. Shows like Clarissa, Degrassi High, Class of 96, Beverly Hills 90210, etc. have an incalculable effect on the direction our young people take in making decisions that will have a life-long effect in their lives.

So I have taken a detour from my usual writing to bare my own soul in the matter. As a reminder to my subscribers, however, I call your attention to my publication, OI-12-92, where I touched on my own research in trend forecasting and the use of the physics of Chaos and Randomness in predicting human behavior. I know most of you were more interested in the fellows from Los Alamos and their use of this science in predicting the Stock Market but my especial interest in the study is the building of a data base which would be useful in my own area, human behavior. The essay of December did spark a lot of interest on the part of readers who had no previous knowledge of the work being done in the study of Chaos and Randomness. So much so that a few told me that once they started reading the essay, they couldn't put it down. One friend, a Senator, said he read it straight through and found it one of the most interesting he had come across.

It is my intention to continue to work on this physics approach to dealing with some of the realities of our lives that seem, on the surface, to make no sense at all. But, in the simplest form, if the most basic facts of human behavior are put in language that people understand, the physics of the needed equations will begin to make sense as well. For example, people, in general, would choose love over hate, would choose to be rich rather than poor, good looking as opposed to being ugly, etc. That such rudimentary knowledge lends itself to such simple formulas as: If A = B and B = C, then C = A seems not to have occurred to social scientists. No one, however, to my knowledge, is working on the possibilities that the new studies in chaos and randomness have opened to us. The fact that we are dealing with "bits and bytes" of an astronomical proportion should not deter us from making the necessary beginnings which would lead us to a better understanding of what are now, seemingly, inexplicable vagaries of human behavior such as the difference between people that care and those that don't, the murderer as opposed to those that love, those without seeming conscience as opposed to those that are tender-minded.

To anticipate you, no, it is not my thinking that the divinity of love can be reduced to arithmetical equations. But I do believe that a far greater understanding of human behavior is possible if submitted to scientific criteria rather than psychological guesswork.

Part of my own fascination with the subject is my own studies in mathematics and astronomy, my dealing with thousands of Teens in the classroom environment, my own experiences with my own children and the need they have for hope of a future. It is my hope that such a study would lead to real understanding of the basis of ideologies that lead to racial strife, to the killing of one another in the name of some belief system, to the betrayal of children and the murder of innocence.

The Frontier of the Mind is one that we have barely intruded into and remains one of the great mysteries. For too long, aberrant behavior, sociological clashes have been treated as things for which only a kind of pseudo-science such as psychology can hope to offer an explanation. The problem has remained, however, that such approaches have left us in continuing ignorance to the point that "expert witness" of such a nature is, rightfully, regarded by the courts as little better than "flipping a coin."

While no arithmetical formula is possible, in my opinion, largely because of the variable of "choice," for the eyes of Diana, Karrie, and Kellie, for the heart's longing for love and trust, this is no reason to discount some of the possibilities to find explanations for otherwise inexplicable behavior patterns. In solving some of these problems, perhaps more of our young people would have a better hope of a future where the things of greater value have a chance at success.

Since TV has such an inordinate impact on the lives of young people, the media has an enormous responsibility. Kellie and Life Goes On is one of the most promising aspects of dealing with this responsibility in a positive fashion. I will be expecting to hear from you, my readers, as to your own thoughts on the subject.

Life is, at best, a bittersweet waltz. Life does, indeed, go on. But how wonderful it would be if all those fathers who are blessed with Little Angels would consider just how precious little time is given us to make the difference in their lives that will give them the chance for growing up with the sense of their true value. If our little girls had such a sense of worth, how different so many things would be. I was fortunate. I was given "one more chance" and I took it. If I hadn't...! But, thank God, I did take it and I won a reprieve from what would have become my worst nightmare.

Parents are not supposed to bury their children. There is something terribly wrong about this. But it happens. Diana's eyes are now a blessing, not the curse they might have been if I hadn't risked what I did. She is the best part of me, like Karrie and Kellie, because I was honest with her. By opening the deepest part of my own heart and soul to her, letting her know how very human her father was and how very precious she was to me, she is with me in a way that gained something of such eternal value even death must bow in homage to it.

If I can help fathers and daughters realize how important it is to be honest with each other, to understand each other, what a difference that would make in our world. Sadly, you can't make people care. But for those that do, it is a different world where there are no tired clichés of love, where the music continues to live in our hearts and hope never fails.

If I have made a fool of myself in sharing these things with you, I sincerely apologize. Most of all, I desperately hope I have not embarrassed Karrie or Kellie. Perhaps it will accomplish some good in the telling; for their sakes I hope so. I don't know.

Hopefully, having said these things, I may be able to get on with the business of dealing with the ordinary things that comprise so much of our lives of quiet desperation. If, as Thoreau said, "If life is only a waiting, so be it" should prove to be the case, I would despair. But, I somehow doubt that such is the case. I don't believe he thought so either. Life is making choices and setting events into action. It will always be better to choose to love than hate, to give than receive, to live for others rather than selfishly, to take the risk of betrayal rather than shelter ourselves in reclusive seclusion from caring.

Will my sons understand? Not until they have Little Angels of their own-how could they? But I pray they will come to understanding in their own relationships with the daughters of other fathers. Only then can they expect any real happiness in their own lives and be able to come to knowledge of their own value as men.

I am not ignoring mothers in the role they play in all this. But I can't presume to speak for them. I'm having a difficult enough time trying to sort through dad's role in all this.

For my readers of some years, you will make the connection between the building of the data base and things like the recent bombing in New York, that *Stream of Consciousness* that is essential to understanding the emerging pattern of such seemingly diverse things like the terrorism of enforcing ideologies, the Kook in Waco, Texas, the exploitation and victimization of girls and women in our society and the prominent role of Hollywood in such exploitation. As my "program data base" grows, the possibility of understanding, of making sense of these things and offering solutions to them becomes ever more hopeful.

It would certainly be far easier to "fictionalize" the things I have said, to put the events and words in the form of "characters" rather than exposing myself. But the most sensitive among you will realize the loss this would represent. So I am taking the risk of personalizing things of such intimacy that the enemies of those things that are pure, honest and of good report may try to use against me.

At the same time, I have an obligation to my readers and friends to let them know that I have not been exercising a departure from the things I have been dealing with these past years; on the contrary, you will recall my continued reminder of the necessity of building an immense body of knowledge which will require an army of qualified scholars to have any hope of success in understanding. Since my part, primarily, is the field of human behavior, this essay was necessary to open the door of understanding in a particularly important area, an area which must be understood if there is to be any enlightenment for the sake of our children and their hope of the future.

The Poet and Philosopher has too often been dismissed to some hazy area of gauzy scenes, ephemeral sidelines of no importance far removed from the place of action where the real work is going on. In truth, there is too much justification for this condemnation. Too many times have poets and philosophers "played it safe" by sidelining themselves and not intruding into areas of life where they might suffer some hurt by speaking out.

This is the "safe" position of the liberal academic. Having done battle in the universities in just this arena, I carry the scars of the maverick that would not be "whipped into shape" and bull-headedly keeps carrying a standard for individual liberty with corresponding responsibility. This kept me in trouble throughout my academic career. But in too many cases, it has been the "well-intentioned" conservative who, without the required qualifications and credentials, has become my enemy because he lacked those essentials of understanding and substituted ignorance and prejudice for them.

I can only say, in my defense, that if people would respond to those things of real value, those things represented by Diana, Karrie, and Kellie, our little "ewe lambs," there wouldn't be terrorist bombs, Kooks in Texas, riots in our cities and inner city hopelessness, the wholesale destruction of young people, especially our girls, by Hollywood and society in general, failure in our schools and homes, in the leadership of our nation.

I have to confess my natural affinity for the theater, for the performing arts. In having to deal with so much "reality" of day-to-day living and ugliness, there is a natural attraction for those, like myself, to a different world where make-believe is preferable to the evil that abounds. My success with young people in the classroom was my being able to involve myself in their world, with the extremes of emotions to which they were so susceptible and understand those extremes rather than condemn them.

Where else is the actual poetry of life as evident as in our young people with their dreams and hopes? They haven't yet been taught what is impossible. We are desperately in need for the right kind of leadership which will encourage them in their dreams rather than a continued pounding of the gloom of the "real world." Prepare them; by all means, but not at the cost of their ability to dream and hope.

There is no other age that is so altruistic and so easily led in hope than the adolescent. All things are possible at this age. I have often said I could move mountains if I were able to exercise the authority to lead young people in the right direction. But our society and schools are the enemies of such direction and dreams.

When you are standing before such a class of young people and you are truthful with them, when they find you believable in caring about them, they are the most open people in the world. They will share their hopes and dreams in an atmosphere of possibilities. It is a wonderful experience to listen to them and encourage them in the sharing.

The idealism of youth is a thing precious in itself, something to encourage and build on. This is the age where the arts, literature, music, the theater and plays should be the basis for life. The very extremes of emotions which attract our young people to the ideals of love and romance should be encouraged in purity of those ideals rather than the utter casting aside of those moral absolutes which would temper those extremes of emotion by necessary reason.

Roll models; here is where it fails. The teachers, families, society, have to provide the basis of the ideals of real love and romance, of the possibilities of the realization of hopes and dreams. Young people reach out in desperation for the realities of those ideals in our society. Hollywood provides the opportunity of expression that should be found in the school environment. Unhappily, Hollywood is grounded in the profit motive whereas the schools should be motivated by the human product of young people who are not only equipped for real life, but able to find their hopes and dreams encouraged during this very brief span of transition from childhood to adulthood.

But such leadership in the schools should be of the kind of people who have not betrayed the best of the child within themselves, who are able to relate, in kind, to the hopes and dreams of the child/adult. The best of such teachers and leaders will still have some of the wonder of Kellie's eyes.

Where does this "gray-hair" get the notion that speaking of such things in this manner can accomplish anything of substantive value? Because I have never given up the same hopes and dreams. "The Play is the Thing!" still rings in my own heart and soul. The tragedy I see in so many my age is the loss of these things in their own lives; even worse, those who don't even know what I am talking about!

Diana, Karrie, and Kellie know. Millions of our young people know. They are the "risk-takers" who know, in their hearts, that: all things are possible to them that believe. How is it that my generation gave up the dream and betrayed it to our young people? I know this, until my generation does the things necessary to restore the dream, we risk losing the only thing that makes it all worthwhile, the very meaning of our existence, our children! As long as it is my part to make every attempt to try to move people to respond in love and kindness to the needs of our children and young people, I will continue to risk it all as a man with nothing to lose.

Christian Perspective

April: Part 2

Psalm 127:3-5

I didn't anticipate the storm that arose around my last essay on Fathers and Daughters hence this Special Edition of CP. Comments ran the gamut of embarrassingly high praise to the calling of my sanity into question. If I were to try to find objective middle ground in the aggregate it would fall to the insanity side. I can live with that.

A number of people inquired of the letter I sent Kellie Martin. This is my reply:

Dear Kellie, the letter was personal, to you, and no one will learn of its contents from me but you have the liberty, with my blessing, of sharing it with whomever you want.

To be called a gifted writer, even a great writer by some whose own sanity might be called into question as a result of such high praise, words a writer would kill for, is heady stuff. Fortunately, for the sake of humility, my detractors more than made up for any inclination on my part to have my head turned. My picture, at least, affords them an opportunity for dart practice.

I knew at the outset that I would have much to answer for by putting such thoughts into print, things which are ordinarily claimed as belonging properly to the purview of the fictions of stage and screen or pulp novels; but for a father to speak so boldly, nakedly, of actual fact and truth from his own feelings and experience? Quite insane! But I've a reputation for being a "high-roller" when it comes to confronting evil. So it shouldn't have come as any great surprise that I was capable of taking such high risks in my remarks concerning love and romance and the entertainment industry. My political essays, by comparison, are relatively safe, personal ground compared to the subjects of love and romance unless their treatment is done in the "approved" manner of fiction.

It is a comparatively easy task for someone like me to confront the evils of Caesar and his cohorts. There has been nothing of courage in doing so because there is no overcoming of fear. But, for the first time, I did have to overcome fear in the essay on Fathers and Daughters. Certainly not the fear of any physical risk, but the fear of doing something which might prove disastrous or embarrassing to others, the fear of betraying a memory, or, more probably, the fear of even being destructively misunderstood.

I knew I was on holy ground in the undertaking. This is an inherently fearful position for any man with even a modicum of common sense and I am far too pragmatic an individual to not be able to weigh the risks of such an effort.

It wasn't but two weeks after I wrote the essay that Siskel and Ebert did a special entitled: "Hollywood's Fear of Love!" Almost serendipitous; for so many to fulfill what used to be exceptional, the knowledge of the price of everything and the value of nothing, this haunts the whole of the entertainment industry as it does our society at large. Movies, as our art and literature, used to glorify love and romance instead of sex and violence. But such a freewheeling society as that of Hollywood, while having enormous appeal, pays a price in violating common sense mores.

One of the biggest problems is that, in such a society as that of the world of entertainment, standards are hard to apply. It stands to reason that if you reprove others, you risk having yourself reproved in turn and your own "art" might fall victim to the assault. As a consequence, since Hollywood attracts, naturally, those of artistry where "anything goes" the "freedom" to express your own artistic talents and temperament too often opens the door to license without the restraining influence of ethics. As a result, the fear of AIDS is now a very real hindrance to relationships in the industry together with the historic fears of betrayal, lack of commitment and trust.

The creed of: He who has the most toys when he dies wins! is not ever going to replace the things of real value. Our beautiful people in Hollywood know this. Those people we view on screen are no less real people for all their vaunted status as "famous personalities" and the envy they excite in others. Being real people, they are sensitive, like all of us, to criticism, to betrayal, to the tabloids like The National Enquirer and Star treating them like commercial products rather than human beings with the same feelings and needs as anyone.

For those who responded to my essay in a negative fashion I ask that you consider the enormous impact the industry has on our children and young people, our entire society, before you judge me too harshly in my treating with the subject in some depth. It will take a conservative such as me with my own rationale and experience to open a door of understanding in the matter. That is not to flatter my abilities but to call attention to the paucity of such understanding, and empathy, on the subject by those who call themselves "conservative."

Some of the responses were to be easily anticipated. Men who did not have daughters yet still felt free to criticize, even vilify. Some who had no experiential frame of reference criticized by damning by faint praise. Some, knowing they were guilty as sin of the very things I called their attention to, cursed me for exposing their own shame in their perversion. Some were angry because of my boldness in attacking the "double standard" of boys and girls (the curse of boys should be "experienced" and girls should be chaste). Some were, obviously, trying to excuse their own immorality by excusing it in others.

Then there were those who responded in sheer spite and envy out of ignorance of the things of which I was writing. The most tragic responses were from people who knew they had betrayed real love and romance and had no hope of it in their lives. Some were angry with me because of my "enviable" single status, allowing me the freedom to pursue those goals, honestly, in my own life.

Some others expressed irritation over my departure from my usual format of political and historical philosophy and the issues with which I have been treating these past years, failing to make the needed connection between my political essays and the one in question.

The most disappointing response to the essay was, really, the non-response of a few who I felt would, as friends, at least offer critical comment. Surprisingly, one of my oldest friends had virtually nothing to say on the subject. I have to attribute this to his inability to deal with such because of his own callous shell which he has spent a lifetime constructing and is loath to examine less it crumble, leaving him vulnerable to the very feelings he has spent a lifetime suppressing. As a result, this was not a "safe" area for his consideration as opposed to things of a more transient and ephemeral nature such as "theology" or "Zen and the Art of Motorcycle Repair."

But a few fathers did respond with the hearts of real fathers. I was especially grateful for the sharing of thoughts and experiences of my old friends, Senator Don Rogers and Byron McKaig, two sensitive men who were not embarrassed to share their feelings about such a profoundly sensitive issue. I want to thank them from the bottom of my heart for their kindness and gentleness in their comments and encouragement:

Dear Don, you blessed my heart so much with relating how very good The Lord has been to you in your own family, it explains a great deal concerning the integrity with which you have dealt with matters in public office.

I also thank the young lady who expressed such appreciation for my saying the things she said meant so much to her. And I thank the young lady who found the essay "unnerving." I know what she meant but her meaning has to go into the category of "privileged information." I am also deeply grateful to the single mother with two, teenage daughters who said she read the essay with tears and was going to share it with her daughters in the hope that they would listen to what was being said for their sakes. I pray they do; after all, they are the ones who need men like me to speak for them, they are the ones who make all the risks worth it.

And thank you, dear "lady at the bank," for the warmth of your smile and your calling the essay "poetry." Your graciousness in your remarks was music to my soul; you brightened my day, you seemed to understand.

Unhappily, the anti-feminists were represented as well in their remarks. A couple of them had the notion I didn't like women and saw the essay as a repudiation and a betrayal of their own slanted ideas on the subject. Granting that some of the writing I have done could be misconstrued in this fashion I still had to defend my position.

Women have certainly done themselves a disservice by intruding into areas where, properly, men alone belong and have lost a lot in respect to the "gentle sex" as a result. Just recently a woman, Lauren Burgess, filed suit in order to force allowing women to take part as soldiers in the reenactment of the bloodiest day of the Civil War. Please, ladies, just be glad you weren't a part of the murderous front line of this national bloodletting. You didn't belong there then and you don't belong there now. That is not misogynistic; it is Fact and Reason.

And we might as well face another fact, if women in leadership roles insist on intruding into every facet of the affairs of society, they will lose all femininity and forfeit all consideration based on gender differences. If men are continually demanded to relinquish those positions of manhood, the result, logically, will be the abandonment of claims to womanhood.

But for those who have read my earlier essays on women as victims in our society, it shouldn't have come as any surprise that I would come to their defense in particular regard to the issues raised in the essay in question. As to the response from the "conservative Christian community," I was pretty well taken to task by those who felt I was departing from a Christian perspective in my comments. This brought to mind a double whammy I suffer because of my position of the past few years in regard to the churches and their failure, particularly in regard to young people.

My readers of some years will remember the writing I have done concerning the "Broadway" productions of televangelism. They will also recall my low opinion of such poor, shabby attempts to compete with Hollywood in the area of entertainment. But I have never disparaged people having "fun" with their religion and few do so as well as the charismatics and, in particular, the Pentecostals.

Such displays of enthusiastic religious fervor only become despicable when The Lord is accused of being the perpetrator of such antic behavior and hysteria. The likes of Jimmy Swaggart, Jim Baker et al. is the logical result of such chicanery trying to pass itself off as a work of The Lord and shames the Truth of the Gospel.

It is no coincidence that Waco Wackos (a well-deserved and earned appellation) come from such religious license that, like the displays of the Pentecostals, lends itself to extreme behavior and excuses itself in the name of religious freedom and expression. How could it be otherwise without any of the restraining influences of disciplined theology or behavior? They are like unruly children playing a game where the rules, if any, are only muddy concepts at best. What is that scene in Texas if not "live theater," and very bad theater at that, where some nut is glorifying himself at the cost of others? The Lord knows I have no sympathy with Feds, Caesar's agents, and their bungling of the whole affair only points up the validity of my criticism of them, but I also criticize the media for giving such unscrupulous persons so much air time. For my part, I won't even dignify this charlatan to the point of using his name (whichever one he currently decides on). What kind of man uses and hides behind women and children?

As an aside, Dr. Ron Paul, Libertarian candidate for president in 1988, a former congressman from Texas, has a very valid point in that the DEA had no business being involved in this situation, a search warrant is still to materialize and, in short, if there was no proof of a crime, just exactly what were the Feds doing here at all? As much as I despise people like this wacko making The Lord look foolish, as much as I despise the shameless way he has behaved in The Lord's name, I think The Lord can handle him. I cannot see any justification, as yet, for Caesar trying to do him in without the necessary evidence to justify such an attack. Seems the media is surprised at the number of calls they are getting in support of this very argument. We'll see.

As a favor to a close friend I recently attended a Pentecostal service only to be reminded, once more, of how closely allied Hollywood and Pentecostalism, and charismaticism in general, are. The fits of hysteria, the "tongues" and "driving out of demons," the "words of knowledge and prophecies," the hand-waving and people being "slain by the spirit," all of this is emotionalism and, as such, is simply "entertainment" and a method of expression which is otherwise denied in the ordinary lives of ordinary people. Religion becomes, thusly, the excuse for that emotional bloodletting of extravagant behavior for every frustrated, theatrical wannabe. This is their Sunday Fix, the High, which enables them to escape lives of quiet desperation, and the deadly sameness that threatens, at times, all of us.

In such a setting, everyone from the youngest to the oldest gets a "part in the play." That little old man or woman, so lonely the rest of the week, gets to sing, dance, shout in wild abandonment in the name of the Holy Ghost. They get to exercise their imaginations and emotions in an approved environment and, like their Hollywood counterparts, get to do so without the normal restraints of either ethical standards of behavior or suffering censure for the display of their "talent." This, of course, explains the success of obvious charlatans such as Swaggart, Baker, Crouch, Robertson, et al.

Every manner of excess becomes acceptable in such an environment. Women and men get to "touch" each other in unseemly ways (a friend once described these as nothing but religiously approved petting parties) and thus their religion is an excuse for even obscene behavior, behavior that would call their sanity into question in any of the ordinary, normal activities of life. And, let's face it, the music of the charismatic most certainly apes its better in the theater, providing the necessary stimuli for exaggerated behavior and the casting aside of any of the restraints of inhibitions. Not unlike a bunch of drunks.

In short, while such people think of themselves as "Christian" and deplore any hint of my defending any part of such a "sink of iniquity" as Hollywood, of the great plays and musicals of the theater, they fail to see themselves in the same light as those who make a living of acting out fantasies or enactments of real life drama. I have to say that Hollywood, at least, does so with a blatantly materialistic motive without the hypocrisy of "spiritualizing" its excesses.

As to the "calmer" brethren among the Baptists, Lutherans, etc., I continue to suffer the "slings and arrows" of those that refuse to do battle from the comfort and safety of their padded pews. But I have already written enough on this subject and refer the reader to my earlier essays. Suffice it to say; when the churches do as good a job of satisfying the needs of people with the same sensitivity that Rebel Without a Cause and Oklahoma and South Pacific do, they will be meeting needs honestly; when they deal with the problems of contemporary life as well as Kellie Martin and Life Goes On, they will prove they understand.

Those with a heart for such things recognized the fact that the issues raised in the essay go far beyond the relationship between fathers and daughters. In watching a segment of Sally Jessy Raphael, for example, some young men were quite vocal in rejecting abstinence as an answer to unwanted pregnancies and disease. The utter selfishness of these young men and their evil intent of continued exploitation of young girls was blatantly, even embarrassingly, to me as a man, transparent. The tired excuse of abstinence not being a "practical" alternative sound so hollowly on the ears of Reason; as I pointed out in my last essay, boys only want one thing from girls and it is my prayer that girls will be given the encouragement of our society to say NO! to such obviously destructive selfishness on the part of these snot-nosed brats who have no sense of responsibility and lack the means or even the intentions of caring for these girls and the unwanted babies which result from their own selfish lust.

Jane Pratt does a good job of letting young people express their views and for that she deserves commendation. I'm sure, astute a woman as she is, she recognizes the need these young people have for family, for those that genuinely care about them. I'm glad she gives them a forum to speak out. I wonder what her views are on the loss of real love and romance in our society and the role of such destructive shows as MTV and personalities like Madonna?

While the New York Times refused to print Bill Simon's short essay about the things I have been writing of, I thank Bill Buckley for doing so in National Review (3/15/93). Apart from the politically correct and patently silly, oxymoronic phrase, Judeo/Christian, Simon might have been quoting from my own essays in his enumeration of the woes facing our young people. So similar was his letter to many of my own, he even uses my "Lincoln quote" in the same context. Uncanny.

Cutting to the bottom line of Bill's letter and my own writings on the subject: "Until Caesar is confronted on the basis of those values that made this nation great there will be no improvement in the chances of our children's future."

I categorically deny Swift's definition of happiness as "The state of being well-deceived" though, at the same time, being an admirer of his genius, willingly accord him the truth of the statement in his context and its application to the theater arts rather than a skillful con designed to both hurt and deceive (God's definition of a lie).

In this respect, I quote Abel's excellent and thought-provoking comments concerning Melville: "Melville characterized Paul Jones as 'a jaunty barbarian in broadcloth,' and saw him too as a type of American possibility: 'Intrepid, unprincipled, reckless, predatory, with boundless ambition, civilized in externals but a savage at heart, America is, or may yet be, the Paul Jones of nations. The character of Jones expresses the savagery still lurking beneath the decorous dress of civilization, and in his comment on the famous battle between the Bon Homme Richard and the Serapis, Melville pointedly put the question he had been agitating ever since Typee: 'In view of this battle one may ask - What separates the enlightened man from the savage? Is civilization a thing distinct, or is it an advanced stage of barbarism?'"

There has never been a subject that has evoked the utter extremes of human behavior as that of the relationship between men and women whether it be father/daughter or husband/wife. Tragically, in regard to husbands and wives, it too often becomes a "battle of the sexes," Clemens' "natural, born enemies," or, at best, my own definition of "armed neutrality." Beginning in the Garden, few have undertaken such a study on the basis of ideological conflict that, in reality, it actually is.

But if there is a single element that would distinguish the savage, the barbarian, from the civilized man it would be in the manner in which men treat women and women's reaction to such treatment. Any discussion of civilized behavior must start here. And this is not to say that women are not able to respond with a form of barbarism of their own, as I too well know.

As the arts began to focus on this relationship, it flowered in European centers of culture culminating in its treatment in England and, later, in America. This was the result of economies that promoted a leisure class that could direct its attention to the finer instincts of men and women who, relieved of grubbing in the ground for daily sustenance, could give the subject the needed effort of definition. Trading on the experiences of a Southern leisure class which had to come to terms with Northern "commerce and trade" as a result of the Civil War, it would be the Southern writers more than any others which would give a literate voice to real romance.

Sidney Lanier could say of his beloved South: "The conceit of a whole people is terrible, it is a devil's bombshell." Lanier exemplified the romance of the Southern traditions but was not blind to its foibles and weaknesses. Yet, cast into the perspective of Thoreau's Northern "Overseers," we are still left with the contrast between Franklin's and Jefferson's estimate of national greatness predicated on the industry of the common man in personal liberty and responsibility and Carnegie's later re-evaluation of the necessary leadership of benevolent millionaires who would "watch over" a nation of "happy serfs." The difference between the two philosophies would be the difference between the ideologies that would either promote or denigrate love and romance and, consequently, define the rolls of men and women in America.

The best of scientific philosophers from Spencer (he should have paid more heed to Franklin and Jefferson on this subject) on could easily discern the fallacy of Evolution as scientific fact but recognized in such a philosophy the possibility of "convenience" which, in their opinion, would free men from the superstitions of religion and lead them to a scientific answer to the world's problems. We live with the failure of such thinking today. No other theory has had such a detrimental effect on the relationships between men and women.

If the "convenience" of Evolution is applied to the sociological problems of abortion (Social Darwinism), for example, the remarks of Dr. M. Joycelyn Elders make cogent sense: "Children who have children constitute America's newest slave class...it must stop...We do the sorriest job of any country in the world providing family planning. We're always running around hollering and screaming about abortion - and abortion is not the issue." Elders calls fundamentalist Christians opposed to abortion "very religious non-Christians" with "slave-master mentality" and once branded two such leaders as "Mean, ugly and evil." Perhaps a backlash to some uncharitable souls labeling her an insufferable windbag (Through all her years with the Arkansas Health Department, it is rumored, no one has ever been able to take her picture with her mouth closed) and unfavorable references to her patently obscene Ozark Rubber Plant.

If, as she says, unintended pregnancy, especially among teen-agers, is the root of nearly every other major social problem, with nine out of ten prison inmates being the children of teen-age mothers together with pregnancy being the number one reason for adolescent girls dropping out of school, the Evolutionary Convenience theory makes, as I said, perfect and cogent sense. But as empirically correct as Elders' statements are, abortion is not an acceptable means of post-contraception unless a society is willing to forfeit any claim to the value of human life and, should that be the case, girls can give up any hope that some young man will ever perceive her as the needed poetry of his life. That, too, is empirical fact and brings with it a host of evils that has undone every previous civilization that fell heir to such thinking.

In fact, if we accept Elders' "evolutionary" expedient we must give the same credence to Carnegie's in respect to the overseership of millionaires who have, obviously, evolutionarily proven that they are the "fittest" to "take care" of all lesser persons. The great majority of Caesar's minions, especially politicians, would whole-heartedly agree.

In respect to abortion, I have to comment on the recent shooting of the abortion doctor in Florida. The argument that the killing of the doctor will save the lives of innocent babies is only valid when duly constituted authority carries out such an "execution". I am not blind to God's use of the leadership, the authority, as His "rod of iron" to exercise judgment against evildoers. Government, for example, in this context, is to exercise capital punishment, not any individual.

I have already made the point in previous essays that if our evil leadership, our evil laws are to be confronted and dealt with according to Godly principles, it will be done exactly as our founding fathers did. A group of patriots will come together in concert to confront the evil and pay the price for such a confrontation just as our founding fathers did. But in no case does the individual have the Biblical right to act for duly constituted authority except in those matters that impinge on him directly as in the case of protection for himself or others when threatened by an evildoer. If Caesar is to be confronted, it will only have God's sanction when the people band together, in concert, as legitimate authority to do so.

But have any groups addressed the cowardly men who would encourage abortion rights just to satisfy their own lust and avoid any responsibility for that lust? Girls, that life within you is sacred. Your body is no longer just yours when you give yourself to a man and the baby that may be conceived from such a union has a right to be heard. I make much of young people being betrayed by my generation, of not having a voice in the direction, hopes and dreams of their lives, but you girls are going to have to face the fact that the betrayal, the murder of the innocent baby conceived has no voice either and mitigates against you when the price of selfishness and lust is abortion.

I have to wonder if Elders will pay any attention to the destructive influences of things like MTV and Playboy, the wholesale destruction of family values by the insanity of our laws and the utter immorality of our leadership? Probably not, such people seldom do and she is already on record as one who will "go along" on Capitol Hill. No hope in that direction.

Is abstinence beyond consideration as a method of confronting the evils attendant on the victimization of young girls and the murder of the innocent? Only if we are willing to concede that love and romance are passé, without any relevance in our contemporary society. If a society has no real love for children and fails to offer the essential discipline in love of its children, if it fails to provide the moral leadership which commands the respect of its young, then the message to the boys and men who exploit our girls, who use and abuse them, is "go to it!" The inherent, degenerate lust of evil boys and men is then given carte blanche to abuse girls in any fashion they want without any concomitant responsibility or penalty for their evil actions. Caesar then has the day and his happy serfs will continue to breed indiscriminately knowing abortion and, logically following, sterilization and euthanasia will take care of the concomitant sociological problems.

Real love and romance are the attributes of a society that cherishes its young. But these are spiritual values, not physical ones, though the price of denying the spiritual values is paid in both spiritual and physical suffering. Nothing but abstinence will move us in the direction of those higher values and it is the way we encourage our young girls, the manner in which we value them and teach them to value themselves, that is the only realistic hope of achieving this. The only other path is Caesar's.

Granted, this puts a lot of responsibility on the girls. But the predominant responsibility is that of fathers and mothers who have to encourage and exemplify the ideals of love and romance in their own lives; and beyond them, the churches, schools and an entire society. As long as the selfishness of divorce is so easy to satisfy, this is not possible. It only exemplifies the selfishness of an entire society when divorce is as easy as buying a bottle of shampoo. But this is why God says He hates divorce and classifies the adulterer with the murderer. There is "murder" involved with divorce; it is the murder of the innocent, the children. They are the ones who are paying the price for the selfishness of those who insist on "having their own way!" or, as one ex-wife said to me: "Having her freedom!" This after exposing our children to her adulterous affair with another man behind my back; the children paid a heavy price for her "freedom."

I have to ask myself; since our laws encourage the perversions of immorality, divorce, what does this tell us about those who make such laws? If men and women prostitute themselves to gain public office, how can we expect moral leadership? Just who, exactly, is going to be able to confront this evil and overcome it?

I'm looking at a recent article headlined: "Children Murdering At Explosive Rate!" A 12-year-old in Monrovia is arrested for robbery and murder. The "experts" in the article can give no reason for the "explosion" of such incidents. The insanity of our laws concerning families and family values has brought this to pass. Will any of those on Capitol Hill make the connection between this tragedy of society and the terrorism of enforcing ideologies (The Twin Towers), the "open border" policy of our flaccid immigration laws, those laws which encourage perversion and "multiculturalism" (read: Cultures in Conflict), with bloated government spending which has forced two paychecks in order to run as fast as you can just to keep in place ahead of bankruptcy and the children can fend for themselves?

These "children" have had thousands of hours of "instruction" through the sex and violence of TV, murderous movies and videos glorifying abuse and mayhem, they have been taught that crime pays by scurrilous leaders in society. They have watched, vicariously, the abuse and torture of girls and women, of other children. They are not from families which had the means to allow them to be children in their own right, they may never have seen a canopy of stars in a velvet sky unobscured by pollution, they have never waded in a sparkling stream or heard the call of quail or the bark of a squirrel or chased a lizard around the rocks. They never lay on a warm, granite boulder gazing down into the depths of a crystal clear pool of a native trout stream and watched the fish lazing about while the scent of pine surrounded them; never felt the electric "aliveness" of a trout rising to take a fly of their own creation. These children never watched the clouds and tried to distinguish the shapes as castles in the air, never related to "Sleeping Beauty" or "Bambi." Where will these children find the caring softness that would deliver them? It isn't in MTV or RAP.

These children have "teachers" who deride the works of Walter Scott and Cooper as romantic "nonsense" and think they have done their job by glorifying perversion as "reality." As a teacher, I always took the risk of "preaching" the ideals rather than risk falling heir to the "prudent pessimism" of Sam Clemens who said: "I, like all other human beings, expose to the world only my trimmed and perfumed and carefully barbered public opinions and conceal carefully, cautiously, wisely, my private ones." Oh, dear Sam; you failed me in this one, singular regard and much as I venerate your genius, particularly as the best, most gifted, natural born liar it has ever been my privilege to know or America ever produced, I take exception to your counsel when it comes to presenting the truth to children!

A word to my detractors: You are absolutely correct; I am the most intolerant man in the world when it comes to fighting for the rights of children and young people. But I am fighting for their rights to be children, to be young people who can have a realistic hope that their own dreams of the future can be met. But unless we make our laws reflect the hopes and dreams of family and family values, we will continue our slide to anarchy and the oblivion of slaves to Caesar.

With the encouragement of good men like Richard Palmquist and Bill Lucas of KDNO in Delano, I continue my radio broadcasts on the subject of the schools because it is within the schools, those communities of young people, that the real difference can be made. I am also going to start contributing to some of the local papers like the Liberty Bell in Bakersfield. Little by little, brick by brick, we may yet make a difference against the tide of selfishness and perversion that is threatening our young people and our nation, doing battle against the edifices of the universities of erudite rot, the monuments to our own destruction as a nation.

Make no mistake; unless we are able to confront the evil in our institutions of higher learning, all else will be of little effect. These, as with too much of the entertainment industry, are the breeding grounds of political correctness, of the undermining of family and national values. In particular regard to the exorbitantly high cost of funding these institutions, if I had the power to do so, I would close down at least a third of these white elephants. This would do two things: It would get rid a bunch of the enemies of our nation and families who masquerade as "teachers" and would go a long way toward solving California's budget woes. What an outcry that statement is going to wring from the left-wing establishment!

The weather has turned mild the past few days. The bright sunshine lifts my spirits; I'm a through-and-through desert rat. I long for the summer. Perhaps the discomfort that comes from the cold weather acting on the wires that were used to hold the bones together after my motorcycle accident and the shrapnel in my right leg have something to do with this.

In visiting with the folks out at the old claim, I was reminded of the bat in the cave. The country around the Lake is riddled with holes and mine shafts. It was just such a day as this that, as a boy, I entered one of these old tunnels nearby.

It was cool inside and the damp earth had a good smell to it. I had only gone in a short distance when, to my surprise, I discovered a small bat hanging from the roof of the shaft above me. Running back to the cabin, I procured one of the ubiquitous Mason jars. Returning to the mineshaft, I entered it again and found the bat as I had left him. Managing to fit the jar over the hapless creature, I shook him loose from his sleepy perch and he plopped, groggily, into the jar. Clapping the lid over him, I took my prize out into the sunlight where I could observe him close-up. Good grief, he was ugly!

Now I had seen pictures of bats and they were numerous, flitting about the area in the dusk of twilight, but this was the first time I had viewed one eyeball-to-eyeball. I had never seen a more hideous face on any creature! But, as with my "pet" porcupine and skunk, what was I to do with the varmint once I had satisfied my curiosity about same? Only one thing to do; I returned him to the mineshaft, a sadder but wiser bat concerning the vagaries of humans.

The bat reminded me of a recent problem I have had to confront with an organization for which I have always had the highest regard, the John Birch Society. Now I have supported the society in its work for over twenty-five years. I used to give invocations for their meetings in Lancaster. The society still does a great job in many areas of its educational format.

It is because of my long years of familiarity with the Society and the fact that I know so many very good people in it that I am most reluctant to address the recent problems with its leadership. But, one of the reasons I have always refused "labels" by not joining organizations, no matter how worthy, is my conviction that I must have the liberty to examine any of them with the objectivity of an outsider.

My problem is this; recent articles concerning Randy Weaver and the Aryan Nations, particularly concerning Richard Butler, just don't make any sense. They are poor reporting at best and outright distortions at worst.

I have vented my opinion about the Society having become a "one-man-show" as per John McManus and, to a lesser extent, Gary Benoit, but egos being what they are; I didn't let this bother me too much. But I have been forced to acknowledge the fact that page after page of terminally boring verbiage might be an attempt to cover a more pernicious fact. Is the Birch Society being led astray from its historic ideals because of its mounting indebtedness to less scrupulous individuals? If, as I have learned, the JBS is in debt to the tune of 8 million dollars, just who are the creditors and what kind of "forced cooperation" is the Society going along with to accommodate these creditors? And, more to the point are "deals" being made just to stroke the egos of a few men who may prove to be unworthy of John Birch and Robert Welch?

In my questioning the lengthy and severely distorted article by Mr. Fotheringham about Randy Weaver and Mr. Butler, I wondered at the time why the JBS was going along with such an obviously poor piece of journalism. My own, personal knowledge of the facts made me aware of the distortions in the piece. This has to lend an element of credence to the accusation of a betrayal of a generation, which has supported the Society, and a betrayal of its historic ideals. This would be sad, even tragic, if true. Further, whatever one's opinion of Bo Gritz, if he is to be believed at all in this instance (and he was there, Fotheringham was not) the JBS did a grave disservice to its members and Americans by a very subversive piece of "yellow journalism." It only acerbates a bad situation when McManus continues to support such a distorted report.

I have read Fotheringham's articles justifying his report; I have listened to his tape. He freely admits having never met with Randy Weaver, Kevin Harris or Richard Butler. No legitimate historian or journalist is going to by-pass the primary sources of his writing or reporting when such sources are available and expect to be taken seriously. This is patently foolish at best. My caveat in my personal involvement in the whole affair was made clear some time ago. Even granting that there is the possibility of some truth in Fotheringham's accusations, my own concerns, legitimate concerns, remain valid and demand an answer.

To all of you good people who have supported the JBS; you should demand an accounting from the leadership concerning these things. You cannot afford to let the leadership of this honorable organization go unchallenged if the credibility of it and its fine work is to be maintained.

I'm a good, card-carrying conservative. It hurts to write these things about the JBS but I do so as a matter of conscience and common sense. I hope you, my conservative readers, will not excoriate me without examining the evidence. In all honesty, how could I maintain my own credibility as a writer, as a conservative, if I did not question those people and institutions that purport to speak for my own views? Those of us who believe in the freedom, liberty and responsibility of the individual have an obligation to question, even confront, any distortion of the truth no matter the source.

My love of The Lord, His Word and His Church makes me the harshest critic of those, like the Waco Wacko, who would discredit or bring shame to Him. My criticism cannot be alloyed by misplaced allegiance in regard to poor leadership in other institutions as well. Neither should yours.

For more information concerning this conundrum and much more, you would do well to get in touch with Criminal Politics: 1-800-543-0486. Tell them Dr. Heath of BitterSweet Publishing suggested you call.

My personal thanks to Arizona State Senator Wayne Stump for his comments concerning Jack McLamb. Quote: "Officer Jack McLamb, ret., is one of the new breed whose dedication to his job, his country, and its constitution goes beyond the usual. Jack's writings to his fellow police officers in the U.S. on constitutional and moral issues have helped to educate many in the need to study and put into practice those values that are responsible for making our nation the foremost bastion of freedom in the world." Jack publishes AID & ABET NEWSLETTER, Box 8787, Phoenix, AZ 85066. I have mentioned this publication before and encourage you to subscribe.

And what of Russia? It is a land going in all directions because it has no direction. It is reaching out to find straws to clutch. Big Brother is no longer looking over their shoulders to make them toe the party line. Production of all goods is down. Forty per cent of the produce rots in the field and granaries because there is no motivation to work hard at distribution. The profit motive that drives the materialistic society of America has not yet taken over the reigns in Russia.

All the Russians I have heard from agree there is chaos in their land. The leadership has been mandated to affect change and embrace capitalism. However, the leadership is crippled by 72 years of socialistic indoctrination. The editor of the popular newspaper Ches Peak (Rush Hour) in Obninsk was shocked by recent moves in the U.S. toward socialism and said, "We are racing away from socialism, why are you going toward it?" Then the deputy editor made a very thought-provoking observation, "Socialism leads a nation into a prison."

There is, indeed, an open door, at present, for Christians to get involved with propagating the Gospel in Russia. But, as with our involvement with so many other nations at this time, we must not get our eyes off the ball concerning the desperate conditions we face in our own nation. It hardly needs to be said that if we cannot do the job that needs to be done here, what business do we have intruding ourselves into the affairs of other nations? Yes, there is the need for maintaining relations with other countries and the need for cooperation where it will produce results. But not at the expense of our own people and certainly not in a hypocritical fashion of doing for others while our own children and young people are being let to go to hell! The truism of Charity Begins at Home better be applied in our own case.

I've been looking through the old photo album I got from my mother when I was visiting with her in Fort Smith, Arkansas (You'll recall my discovery of the fact that the quality of poverty in the South to be far superior to that of California). Because of my mother's rather heterodox marriage habits, she found herself in Pearl Harbor when it was attacked. My brother and I had been left with the grandparents in Bakersfield. Probably just as well since a shell landed in Mom's kitchen. Many of the pictures are scenes in Hawaii including some of the harbor after the attack. These were probably "contraband" at the time.

Included with the photos are many of the newspaper articles of the time. Things of intense interest to us boys and they still have interest to me. War is always a fascinating commentary on the human condition.

With so many things happening in present world affairs, I note, at my age, the sameness of many of these things. People still do things for the same reasons they always have. Ego and greed certainly haven't changed.

A recent article concerning Hitler's bomb expert, Werner Heisenberg, caught my attention; the vagaries of the inexplicable turns of events that determine the outcome of history. Had Albert Speer pressed Heisenberg, no doubt Germany would have had the "bomb" first and, as a result, Hitler would have ruled the world.

As a believer, I see God's hand in the affairs of men and history. But I'm not blind to the facts of human behavior that lend so much predictability to human events. Odd, isn't it, that one of Britain's best-loved poets, Philip Larkin, has just been discovered to have been a Hitler advocate, accused of misogyny and racism? It was well known that Larkin's father was openly sympathetic to Hitler. This, of course, in today's political "correct-speak," makes him, automatically, anti-Semitic as well.

Reminds me a bit of the Negro fellow in Sonoma who ran an ad with a bogus mug shot of himself captioned: "What would you do if you saw this man riding a bike through your neighborhood?" The fall-out of the bogus ad was an instantly formed Cultural Awareness Committee, pressure on the city fathers to recruit minority bidders on contracts, committees to develop minority support groups and an answering service to field race-relations complaints.

Like the Dutch vandal who desecrated a holocaust monument and fooled people into thinking it was an act of racism, the good Dutch people, the government, the press, everyone jumped on the bandwagon to prove they weren't "intolerant" Nazis. But The Hague just approved a broadening of the guidelines for euthanasia to include "severely handicapped newborns and the mentally ill!" But don't call them Nazis.

A first grade teacher in Pennsylvania gets herself in a jam by trying to expose the inhumanity of the old slave auctions. Problem was that she used some of her Negro pupils in the demonstration. Did anyone communicate this tidbit to Zoe Baird?

State Rep. Liz Van Leeuwen of Oregon is sponsoring a bill to require mandatory gun ownership; makes more sense than trying to disarm responsible citizens. One can hardly fault her logic; criminals have indeed learned that crime pays! And it took our judiciary to make this true!

We have our own version of the Waco Wacko. Billboards have been springing up in Kern County denouncing the Pope as the Man of Sin. Nothing new in that concept but one wonders who finds it worth all the money to spring for such expensive (at last count, five of them at 4 to 5 thousand dollars a month each) advertising? They call themselves Barn Ministries. I wonder if they would be interested in a scheme for Mormon and JW repellent in ecologically correct aerosol cans?

I really think NBC should pick up on this. Look at the job they did on General Motors. TV's hunger for hype lends itself to such chicanery but goodness gracious, if you can't trust either NBC or General Motors, just who can you trust? Rhetorical, of course.

But it does remind me of something I said to Gary many years ago; I would like to do business with Christians, I just can't afford to. His letter of last month (the whining for Jesus was a nice touch, Gary) reminded me of this once more. Quote: "It is time for prospective Christian leaders to beat the competition, not just equal it. We have three generations of a well-deserved reputation for incompetence to overcome." I wish Gary would cut to the nub of just where this "overcoming" is to start- in our own backyard. I'm sure he is aware of this; I just wish he would address it with the needed candor.

Remembering Audrey: Audrey Hepburn's career, her work and obvious tender caring with UNICEF on behalf of the children of Bangladesh, Ethiopia and Somalia, her Jean Hersholt Humanitarian award, her remarks concerning Cary Grant: "Cary is immortal, undying, unfading and constant for us all." And, to quote Parade: "So is Audrey."

In response to those of you who expressed the wish that I would write more of the kind of essays like Fathers and Daughters, I would like, so very much, to do this kind of writing that my soul and heart responds to. But, lacking the warmth and inspiration of that "Lady" in my life, I have to wonder how far, in reality, I could carry such a thing on my own? I fear, not far. I could never delude myself to the extent that a man of my temperament without such inspiration can do such writing. Lacking that needed dimension; I'm not sure where another installment of such a nature might come from.

If you missed, for example, my comments on the show Northern Exposure, you might read Woody West's excellent article in Insight (3/22/93). I only wish he had included Life Goes On in his plaudits. But Woody did put the better part of what TV has to offer in a proper perspective. Such shows offer hope that the industry, with some input from conservatives like Woody and me will offer the public more than the usually biased, liberal agenda. Not all of us conservatives have horns and run around in red union suits with a tail and pitchfork. Further, not all of us are insensitive to what well-intentioned liberals have to say or are incapable of appreciating their point of view.

Whether liberal or conservative, however, I won't hesitate to strip the mask of the hypocrisies of self-serving egos and selfishness in either case where I find it. I don't have any sacrosanct oxen in my stall and this gives me great liberty in calling a spade, a spade. And I'm constantly aware of the necessity of the thorns on my roses; you take the one, you take the other.

I think Art Spikol is correct in his statement that a good writer will take a walk and come back with an idea; a great writer doesn't need the walk. Perhaps this is why I have never been given a forum by any conservative group to speak out for our young people and the schools. Tragically, the conservative camp too often restricts itself with a far too narrow view of the truth.

The fact that I have never heard a sermon so eloquent in the truth of God's love through the Gospel as Kellie Martin's treatment of Rebecca dealing with the boy with AIDS is a case in point. The fullness of God's love, the very center and core of The Gospel, is more easily discerned in Kellie's portrayal of the very essence of God's love through others than in any pulpit rhetoric I have suffered (and, to my own discredit, uttered myself).

Will my conservative "brethren" accept this? Not a chance. But our young people suffer the lack of relevance in the churches because of this conservative blind spot. Kellie's "sermon" gets to the very heart and intent of The Gospel. This is where it reaches into the hearts of our children and young people, not in being "preached at" regardless of the well-intentioned rhetoric and the number of "proof-texts" applied meaninglessly and numbingly. Audrey's "Words, Words," should be a warning to religious people that our young people need examples of Christian living and charity, not just words. And that is all John 3:16 will ever be to people without the proof of it in our lives, Words, Words.

Priests and Pedagogues do, indeed, league with the "masters" of the people and, as a result, the answers seldom come from these sources. Tragically, neither the artist nor the poet will provide answers where the dreams of ideals give way to the vulgarities of the so-called "popular" tastes. By their very definition, ideals are never the domain of "commonness." Whitman failed miserably as a poet in this regard; he profaned real love and romance and, as a sop to "evolutionary expedience," traded on the base vulgarities for "success." In that sense, God forbid that I ever become "popular!"

When it comes to confronting the evils of perversion my conservative credentials are impeccable. But don't anyone dare make of my denouncement of such evil the narrow-mindedness of those who have no empathy with those that suffer the estrangements of society brought on by prejudice or bigotry. My peculiar brand of conservatism deals with the issues on the basis of Truth, Fact and Reason tempered by the mercy and love of God as well as His righteous judgment of the evil that men and women do. And I will never recant of my denouncement of the kind of perversion that preys on children. There is a hotter place reserved in hell for such spawn of Satan.

But, if the churches and many conservative groups were, themselves, free of the perversions of twisting and distorting God's own heart and Word, I would have friends. It is in confronting the evils here as well as in the liberal camp that keeps me estranged from the common comforts of gentle conversation with those like-minded in so many things. I sorrow for this loss because I am a man who would like friends. I just can't seem to practice the kind of self-deception that would buy friends at such a cost any more than I could bring myself to "buy" the love of a woman through an even baser deception. Men that do so make me, as Sam would say: "Ashamed of my species."

The Jefferson Memorial in D.C. is visited by thousands of people annually. But the inscription on the memorial is purposely misleading. After the words "to be free" there is omitted the rest of the sentence that reads: "nor is it more certain, that the two races, equally free, cannot live in the same government. Nature, habit and opinion have drawn indelible lines of distinction between them. It is still in our power to direct the process of emancipation and deportation reasonably." How many people know Jefferson was a leader, like-minded with Lincoln, Madison, Monroe, Jackson, Clay, Webster, Douglas, Grant and many others, of the American Colonization Society and wanted all Negroes returned to Africa?

Why do I get the distinct impression that House Joint Resolution 438 which was introduced in the House of Representatives on March 11, 1992 by representative Major Owens calling for repeal of the Second Amendment of the Constitution and Senator John Chafee's bill prohibiting the sale, manufacture or ownership of handguns nation-wide are somehow tied in with the omission on the Jefferson memorial? And why am I not surprised that Mr. Perot will not respond to questions on these issues? Tragically, a slave mentality does not deal in Streams of Consciousness. Only minds and hearts free to dream and hope and are capable of seeing eternity defined in the eyes of a child and in the stars, in the fidelity between a man and a woman, are able to exercise the kind of maturity that can deal with such issues honestly.

I have never deluded myself that the information I pass on in my essays isn't, for the most part, covered better and in more depth by those publications which are specifically oriented to those issues. A good example of this can be found in Nord Davis, Jr.'s "On Target," the publication of Northpoint Tactical Teams. My readers are those who respond to my down-to-earth way of dealing with these issues, not my peculiar genius in their specific definitions and, especially not, in originality. I read a lot. In fact, my desk seems to have developed its own progeneration, a life of its own where stacks of material are never depleted but grow and grow.

In attempting to absorb this sea of information which seems to threaten a flood of Noahic proportions at times, I have a self-imposed duty to make a synthesis of it, to put it into a perspective where people can relate to it without drowning, themselves, in a sea of particulars. Quite a challenge, you must admit. Most importantly, I have discovered a readership that appreciates not being put upon by recitations of reams of dry data important as it is.

My particular concern, the thing that motivates me, is my love for children and young people, my hope that kindness, gentleness, love and romance are still possibilities in the face of a sea of ugly "realities" that threatens to overwhelm us. I try to give a voice to these things.

A good teacher is a performer. I "perform" in my writing. Teaching shop classes, it was easy to perform for the young people; the props were numerous and right at hand. Demonstrations of how machines could hurt, maim or kill were real attention getters. I could make a real performance of lighting an acetylene torch or the foundry furnace and explaining the intricacies of avoiding blowing the entire shop up in the process.

I even discovered how to "perform" in teaching algebra classes in high school and college. Now that was a challenge but I discovered I could do it. Again, it was "live theater" to be most effective and I made sure everyone had a part in the "play." And young people learned, and, most importantly, they learned to value themselves and regard others. And I never neglected the necessity of a disciplined learning environment and the need for well-defined authority, respected leadership, in the classroom. This held true in the Ghetto of Watts, the Barrio of East San Jose and Lily White (then) Lancaster and Castro Valley. Since I have written so much on the subject, I am loath to do more but feel constrained to do so; this in respect to the evils of the failed systems of both education and welfare.

The Bakersfield Californian has spent several days giving broad coverage to the subject of "The Vanishing Black Man." The dry statistics paint a horrid picture of the destruction of the Negro family. It simply, for all practical purposes, doesn't exist. Sally, Geraldo, Williams and others continue to throw Negroes, Mexicans, Jews, Asians and Whites in gonzo confrontations that only acerbate an already deadly situation. No one of any degree of intelligence can say this accomplishes anything but a deepening of the hatreds and higher ratings for the shows.

When cultures and ideologies come into conflict, as they always do, there can only be one predominant "winner." America is under siege without a doubt. It is one thing to make the plea for Truth, Fact and Reason to be the arbiters of solutions; quite another to find the leadership which can act on these absolutes in the face of what is happening in our country.

The Balkanization of America has become, in so very short a time, a stock phrase. Yet, people like me, who have worked in the ghettos and barrios, have long known this to be the case. The Why of this is something that no one in the leadership wants to confront with the required honesty.

The Gospel is colorblind because it is the Truth. No other religion or ideology possesses this characteristic. But our nation has forsaken the Gospel of Jesus Christ and tried to substitute the institutions of "social programs" which, because of the inherent greed and selfishness of evil men and women were doomed, as ideologies, to failure.

If one is to countenance a "conspiracy" of pitting race against race in order to bring about a race war in this nation, there is evidence aplenty for such a thing. It is, in fact, already going on and has been for quite some time. Only the most obtuse or willingly ignorant can deny this.

Facts are stubborn things. America was founded a White, Protestant, Christian nation; that is a fact that won't go away no matter the erudite rot of revisionist "historians," the multitudinous failures of our forbears or the agendas of evil persons. All the social "tinkering" in the world cannot erase this fact. If such a fact is unpalatable, you must, honestly, ask yourself why and to whom? Legislative attempts to enforce a multi-cultural amalgam have only succeeded in bringing to pass the ripening conditions of the threatening holocaust.

No minority of race, creed or "lifestyle" can hope to do anything but alienate the majority when these things are used as a goad or whip against that majority. The backlash against such a thing is easily predictable and all the wishful thinking, all the "liberal" laws in the world won't change this and until a mechanism other than the Gospel is found to change human nature, it isn't going to change. Lots of luck. Unhappily, most of what tries to pass as The Gospel is just "another gospel."

The majority is content to let minorities kill each other and founder in a sea of drugs, prostitution and all other manner of crime, attend schools that have become killing fields, as long as they do it in their "place" and it doesn't spill over into the suburbs. You can imagine the backlash if it should. Powerless, stymied of reasonable solutions, Caesar will continue to augment the disaster by punishing the vastly predominantly white middle class until the situation hits a "flash point." This is an historical imperative, as I have said many times.

Is civilization only a thinly veiled barbarism? If one looks at the history of nations and the present, ideological battles going on, a good case for this can be made. I have already made the point a number of times that only one culture, one ideology, can survive in any nation; another stubborn fact that won't simply go away.

Moslem, Jew, Hindu, Shinto, Protestant, Catholic, Black, Brown, Yellow and White, fanaticism in all of these ideologies of supremacy of race or creed are in conflict. There is no possible "amalgam" of such diversity no matter how many "equity of fairness" laws are passed; only one can prevail within any geographical boundary. No amount of striving for an appeal based on intelligence can make people care, can make the fanatic give up his terrorist tactics of threatening, killing those that oppose him; another ugly, stubborn fact of human nature that no laws of men can change or circumvent. But the further fact that unless there is voter eligibility reform enacted, until we have control of our borders, the masses will still howl for bread and circuses and evil leaders will still, as Caesar has always done, cater to their whims until Rome burns.

Melville may have prophesied better than he knew. America has certainly behaved as the Paul Jones of nations. The philosophy of Social Darwinism ala Carnegie holds sway and incurable romantics such as me find little voice against the tide of Commerce which is most surely destroying our nation; the bottom line remains a dollar sign and those dollars give power to the enforcers of barbaric ideologies.

Goodbye Helen, you graced the stage and screen as their First Lady for many years. You, among so many others, gave hope of a reprieve from the ugly residue of the Gilded Age. Maybe, if Clemens and Warner had not themselves been so much a product of the very evil they tried to address, the message might have been clearer, more effective. But the churches, even then, having given up their authority to confront evil, who was there to do it except those gifted artists like James and, later, Lewis? But their warnings were lost to those who insisted the message had to be properly packaged in the accepted religious mode complete with hoary, proof texts and "untainted" by the profane lives and heritage of such prophets.

Kicking against the goads, I will take my text from South Pacific and Life Goes On and continue to be the outcast from among my brethren; not from conscious choice so much as from the child within me who cries to be heard in the face of the mounting, screaming chaos of "adult" ideologies. In short, I refuse to "grow up" by the definition of the betrayers and enemies of children and young people and The Lord God of Heaven to whom they are His Peculiar Treasure!

Of course, in attempting to be the voice of those who have no voice, the children and young people, I have had to forfeit the needed "pulpit" of both the liberal and conservative "adult" camps. It isn't unlike the battles I waged in the schools against all those administrators who hadn't the slightest idea of what children really needed in an effective and relevant education; and the universities and state legislatures? They are even worse! They are the institutions that produce the Honig's with no hope of anything better in sight!

I'm looking forward to the spring and summer lecture circuit. I have some interesting groups to speak to and hope this will afford the chance to make a difference for the sake of the future of our children and young people. I have to admire the courage of those who extend invitations because they know I will not temper my remarks to encourage any "special agendas" but will "tell it like it is!"

But I continue to live in the hope that I will meet those with whom I can engage in gentle converse, people who will respond to the child within themselves and, with the maturity of years, help give a voice to both Reason and Love in the practical working out of the problems for which my generation is responsible. Please continue to give me your thoughts on these things. They are much appreciated.

Chapter Five

Christian Perspective

May

Ephesians 6:10-18

Because of the extraordinarily mild weather coupled with the recent rains, our area is ablaze with greenery and wildflowers. I never cease to marvel at the variety and colors. Some of the flowers are almost microscopic, so very tiny and delicate that I tread carefully in my sauntering and thrill to the abundance of such an array of natural marvels that so delight my heart, mind and soul.

Long dormant springs are running, providing for the critters. The river and lake are higher than they have been in years, the snow pack promising a good fishing and boating season. As I write, I can watch through my sunlit windows as a beautiful grey tree squirrel romps among the pine and oak as well as the shaded rocks. Life should be good in such an environment but, as with Thoreau: What is nature to me if I have no one with whom to share it? So, lacking that "one," I share it with you, my readers.

Not surprisingly, I continue to get responses to my essay on Fathers and Daughters. I am most grateful for this because the essay raised issues that touch on all of our lives. And, in answer to some of the more insightful of my readers: Yes, the essay was "unfinished." Not only did I not explain the events that led to my sharing the story with the children, I did, in fact, have to draw back toward the end and left much unsaid. This is why I have told some of you that I considered the essay only the "first installment." You will remember what I said would be necessary to carry it further.

In respect to Hollywood, "Inside Edition" just aired a segment on the stalking of celebrities. And before you ask, no; Inside Edition is not on my mailing list; just a coincidence. But I repeat; there is no other industry that has as much justifiable fear of the Kooks and Cranks as the one that employs our beautiful people in the entertainment field. It is certainly fearful to know that if someone wants to know where a celebrity lives, and is willing to spend a small sum of money, he can find out!

It is equally fearful to know that the "Mansons" are increasing in number. The "Killer Exhibit" in Pembroke Pines, Florida, an exhibit and sale of "memorabilia" of the likes of John Wayne Gacy has some of the inhabitants angered. Rightly so I agree; such a thing is an outrage! Such a thing only mitigates further crimes for "media immortality" by crazies attacking celebrities.

Another note along the line I followed in the essay: "Hollywood has become a victim of its own greed." A quote from Ismail Merchant who produced "Howard's End"; Merchant made this comment in respect to the Hollywood focus on sex and violence for the sake of wider profit margins.

Seventeen Magazine following my own views on the subject had a lengthy article exposing the widespread sexual harassment of girls in the schools. I could have offered them considerable material on the subject from my own experiences in these institutions that have become "stalking and breeding grounds" and, in too many cases, killing fields. This includes sexual harassment by school personnel that is woefully underreported, not unlike the "teacher" of my experience that I mentioned some time back who divorced his wife so he could marry one of his pupils.

Tragically, our young girls are not getting the needed leadership and role models that would teach them modesty and encourage chastity. On the contrary, we live in a society which steals their childhood and forces them to think, dress and behave in sexual ways, cloaked in a pseudo-maturity without the knowledge and life experiences which promote responsibility and, consequently too often invites such attacks.

In such an environment it is not surprising that Norplant and condoms are being used as the panaceas of a lost battle against rampant immorality and abuse of our girls. It's somewhat like trying to "reform" our schools and political system without moral leadership: Not possible!

The boys are taught to expect girls to give in to their lust and abuse. As a result, neither have much chance to learn the things of greatest value in a genuine, mature, loving and committed relationship.

We have an evil system that must be confronted. When I refer to "Caesar," I hope you understand that I am speaking of that evil system, not some individual. While it is painfully obvious that the system is filled with evil men and women, it is the system of evil itself that is destroying us. Without moral absolutes, how could we expect any other kind of system to fill the void? But, in confronting the system, individuals and specific agencies must be confronted in their evil.

I think my readers will appreciate knowing more of how my son Daniel, Diana's brother, responded to the essay.

Dan is a sensitive and intelligent young man and I heed his input and criticism. The love between a father and son, while quite distinct from that between a father and daughter, most certainly shares some of the same characteristics. I am most fortunate to have children with whom I can share, openly, the feelings we have on such a wide-ranging field of various subjects, feelings and subjects that are often in concert.

My son remembered the conversation in the restaurant quite vividly, as I was sure he would. And, while the "story" focused on Diana, it couldn't help but have an impact on Dan as well. One point he brought up prompts me to clarify something of which my readers might have a wrong impression. I do not hold it against anyone who has not experienced the romance I told of. That would be eminently unfair. There are "eunuchs" born of God for whom, through no fault of their own, such a thing will never become a part of their own life experience.

But apart from such exceptions, so very much of this kind of thing depends on the childhood experiences of the person. If that childhood is not filled with the kind of caring love, the opportunities to explore, has not had the chance of being immersed in good music, art and literature, the experiences which lead to the expanded imaginations which result in the wonderment of God's creation, it is highly unlikely that true romance will find fertile soil in that individual's life. It is even more unlikely to flower when that child is exposed to the cruelties of divorce, of not having a father and mother who have exemplified the realities of such a thing in their own lives and, as a result, failed to pass the torch to their children. This, naturally, explains the dearth of the realities of genuine love and romance in the present generation. It is, tragically, an unknown factor in their lives.

I'm an inveterate storyteller. My maternal great-grandmother and grandparents who were themselves marvelous storytellers raised my brother and me. We were raised with radio and books, the classics of literature and the old Colliers and Saturday Evening Post, National Geographic. So much that allowed us to exercise our imaginations; most importantly, the sincere love that surrounded us. As a result of this, I raised my own children with stories of my childhood in the wilderness. I often took them to the mountains and desert and tried to introduce them to the wonders that can only be found in such places.

But Dan pointed out the fact that there is an interest as well in my enviable Camelot experience of the South Bay of the 50s, something I hadn't dwelt on much with the children. Maybe because I felt the time I spent in the wilderness to be more important. Part of my feeling this way, I know, is the fact that the solitary pursuits of mountain and desert provide an escape from the relatively transitory "monuments" of civilization. Also, when the children were young, the stories of my wilderness experiences were far more suited to their fancy and imaginations, they could relate more easily to these as opposed to those that would become relevant to their adolescence and young adulthood.

However, unless one is of an inherently hermit or monkish disposition (I am not, though I admit to the need of a good deal of solitude), it is the experiences of involvement with others that makes us what we are. It is how we live in relationship with other people, our interaction with them that becomes the predictor of our own psyches and actions.

Just recently I was told of the serious illness of the wife of one of my oldest friends. She has had a mastectomy and one never really knows the prognosis of such a thing. This is the third woman I count as a close friend to whom this has happened. It is a further tragedy that in all three cases the woman has been a good and faithful wife and mother, an all too unusual virtue and commendation among the women I have known. One fails to see the justice in such a thing.

Among men, it is the prostate that is doing us in. As I grow older, I am experiencing this condition among the men I know. One of my ex-father's-in-law died at 60 of this. While none of us are going to get out of this alive, it still angers me that good women like my friend's wife have to suffer such a thing so seemingly unfairly. If He had asked me, I could have told the Lord of some I consider far more deserving of this kind of attention (like myself). But He didn't ask me. For example: live hard, die young and leave a good-looking corpse is beyond my own scope now. The living part, if anything, has gotten harder but the rest is moot; if I had known I would live this long, I would have taken better care of my carcass. Oh, well.

I will never undervalue the effects of my wilderness experiences in the forming of my own character, the way I perceive life and the values I maintain. I have written much on this theme. But it is in living life with others that gives the "voice" to our character.

For example, as Thoreau pointed out, if you are not sharing the things that delight your own soul with others, there is a missing dimension in your life; the real joy is not there. Too many people today fail to find that sharing of mutual delights in their own lives. There has to be someone who gives the color and scent to the flowers, who will make the music meaningful, the moon and stars shine brightly, who makes life a living experience and redeems it from mere existence. The single most important thing to come from such a relationship is the learning to live for the benefit of others rather than selfishly. The family is supposed to be the ultimate expression of this kind of love.

Obviously the color and scent of the flowers is there whether you notice them or not. But it is love that causes you to notice them in all their glory that gives real meaning and value to them. Destructive fanatics of various stripes and ideologies fail to find such a thing and, as a result, turn their energies to hatred of those that oppose them. The "leadership" within our own political system and our society at large exemplifies this tragically missing ingredient and, as a result, selfishness abounds. I believe this is the reason I feel compelled to address the subject even at the risk of appearing foolish.

But even in my own case, too often, as with most writers, some of the bitter parts of experiences come pouring out in invective because of frustration, disillusionments and disappointments, a too-often prosaic present vying with a romantic past, both in my life and our nation. As a result, I have to guard against living too much in reverie and pay close attention to the tasks of the day. Admittedly, I do find the better part of those softer and kinder memories of that past far preferable to the ugly realities with which we all have to contend in our contemporary setting.

In respect to Camelot, It is hard to recall the fact that Torrance, for example, used to be a "countrified" area. I started flying out of the old Torrance Airport in 1958. My first instruction took place in a J-3 Piper Cub with an "armstrong" starter. It was on the old strip that I discovered my DeSoto convertible with fluid-drive would, in fact, upshift in reverse! That is how laid-back the place was in those days.

I would arrive at the airport to begin the lesson in the morning hours. The instructor would give me the privilege of swinging the prop to fire the old bird up. Quite a transition from the model airplanes I was used to but at least they had taught me some of the essentials.

Climbing out, slowly and noisily, at about 700 feet AGL, we would head for the shoreline. Being Summer time, the weather was absolutely beautiful. Passing over the beach along Palos Verdes and Portuguese Bend and heading out over the ocean, I would look down at the marvelously white sand only sparsely peopled and the contrasting, huge expanse of a sparkling, sapphire blue Pacific dotted by boats, the waves foaming and breaking against the beach. Magnificent!

Flying can be terribly monotonous as Pappy said. It is those moments of stark terror that delivers from the boredom and keeps one on his toes. But, the usual drill in training is interminable maneuvers, repeated over and over, essential but boring. There are four drills, however, that deliver from the boredom. One: Taking off. Two: Stalls. Three: Spins, Four: Landing. Acrobatic work comes after the license.

The stalls and spins were something I learned to look forward to. Once over the ocean it was "stall time." A punch in the shoulder and a shouted command from the instructor in back and I would start to gradually pull the nose of the old bird up, and up, and up until the world dropped out from under us and the Cub would, wrenchingly, fall out of the sky trying to slide back down on its tail. In those days, spins were also required but were later discontinued by the FAA due to some unfortunate incidents. But I enjoyed them.

The stalls would be straight ahead, to the right and to the left. They would be full power, partial power and power off and provided some variety. Apart from relieving the boredom of less enthusiastic maneuvers like S turns and turns around a point, the stalls familiarized you with the position the aircraft would impact the ground should the plane stall in too close proximity with same on an approach. Just how useful this information was might be a matter of conjecture. But the real purpose, of course, was to become expert at the recovery from a stall just in case you had enough altitude to perform the maneuver before auguring in. It was also necessary to familiarize you with unusual attitudes of the aircraft if you, in a moment of insanity, decided to fly into a thunderhead or encountered extreme, clear air turbulence. I have never been a cruel or malicious person. As a result, when I would take my children or others flying, I never "treated" them to such maneuvers.

Torrance has always been important to me. When the ex-wife returned from Hawaii with Daniel and Diana, she located in this city and here is where the children remained and grew up. This is where Diana suffered her fatal accident. Daniel still lives there. It is, predominantly, for this reason that I still visit the area occasionally.

The city of Torrance is a "white ghetto." Surrounded by minority enclaves, it is ripe for attack by the surrounding hoards of "vandals." The threats have been made and the Torrance P.D. is certainly aware of this and is training and preparing accordingly.

I was just thinking of the car I had after the Cad convertible, a Continental Mark III; beautiful, comfortable car; full leather interior and sheer delight on the open highway with 400 horses to push it on trips to Vegas or wherever the spirit led. The only car I ever owned in which I could lay my six-feet on the seat full-length and not touch the doors with my head or feet.

But Detroit, in its betrayal of American car-buyers, didn't provide disc brakes on these behemoths of the highway. As a result, I would have to cool the brakes when I would come down from Trancas Canyon and other steep roads.

I had a state of the art radio with reverb installed. What a joy that was in listening pleasure in that big vehicle. Talk about audio acoustics! I also had an LP record changer in the thing. Now that was really first class in those days.

In harking back to this time, I find my anger stirred that in such a comparatively short period, my children have been betrayed of the opportunities

I enjoyed. It takes two paychecks, if jobs can be found, to do the job of the one when I was young.

In my travels throughout the country, I hear people my age complaining, often thoughtlessly, of the attitudes and actions of young people today. I speak myself hoarse in trying to direct their attention to the huge loss our young people have suffered and the responsibility my generation bears for that loss. I don't win many friends with that apologetic.

It angers me further that I seem compelled to do the kind of writing that addresses the causes of the betrayal of our children and young people. How much I would rather write of the softer things that stir my heart than those things that are required to confront the evil that threatens to destroy America and any hope of a future for our children.

If you want to know what is wrong with our inability to deal with drugs and aliens, read the article in The New American, (3/22/93) "Strange Justice", concerning Joseph Occhipinti. Here is a man who is being "lynched" because of trying to honestly do his job in the INS. One of the primary players in the lynching is New York Mayor, David Dinkins. I earnestly want you to read this article so I won't go into the details. Suffice it to say that any real American Patriot can't help but be enraged by the injustice, the insanity of the situation and further enraged by the abuse of power, the political chicanery involved. The depth of the perversion of every tenet of our founding fathers, of every scruple of honesty, is almost beyond belief. If Caesar wants to promote anarchy all He has to do is to continue to countenance such lynchings of the few honest men like Occhipinti and continue toadying to the "Dinkins'," illegal aliens and drug lords.

My "thorn on the rose" in the case of the JBS is that in this same issue, R.W. Lee gives Gary North full credit for his comments on school vouchers but both he and Gary ignored the input I had provided which Gary used. However, knowing how Gary and the leadership of the JBS perceive me, I am most certainly not surprised at their journalistic dishonesty and plagiarism. But I am not going to let up on John McManus and the leadership of the JBS until I have a satisfactory answer to the questions I posed in my last essay. I have too much regard for the noble job the Society has done in the past and the service it continues to render in its educational format to let those questions go unanswered.

My real concern is that as long as they use the material that others and I provide them without crediting their sources, they do a real disservice to the cause of conservatism and provide the enemy ammunition to use against worthy causes. But, tragically, egos too often prevail when men seek their own selfish interests rather than the cause of liberty.

Another strange "coincidence" of a like nature; since I communicate with National Review, I found it odd to read Anthony Lejeune following up my essays (with no comment on them) in his article of 3/29 entitled: "No More Enchanted Evenings." But rather than chaff under the slight, I soundly applaud the excellent article which gave a much broader voice to my own thoughts on the subject of what I consider, with Lejeune, the greatest American art form of the twentieth century; the musical play. He, as me, pays homage to the genius of such great artists as Jerome Kern, Sigmund Romberg, Rudolf Friml, Victor Herbert, Rodgers and Hammerstein and mourns their passing.

"The musical-comedy lyric," mused Wodehouse, "is an interesting survival of the days, long since departed, when poets worked." But for the great Broadway musicals like Showboat and Oklahoma with their emphasis on True Love conquering all to survive required a national Ethos that, with the betrayal of our nation by the evil leadership of an increasingly evil system of government, fell into dark decline. There remains no more "...bright, golden haze on the meadow." To have traded I Walk Alone and Younger Than Springtime for A Tear In My Beer, Ice T, VH1 and Madonna borders, to me, on sacrilege and speaks volumes for the conditions our young people face and the tragedy of their betrayal and loss.

But poets and philosophers do not flourish in ideological hatreds, in systems of evil where the value of the individual is sacrificed to the vulgar, common cry for unearned bread, in systems where slavery to such evil punishes all efforts to live responsibly and cheats a man of his manhood, victimizes a woman of her womanhood and children of their childhood.

It takes a common culture to produce the great works of art, of love and romance that the great Musicals exemplified. It requires the genius of that culture to produce hope of the ideals of commitment and fidelity being fulfilled, of a family being able to work with the hope that they are building a future for their children. Cultures in Conflict result in the base obscenities with which we live in America today.

I realize that in order to maintain good "liberal" credentials many leaders in this camp have to give "lip-service" to things they know are untenable; conservatives likewise. But the hard choices remain to be made. A French Revolution looms in our future if those choices are not made. It was The Gospel that saved England from suffering the same fate as France but we have no certain trumpet sound in the land of a like nature to save us. The churches gave up their authority to confront Caesar by selling out for tax-exempt status thus becoming Caesar's "dogs," eating at his table.

I endorsed the LEARN program for the L.A. Schools not because it is an answer to the problems but because it offers some opportunity to make necessary changes. The real problems remain, problems like the whole system of education being staffed by those who still have no real knowledge of the real world our children have to contend with together with the lack of any moral absolutes which dooms all strictly mechanical attempts thorough merely pedagogical approaches to solutions.

Once more, social "tinkerers" are in the driver's seat and the hard facts; the hard choices are ignored and delayed. But the problems won't go away anymore than the historical imperatives which reflect human nature. They will continue to consume like a cancer until it is cut out by increasingly drastic surgery or destroys us.

I entered the state Senate race to call attention to the desperate case of our schools and our young people but no one, the media or the other candidates, would pick up on the issue. They still won't. They still don't see that this issue, more than any other, is the battle for the soul of America. But I did learn something of great value. As long as the vulgar masses have the franchise, as long as people have to prostitute themselves to gain public office, so long will there be no hope of anything changing for the better and will only force this nation all the more quickly and devastatingly to confront the only choices with which history and human nature leave us.

Apart from The Gospel upon which this nation was founded (like it or not, historical fact that won't go away in spite of revisionist "histories" and subversive courts), we face only two other options: Worship of the State (slavery to Caesar), or the anarchy from which dictators, tyrants and despots always arise; those that beat the "Global Drum" do so in the hope and expectation that they will be the Darwinian inheritors of world rule. My past essays cover this subject so I won't belabor the point.

Diversity is a good thing when hateful agendas of ideologies are able to be separated from it. Our evil leadership, the evils perpetrated by evil courts and laws, have robbed us of the culture which produced the great art, literature and music of the past, have cheated our children and young people of hope of the future and the betrayal leaves us with only the three options history and I keep enunciating: Anarchy, Abject Slavery or Confrontation by Duly Constituted Authority in the form of our founding fathers.

Bloods, Cripps, Nuestra Familia, Tongs of various descriptions are providing graphic illustrations of the failures of the leadership to come to terms with the three "choices" we face and a disastrously diseased society. Police agencies, especially the honest people within them, are being overwhelmed by the growing enormity of the problems. The cops are in a no-win situation; damned if they hit or shoot and dead if they don't.

When 12 year-olds are in the front lines, as they are as a matter of cultural fact in third-world nations, and now, within our own third-world "nations within the nation," in our own society, when these child/adults, 12 going on 25-to-life have no other life but crime and killing, you would think the leadership would start talking common sense. But I'm not hearing it.

The media "treats" us to inside coverage of minority children being instructed in the use of weapons but what, do you suppose, would be the result if the NRA were to single out a bunch of white children in the use of automatic weapons? Imagine how that would play on 20/20!

The leadership of the NAACP still touts the "progress" it has made. They still sing the praises of forcing laws that have only made the situation for minorities increasingly hateful to the taxpayers who are forced to pay for insane programs like Welfare as a "lifestyle," Affirmative Action and Quotas in hiring which have done so much to gut our industries and bankrupt our nation. The Willie Browns, Rangels, Dinkins' and their ilk bow and scrape to the vulgar masses who feed off responsible, law-abiding workers and take "credit" for making it so much "better" for "their people." They might as well be honest enough to take credit for gutting our industries, stealing from honest workers and for making the schools, ignorant, diseased, drug, breeding and killing fields and enslaving "their people" to a far worse taskmaster than any Southern overseer, to a form of slavery far worse than that of the old South.

The agents of Caesar, lacking reliable information on groups like The Aryan Nations, the KKK, The Order, Posse Comitatus, etc., will continue to blunder into situations like murdering Vicki and Sam Weaver, be made to look downright stupid as in Waco, will expect the Serbs to bomb N.Y. and the Iranians or other fanatics, sneak through instead. I wonder if they are really prepared for the suitcase nuclear devices that are being planned? I doubt it.

What I mentioned concerning the near nuclear exchange between India and Pakistan some months ago is now being trumpeted by the mass media. The evil of leaders and fanatics will keep this "option" boiling. South Africa, Israel and North Korea are key players in this scenario not to mention the continuing deterioration in Russia.

And any agencies which can come under the sway of the likes of a Hoover, any agencies which would cooperate, with presidential blessing, in the murder of children, missionaries, nuns, priests most certainly is inviting the scorn of all civilized people throughout the entire world!

Do Jews in this nation have a justified fear of increasing anti-Semitism? You bet! As long as we have to contend with Congress being Israeli Occupied Territory, as long as ignorant people, ignorant preachers continue to use the moronic, oxymoronic phrase "Judeo-Christian," as long as such a minute fraction of the population continues to intrude such a hateful and inordinate, grossly disproportionate influence in our universities, the legal profession, the fields of psychology and psychiatry, the entertainment and media industries (have you noticed how many Jewish children and young men and women have, vastly disproportionately, been appearing on TV lately?) they will become increasingly hated just as they have become in virtually every nation in history where they have exerted the hateful influence of their peculiar ideology and agenda.

Just as those Jewish leaders used Caesar as their instrument to crucify Christ they use their influence with Caesar today to press their evil agenda. Just as they flaunt their hatred and attack Christ and every Christian symbol from the Cross, Christmas and Easter on with their Brown Shirt ACLU, proving that they despise the very ideology upon which America was founded, despise the culture which gave them the very liberty, which they pervert, to act destructively against it through betraying, treasonous courts, attacking America's very foundational culture and beliefs, they become the targets for retribution. And nowhere is this more pronounced than among the Negro population. This is certainly a two-edged sword in the nation.

And I always make the careful distinction between Jewish believers like the Apostles and those that established the early churches. It is the "Judaizers," past and present like those "Jews" who Paul and others referred to, the early enemies of the Church, who, like The Lord and the Apostles, I confront in their evil agenda and anti-Christ ideology.

From Franklin and Jefferson on, these great statesmen knowing the disastrous effect of the Jews in England and France, the intent of our founders was made indelibly clear that the Jews were never to be given an opportunity to gain any kind of influence in our nation for the very reasons already cited. And if you take exception to the rationale of these great statesmen, I would ask you to try to think of a present leader in government who could be favorably compared with them, let alone one with the backbone to articulate such things!

I am not a "hater" of people. I am a hater of evil. I am the enemy of any special ideology or agenda which seeks to destroy my America, the America of Franklin and Jefferson, of Hale and Washington. That does not make me anti-Semitic any more than it makes me anti-Arab, anti-Slav, anti-Mexican, anti-Eskimo, etc. I am opposed to any culture, any ideology which insists I betray and disavow my own, the one upon which this Republic was founded in the liberty and responsibility to pass that same culture and Christian ideology on to my children! The enemies of this heritage that made America the freest and most unique nation in history in the exercise of liberty are my enemies!

It is well past time that serious thought be given to the fact, devoid of emotion and name-calling, that the emphasis given to the glorification of cultures inimical to our historic American culture be questioned and the advocates of such a destructive thing be called to account! Just who is behind this conspiracy of trying to make me ashamed of our noble forbears, our noble beginnings as a nation, of being of Caucasian, European, Christian ancestry?

It was equally clear that the franchise was not to be given to any who would use it to subvert the intent of our Constitution and Bill of Rights, to any who would not be able to knowledgeably and intelligently vote for those things which would encourage liberty and individual responsibility with a view to posterity. Who, in the "leadership" today, dares face these facts let alone utter them? On the contrary, Caesar and his toadies would have us betray our heritage, even disown and disavow it and betray our children and our nation for the sake of the vulgar masses, the hoards of vandals that threaten to destroy us!

Why do I write in such anger of such things? Because only a strong nation, a strong America will offer my children any hope of a future, because only a strong America can offer any hope for the oppressed of other nations and unless these issues are addressed with the utmost candor, factually, such an America is not possible!

Just as perverts who try to coerce "acceptance" for their depraved and destructive behavior by "liberal" legislation make themselves the targets of wrath, Jews and all minorities who try to gain acceptance of their own ideological agendas through the courts will only succeed in heaping coals of fire on their own heads, will only succeed in hastening our own French Revolution! You can input the Willie Browns, et al. in the database as well. Of course, people like Sam Nunn and me together with our founding fathers are the "Bigots, Intolerant, Xenophobic, etc." I say again: carefully mark those who are calling us names in the face of the irrefutable facts of history and consider their own agendas!

I write and think as a Caucasian, Anglo Saxon Protestant Male, and one who is proud of our history as a nation, proud of what my race has achieved. I am thoroughly imbued with the sense of the priorities of Liberty, Freedom and Responsibility of the individual, with the sense of wanting a future for my children that reflects the best of my Caucasian, Anglo Saxon heritage and the principles of freedom espoused by our founding fathers. I am the sworn enemy of any ideology that is antagonistic to these things. I am ready to bear arms to confront the enemies of my America, the America that became the freest beacon of hope to the rest of the world that the world has ever seen because of those historic ideals that made it so. Put my name at the top of any list of those, including Caesar and his minions, that is looking for "enemies of the State." Like Thoreau, I go around with murder in my heart of such a State that would betray the hopes of a future for my children, those ideals, those great men and women who delivered us our Republic. I will not sell out to the cry of the vulgar masses, to those who betray and steal, who cry out to Caesar for unearned bread!

It is definitely "whistling through the graveyard" to think that America will ever become a "global society." Name one nation now or in history where this has ever happened! On the contrary, as minority races and illegals with their own fanatics and ideological hatreds of Christ and Caucasian, European ancestry continue to erode the foundational principles upon which this nation, this Republic was conceived and came into being, the conflict will become ever increasingly confrontational.

The very fact that so much killing of "brother against brother" is going on the world today should force people to face the fact that I keep repeating: One, and only One ideology can survive in any geographical setting. And if ours is not to be the one delivered us by the founding fathers, what is it to be? It will not be a "global one." That is not an option and anyone who thinks it is and tries to force it on America is either a traitor of our nation or so willingly ignorant, prejudiced or mentally retarded as to be beyond redemption!

Leave it to rags like Newsweek to accuse us Caucasian males of White Male Paranoia. Accusing us of succumbing to the onslaughts of feminism, multiculturalism, affirmative action and P.C. zealotry and using Falling Down as its foil, Newsweek hangs itself on its own petard; its list of reasons for Caucasian males knowing they are under attack is hardly all-inclusive but complete enough to force the truth of the statement: If you're not paranoid, you just don't see the whole picture!

Who is more at risk; the Caucasian person trying to drive through Watts or the Negro or Mexican driving through Beverly Hills? Now who is the "civilized" American citizen? Who is the "enemy?" Why of course! It's those "abusive and uppity white folks!" Unhappily, it is the white "leadership" which is proving to be the enemy of the white citizen and, especially, the white male. I've got a bulletin for such "white leadership:" You are never going to make me ashamed of being a Caucasian male with Christian, Biblical values and principles and I will never buy into your hateful agenda of trying to make me so!

The gang of high school "students" in Lakewood who scored gang "points" for raping and abusing girls should give us pause for thought. Also for your consideration: Mike Hynes, an 18-year-old senior who played football with some of those arrested at Lakewood High School wore a T-shirt emblazoned "We support you Kris." This was a reference to the one so-called "adult" arrested, one Kristopher Belman. The excuse offered: The boys were the "victims;" the girls "consented." The L.A. County sheriff's department has a grimmer picture of the facts including the abuse of a 10-year-old-girl! I have to wonder what she "consented" to with these monsters?

The brutal sexual assault of a retarded girl in Glen Ridge, New Jersey by a bunch of teenage boys has been called a "Failure of Conscience!" Like the brutal rape and maiming of the jogger in New York by a gang of roving Negroes, if it is a matter of "conscience" then all is lost. What good are laws and police if the law-abiding, if the innocent, are prey to such animals? You don't have to be a student of history to understand where such unrestrained violence is taking us as a society.

The law-abiding citizen faces more risk at the hands of our anemic courts for carrying an "unlawful" weapon for personal protection than these beasts do for their malevolent depredations! And for a responsible, tax-paying citizen to use force to protect his property? Throw away the key! Let them steal your car, your goods, let them force you to be a prisoner in your own house and live in fear of walking your streets, going to the store or driving your car! The "Law" will make sure you pay a heavy price for trying to exercise your own "liberty!" And God help you if you point to the causes of such insanity! The Feds will have you up for "Intolerance, hate crimes" or violating someone's "civil rights!" Dear God in heaven, what direction is a society headed, whither such a "civilization" which violates every rule, every tenet of civilization, common sense and justice in the cause of such obvious insanity! Try to move to Idaho to escape and get murdered or face a kangaroo court by Caesar's agents. Color yourself intolerant, bigoted, prejudiced, homophobic, or xenophobic for trying to deal with the facts or protect yourself and your family from the insanity of it all!

The gang at Lakewood High School, calling themselves the Spurs Posse, certainly makes my point for me in relationship to the heinous attitude our society is teaching boys about girls. Of course, as per my own experience in the schools, this utterly abhorrent, criminal abuse had been going on for quite some time, was common knowledge among the young people but the faculty and administration "knew nothing about it." In the wimp, limp-wristed atmosphere of the school's "leadership," it is "Hear no evil, see no evil, speak no evil," or, in other words: Maintain the status quo and make no waves. A "good" teacher is one whom the administration never hears from in regard to "discipline" problems; and lord help the teacher who really tries to make school relevant, and learning exciting, outside of such "leadership's" approved guidelines!

As an aside, the only two times (once in Watts and once in Lancaster) I had to physically save a teacher and a VP from attacks by pupils, literally, physically pulling the young men off the "adults," I regretted having to do so. In both cases, the "adults" had invited the attack. It was fortunate, in both cases that I knew the kids and they knew me. In several other cases, I was able to intervene before any physical violence occurred.

While some are questioning breaking up the massive L.A. school district in order to restore "order," the larger issue of morality goes begging. Granted the fact that the closer control a local community has on its schools the more likely it is that such things as the Spurs Posse aren't going to occur, unless an entire society can provide the moral leadership required, unless we can restore those Ancient Landmarks of individual responsibility and liberty, nothing is going to save our children from such creatures as Spurs Posse and others!

Just as the treasonous enemies of America have encouraged hoards of illegal aliens to invade us and encouraged generations of welfare-dependent slaves, so our young people are facing a hopeless future unless Patriots confront Caesar. The American Dream has become an American Nightmare. Cut spending? When and where? Listen up you self-serving, bloated, tax-fattened hyenas; start with cutting out government intrusion into our lives where it has never belonged! Close our borders and restore the rights, liberties and responsibilities of the American Citizen to provide for his family by getting rid of the bloody, tax-bloated bureaucracies and petty bureaucrats that stifle, penalize all personal incentive and initiative through the insane multicultural, equity of fairness laws, etc. and it can be done!

Seal our borders from all immigration and get the illegals out. We will never be able to provide for ourselves or protect our nation from terrorists or a deteriorating economy unless this common sense action is taken. Do away with all government forms in an alien language, especially in our post offices, welfare agencies and ballots!

Put the franchise in the hands, once more, of law-abiding, English-speaking only, responsible, working American citizens by enacting voter eligibility reform. Set the salaries of elected politicians at the median of their constituencies and eliminate the perks and retirements thus ending the "professional politician" and restoring Citizen Representatives, Statesmen to government. This is what our founding fathers intended, what they, in fact, were, warts and all!

"You have rights antecedent to all earthly governments; rights that cannot be repealed or restrained by human laws; rights derived from the Great Legislator of the Universe." John Adams.

"The law perverted! And the police powers of the state perverted along with it! The law, I say, not only turned from its proper purpose but also made to follow an entirely contrary purpose! The law becomes the weapon of every kind of greed! Instead of checking crime, the law itself guilty of the evils it is supposed to punish! If this is true, it is a serious fact, and moral duty requires me to call the attention of my fellow-citizens to it.... But there is also another tendency that is common among people. When they can, they wish to live and prosper at the expense of others...

"Away with the whims of governmental administrators, their socialized projects, their centralization, their tariffs, their government schools, their state religions, their free credit, their bank monopolies, their regulations, their restrictions, their equalization by taxation, and their pious moralizations...

"And now that the legislators and do-gooders have so futilely inflected so many systems upon society, may they finally end where they should have begun: May they reject all systems and try liberty; for liberty is an acknowledgement of faith in God and His works." Frederic Bastiat: The Law. Ibid: Don Heath and every other patriot in America!

"Prudence, indeed will dictate that governments long established should not be changed for light and transient causes; and, accordingly, all experience hath shown, that mankind are more disposed to suffer, while evils are sufferable, than to right themselves by abolishing the forms to which they are accustomed. But, when a long train of abuses and usurpations, pursuing invariably the same object, evinces a design to reduce them under absolute despotism, it is their duty to throw off such governments, and to provide new guards for their future security." The Declaration of Independence.

That "long train of abuses" more than qualifies a New Boston Tea Party, more than qualifies a New Sons Of Liberty to come together to take action against the despotic tyrant. The conditions we face today are far worse than those that caused those early patriots to take up arms.

As I have said, the literature has all been written long ago for a New Revolution against the tyranny we must now confront. It remains for those of us who are patriots of the same mind and thirst for liberty as Paine, Franklin, Jefferson, Hale, Hancock, Washington, to be called "traitors and rebels" for coming together to confront Caesar and the evil system of government that is crushing the life out of any vestige of liberty or hope of a future for our posterity!

And just in case you bloated, treasonous, tax-fattened hyenas missed it, the message is: No New Taxes And Cut Spending, Stupid! If I were not such a mild-mannered individual, I could truly indulge myself and wax lyrical on this theme.

Congress is sure to pay very close attention to the "Violence Against Women Act." It boggles the mind that this hypocritical body is going to give serious attention to an invitation to involve the FBI in spousal abuse and put another club in the hands of man-bashing feminists (You don't suppose the Iron Busted Maiden has anything to do with this do you?). And, like pointing out the fallacies of "Israel is our friend" and so-called "cultural diversity" is good for a nation, anyone who tries to face up to the lunacy of this proposed legislation is sure to be lynched by the liberal establishment.

No one is more opposed to men taking advantage of women than I am. I have made my position abundantly clear in regard to the abuse of our girls in our schools and society. But I have not lost sight of the fact that society must accept the obvious that as long as our girls and women are encouraged to invite lust by the way they act, talk and dress, unless reasonable approaches to these things are faced and dealt with, such things will continue to provoke violence against them.

One of the most devastating things we have to confront as a society is the proliferation of pornography in the guise of "free speech." Whether it is the pornography of destructive trash like Playboy or the sex and violence of TV, so-called "music," videos and movies, if a society and its leadership is going to force a mode of inviting and inciting the violence and lust of human nature in men on women by promoting such things, as long as girls and women buy into such a thing and lend themselves to the encouragement of inviting and inciting such attacks, by selling themselves so cheaply to the animalistic urges of boys and men, there will only be an escalation of such things no matter how many laws are passed!

Face it; if girls and women talk, dress and act like prostitutes, they are going to be treated as such no matter how they and the liberals howl against the very abuse they are, in fact, subjecting themselves to. Our young girls are deceived and encouraged into dressing immodestly and "displaying their wares" long before they have the maturity to handle the power of their sex. Then, when the situation gets out of hand, when the boys take advantage and respond according to their own nature, both may become victims (the girl most surely, the boy?) and, in too many cases, a baby (and society, in the form of ruined lives, welfare and disease) has to pay the price for that society's wicked lack of morality and its hypocritical double standard.

The trial of Randy Weaver is supposed to start April 13.

I'm taking another look at David Bergland's book: "Libertarianism in One Lesson." While I have some deep, philosophical differences with some of the tenets of the Libertarian Party, it remains the only Third Party on the ballot in all 50 states. Given some modifications, it could attract people like myself to the ranks and become a force with which to contend by the entrenched, self-serving despots which have betrayed America.

While I chide Gary unmercifully and rightly so, he and The Freeman is an asset, in the whole of things. I just wish he could refrain from using a page for a sentence's content and quit speaking *ex cathedra*.

M.E. Bradford, along with Locke, Smith, von Mises, Hazlitt, Rothbard, Hayek, Rand, Hoiles, Bourne, Faulkner, etc. would agree on the concept of *habitus*, a way of life that is in agreement with the philosophy of our founding fathers and our great literature. The best, most productive and reasonable philosophy of government must begin with the foundational fact of the rights of the individual to self-ownership. From that basic premise, springs all that flowers into self-discipline and the kind of morality that leads to respect for the worth, the value of the individual, the rights of others and the right of self-determination.

In respect to leadership, such leadership should be proven to support this concept of self-rule and self-responsibility. Such leadership should be of the kind which, as the founding fathers so well said, would be capable of governing for the sake of the nation's welfare and its posterity, encouraging and promoting the ideals upon which the nation was founded.

But we live with a monster, a leviathan of government that repudiates, is the enemy of, this foundational fact, is utterly alien to it and is, itself, mindlessly out of control like the wounded animal I compared it to in an earlier essay. Such a rabid, immoral, mindless, wounded animal must be put out of its misery before it destroys all around it.

No one questions the need of a governing power that would restrain the abuse of liberty, which would prevent liberty from being perverted to license. Our problem is not the perversion of personal liberty, it is the perversion of a government which has, itself, perverted its power to license against the individual, stealing from those that work to provide for those that can't or won't, stealing from its citizens in order to promote an ever burgeoning, bloated, utterly selfish and self-serving bureaucracy which has no other intention but enslaving those it was supposed to serve.

The perversion of the Supreme Court which has denied our Constitution, has perverted it to serve the ends of this monster must be confronted. But this would require men of integrity and morality of the kind that gave us this Republic. Such men, obviously, are not going to get elected to office because of the prostituting system which encourages only small-minded men, men of spineless inability to confront this evil; selfish men, to run with any hope of winning. And the primary reason that such a system exists is the howl of the mob, the vulgar masses which cry to Caesar for unearned bread. And just who is going to lead us to the necessary reform of eligibility for the franchise in order to correct this perversion of the intent of our founding fathers? Who is going to confront this monster that has been primarily responsible for the nation's bankrupt and enslaving status?

If such men cannot be elected to the necessary offices, we face, exactly, the conditions our founding fathers faced. Cut off from any effective voice in the affairs of deciding their fate, their future, being forced to submit to the tyranny of despotic rulers, they came together to make the decisions which they felt constrained to make and confronted the monster which would enslave them. So it was that, lacking any alternative, facing the increasing force being used to silence them, they saw no other option but to take up arms against the monster.

By God's grace and with His help, they succeeded and founded a nation in liberty without peer in history. How they would weep, would cry out in righteous anger against the perversion of such liberty in the hands of Caesar and his agents of slavery today!

If the logic of the situation is irrefutable, if the insanity of uncontrolled borders, of increasingly bankrupt families and government, of failed schools and criminal justice systems, of suborned and suborning men and women in government, unrestrained violence in our cities, burgeoning ideological conflicts, the hopelessness of anything like a future for our young people, if these things and so many other indictments against Caesar are not evidence of the need for a "revolution," of another war for independence, the sun will not rise tomorrow!

The historical imperatives will not, cannot, be denied; the three, inescapable options confront us and won't go away. It only remains to see which will prevail. My expressed hope has continued to be that men of good will can come together to confront Caesar on the basis of Fact, Truth and Reason. This was the avenue by which our founding fathers, first, tried to approach solutions in their time. My prayer continues to be that such an effort would be more successful in our case than in theirs. But I am not seeing or hearing anything that would foster such hope. On the contrary, I see an intolerable situation becoming increasingly intolerable.

No one of any knowledge of the facts would deny that the world is a far more dangerous place at this time than the one our founding fathers faced. Nuclear proliferation alone makes this true. It is a further fact the U.S. must play a prominent role in world affairs for this reason if no other. But any hope of success in this arena still relies on scrupulous, courageous Statesmen to lead. It is in this area that we lack the essentials for moral answers to the problems. If such men are not found, are not promoted to leadership, world tyranny looms.

In private conversation with many of those in government I find broad agreement with my concerns; what is lacking is the climate in which those shared concerns can find a voice. This comes back to voter eligibility reform. This nation was founded a Republic, not a so-called *Democracy*. The universities, the schools, unscrupulous leaders who cater to the howl of the mob, have destroyed this distinction.

If our Supreme Court itself had not lent itself to this betrayal, how different things might be! But any hope of a return to the principles upon which this nation was founded, any hope of getting Citizen Representation of real American Citizens of the kind which led this nation to greatness, depends on an enlightened, knowledgeable, responsible, unselfish electorate. I don't find even the "best" of conservative leadership or conservative writers addressing this pivotal issue. But if it is not faced and dealt with, there is no hope. The Clintons, Willie Browns, Rangels and Dinkins will decide our fate!

As a Christian, I see our real hope in the Gospel Jesus preached. But the churches have failed to lead with a concerted voice, that "certain trumpet sound," which would give me hope of this solution. Lacking that hope, I would hope that men of the kind that made up the body of our founding fathers would come together to confront Caesar and deal with the situation. Even at that, they owned their allegiance to God and relied on the righteousness of their cause for His help of redress. Can we hope to do the same? Not unless such men lead. Keep in mind the indisputable fact that God alone provides the motive force for moral, unselfish behavior. And only the God and Father of Jesus Christ owns love as the motive for His own actions and requires those who espouse His Name to act on that same principle. But that love is never to be perverted to serve "special agendas," not even that of those who would be the Apostles of that love. The Gospel is not "conversion by the sword" like the religions of Judaism or Muslimism.

Christian principles are those upon which this nation was founded. They are the principles which were recognized as giving the greatest liberty to the individual to live by the dictates of his individual conscience and his right to self-rule, self-discipline and individual responsibility with due regard to those same rights for others. Never in history has a government been formed which has had so much success as that which owned allegiance to these Christian principles. Why? Because the emphasis in those principles is placed squarely on the shoulders of the individual, not another, not a group or a society or a government, for his actions! Self-determinism with the concomitant liberty and responsibility for those decisions and actions!

Unlike so-called "democratic" mob rule, the Republic of our founding fathers relied on this basic, Christian principle and recognized the irrefutable fact that only an enlightened, responsible and knowledgeable electorate could keep it intact. The betrayal of this principle has led our nation to ruin. And as long as we are subject to that "mob rule" as espoused in insane so-called civil rights and equity of fairness laws, quotas, slavery through welfare and socialism of all descriptions, betrayal of our heritage and our young people, so long will we be betrayed of any hope of a future as a nation, so long will the value and liberty of the individual be exchanged for the worship and tyranny of the state!

The recent Conservative Summit gave a voice to some of my concerns. Able speakers like William Bennett and others certainly are eloquent of such concerns. But, here again, the necessary candor of the root causes of our hopelessness and betrayal is lacking. As I said, who dares to confront the "vulgar masses" of so-called "democracy" knowing they will be pilloried by the media, the JDL, the ACLU, the NAACP, etc., for saying what must be said? Once more Fact, Truth and Reason must be set aside for cultures and ideological agendas and, not unexpectedly, the egos set on elected offices! The fragmentation and egos of the conservative camps does not give one much hope from them.

I cannot explain the compulsion by which I am driven to write such things. I have to wonder if Paine, Jefferson, Adams could explain it in themselves. A thirst for liberty? Certainly! But perhaps it is the product of wanting more for our posterity, of wanting a future for our children. Maybe my own study of history, literature, the Bible, my own freedom in wilderness places and the raising of a family, all this and more surely play a part. I know I am not the stuff of martyrs. But not to the point where I am not willing to fight for the future of our children and young people, for the hopes and dreams which better men than I paid the ultimate price. Here is where "reason" fails of the prudent discretion that would keep me from harm's way. To that extent and for those reasons, I seem compelled to play the fool.

But if I am to play the fool, I will choose to do so in the mode of those men like Tom Paine and Patrick Henry who gave us our Republic. I have to bear in mind the fact that Franklin, Jefferson, Clemens and Thoreau came to the end of their years with a very low opinion of the human race. In fact, they questioned whether the species was even worth saving! These men, so diverse in so many other ways, came to this common conclusion and it is that conclusion which must be honestly faced in the light of our present, dismal, prospects.

When I refer to the "vulgar masses," I realize I am speaking the mind of those men who pledged their lives, honor and property to deliver us our Republic. They were, in all, a very "elitist" group. They were a well-to-do, propertied and educated class of people. In short, they, as opposed to "sunshine patriots, Joe Six-pack" and our own present, mongrel and welfare hoards of slaves, had much to lose in taking the position they did. As such, they spoke to those issues that would promote the freedom and liberty that would encourage the value and responsibility of the individual and worked to promote a government that would give men the essentials of being able to provide for themselves and their posterity, the nation, without unnecessary or punitive restraints. But their failure to exclude slavery for the sake of profits may yet be our undoing.

The present government is 180 degrees off of this intent of our noble ancestors. The present Trojan Horse comes to us pretending to "care" for children and family and the "incapables" as it too often has done. In this guise, Big Brother will "take care of us poor sheep" since the present elite have no interest in anything but ruling. As to the "species," it is replete with enough "sunshine patriots," etc. to give Caesar reason enough to think in terms of sheep.

I am not a mongrel and I know the mongrelization of America, i.e. multiculturalism, unrestrained immigration, the enfranchisement of the "vulgar masses" of Rome's destruction, spells nothing but anarchy or slavery. While the present leadership isn't fit to wipe the shoes of our founding fathers, they consider themselves to be above the law of God and the obvious intent of our Constitution. Committed to the idea of mongrelization (they call it a "global society") they lead us to destruction or enslavement.

You search in vain to find this analysis in publications that tout themselves as "conservative." While the facts of the case are indisputable, such facts in such plain language are too fearful, too inflammatory, for the faint-hearted. National Review, Reason, The Spectator, The Freeman, The New American, etc. all fail in this regard in large part because of the cowardice and egos involved. Not even Robert Ringer in his excellent and very important book, which I urge everyone to read: "Restoring the American Dream," confronts these things.

While we are demanded to "contribute" and "invest" by the tax-and-spend philosophy of our evil leaders, they seem to be utterly blind to the path they are leading us on. And, as blind leaders of the blind, the chasm yawns ahead and they will most assuredly lead our nation into that abyss unless men of good will, men like those early patriots, confront this evil and do battle against it.

But where will the righteous men come from to do battle, men like those noble ancestors who set aside their differences, restrained their egos and selfish interests in the cause of liberty? Caesar is counting on this not happening, in fact, impossible of happening. There is far too much evidence of his analysis of the situation. Conservatives are splintered, fractured in a thousand parts. There is no "certain trumpet sound" to call to the battle.

So it is that I write in plain language, devoid of flowery rhetoric, in order to make the issues plain enough that all people can understand what is being said. The literature of resistance, of the confrontation of tyranny is in place. The dry, sober statistics of our ruinous, national policy of the betrayal and destruction of our Republic are there for all to examine.

It only remains for enough men of good will to come together as those early patriots did in a duly constituted body of authority to confront the evil.

Unless some unforeseen event should miraculously intervene, these men will not come, any more than those early patriots did, from the elective process of the present evil system.

What is required then? The leaders of the many, diverse conservative camps could begin to agitate for their own "Continental Congress" and with common cause, once more, face the necessary facts and determine a course of action to reclaim our Republic from the hands of its enemies. My contribution is to continue to play the part of Tom Paine, to be the "pamphleteer" of "Independence." Were it not for the fact of God proving that He thought the "species worth saving," if it were not for the fact of my children and my hopes for their future, I too could take the pessimistic view of Franklin and Jefferson in regard to humankind. But my love for my children, my love for others and believing God's view, I will do battle the best I can against the evil system which threatens to destroy our nation. The question is whether I will become too articulate in such a cause; will I become enough of a thorn in the side of Caesar to be allowed to continue the battle? In short, will I become dangerous to Him?

My peculiar affinity for browsing through tomes like Snider and Osgood's "Semantic Differential Techniques" and "Biblical Archaeology Review," my knowledge and love of good literature, art, music and the Bible, my experiences in the schools, in industry and business, the freedom of wilderness places, the joys of the old South Bay of the 50s, my love of children and young people, my refusal to pledge unquestioning allegiance to "personal agendas," my love and knowledge of liberty, my knowing how things used to be and how we have betrayed the ideals of my America, all these things and so much more make me the most dangerous kind of man to the system of evil which we must confront.

I recall living in San Pedro for a while as a child. I remember the awe of watching those huge, gray warships come into the harbor. Such a time and such events fired the imagination. I would sit on the grassy hillside near the shore and fill my mind with the scenes of the activities of a world at war.

Much later, as a young adult, I would take my boat out of this same harbor and, with some friends, we would water ski in the ocean, skipping the wave tops and cutting the troughs of the waves and the boat's wake. This kind of skiing, of course, ruined you for the tamer pursuits of the lakes and rivers. I took a spill once that ripped my trunks off; quite embarrassing.

It is in remembering a time when one paycheck took care of a family, when I could enjoy the delights of San Pedro in a clean, crime-free environment, that my anger against Caesar is aroused. Seems Clinton is firing those who would help bring the criminals, Rostenkowski in particular, to justice in the Congress and replacing them with "safe, approved" vassals.

This reminds me of the tirade Patton suffered for using Nazi party personnel to get Germany back on its feet after the war. Yet, here is a situation far worse and it has the leading and blessing of our president! Surely Clinton knows that our "deficit" is the result of insanely treasonous spending, that the greatest part of that $4.37 trillion is "owed" to private money lenders in the guise of the Federal Reserve System! Surely he knows that the IRS is a "private" collection agency that operates unconstitutionally without any of the restraints of common law!

As the battle heats up in regards to abortion, racial and ideological warfare going on right now in our cities, as terrorism looms as a reality, as the monumental structure of unenforceable law as per drugs, etc. threatens to topple, the yawning, black hole of immorality rampant in our nation, the hopelessness of our young people, so much and more hastening the crisis of America (Babylon?), where is the voice of Reason to be found yet alone, prevail?

Recently, an L.A. County sheriff's deputy gunned down Donald P. Scott; his suspected crime? An "informant" had accused Scott of growing marijuana. In actuality, according to the Ventura County D.A., Michael Bradbury, the underlying reason for the Gestapo breaking into Scott's home was to confiscate his 5 million dollar estate! No, Scott was not some "little guy" who was picked at random. He was a wealthy man living on a palatial estate. Reminds me of that wounded animal, gnawing off his own leg to get out of the trap and attacking, blindly, anyone near at hand; not even the wealthy escape in Rome's last days!

Of course, the deputy who shot this innocent victim did so in "self defense!" But the D.A. says the Gestapo had no legitimate reason for even being on the man's property! Sound familiar; all too familiar and, increasingly so in the light of that mindless, paranoid, desperate animal and its cohorts. Randy, Vicki and Sam Weaver, Kevin Harris, the list of "enemies" of the state is mounting and, tragically, so is the number of victims of this mindless animal I call "Caesar." Not a single one of us is safe or secure from the depredations of this animal. You can easily be "set up" in any number of ways if he wants to dispose of you.

Now when your door is broken down at 2 o'clock in the morning and a bunch of armed thugs come crashing into your home, what will your response be? Like so many already have learned, if you try to defend your home against the Gestapo, you will be gunned down in "self defense!"

Where, in the mercy of God, the "Moses" to deliver from this kind of bondage? We are already commanded to make bricks without straw, our children and grand-children sold into slavery by unconscionable taxation, the vulgar masses having, by their selfish votes for unearned bread and abetted by the traitors of America in The White House, Congress and the Supreme Court and the host of Egypt (numberless bureaucrats and functionaries), put the sword of our destruction in the hands of cruel taskmasters! How much worse is it going to have to get?

That train of abuses, those usurpations of our liberty more than constitute a call to arms. But University of California "researchers" have determined that minorities believe "American Society (predominantly that white society) owes them a better chance in life than they currently have!" The blindness of such so-called researchers and their respondents is the fact that only that White Male Dominated Society of the past could hope to offer anything like that "better chance." The betrayers of America have nearly succeeded in killing off any opportunity of the kind of improvements in society that might bring this to pass.

The equally blind liberal media will continue to beat the drum of "equal opportunity" and "multiculturalism," failing, miserably, to offer anything like an explanation of the miserable failures of their own agendas to promote anything but increasing anarchy or slavery to the state!

And howls of White Supremacy or White Separatism or White, Male Dominance aside, human nature being what it is regardless of gender, ethnicity or ideology, if you steal from someone, he will hate you for it; if you cheat someone, he will hate you for it; if you hurt or kill one of his family or friends, he will hate you for it; if you try, through unscrupulous, unjust means, to gain an advantage over him, he will hate you for it; if you destroy his property, he will hate you for it; and so on.

It would seem that these irrefutable absolutes would be clear to all. How is it, then, that Caesar refuses to see it and does all that he can to encourage the insanity of so-called "equity" which encourages these abuses that can only lead to his own destruction? Only that mindless animal acts in such a fashion or, as Gore Vidal so well put it: "Empire that is beyond Reason!"

I'm not sure how much longer I will be "allowed" to give a voice to these things. No one is safe, as I said and daily events make patently obvious, from Caesar once he perceives a threat to his rule. In any event, being a man with nothing to lose and, being alone, not drawing anyone into harm's way with me, I will keep on keeping on as long as The Lord permits. Your input, as always, is most welcome. I am not, as I also said, the stuff of martyrs. But if you happen to think the things I am saying speak for you (or not), your encouragement (and criticism) will be much appreciated.

I enjoyed watching Hollywood, in spite of Streisand and a couple of others in all its splendor for Oscar Night. Congratulations Clint. I especially appreciated the tribute to Audrey and I really do appreciate what Liz is doing for AIDS patients regardless the liberal agenda. I will never get over the romance the silver screen once offered a kinder, gentler America. Neither will I forsake my empathy for those in the industry who suffer for their art. "Valley of the Dolls" is still too true of the common frailties and needs of humanity to do so.

I'm planning a trip to Torrance this weekend. A very sophisticated bomb was discovered under the set for a scene of Beverly Hills 90210 at Torrance High School. Will terrorists begin to target our schools and those in the entertainment industry? I fear so.

Christian Perspective

May: Part 2

Isaiah 3:12

During a licensing exam a trucker was asked, "What would you do if your brakes failed on a narrow mountain road and as you rounded the bend you were staring head-on at a tanker coming up the hill?"

"I'd pull her to the right."

"But suppose there wasn't any room?" asked the examiner?

"Then I'd pull her to the left."

"No room there either," said the examiner.

"Then I'd wake Wendell."

The examiner paused. "Who's Wendell?"

"Wendell's my relief driver and he ain't never seen a wreck as big as we're fixin' to have."

"Welcome to Sacramento, and get ready to watch the biggest wreck you've ever seen." California Political Review.

The above gem was told in respect to the looming budget crisis in California but holds true at the Federal level as well.

I really like Mark Russell. Two of his gems before I get into the essay: "Every day - more sex scandals involving Catholic priests. If the church really wants celibate men, why don't they get guys who have been married for 30 years?"

Our new president doesn't seem to be getting on too well with the military. The Army mess halls are featuring a new breakfast: Clinton-on-a-shingle!

It is a hard thing to see hope die. In my travels, my conversations with groups and individuals, as I watch various programs on TV, as I read the papers and periodicals and listen to radio, as I read letters from those who respond to my essays, I'm watching hope die in our nation and the world. William Dean Howells, in his climactic novel "A Hazard of New Fortunes" writes of the New York tenement district as "...his sensibilities were dragged in a coupe through a tenement house street: It was not the abode of the extremest poverty, but of a poverty as hopeless as any in the world, transmitting itself from generation to generation, and establishing conditions of permanency to which human life adjusts itself as it does to those of some incurable disease, like leprosy."

Even in 1890, the time of this novel, and earlier as per Emerson, Thoreau, Howells, Clemens and many others recognized the greed of the plunderers of America's resources and its corrupt politicians as the causes of the "incurable disease" of poverty; and if they could have foreseen the welfare slavery of today? It would be up to men like Mencken to address the root causes such as rampant socialism, immigration and racial characteristics, alien cultures, as the threat to anything like the Americanism of the founding fathers.

But it is the failure of an entire society that has given rise to anarchy in our cities and the growing need for civil disobedience as espoused by Thoreau and providing fertile soil for publications and organizations like The Cause Foundation (Kirk Lyons), The Pilot Connection and The Citizen's Claw among a host of others, my own included. And let's not forget the utter hypocrisy of the attitude toward South Africa!

While I'm at it, compare the rulings of the Jewish judge, Jack B. Weinstein, in the case of Khaled Mohammed el-Jassem in New York with the recent discovery of the fact that B'nai B'rith has been spying on us for over 40 years! Guess who will suffer in these two instances?

The recent atrocity by those Negroes in Florida who dragged that poor, German mother to her death while stealing her car and money and her children and others watched in helpless horror (the Germans, understandably, are warning tourists to avoid Florida), the lines in front of gun stores in L.A. as we waited for the verdict in the Rodney King case, the necessity of Ellie Nesler taking the law into her own hands with community support and approval, the murders of Vicki and Sam Weaver by the Feds and their stupidly unconscionable, unconstitutional stand-off in Texas, the Negro who recently murdered a young, pregnant white woman, Sherry Foreman, stabbing her in the stomach and killing the baby as well, as he tried to steal her money and car in Sherman Oaks, another young woman in Alhambra, Kathy May Lee, shot to death in her car while her mother watched, the huge increases in violent crime, add the recent innovation of carjacking, across the nation, all of this and so much more, is a testimony to the utter failure and breakdown of law and the shameful, despicable failure of our leadership across the board to face the hard choices which must be made or we will continue to sink into anarchy or slavery. In the face of such insanity, France, Germany and other countries are doing what they need to do. Will we? One way or another.

What does the "leadership" do? One has it figured out. A Senate committee in California decided to approve $900 a month for a bodyguard for Senator Teresa Hughes, a Democrat. I guess the rest will be getting in line for this fulfillment of one of my "prophecies:" To hell with the unwashed, let's protect ourselves! As I have often said, the leadership isn't that stupid, they know they are the legitimate targets for our new Minutemen! Caesar wants to take away our guns so we can neither legitimately rebel against his enslavement and abuses nor protect ourselves and our families but he wants to do all in his power to make sure his "servants" are well-protected.

Consider the insanity of a security officer turning a school troublemaker into the INS and being censured by school administrators, Mexican "rights" advocates of all descriptions and, of course, I expect every other liberal connection to join in the hue and cry.

The fact is that the Mexican was an illegal, feeding off taxpayer money and the schools are forced to break the law by not reporting illegal aliens! And when any school personnel are involved in acting according to law by reporting illegals? They are the ones that get into trouble! Insane! But I have learned to expect no better from the wimp, limp-wristed "leadership" in the schools and government in general. One could wish Richard Viguerie was correct in: "The New Right: Ready to Lead!" But I don't see any evidence of it.

I think my old friend, Gary North, hit the mark when he wrote: "...each of us needs to be preparing for the crisis that lies ahead...believe the court prophets or believe the Bible!" And neither Gary nor I are talking about the Bible as distorted by the TV charlatans or Waco Wackos. God gave us a mind of reason and expects us to use it, particularly when we are dealing with God who possesses the purest essence of reason and gifted man with the ability to respond in kind!

As I taught in the schools for those many years, I saw the gradual erosion of hope among young people and I was stymied of doing anything about it beyond those I could touch personally. The utter blindness of the entrenched, ivory tower bureaucracy prevented meaningful, relevant education. Most refused to see what was happening in their own schools and had no experiential framework of the real world with which to comprehend the accelerating crisis in education. And, of course, the politicians were, and continue to be worse.

It is a further pity that well-intentioned folks think some kind of "voucher" system will work in education. Tax money in any way, shape or form is just another coercive effort of Caesar to steal our children and force his ideology of the worship of the State upon us. Since this is such an obvious fact, I have begun to wonder just how well intentioned these "good" people really are who are espousing such a thing?

I started three Christian schools myself in retaliation to a failed system of public education, two in California and one in Colorado, and also to assure my own children a safe, moral and disciplined learning environment and a solid, basic education. I told parents: If you have to live with sheets in the windows instead of curtains, if you have to eat beans and rice instead of meat, make the necessary sacrifices to place your children in a private school! The wisdom of my pronouncement is all too readily apparent today. And, further, my own schools had nothing to do with tax-exempt status or any handouts from Caesar in any manner.

One of the more disturbing things I am seeing and hearing is the growing number of people, good people, law-abiding, responsible, and hard working who are giving up. One man, a conscientious and honest businessman, a close friend and Christian, was almost in tears as he shared the horrible thoughts he was having, thoughts utterly alien to his Christian beliefs, of taking personal action against the evil that surrounds us for the sake of his children's future.

As a Christian, I see the events of our time pointing the way to that time Jesus warned of, that time like that of Noah's which presages the end of the age. Caesar seems to, mindlessly, be giving such hastening destruction his full cooperation and, in the process, forcing real Christians to separate from the goats and false shepherds.

I have a sign in the back window of my station wagon. It reads: "Good Shooting Ellie!" Bumper stickers are appearing with the same message.

Seems Ellie Nesler from Jamestown way, an area with which I am thoroughly familiar, shot and killed the creature that had molested her son and a number of other children. She did this in the courtroom in front of God, the DA and a number of other witnesses. Good Shooting Ellie!

Her bail, $500,000, was actually posted, personally, by a bail bondsman! Something virtually unheard of! There is already a movement to nominate her for Mother of The Year! She will get my vote. This leaves the courts of Caesar with an insolvable conundrum, a problem of huge magnitude and unthinkable consequences.

One of Ellie's attorneys, David Lewis, said it well: "I think the public is demanding that the law catch up...One of the ways it catches up is by saying what she did is justified."

Without question, what Ellie Nesler did was certainly justified in my opinion based on the higher law of God and on the basis of what our founding fathers did in confronting the tyranny of the laws of the Crown in their time. And there was the usual hand wringing of the "good" churchmen then with their liberal cant and false piety mouthing: Vengeance is mine saith the Lord! and refusing to recognize the context in which God made this pronouncement. Things haven't changed much since then in this regard.

But the thing that makes Ellie's actions of such monumental import is the fact that Caesar simply cannot allow her to get away with this. In this respect, the case in Jamestown (what a coincidence of place-names!) is the single, most important judicial proceeding of our time, far outweighing the Rodney King trial, the Waco Wacko or any others.

Obviously, if Ellie wins on her plea of justified execution of this creature that continued to threaten her, her son and other children with his depredations, it might well become "open season" on other such animals and no hunting license required! Face it folks, there are a whole lot of "creatures" out there that just plain need killin'! They are rattlesnakes and there is no successful appeal to any kind of "reform" for their "nature." And many wear black robes and hold high offices!

Federal judges have already petitioned Clinton for permission to carry firearms at all times (so far they haven't asked for bodyguards like Senator Hughes but I guess that will be next). I said long ago that these agents of Caesar had every right to fear the new "Minutemen" who are arising about the nation. Now they prove that justifiable fear with this request. And, they will try all the harder to disarm the honest but aroused citizenry they fear because of the abysmal failure, as in Ellie's case, to protect law-abiding citizens from such predatory creatures like the one Ellie took care of and that other long train of abuses and usurpations of liberty of which Jefferson wrote.

As the vision of evil daily unfolds all about us, despair and depression is often the result. You simply cannot swim in these murky waters on a daily basis without sinking, at least occasionally, into the depression and despair of the slough of despond. So it was that I recently determined to try a new tack to shake off the bouts of my own depression by mixing with some folks who inhabit another sphere of life- the barflies.

Now, to put the best face on my actions, let me explain it this way; I picked up a young prostitute in one of the bars. How's that? I'm sorry, that might be a tad misleading, a little overdrawn. Perhaps I'd better start over now that I have the interest of the "brethren" and some who seem to enjoy heaping abuse on my good name.

Notwithstanding the fact that my good Baptist brethren have already consigned me to the outer reaches for other monumental breaches of their own peculiar ideas of "holiness," I add this to the litany of woes pronounced against me. However, Gary North sums it up neatly for me in this little gem: "The only way you could get Baptists in East Texas to picket an abortion clinic would be to spread the rumor that after the abortion, the physician always gives a glass of beer to the woman to steady her nerves."

Now don't misunderstand me, my personal doctrine and beliefs are more closely aligned with that of conservative Baptists than any other. But to give you an example of the problem, I recently visited the largest Baptist church in my area. Yes, I do attend church now and then.

It was obvious that the congregation was really into "comfort" and "comfortable sermons." Nevertheless, I passed a couple of my essays on to the pastor with a request that we might get together and discuss some of the issues I raised in my writing. I can hardly blame such pastors for thinking me a dangerous man and a pagan; my writing doesn't do much for the sake of promoting easy consciences and, from the view of many, I am irretrievably "lost."

To the pastor's credit he not only read the sample essays but also actually agreed to meeting with me to discuss some of the issues raised; the most prominent one the deplorable condition of the homeless and helpless young people in our area. It became obvious that this good man was in tune with the Lord's heart in the matter but we agreed that in too many cases Christians find themselves becoming so comfortable in their well-ordered lives, free of real want and grief, surrounded with friends and family and, as a result, become insulated from the tragedy all around them in their own communities. And, it should be openly admitted, we don't really want to enter into the sufferings of the "rejects" of society. Unlike Jesus Himself, we would far rather insulate ourselves with our "own kind." Further, the problems are of such a magnitude, we would far rather leave them to Caesar and welfare to dispose of thus salving our consciences that we are doing our part with an occasional "loaf of bread" or writing a check.

We prayed together as I got ready to go. I left with the most favorable impression that this good man and shepherd would not dismiss the things we discussed but would pursue them as best he could. I can hardly ask more of anyone; but to return to the matter at hand.

In spite of my seeming "tolerance," I remain largely of the opinion of Billy Sunday who said; "Booze has its place but its place is in hell!" I have witnessed far too much of the human tragedy for which liquor was the cause not to have such an opinion. But, as with others whose opinion I respect on the subject, it isn't drinking that constitutes sin, it is drunkenness. The alcoholic isn't someone who needs a drink; it is someone who needs not to drink.

I'll never forget walking into a bar and sitting next to an old man whose wheelchair was folded next to his barstool. The old man, to me, was doing nothing but drinking himself into the grave with nothing better to do. Tragic. As a Christian, I recognize the God as the only viable hope for all of us and, especially, for those like this old fellow. But, sorrowfully, it isn't likely he will find himself going to church or moving in circles where the Lord is openly discussed and presented in all His reality. I was reminded of the fact that the Pharisees accused Jesus of being a drunkard and reveler among sinners, a "Party kind of guy." If only they had had a comprehension of His Reality among people such as this old man. But lacking real hearts of compassion for such "sheep," all they could do was condemn his lack of "spiritual discernment" and his consorting with the "unclean."

In conversation he discovered I had access to some of the local politicians and asked if I could do something about getting a street light for the entrance to the old folk's trailer park where he resided. I explained that until the budget mess was settled in Sacramento, it was unlikely that the county would approve any expenditures.

In reply to my explanation, he uttered the familiar oaths and anathemas against politicians and returned to getting crocked. I had ordered a cup of coffee but the old fellow hadn't heard me apparently because, as the barmaid brought it to me, he looked at it with disgust and said loudly: "Hell, I was gonna buy you a drink but I sure as hell ain't payin' for that!"

There is no one out there, having witnessed what alcohol has done to a loved one or been abused by some drunken bum or has lost a loved one to the drunk driver, who doesn't rise in righteous wrath against the evils of the stuff. Again the hypocrisy of the "leadership" rears its ugly head in making marijuana illegal and turning its head to the greater evil of booze. My own personal experience of watching people destroy themselves with alcohol has been sufficient to warrant Billy Sunday's dictum.

I have never been a habitué of bars and even when I did go it would be places like the piano lounges of the old South Bay. Quiet, civilized, congenial atmosphere with good music and interesting conversations and the men and women acted like ladies and gentlemen.

But recently, I decided to reconnoiter some of the local bars to find out what is happening among the "unwashed." I realized the local "cuttin' 'n' shootin' joints might be a tad rowdy and so it turned out. One in particular offered all the "entertainment" with which the locals amuse themselves. The night I visited I was treated to a live band consisting of two guitar players and a drummer. About twenty minutes into noise that would sterilize frogs, a couple of the boys began to whoop it up with a wrestling match around the floor that, coming too close to the amps and drums prompted an announcement that any damage to same would require the intervention of one of the guitarists, a huge, heavily muscled guy who could obviously do some hurt if his artistic endeavors were interfered with.

Having put a terminus to the spirited play of the combatants, a search was conducted in an attempt to discover a pair of missing glasses. The miscreant who started the fight was evicted and things returned to what constituted normal in the environment. Not being much of a drinker (I can make the lightest draft that still has enough alcohol content to qualify as beer last an hour) I was on a cup of coffee when one of the locals approached and said: "Hey, aren't you the guy who was running for state senate?"

I confessed to the crime and the fellow began a litany of the abuses in government and heaping of anathemas on the so-called "leadership." He had lost his business in Bakersfield because of the abuses in Workman's Comp, the slowdown in construction and the enormous tax burden of trying to do business in California. An all too familiar story. He had come up to the lake because he had lost his home and could live in his tent along the river. He was drawing food stamps and general assistance to keep alive. Oddly, such people always seem to come up with just enough to frequent the bars.

But, rather than be condemnatory of such, I realize the loneliness that draws these people to the temporary camaraderie of so many others in the same circumstances. It is tragic the churches aren't able to offer the friendliness of the bars. If they could, they would be crowded. And, I have discovered, many of these people espouse Christian beliefs and backgrounds but the churches don't seem to be able to offer them the help they need. Too often, such help is wrapped in hypocrisy. Also, as I will explain further on, the churches too often operate on a false basis of simplistic "fixes" and simply lack the reality with which to help these kinds of people.

This fellow, drunk as he was, profane as he was, was no different than the good Christian friend and businessman who had, in the same case of despair, shared the same feelings of frustration and desperation. They might never meet in the same social circles but the mind-set was identical.

His one repeated question to me caught my heart: "Do you think there is any hope?" It was a rational question through the alcoholic haze. Why? Because he wasn't too drunk to realize that people like me, educated and conservative, not double-minded on the issues, not given to political rhetoric, not sold out to the prostitution of public office, were the only hope of people like him. He knew his kind of people, the victims, the sheep, the unwashed, could never speak for themselves, had no voice before Caesar, apart from taking up arms. But, let's return to the "entertainment."

"Dancing" in such an environment requires the broadest interpretation of such. Apart from waltzes, I don't dance. The wires in my bones because of my motorcycle accident and the odd configuration due to uneven healing of a couple of ribs prevent me playing golf and from the kind of gymnastics that constitute dancing of the variety the natives engage in. As the "music" blared at a decibel level that would put a 747 to shame, the dancing was done not by couples as such but an array of people who moved and intermingled at will as the spirit led. It might have been "revival" time at a Pentecostal tent meeting.

Not being eligible, yet, for induction into the Over-The-Hill Gang, I notice pretty women. Ah, the weakness of the flesh! One young woman in particular caught my attention. She was quite lovely and seemed, oddly, out of place. I was introduced on arrival as "Mike's father." Now that has relevance to anyone who knows my son. As a consequence, I had all my defenses up, prepared to defend myself from any resulting misunderstandings or calumny. Happily, the young lady had no such misconceptions and even liked Michael. I breathed a sigh of relief.

In conversation with her, and having learned I was a writer and publisher, she asked if I would read some poetry she had written. Due to the circumstances and respecting her confidence, I won't tell of the events by which she happened to have a collection of her work in her purse.

She sang with a couple of the local bands and wrote lyrics as well. She did have a very lovely voice and, when the infrequent, mellower tunes were played, I could tell she had a real gift for music.

But, as I began to read some of the poetry she shared with me I was astounded! Here was a young lady with a very real gift for language and with the extreme sensitivity to express her feelings in a way I knew people could respond to. I asked her to get in touch with me the next day and see if we could work together to get some of her work published. She said she would.

But I didn't hear from her the following day. So, that evening I went back to the bar and inquired of her. The bartender hadn't seen her and I asked him to have her call me if she came in. The tragedy of this situation is the fact that there is nothing more common than for people to have a gift such as this woman's only to have nothing come of it because of their falling into a lifestyle like that of the bars and continued dissipation of their minds and bodies. What a terrible waste! Will I ever hear from her? Will I be able to help her if I do? Not unless she is willing to come to terms with the dead-end course she is presently pursuing.

As I was getting ready to leave, I noticed a young girl at the end of the bar. Some drunk was trying to pick up on her, an old fellow who should have known better and probably would have if he had been sober.

My natural, protective instincts for young people caused me to intrude and the drunk left. But that left me, as protector and deliverer, to do something about the young lady. We struck up a conversation. She was grateful for my intervention and, as it turned out, she had come into the bar because she was new in town and lonely. She had arrived from Florida just two weeks previously and was staying with her mother.

Hers had not been an easy life even at her tender years. She did not have a car and suffered walking due to an injury that had left her leg with steel rods in it. As a result, she couldn't even ride a bicycle. And, due to extreme circumstances, couldn't really afford to take the bus. But, again, the conditions led her to find some solace from the extremities in the bar. Having obtained some emergency food stamps upon her arrival in the area, she had managed to sell some for a small amount of cash. I knew, but for the grace of God, she could have as easily been my own daughter, the primary reason for my "rescuing" her. They were the same age but, unlike this girl, my daughter, while making disastrous choices in her young life, had had the benefit of not knowing want or abuse while she was growing up. How different might this girl's life have been if she had had such an advantage?

In any event, discovering that she hadn't eaten in quite some time and was obviously hungry, I declined to buy her one of the bar's cardboard pizzas and offered to take her to one of the local coffee shops to get her a real dinner. She readily accepted.

As we sat in the restaurant, she shared a good deal of her young life with me. The all-too typical tragedy of broken home, abusive father and men, molestations was all there. She had had to resort, as most of these young girls do, to prostitution. Lacking education and opportunity and being young and attractive, her only assets, the "oldest profession" offered her the means of providing for herself.

As a Christian and having so much personal experience in dealing with such young people, there was no necessity of "preaching" to her. She hated what she was doing and had the dream of all such young women that somewhere, somehow, there would be a decent man who would deliver her from the hellish prison she had lived in all her young life. But as my daughter and most of the young women her age keep telling me, they can't seem to find such men in their age group.

My conservative Christian friends will always pronounce the obvious: "They aren't going to find such men in bars!" And I agree. Tragically, the churches don't meet this need either because they are failing in meeting the realities, the actual needs of our young people just as the schools.

I took the young woman home to her mother where the truth of all she had told me was confirmed. Her mother was in dire straits, living on welfare and unable to provide anything for her daughter. The mother had a similar background and had accepted the inevitability of her own daughter's life in the bars. It may seem strange to my "civilized" brethren in comfortable circumstances and their padded pews that people can be so candid about such sensitive matters. But my own experience with such people confirms their openness about such things when they talk with people like me. They no longer have any pride or self-esteem. An ugly system and ugly men that they have no value and "deserve" all the abuse and victimization they are subjected to have taught girls and their mothers such as these.

The mother showed me a doctor's certificate that stated that because of the severity of the injuries (including some brain damage) the girl had received; she was unemployable and eligible for disability. A further complication involved probation from a drug arrest back East. Could I help with this? The mother was in fear that if she pursued the girl's eligibility for disability that the system would put the girl in jail. I told her I would do what I could but the circumstances and the way the system works, I know, can really chew such people up.

Another tragedy of the "system" is the fact that such people as this girl and her mother, woefully undereducated, desperately need someone to literally lead them by the hand through the labyrinth of almost Byzantine rules and regulations. And who has the time or necessary empathy to do such a thing? But I would do what I could.

I was able to offer one thing of substantial value. The mother owned a broken-down van and a rusting hulk of a Chevy sedan. As it happened, I was able to "broker" an exchange that would solve the transportation problem.

This came about from the fact that my place has become a kind of refuge for homeless, young men when I am here. This began with my own son, Michael. Shortly after retrieving him from the open and cruel streets of Stockton, he was involved with young people in similar circumstances here locally. I awakened, recently, to find three of them sleeping on the cold, slab floor of my living room. Going outside, I found another one asleep on the seat of my truck. This was cold weather but, as it turned out; the young fellows at least were protected from some degree of the elements and had a place of safety for the night and a cup of hot coffee in the morning to look forward to.

My son, knowing the rules, I don't have any trouble with alcohol or drugs on the premises. These young people, some as young as 13, need a place of safety out of the elements and are quite willing to abide by my "rules."

But one young man, D----, was unique. He was 26 and had actually been a Utah Highway Patrolman. I won't go into the circumstances, which I confirmed, that had brought him into the world of the "New Poor" (as tragically usual, alcohol played a part) but he proved to be an able mechanic.

He had been drinking, the too-often curse of the down-and-out, and had managed to run over a telephone booth with his pickup in Bakersfield. Fortunately, the booth had been unoccupied at the time but the local constables still took a dim view of such things and D--- wound up in jail for the night.

When he was released the next morning, he discovered his truck had been stolen. He called my place and talked to Michael. Somehow they arranged something that managed to get him back to Lake Isabella.

Well, to make a long story short, the young man needed transportation and the girl's mother needed at least one of her vehicles put into operation; so

I affected a "swap." The young man would repair her Chevy in exchange for the van. There was one glitch; the Chevy was at a local storage yard that had a lien of $135 against it. Also, I discovered, the car was missing the starter and needed a battery.

Having come to know D--- as an honest and hard-working young man, I fronted a loan to cover the storage fee and a starter and he came up with a battery. I had to do a lot of driving back and forth and supplied the necessary tools and the outcome was a serviceable vehicle for both the girl's mother and D--- for a lot of hard work and a small loan from me. This is the kind of real help such people need but won't get from the churches or welfare.

Tragically, I know the young girl will be back to the bars, risking AIDS, and alcohol will continue to play its evil part in the young man's life until opportunity is provided to escape by both of them. But in a devastated economy, with welfare playing its ugly role of bare, slave subsistence, the lack of education, the prospects are exceedingly dim. Flipping hamburgers will not support a man or woman without additional help from family, friends or society. The willingness to work is there among such young people like this young man and woman, but the work, the opportunity isn't there for them as it was in my time.

God made us in love. The beautiful and exquisite intimacy of real love and romance is denied people like this young girl and young man. In the inner cities the "high" of war, the gangs, police actions, has replaced such things. But for Caucasian young people like this boy and girl, they awake each morning with only the hopelessness of their situation to face another day. And, as it was with my brother's sudden revelation that "stealing is wrong," this when he was well into his 30s, what we know by our intellect can only be translated to our consciences when the circumstances allow it. As with the Psalmist's own revelation: "Neither too rich nor too poor lest the righteous put forth their hands to steal!"

Another most tragic human-interest factor: While I was visiting with the girl's mother, I was shown a broken-down, 12-foot travel trailer in the yard. She had lived in this before she had enough from government subsistence to rent the small, mobile where she now lived. Even though she was hard pressed for money, she was reluctant to sell it for fear that she might be homeless once again and it offered shelter in such an event.

As we talked, the girl received a collect call from a "boyfriend" in Florida. She had already learned enough of the system to assure him that if he could get to California, he wouldn't have to work! The mother was quite agitated. The phone company was threatening to disconnect because of non-payment and the mother told me the boyfriend had abused the girl while they were together, had, in fact, kicked her in the face and broke her nose among other things. And she still wanted him to come to California and join her! And there were the drugs. Her daughter was "straight" now and the mother feared that if the man showed up it would all begin again. Later that day, the phone was, in fact, disconnected. One can hope the "boyfriend" doesn't make it out here. It's things like this that really make me feel my age. Plus.

The girl has a sister. She is also trying to make do on welfare but has the added burden of a child, a little girl. No husband and a "boyfriend" who drinks and abuses her. This young woman lives with her daughter in a small, 14-foot travel trailer in a disreputable "park" with a group of others in similar circumstances. The sister is a beautiful, petite, young woman. But life had treated her cruelly. She had worked as a truck driver and firefighter, anything she could get to keep her and her daughter in food and shelter. But like so many who never had a chance because of the circumstances of their childhood and lack of education had fallen into the same syndrome of believing she had no value and deserved her humiliation and all the abuse she had suffered. The flow of alcohol and a "green, leafy substance," as usual, were predictors of continued failure and abuse.

I think I should mention the part language plays in these tragedies. The young girls I have mentioned have the dreadful and destructive habit of using every manner of profanity and vulgar expression in their speech. As attractive as they are, it is painfully obvious that, with their background and lack of education, having a lifetime of abuse, they have had to become tough to survive; their speech is a part of this survival technique.

Without family, without those who cared, the girls grew up having to confront the enemy the best they could. Aided to a large degree by the so-called "entertainment" industry, TV, Rock, obscene and profane movies and videos such as MTV and VH1, they are a product of a wholly self-destructive way of life. No one taught them to be ladies; no one sheltered them from the vile actions of men. They had to learn to cope in an environment so very alien to those of us who were blessed with caring and loving people in our lives where the absence and disapproval of obscenities, perversion, and alcohol were the moralities which gave us a real chance at life and self esteem.

Such young women don't even know anything of the society where such language is disapproved. They lack a background of association with moral and sophisticated, educated people where language is the primary judge of breeding and manners.

As a child, it was virtually unheard, unknown to me, absolutely unthinkable, to use the names of God and Jesus as epithets. Even after all these years, no one has ever heard me use the name of God or Jesus in such a manner. Virtually unheard also were the vulgarities and profanities so common today. But where, I have to ask myself, are these young people going to find the essential, caring leadership, trustworthy authority to lead them out of such self-destructive habits?

The other day, as I was driving to town, I saw a young couple with two babies, one being carried and the other in a stroller, walking alongside the road. It was a cold and blustery morning so I stopped and offered them a ride. The boy must have been about 20 and the girl seemed no more than 17. They were on welfare and, without a car or even enough money for the transit bus, had to make the long walk into town to the welfare office. There are just too many of such young people, children themselves, actually, in just such "slavery" to an evil system that seems determined to keep on producing such hopelessness. I was reminded of the scene in Life Goes On where Kellie Martin stands before a crucifix in the chapel and cries out to The Lord: "You aren't supposed to let these things happen!" Ah, Kellie, regardless of all the theological "explanations" and apologetics, you expressed all of our feelings in this regard. So it is that I am drawn into the battle of confronting the evil system and the evil people that support it. I was reminded once more of the truth of the statement: It is not enough to discern evil; action is required.

I'm not altogether certain what the reaction to this essay will be. My conservative brethren will, as with the essay on Fathers and Daughters, undoubtedly take me to task for frequenting "gin mills" and associating with the "unclean;" after all, "Can a man take fire in his bosom, and his clothes not be burned?" Too true; but the "burning" in my case is knowing the desperate need of so many and being able to do such a pitifully small part to offer hope and alleviate the suffering. I don't delude myself that I am sufficient for all these things.

But, as with Jesus Himself, I am not calling the "righteous" to repentance, but sinners. These people, the "unwashed," the victims of a cruel system, have no pretense of righteousness and, as a consequence, are much easier to speak to about the hope the Lord has for them in the Gospel. The task is to break through the cruelty and become believable as someone who truly cares and is not seeking his own advantage, something such people have been taught is always the case.

Closer to home, my two youngest children pay the price for their mother's divorce and their own rebellion and bad choices. Due to the tragic circumstances, I had custody of the children but failed, miserably, in the attempt to do the job that only a mother and father can hope to do together.

Currently, my 19-year-old son, Michael, is staying with me in my bachelor pad. It's a little crowded but we men are tough and make do. Without formal education, his job prospects are poor. He is intelligent and literate, thanks to my being able to provide him Christian School training in the early grades, and a hard worker and earnestly trying to find work. But with so many seeking the kinds of jobs for which he can qualify, the prospects are poor, particularly in construction.

My eldest son, Daniel, lives in Torrance. Mike is with me, this would provide him an opportunity to visit with his brother as well. I also wanted first-hand information on the bomb that was planted at the set for Beverly Hills 90210 at Torrance High School and talk with people about the anticipated riots pending the Rodney King verdict. Since I know so many people in the South Bay, I knew I would get substantial input about the situation.

It was one of those marvelous, balmy, South Bay days with a fresh, salt, ocean scent in the air. I have always loved the weather down South. At least that has remained a constant. The two biggest, new items of interest at Dan's place was his acquisition of a beautiful, '40 Packard and his engagement to a lovely girl, Patty, an Irish Colleen. I'm not exactly sure which item had precedence of priority but assumed Patty did.

As we discussed various topics of mutual interest, the subject of AIDS came up. I mentioned the discovery of a hitherto unknown vine in Cameroon that showed promise by blocking reproduction of the AIDS virus in a test tube. According to the scientists involved, even if the newfound chemical is effective, its actual use would still be years away. This led to my relating the fact that we must still do battle against perversion in spite of empathy with those that suffer from this dreadful disease. For example, "...even though the best estimates place homosexuals at 2% of the population, they account for 93% of AIDS deaths, 66% of serial killers, 40% of child molestations and about 50% of suicides." Sword of The Lord, 4/9/93.

As for Clinton's disposition to play to the pervert crowd, whom does he choose to punish the Boy Scouts of America for their stand against perversion? Lesbian Roberta Achtenberg. She is now Assistant Secretary for Fair Housing and Equal Opportunity! Oh, well, what can we expect from the man who picked the mass-murderer, Janet Reno for our Top Cop!

We had some fun talking about the guy in Santa Ana who won an award of $242,000 from an ex-wife because she lied about loving him and, as a result, was not entitled to community property. The "fun" of this was prognosticating where such a court decision might lead in millions of such cases should they be brought to court. In my own case, I wondered if I might be able to do so and collect damages from ex-wives who had jumped in bed with other men. But we agreed that cut too close to home.

There was the matter of Jerry Falwell having to reimburse the IRS $50,000 because of a ruling that he had engaged in "political activity" through his broadcast ministry. I can only shake my head over the failure of the churches continuing to ignore the obvious: If you eat at Caesar's table, you are Caesar's dog!

The shooting death of Brandon Lee was also discussed. My warnings about those in the entertainment field being such easy targets for Kooks were brought forcefully to mind. There is no doubt of L.A. and its environs being a qualified war zone. The evidence of such is everywhere you go. If you are white, especially, you simply take your life in your hands traveling in most sections. When will the "leadership" acknowledge such racism publicly? It is to laugh. I admit to the feeling of relief in getting out of the war zone and returning to the relative sanity of my mountain home where poverty and stealing are the main threats and the people are Caucasian, the main reason that crimes of violence are very few.

Whenever possible I meet with a group of patriots in Bakersfield. They are a diverse group of people and meet on a weekly basis to share information and discuss the options we face in opposing Caesar as Americans. I say "diverse" but that is only in regard to the specialties of the individuals. One man is expert in dealing with the coining and exchange of silver in opposition to Caesar's fiat money. Some have become expert in dealing with the unconstitutional Gestapo agency of the IRS (The Pilot Connection). Many of these have not paid income taxes in years and might be called tax protesters. Some deal specifically with state constitutions and agencies like the DMV and court systems.

The body of literature that is being amassed by patriotic groups across America is awesome. It still remains, however, for a concerted voice of opposition to Caesar, together with the required leadership of "Enlightened Self Interest," to arise with a specific agenda of redressing his "long train of abuses and the usurpation of our liberties" through the "legal" perverting of our Constitution and the subverting of virtually every tenet of our founding fathers.

I'm looking at my RSVP from the Claremont Institute and National Review. Special guests are Charlton Heston, Ricardo Montalban, William Rusher and William Bennett. The meeting will honor Henry Salvatori. But, as with so many such invitations, it is unlikely that I will attend. I admire these men very much and applaud the job they and the Institute are trying to do for America. However, it is not very probable that the basic, fundamental issues will be addressed with the required candor. Even the best of conservative men and organizations are tied to a mind-set that believes there "must be another way" than that of our founding fathers. I wish I could agree if for no other reason than to find myself in fellowship with such men as these. Tragically, I can see no other solution and, as a consequence, generally avoid such meetings where my own input would be, to say the least, abrasive if not, in fact, an embarrassment to them.

I have missed several meetings of late with several good men like Don Rogers, Dan Lungren, Phil Wyman, et al. for this very reason. Their public, political positions deny them the opportunity to speak as candidly as they would have to in order to confront the real evil of Caesar. Recently, for example, Don Rogers was taken to task for making the point that the founding fathers gave us a Republic, not a so-called *Democracy*. The left-wing liberal, California State University (of course) political scientist Ray Geigle attacked Senator Rogers' historical fact with his own interpretation, the usual liberal revisionist "history," saying that the difference is only "...an esoteric argument and it's a lacuna that only political scientists would worry about because it does not have any practical value!" Sorry Mr. Geigle, your "gap argument," your well-studied propagandist line of the difference being only a lacuna, of not having any practical value, has plunged our nation into the present choices of anarchy and slavery! This with the fact that I still hear nothing about the fight for the soul of America, our young people and the schools, doesn't exactly make me the life of any party. I am, confessedly, not an amiable man on this issue.

Since my essays go to the governors of all 50 states I have been discussing the possibility that one of these or their state legislatures might be willing to do battle with Caesar on the basis of the state's constitution. The plausibility of this is contained in the Constitutional basis of Individual's and State's Rights as opposed to Federal together with the fact that there are many states which would be far better off without Federal intrusion in sum. Since California and New York would not qualify in view of their being welfare states, i.e., Federally Dependent, states such as North Dakota, Wyoming, Idaho might be possibilities.

In my own attempts to gain understanding and make the situation plain to the public, I meet with many people and groups that, on the surface, have nothing in common with each other. For example, I recently sat down with The Rev. Dr. Charles R. White, an ordained minister in the Presbyterian Church (USA), and we had an extended conversation concerning Multifaith Resources of which he is the president.

I learned of Dr. White and his organization just recently and, as a prelude to our meeting, I supplied him some of my essays. Because of this, I wasn't sure he would meet with me but, on the basis of my being honestly candid and transparent in my views, well-educated and my lack of "labels," he agreed to the meeting, though, as he confessed, with some trepidation. I counted on my own experience in working with people that Dr. White would welcome a dialogue with a conservative such as me to further his own understanding of the issues involved.

Dr. White had just returned from New York where he had attended a meeting at Stony Point concerning the problems of the multifaith approach to the problems of pluralism and multiculturalism. Probably the most interesting thing to come out of our meeting was the agreement we found on the basis of the three, historical imperatives we face as an Empire: Anarchy, Slavery or a New Continental Congress. Naturally, there was broad disagreement in regard to our belief systems and our personal views but, as educated, civilized men our discussion was friendly and in good faith of mutual respect for each other's positions and honest attempts to understand and learn from them.

He had mentioned the fact that Hans Kung and others are agreed, as I myself, that there will be no peace among nations as long as there is conflict in ideologies, as long as religious pluralism remains stalemated. His organization, Multifaith Resources, is dedicated to dialogue and training to overcome this obstacle of religious intolerance; an admittedly noble undertaking. Many others like Wade Clark Roof, professor of religious studies at the University of California, Santa Barbara are researching this very thing. It is also a significant part of my own database in Human Behavior. In spite of our agreement on many issues, those such as the literal truth of the Gospel, the murder of millions of innocent babies by abortion as a means of contraception and the plain word of God's judgment against perversion there will remain irreconcilable differences between us.

The following is something of which I had no knowledge at the time. If I had, I would have asked Dr. White if he knew anything about it. A most interesting article in issue No. 18 of the Aryan Nations well deserves to be passed along if for no other reason than the fact that I haven't found it mentioned in any other conservative publication; quoted in The Way from Destiny Magazine, Oct/Nov.:

"If you are one of those who don't have time to worry about the matter of the spirit, not to worry, the U.N. is working to take care of that for you. Living up to its charter - to be an agency of the world - it has assigned Donald Keys, President of Planetary Citizens, to fade individual worship out and to replace it with one religion for everyone.

"Mr. Keys explains the need for a single religion for all mankind. 'The United Nations is the chosen instrument of God. Because of this fact, the world must come to treasure the soul of the U.N. For it is a soul that is all-loving, all-nourishing and all-fulfilling.' In the major cities of the world, temples have already been built in which to worship the U.N. god. Without any news coverage, similar temples to the one in the U.N. building in New York are being constructed throughout the U.S." If this is true, and I suspect the U.N. of any anti-Christ evil imaginable, why isn't it being talked about in publications like The New American?

A most important facet of my meeting with conservatives, moderates and liberals, labels that are, for the most part, meaningless, is the commonality of concerns, of agreement on many important issues. Not really surprising since we are all in this together, since we are all, in fine, human beings. For example, as I write, we are awaiting the Rodney King verdict. All of us are agreed on the fact that any rioting will only inflame passions on all sides, will only increase racial hatreds and encourage further erosion of our freedoms as Caesar tries to deal with the situation in the usual manner of more "laws."

The gun ranges are packed in L.A. and the gun stores are doing a brisk business. As I sat and chatted with Dan in Torrance, a friend of his came by and borrowed a shotgun to protect him and his family from the anticipated hoard of black and brown vandals. If this should occur, it won't be a matter of fine distinctions between Christian, Muslim or Buddhist beliefs; it will be anarchy and my inside sources tell me that the law-abiding citizen will have to protect himself, the police will not be able to do so. And should the cry of the vandals "Next time, Rodeo Drive!" be fulfilled? It's only a matter of time in any event.

The Crime Control Act of 1993 is a thinly veiled attempt of Caesar's to bring every act of trying to deal with the insanity of an Empire beyond Reason under the broadest umbrella of criminal activity. In sum: Will Citizens exercising their Constitutional right to free expression and association be targeted by government agents who know their jobs are dependent on property seizures, fines and arrests? Count on it! For all practical purposes, we already are targeted: Kahl, Terry, Randy Weaver and Kevin Harris, Donald Scott, the Waco Wacko, Lyndon LaRouche, etc., are glaring examples of the madness.

APOCALYPSE IN WACO

So reads this morning's headline in the newspaper. By now we all know the outcome of the shameful and despicable actions of Caesar's Storm troopers and Gestapo in regard to the flagrant disregard of every tenet of liberty and humanity in causing the deaths of men, women and children in the tragedy of Waco. How very magnanimous of Ms. Janet Reno to take full responsibility for these murders. Lacking any background of real understanding or genuine concern for family, let alone any of what was really going on in this instance, she showed her utter disregard for the Constitutional rights and lives of those in Waco by her callous decision to attack. Mr. Clinton, you sure know how to pick them! I shudder to think of the consequences of some of your other "picks" for positions like the Supreme Court! But, then again, the Court is so perverted already can you really make it worse?

In respect to Waco, consider the utter hypocrisy of an FBI official's statement concerning "taking out" Koresh by a sniper: "It would be a terrible precedent for law enforcement officials on the scene to be judge, jury and executioner." Now why didn't this argument hold true for the murder by the Feds of Vicki Weaver? This hypocritical fool, whoever he is, wants us to believe such a "precedent" hasn't already been set? I've got a bulletin for him and the Feds; Those of us who will "Never Forget" will keep writing and speaking out against Caesar and his murderous agents as long as we have life and means to do so!

Because of the obvious bias of the liberal media, it is highly unlikely you will hear about the arrest of Louis Beam in Waco; seems Beam, as a reporter, is "tainted" by speaking and writing for the cause of White Americans. He was at the site representing a paper, "The Jubilee," which is unabashedly White American in orientation.

As reported in The Jubilee, the arrest came about because of the following question Beam asked FBI agent Dan Conroy: "Many people who viewed the video of the initial ATF action against the church complex, view the tactics as something very similar to those used both in Nazi Germany and the Soviet Union by the KGB; as you well know there is much talk in the country about that. Are we seeing the emergence of a police state in the United States?"

Well, it seems you just don't ask such an obvious question of Caesar's agents and get away with it. But it was answered in full, in my opinion, by one Melissa Sims, a Waco police Sgt., who badgered Beam about The Jubilee and his connection with the Klan. He was arrested by Sims. But to the credit of a Judge, one C. Evans, the question for which Beam was arrested was acknowledged by the judge as one "Needing to be asked" and he was released on his own recognizance. I'll let you know of any further actions against Beam.

I am as repulsed as any normal human being can be concerning the stories of abuse of children by this religious charlatan, Koresh. Perhaps they are true. As I wrote in my last essay, I despise any man who would hide behind women and children. If this Kook is responsible for the deaths of those children I hope the Lord has an even hotter fire prepared for him in eternity. But coming against someone solely because of their peculiar religious beliefs is most certainly not part of my belief system unless those beliefs pose a threat to enslave me to them. I am the enemy of all religious charlatans who would shame The Lord and His Word; but not to the extent of ever perverting The Gospel as a message of the sword.

In any event, are any of my readers gullible enough to think we are going to be told the whole truth about this affair? I don't think so. But thanks to Caesar's actions against people like the Weavers and so many others, his protestations of innocence and his "justifications" for the actions taken will fall on increasingly deaf ears.

The hard choices which responsible and honest people are going to have to make still lie before us; the mounting terrorism (Was the poisoning of the municipal water supply in Milwaukee really "accidental?") of Caesar and the hoards of vandals that are murdering, stealing, plundering and destroying our Christian culture are propelling us to the moment of crisis when such choices are going to be made whether by force of circumstances or design. I will continue to work and pray that men of good will who will come together, just as our founding fathers, to confront Caesar and take back the Republic they gave us and the liberties that have been stolen from us by America's betrayers, will make the choices.

The recent opening of a Holocaust Memorial Museum recently in Washington augmented part of this betrayal. World leaders gathered to pay homage to this Trojan Horse. This is only going to attract more of Abu Nidal's attention to America. But a curious thing; Croatian President Franjo Tudjman who has written a book claiming that fewer than a million Jews died in the so-called Holocaust and has called Israelis, most appropriately, "Judeo-Nazis" was in attendance for the ceremonies! As I have said many times, there is a dark purpose in all these things that the "leadership" refuses to acknowledge. But it hasn't gone away in 2,500 years and it isn't going to until The Lord returns. And there is too much truth to the comparison of Warsaw '43 and what has just happened In Waco.

And, speaking of perverted courts, the Rodney King decision is in at last. The jury played it safe by convicting two of the officers. This together with the warnings of the amount of firepower in waiting should rioting break out cooled the ardor of the hoards of vandals; they aren't altogether stupid, just lawless. I wonder if anyone is going to give any serious consideration to the Double Jeopardy under law by which the officers were sacrificed? One thing is certain, police are going to become eunuchs by having to stop and ask themselves whether it is worth the risk to even stop drunk drivers anymore. If one such punk as King can do such monumental damage to law enforcement, you have to wonder what other insanity lies in wait for police who already face an impossible task?

This is in no way to excuse police brutality. But when a jury already decides an issue and Caesar can step in and have it his way regardless, you know you have Empire that is beyond Reason. Such Empire always results in the insanities of the King affair, Randy Weaver and Waco.

Not many people of any "standing" will admit of receiving publications from the Klan and Aryan Nations. Most don't even read Aid & Abet in spite of the most valuable information contained in it regarding the rights of all citizens (Jack McLamb, the editor, is one of the most patriotic people we have working for us as Americans). As a result, they lack a point of view that could be of help to them in their own publications. I am one of the few that openly admit of receiving and reading such and suffer a good deal of "polite ostracism" by my colleagues as a result. This is most unfortunate because anyone who claims a knowledge of "conservative" views and ignores such publications remind me too much of those critics of the Bible who have never read it for themselves and those that complain of government who never vote. Brethren; ignorance is ignorance!

The case of Ella Mae Buren disclosed in issue No. 18 of "The Way", a prison outreach newsletter of the Aryan Nations, as a result, may not find publication in the more "polite" periodicals like National Review or The Spectator. The story of Mrs. Buren is not unlike that of Randy Weaver and so many others who are political prisoners of conscience right here in the U.S. If any of my readers are in revulsion over recent events such as Waco and King, and we should all be, I encourage you to write: Aryan Nations, P.O. Box 567, Hayden Lake, Idaho 83835 and ask for this issue.

If you do write for this publication, you will also read a very informative piece by Adam Starchild that was originally published in Aid & Abet Police Report. To give you some idea of what it is about, I quote Starchild's concluding remark: "It seems obvious that the argument about cameras in courtrooms is a red herring, designed to conceal the real issue of doctoring of court transcripts by judges and prosecuting attorneys, especially the latter." What? You didn't know this is common practice with Caesar's agents? Anything you say in a court of law may be held against you! Sound familiar? What you didn't know is that regardless of what you say, if they want you, they can get you whether you said it or not!

My good friend, Byron, the Episcopal Priest, just brought me a copy of Phil Donahue's book, "The Human Animal." Being on my list of "must reading," I was quite grateful.

In the minds of many, if you want the Point and Counterpoint of conservative vs. liberal, you would probably choose Donahue vs. Limbaugh. It was quite revealing to watch the two of them together on Donahue's show. Thus it behooves conservatives such as me to continue to be familiar with people like Donahue. And, since he, like Limbaugh, has such a large coterie of devoted followers, it helps in keeping your finger on the pulse of public sentiment.

In spite of the pervasive shallowness of personalities like Donahue and TV in general, a seeming by-product of such a media and not a criticism of the individuals, there is still an essential depth of such in the approach to the problems of society and Donahue does a good job of summing up the general, humanism approach to their solutions. I use the "humanism" term because it is not, properly, a *Weltanschauung*, falling far short of such. Humanism on the other hand having the approval of the liberal community offers a broad enough brush to accomplish the task of providing shallow and simplistic answers to otherwise profound questions.

Like Schuller of the Crystal Cathedral, Donahue, and humanism in general, doesn't demand, as Heine and Goethe, any real depth of understanding or insight. His book, like Schuller's sermons, is designed to leave you feeling good about yourself and the world; the old God is in His heaven and all is right upon the earth. Of course, in view of the obvious contrary facts of the case, this is, on its very face, ludicrous. But it promotes snake oil salesmen like Donahue and Schuller.

A friend recently made the criticism of my essays; "You have to read them twenty times to get their full meaning!" I couldn't argue his point. In fact, I shared with him the truth of his comment as it applied in my own case; I have to do the same thing!

To explain, as I did with him, the essays are a product of a life-time of reading broadly, of more than the usual experiences of life and the sharing of your life with so many others, people of widely diverse backgrounds themselves and a wealth of such diverse experiences and interests in my own life. Much of the writing I do is the product of drawing from the "unconscious well" of the mind and, as a result, I often have the feeling that someone else has written these essays; so much is not a product of conscious thought processes but flows from the "well."

As my readers know, I often walk where Angels fear to tread. Foolish, I agree, in many cases. But the result is an on-going dialogue with these people of diversity and, a continued interest in life itself apart from the contemporary conditions that, often, take our minds off those things of real, eternal value. As I have often said: God's business is a people business. Unless you are involved with others, you are missing the essential element of what "humanity" is all about and what God, Himself, is all about.

I've been cleaning out the little cabin in back of my shanty house. Hoping for continued good weather, I have taken out what I can to the side of the house and placed a tarp over it in order to set up a bed, chair and a few necessaries in the cabin and make it at least a place where some young person can sleep in some degree of comfort and shelter.

Doing these little things isn't, perhaps, unlike mopping a mud floor but it is the best I can do under the circumstances. I'd build a storage shed but with my limited resources, what little extra money there is has to go for food rather than building materials at present.

I'll continue to do the little I can to alleviate some of the suffering of those "sheep" that have no voice or choice, the "rejects" and our children and young people. At the same time I will keep in touch, with continued revulsion, those who are involved with their own egotistical and selfish agendas of enslaving us to Caesar or thrusting us into anarchy. All the while, I will beat the drum for a new Continental Congress to confront Caesar and his agents.

I have just watched Evans and Novak discussing the issues with Pat Robertson. My readers know my view of Robertson. A millionaire himself, he can, nevertheless "aw shucks" with the best Foggy Bottom has to offer in gulling the public. But, as I have also said, no one who "hears voices" and whole-heartedly subscribes to the charismatic heresy is going to be taken seriously by any of Reason and sound doctrine.

As with Perot, Robertson and others are saying many of the things that need to be said. But, as I have also said, repeatedly, the really hard facts, the really hard truths and choices are not being dealt with by any of either the mainstream conservatives or liberals. They are far too inflammatory in the face of what the media is capable of doing with even the hint of such. But let's face it folks, those imperatives of history are not going to go away by fiat of wishful rhetoric. They remain; adamant, unyielding and the choices will be made willingly or unwillingly, consciously or unconsciously, to our salvation as a nation or to its destruction!

The sun shines brightly through my windows as I write. The squirrel in my backyard has found a mate. Last evening I sat out front and enjoyed the thin, cirrus mare's tails blow into intricate, charcoal traceries against a sky of platinum, giving way to silver and pewter in the setting sun, the mountains beginning to be silhouetted in the fading light.

As usual, my mind reaches into the reveries of life past to find some degree of solace from the evils of our world. Quiet music of that gentler time plays in the background. It saddens me that our young people don't know of such a time, don't understand the music, and have to face the horrors that surround us without the inner strength of real love and romance, without a living relationship with their Creator, without hope. Will good men and women of good will finally come together to confront these evils of the age? I pray so. Unfortunately, so many I talk to don't entertain any hope of such a thing happening. But, if it doesn't happen in the cases of the individuals first, how is it to happen in the population at large?

So it is that I continue to work and write as one individual and live in the hope that God will bring genuine repentance to those who have given up and turn them to righteousness in their own hearts and cause them, as individuals, to start doing those first works over again, returning to their first love and start producing those fruits meet for repentance. If not you, who? If not now, when?

Chapter Six

Christian Perspective

June

Psalm 104:14,15
A Christian friend of mine recently surprised me by sharing that he read my essays as "devotional literature." He explained that he found the sensitivity and significance with which I wrote of many people and subjects suited to his own meditations. I was grateful for this even though I had never thought of the essays as devotional in any respect. It did cause me to wonder if others found them so? I have received correspondence from readers that might indicate this but in most cases they use phrases like "thought-provoking."

Like most writers, I like to think my own writing is found profitable to people's thinking, of some value in their lives and worth their time. My own view of my friend's comment is that if I am "devotional" it is the devotional writing of revolution, of the poetry of confrontation with Caesar and his agents, the prose of Tom Paine and Patrick Henry.

But the writing I prefer to do might very well be devotional in respect to my wishing I could contribute to the joy and happiness of others full-time rather than the hard labor of addressing the evils of our world and nation. How much rather write of those things which would inspire the joy and happiness of God's creation, of the best of the child within us, of the music and poetry in ordinary lives, the love and romance and the kindness I find in lovers, friends and families.

Ah, but the beat goes on and evil men and women, the evil that they do, must be confronted and this burns in my bones and the fire is released in those hard things that I am compelled to write of rather than the soft and gentle things that would be the joy and happiness of my own soul and heart. It is the evil that stifles the music and poetry that I would far rather compose and enjoy. Once in a while, however, as my readers know, I let fancy have her wing and go off on a tangential journey of the heart and soul. So: I'll call her Rosie.

She sat in the cheap, plastic-covered recliner; its cotton guts oozed from the various rips and tears in its hide. Rosie was wearing a thin, nondescript, threadbare robe that didn't obscure the fact that she was overweight. As she said, when you are poor and stressed, you eat and cheap food is fattening. But she was going to get her weight down in order to attract a man. "I'm not someone who has to be alone." She said this with a voice that trembled in an effort at pride and conviction.

I would guess Rosie's age about 57 but the years had been cruel. Her face, marred with the veined and seamed tracks of the alcoholic, had once been quite lovely. She sat there, playing with her hair, twisting the thin wisps in nervous fingers. Two plastic curlers were stuck, like an afterthought, in a few entangling strands on the right side of her head. I wondered if she was even aware they were still there?

"You've been a good friend, Don." I didn't know how except for the fact that, knowing of her desperate circumstances and how she had suffered to try to make a life and care for her children, I had brought some groceries and listened to her try to talk about her life. I had also taken her to some essential appointments. She couldn't afford to register her old, rusting Chevy. It needed a good deal of work and a smog check anyhow, which she couldn't afford either. Insurance; what's that? People like Rosie, about 50% of California drivers, among them the host of illegal aliens, not only can't afford it they wouldn't buy it anyhow. The taxpayers, the workers, the "system" will take care of them. They have nothing to lose so why worry?

It looked like Rosie had been a lovely girl and woman once. You needed to look beyond what the years had done to her. I had no doubt that she would, indeed, find another man. But, in all probability, he would be one of the many drunken leeches looking for someone to support him on her welfare check.

I knew of too many young men looking for the same "meal-ticket" and preying on younger women, especially, with children who could never expect anything much better and actually had been taught to believe they deserved such a life with their continued abuse by evil men.

Rosie wouldn't say it. It lay unspoken between us. She would never have a chance at a decent man. Neither would her girls. Once youth and beauty are gone, the pickings get slimmer and slimmer. This together with the fact that vulgar language, drinking, lack of education dooms attracting young men of value in spite of good looks and a nice figure. Sex may be the prominent commodity of exchange while girls and women retain their youth and beauty but once that is gone, what is left for them in our culture and society?

There is no idle, philosophical double-talk about so-called "equality" between the sexes in Rosie's world. She knows the truth, at least in this regard, when it comes to the value of older, wrinkled women with no well-turned ankles or trim figure to catch the eye.

It reminds me of the pitiful scene I witnessed in a bar. The young lady was very attractive. She had been dancing and all at once she stopped. I don't know what caused the outburst but she said in a loud voice to her partner: "Quit looking down there, look up here (pointing to her head), I'm a person, not 'that!'" Ah, young lady, you had my deepest sympathy. Tragically, you aren't a "person" to most men; you are only "that!"

Rosie was staring out the dusty window of her small, drab trailer. Cheap rent, welfare and a collection of neighbors in similar circumstances were her world. Her absent-minded gaze told me she was lost in another time and place where she had been young and full of hope.

The small black and white TV had a snow-filled picture making it virtually impossible to tell, apart from the audio, what show was on. No money for cable and the rabbit ears didn't respond well in this mountain community. But Rosie was used to not really watching TV. Just the voices were needed for companionship, not unlike the way we used radio in my youth.

There were no books or magazines about. Rosie didn't read much. Neither did her daughters. There was a son. He tried to make money cutting and selling firewood. But he often didn't have enough money for the gas to take his decrepit old pickup out to find the wood. He seldom went by to see his mother and sisters and couldn't help them in any event. I recalled seeing him, along with a few others of the same "brotherhood," on the boulevard occasionally with his truck; a small pile of wood in front of it with a Firewood For Sale sign against the meager stack.

Years ago, when I was a freshman, high school teacher at Jordan High in Watts, I would visit families in similar circumstances, my white face being a real rarity even then. Drugs and alcohol were the curses of welfare slavery then as now and had no distinction of "color." I was thoroughly familiar with the lifestyles of those who victimized, preyed upon one another, a "fix" or bottle not having any respect of persons, not even family or friends.

My introduction to Rosie had come about with my finding one of her daughters in a bar. The circumstances of my being in the bar were explained in my last essay.

Rosie had called me and asked if I would please bring her some wine. She complained of an anemic condition and stomach problems that the wine would alleviate. Now I have had enough experience with alcoholics to know the stories and the symptoms. I worked with a drug and alcohol abuse group in a professional capacity once.

But there is more to this than allowing yourself to be taken advantage of by the scheming of a boozer. Those who are familiar with "The Winter of Our Discontent" and "Cannery Row" will understand why I bought the wine and went to see Rosie.

What I didn't know was that she and her daughter had gotten an early start on the evening by consuming a twelve-pack. Now, with the wine, their life was full. They knew I wouldn't drink with them but had, thoughtfully, made a pot of coffee for me.

Rosie's Mexican live-in was there. But, unlike them, he drank very little and was not an addict. I had gotten to know him as a good man, unlike many I have met in similar circumstances. I could tell, through our broken conversation, that he deplored the drunkenness of the women. Jose was probably in his early 60s and retained some of the better qualities of civilized manners of his native country.

Rosie was at that point of inebriation where "confidences" were shared, congeniality reigned and all was right with the world. But the combination of the wine and beer were about to have the anticipated consequences. The music was being played louder with each glass consumed. The daughter was dancing with drunken abandon to a variety of Mexican and English tunes. She was obviously an experienced and talented dancer. She had done quite a bit of professional dancing, topless, in a number of bars and, being intoxicated, was displaying all her "talent," the loss of inhibitions, one of the curses of drunkenness, betraying all sense of decorum.

Rosie soon joined her daughter and, grabbing a most reluctant Jose, made it a threesome. I sipped my coffee and watched the whole thing deteriorate rapidly. Evening had passed into nighttime. Rosie's other daughter called. After a mostly incoherent conversation with her mother and sister, she asked to speak with me. She asked if I could possibly spend the night with them, as she feared what might happen if things got out of control. I said I would attempt to do so.

Jose tried to maintain some degree of sanity in the situation. The women couldn't even pour the wine in their glasses now without spilling it on the table or floor. Rosie knocked her glass over and slipped off her chair. Jose struggled with the near dead weight of her bulk, finally getting her back up on her now precarious perch and grabbed a towel to clean up the mess.

The daughter was making drunken attempts to use the telephone to call someone but her eyes, mind and fingers weren't cooperating. She gave it up and returned to the wine and the dancing. The music was blaring painfully now. I went outside to escape the noise and the smell. Jose joined me.

He spoke sorrowfully of his circumstances. Fists clenched and clutching his crossed arms to his chest, he articulated in broken English the feeling of pain he was enduring, far from home and family, a virtual prisoner of Rosie and her welfare check, of his fear of deportation and his fear and repugnance of having to live any longer in his present surroundings, of enduring the humiliation of what we were presently experiencing.

The daughter came to the door of the trailer and shouted at us to come back inside. Jose, shoulders stooped and his head bowed down, went inside. It took a while longer for me to gather my strength to follow him.

Upon entering, I discovered Jose mopping up Rosie's vomit. She lay on the floor in it passed out; not unexpected result of the beer, wine and dancing. We managed to get her up on the couch and left her there to sleep it off.

It was now quite late and I had to consider where I was to sleep. But the daughter had disappeared and Jose wasn't sure where I could bed down. If Rosie came out of it during the night, he would have to take her to the bedroom. Fine. But I couldn't stay awake long enough to use the couch she presently occupied. The stench from the floor would prevent me laying down a blanket there and sleeping.

It was now 11 p.m. The phone rang. Jose answered. It was the elderly couple in the trailer next door. The daughter was over there and if someone didn't come and get her, they were going to call the police.

I went. The girl was incoherent and staggering. The old folks were incensed. On the way back to the girl's place, she fell down a couple of times in spite of my efforts to keep her upright. Somehow, she had managed to add a pipe or two to the combination of beer and wine. As a consequence, she was well wired and I considered whether it would even be possible to spend the night. I've known people in her condition to last many hours without sleep before crashing.

As it turned out, the decision was made for me. The girl began to insist that I go to the store for more wine. I refused, pointing out the fact that even if I were to do so, the stores were now closed. She turned to Jose. "Walk to the store, Jose, and get us some more wine!" In her intoxicated mind, what I was doing was refusing to accommodate her and making excuses. Jose tried to explain to no avail. Then she turned abusive when cajoling failed. At that point, I had no choice but to make my exit.

Leaving Jose to the nightmare of attending the two women, I took my leave into the cleansing air of the mountain night, sorrowful for the tragedy I was leaving but so very grateful that I could leave it. Also, I have learned that no matter how bad something is, with just a little effort I can make it worse. So I left.

Sally Jessy Raphael had a good point in "Living Without Answers." So often in life we are left in exactly that position. Even in the working out of so much pain and grief, we are still, too often, left with no other answer than to just keep on keeping on which, of course, is no answer.

I'm reminded once more of the exceptional good fortune of my own birth, That from a child I have known the Holy Scriptures which are able to make one wise unto salvation, that I was born to loving people like my grandparents and others, free of abuse, illiteracy, alcohol, profanity and extreme poverty.

But I have had to work through so much betrayal and pain in my own life, I have had to live so long and often without answers, it has made me very empathetic to others who face the same things, for others who have not had my good fortune, for those "incapables" who cannot do for themselves.

I have the tremendous benefit of being able to look to The Lord and His Word for the ultimate answers of life and death, of many of the even smaller things, the things that constitute the morality of everyday life. But, in far too many cases, life seems a "proving ground" where we must work through to our own answers. I hold to the belief that God's Word and Holy Spirit gives the child of God great advantages in these things as well. But, still, there is the seeming responsibility to use the faculties God has gifted us with to come to terms with many things for which no ready answer is available.

Rosie and her daughters will call me tomorrow. They will be profoundly sorry for what they did and, they will be sincere in their apology. They will tell me it will never happen again. And they will mean it. But it will; as sure as the rising of the sun. Pathetically, they know very few, if any, people like myself-educated and caring, self-supporting. The advantage they try to take of me is, pathetically, child-like as in Cannery Row, the subterfuge of acquiring the wine, for example. But the lengths to which they would go, equally pathetic, no, tragically, in order to give something in return can best be understood by the following: I could "have" the daughter for $20 or even $5 if necessary. Make no mistake, this is not the hiring of a prostitute, this is not "Love For Sale," it is an offer of friendship by those that have nothing else of value to offer. Also, I present the image of a wealthy man to such people because of my education, independence, of owning a home, a car in no need of repair and being free of debt. Further, as a writer, they hold me in near superstitious awe. I not only read books, I write and publish them! They don't understand, of course, but they know this is somehow terribly important. As a consequence, the daughter would be "honored" to do this for me and I would honor her by complying.

Now I am far from immune to the need of the warmth and softness of a woman in my life. But, notwithstanding the common sense avoidance of the risk of disease, those who know me will understand my being able to forego the daughter's offer. The key element here is the need for a woman in my life! I am not, and have never been, given to promiscuity. Rather old fashioned that way. In fact, many consider me a "moral dinosaur" as a result.

Such folks as Rosie and her daughter know nothing of the world of F. Ross Johnson or "Barbarians At The Gate" but they understand his reputed methods of earning money the old fashioned way; Steal it! However, they will never have the opportunity to steal, legally, on such a monumental scale as per the S&L and BCCI thieves and congressmen. They won't even have the opportunity or know how to steal on the more equitable scale and level of lower echelon, prostituted politicians, judges and crooked cops.

To be sure, Rosie and her daughter steal. They steal every chance they get. It is a part of their "lifestyle." One has to be very cautious around them. Human nature being what it is, envy and greed are alive and well in their lives, particularly since they are undereducated, have no job skills and face a hopeless existence, hopeless of anything ever being any better than what they now have. But the evil of welfare robs them of any of the "nobility" of poverty. Irrespective of color, those within the welfare "society" victimize each other simply because those outside the society usually have nothing to do with them, leaving one another the only choices of victims. And, admittedly, it is risky to associate with them. I have no illusions on that score.

As I drive "home" in the clean, crisp, late night air, there is the leaden weight of the feeling of failure, of the vague uneasiness of knowing I should have been able to help in a way that utterly eludes me. I know full well the futility, the heartache and grief, of trying to help boozers. But the tragedy of the scene keeps playing over and over again like a video stuck on replay. And, over the years, I have had to witness the same tragedy too many times in too many other lives. I'm far too well acquainted with "The Days of Wine and Roses" to give in to futile and wishful thinking of "what might have been."

Once at my small cottage I put on an album of the kinder and softer music of a gentler time to try to wash out the destructive noise I left behind with the women and Jose. I move a folding chair out front and look up at the stars, the music providing the background I often need in order to fully appreciate God's glory and promises in the heavens. The thought stabs in my mind that Rosie and her daughters are denied any real comprehension of the joy of such a quiet and contemplative lifestyle. They would, doubtless, consider it "boring." But, I have discovered most women find a poet boring to live with. They become quickly aggravated and frustrated with his lack of "common sense." Even most men would agree with women in this respect.

The Russian poets have well described America as a nation without a soul. I fully understand what they mean. A nation's soul consists of those gentler, and even, heroic things that are expressed in the genius of its poets, philosophers, composers, writers, and artists. Tragically, America has never recovered from its Gilded Age. It takes, certainly, building that part of the house that will accommodate the material needs of warmth and shelter before the study, the parlor, the reading and music rooms are added. But America became so preoccupied with the material successes that the "Business of

America became Business." We passed by the needs of the soul that would have sustained our greatness as a nation.

I am a racial and ideological "separatist" because of the fact that no nation can have a "soul" which is divided on racial and ideological lines; as Abraham Lincoln so well and wisely said of the Negro: "But for your race among us, there could not be a war, although many men engaged on either side do not care for you, one way or another...it is better therefore for us both, to be separated. You and we are different races. We have between us a broader difference than exists between almost any other two races. I think your race suffers very greatly, many of them, by living among us, while ours suffers from your presence. In a word, we suffer on each side. If this is admitted, it affords a reason, at least, why we should be separated." I underline the phrase *If this is admitted*, for the obvious reason; what politician dares voice, as Lincoln, this inescapable imperative? Yet, there it is in its fullest and clearest candor and it will never go away! But Lincoln might have recognized, as perhaps Benjamin Franklin may have, that the seed of America's possible destruction might have been sown in slavery.

For example, a lengthy article in a large Metropolitan newspaper featured a Negro woman's comments on Lincoln; her conclusion, quote: "President Lincoln believed the white race was superior to any other. That describes a bigot and racist, to me." Not surprisingly, this woman is a "student" at a university and is being taught the usual, liberal, revisionist, so-called history of our nation. But she does, as far as it is possible for her to do so, cut to the bottom line of what politicians are so afraid to talk about.

Lincoln made it clear that he considered the Negro an inferior race. It is, as I have often said, a tragedy of monstrous proportions that Franklin's and Jefferson's warnings were not heeded, that slavery was not abolished by the Constitution resulting in a fatally flawed document, that this omission constituted our Tragic Flaw and led to the Tragic Era and beyond. The seeds of our own destruction, as I have also said, were sown in that corrupt omission. And why was it omitted? Because the seeds of Commerce, the seeds of The Gilded Age, Business and Commerce were preferred, were the selfish goals of a few of the founding fathers. But those few had held the key to the battle against the Crown and their blackmail prevailed in forming the Republic. And that other flaw, exclusion of the Jews? Had that prevailed?

Bill Lucas and I were discussing the issue of the Hyphenated American just before we went on the air on KDNO in Delano. We asked ourselves the question: Just what do we mean when we use the term American? What do people, in general, mean when they use the term? What should it mean, what should its definition actually be? Is it any longer even possible of definition?

Bill is an outstanding example of a Christian Man. He is vitally in tune with the Christian Community and has a heart for young people as I myself. We relate very well on this level. But I am in touch with organizations with which very few of Bill's background have any acquaintance, like many of the White Separatist groups and Patriotic groups such as Aid and Abet, Common Cause, Posse Comitatus, etc. As a consequence, I add another dimension to the discussion of American that is too often lacking among Christians.

Henry James, around the turn of the century wrote: "It's a complex fate, being an American." If he could only see us now! From my self-imposed exile from so many with whom I would like to have fellowship, that fellowship denied me on the basis of my refusal to subscribe to their peculiar definitions of "American" or "Christian," I write as one who, without labels, prefers the liberty to say what I believe needs to be said without the restraints of "labels" or even the risk of offending friends by appearing to betray their own labels through "belonging."

I asked Bill if he could accept "American" as defined by our Founding Fathers? Since that definition was based on White Anglo/Saxon Protestantism, Men Only. Propertied Only, could that conceivably be, once more, a possible definition? He said it could not. Our discussion included my own premise that only with voter eligibility reform could any hope of an enlightened electorate, that Enlightened Self-Interest, be, once more, possible. This would be essential, as he agreed, to have any hope of returning the Republic our founding fathers gave us and eliminate the selfish, Unearned Bread Masses which keep feeding off the productive workers in society and keep the same-minded tax and spend betrayers of America in office.

But if the Americanism of the Founding Fathers is impossible then what; what of the Americanism Bill and I were taught as children? Was that possible? We were born to a generation that had experienced a World War and the Great Depression. We grew up with World War II. We had witnessed Korea and Viet Nam. How was American different to us as children and American now?

It was, admittedly, quite a conundrum. The hyphenated American, we agreed, was totally unsatisfactory, leading only to conflict and the resulting Balkanization of our nation. Was Separatism even, as per Lincoln even a remote possibility? Again, we agreed, not without bloodshed, another Civil War. And why; because, it was also agreed, good men who would recognize the necessity of voter reform, the necessity to address this issue with the needed honesty, integrity and resolve were never likely to be elected to office.

By what definition, then, could Asians, Negroes, Mexicans and Caucasians be brought together as Americans? Never without a common culture, a common belief system, a common ideology, a common language, all dedicated to the common good and common goals and objectives with agreement on the methods with which such things can be achieved. The Platonic Reasoning, the very historical dictates, human nature itself, of such simply cannot be denied notwithstanding all the wishful rhetoric to the contrary. The All-Encompassing Brotherhood of the U.N. god? Again, not without bloodshed on a historically unparalleled scale; but we agreed that such a thing could not be discounted. It certainly seems the direction we are headed.

"Skinheads USA: Soldiers Of The Race War." This TV special is said by one commentator to offer "...television viewers an amazing look inside the world of the Alabama-based Aryan National Front neo-Nazi 'skinhead group'..." As to be expected, the "special" presents the liberal view of such things and casts the people involved in the worst possible light. Not particularly "Amazing." Fanning the flames of anarchy, the media, as usual, is more concerned with "hype" than truth. Could they be so ignorant as not to know that this kind of thing only foments more hatred along racial lines? And they will air this show in the "public interest?" Just who is kidding whom?

Women in combat? Perverts in the military? Abortion on demand? Just how much of this kind of thing can society survive? Crank in the flames of the utter failure of the schools, the failures of the courts to deal with crime, the fomenting of racial and ideological conflict and you have the essential ingredients of another Civil War in this nation! Ellie Nesler, Skinheads USA, Ruby Creek and Waco only help to draw the battle lines.

In "Biblical Horizons" I find James Jordan making this interesting statement concerning the wicked: "Christ is restraining the wicked at present by promoting AIDS among them...God has given them over to folly. We must do our duty and bear witness to them, urging them to advocate chastity, but so far they refuse to hear us. Thus, they promote AIDS and other venereal diseases through their sex education programs, etc. By this means, God is wiping out many Canaanites, making room for His people to have greater influence in the next generation. Similarly, Christ is restraining the wicked by causing them to kill their children. If thirty million babies have died since 1973, that is 30,000,000 fewer pagans our children will have to deal with. Over time, the percentage is running favorable to the Kingdom, since Christians don't kill their babies." Dec. 1992.

Pretty cold-blooded calculation: Christ is "causing" the wicked to kill their babies? I understand where Jordan is coming from but...? Part of his reasoning is the "hardening" of Pharaoh's heart. I understand that and more; but an interesting argument in all. I do take exception to Gary North's and James Jordan's doctrine of Christians making the world a better place for Christ's return. Too many statements of Scripture lead to the conclusion that, in the words of Jesus, "When the Son of Man returns shall He find faith in the whole earth?" The Lord's return, whether post-mil or pre-trib, won't keep me from fighting evil with all my means and might regardless. But it is fascinating to contemplate the wicked doing themselves in by any and all means including AIDS and the perversions of divorce, homosexuality and abortion.

This leads me to point out one of the many lunacies we find in the Congress. Seems Foggy Bottom is just coming to realize the fact that Negro legislators align themselves with other minorities like Mexicans and, as a consequence, ignore the needs of their own people. This, together with the gutting of our industries by tax and spend betrayers of America, has helped to lead to low-wage-slaves, particularly young people, black and white.

When you lump the likes of a Rangel, Brown and Dinkins you begin to get the picture, quote: "Blacks have been hurt since Emancipation, politically and economically, by various waves of immigration...but black members of Congress identify with members of the smaller and more newly arrived Hispanic Caucus, rather than with the black working poor in their own districts." It's like the attitude I discovered among minority teachers and administrators while teaching in Watts and East San Jose: "To hell with them (their own people), I got mine!"

The lengthy article from which I quoted pointed out the obvious fact that cities are hurting badly from immigration, a point I have long tried to get legislators to face. When aliens will work for minimum wage or less and you can't possibly take care of a family on that, such "workers" doom citizens from improving their own financial status. This has become an issue, finally, not because legislators give a damn about the poor sheep in the inner cities but because of the professional aliens who are coming in and taking $50,000 jobs away from citizens by working for $35,000. It is that professional, invariably well educated, who has lost such a job to an alien that gets the ear of Caesar.

I have been making the rounds of the bars. This, together with trying to deal with the plight of the homeless young people in our area, led to my involvement with people like Rosie. Most of the bartenders know I am writing about life in the bars, welfare, the homeless and "rejects," that I am not a "drinker" and, as a consequence, usually draw a cup of coffee when they see me come in. Seems it is not that unusual to find people who come into the bars just for coffee. Many of such simply come for something to do or to dispel the loneliness of their lives and find some friendliness and companionship. I could well, often, include myself in that category.

Having just re-read my opening comment in this connection, it is surprising that I am still blessed with a few good friends who are outstanding Christians. I know, however, that I am often a trial to them and wish it were otherwise. But they still love me warts and all and still credit me with a living relationship with The Lord. For this I am most grateful. It would be a far lonelier task without their love and friendship. To their surprise, however, they will hear comments from their own pastors in sermons that have been taken from my writing. Of course, the pastors don't acknowledge even reading anything I write, let alone, knowing me or knowing of me. A few "blue noses" even object to one of my publications being named "Christian Perspective." Oh, well. I don't hold this against them, I thoroughly understand.

In conversation with one of my closest friends recently, he expressed the thought that I had a poetic appreciation of Creation, Nature and people that he lacked. He didn't say this in envy; he was well satisfied with his own gifts. And it wasn't that he lacked such appreciation, it just didn't take the turn in him that it did in me.

But, as I pointed out to him, he has been abundantly blessed with a loving and faithful wife, obedient children in whom he could take justifiable pride and a host of other things that brought him real joy and happiness. It was that point upon which the conversation turned. Real joy and happiness are no longer a part of my own experience. However, unlike my friend who had family from which these things, largely, derive, I had known such things and had a full appreciation of the loss of such whereas he hadn't had to suffer the grief and tragedy of their being violently wrenched from him. As a consequence, while I may be gifted with the poetic appreciation of Nature, of people and Creation, the ability to articulate this is lessened considerably by the betrayal of love, fidelity and commitment; As Thoreau so well pointed out: "What is Nature to me if I have no one with whom to share it?"

As a result, I am well suited to campaign against the evils that decimated my family, of the evils of Caesar and his Gestapo, of the evils which betray and rob our young people of a future, the evil system that is attempting to throw us into anarchy or slavery. Oh, but how much rather do the work of the Poet, the "Maker," for which my own heart longs, to string words like pearls and hang such a precious necklace around the ivory throat and upon the alabaster breast of my own heart's desire! But where the faithful and inspiring spirit worthy such adornment? That, for now at least, is denied me. And later? Foolish; for a man "lacking common sense and practicality" to quote an ex-wife, for a man who still thinks giving a rose to a woman says she is special to him, a man to whom a kiss and a touch are promises not lightly made but made in tender good faith and to be kept? Oh well, to continue, not because my heart of hearts is in it but because it's a job that still needs to be done and I have enough heart, at least, to do at least this much.

Before I go on, I want to make it clear once more, I am not a drinker. As I have said, I can make the lightest draft that still qualifies as beer last an hour. Very seldom do I have anything more than my "staff of life," coffee. I don't say this with pride because I have been fortunate to have been raised by grandparents who never drank and I don't have the necessary "gene" of the alcoholic. Thanks to a number of other factors, especially the place The Lord and His Word holds in my life, I even lack the "personality profile" of such addiction. It is not flattering to me, as a consequence, that I have never been hooked on the stuff, circumstances of birth and family have prevented it; not something to boast of as some accomplishment on my part.

As with profanity, alcohol was never used by my grandparents. My grandad, the idol of my childhood, was never seen to take a drink or utter an expletive. My brother and I, accordingly, were raised with a morality that precluded vulgar language or drinking. This has been one of the great blessings of my life; now, on to the sordid business of my "bar-hopping."

When a bar is crowded, the bartender really earns his or her keep. I have felt tired just watching them do their job. They also have to keep an eye on people who are likely to become boisterous after "one too many." I am especially in sympathy with the women bartenders.

I have said to some of these that theirs has to be the more difficult task since, if they are attractive, especially, they become targets for men "hitting on them." They have to walk a thin line of friendliness and aloofness so as not to encourage some man's advances. I do wonder why a woman would want the job but it often comes down to the circumstances in which they have found themselves and "one thing leads to another."

Bar life is different at different times of the day and night. There are the "regulars," some of these can warm a stool for hours and drink till you would swear they should be falling off their perch. The time of day is of no consequence to many of these. But there is a difference in the night crowd, it is usually more boisterous and the liquid camaraderie can be punctuated by acrimony, even physical violence. This, in most cases, is, not surprisingly, over women.

Since the drinking woman knows she is the object of male attention, it can become a "sticky wicket" at times. For example, I was recently drawn into a "quadrangle" with an onerous conclusion.

The lady was young and attractive but liked her liquor. We were having an amiable conversation when a much older woman came in. The young lady knew her and invited her to join us. Both of the women were interested in my being a writer and enjoyed learning about such a life. Then "trouble" came by in the form of a man who used to be a "friend" of the girl.

She suggested we go to another bar. The friend followed. As the hour grew late, the girl was becoming some agitated about where the evening was headed. As an observer, I had some question about the same thing. The old lady was having a good time and had taken on enough of a "load" that she didn't notice the problem between the girl and her unwanted ex-friend whose advances were unmistakable and becoming more objectionable with each drink consumed.

It was worked out by the old lady suggesting going to her place. The girl "suggested" that the unwanted suitor follow with me in my car. This brings up one of the problems men like this commonly have; he didn't have a car or he was on probation with a DUI and couldn't legally drive. I find, many times, women driving men around as a consequence. Some of the men in this category even resort to using bicycles. This being a relatively small area, the local cops know who can drive legally and who can't. One of the advantages of small town living.

In any event, he didn't have a car and the arrangement was made. Going out to the vehicles, the girl whispered to me, "Please don't follow us, please try to 'lose' us and I'll call you tomorrow morning!" This put me in a somewhat vulnerable position but the unwanted man was drunk enough by now that I was able to accomplish the request with only minor difficulty. He was incensed by my "inability" to follow the women but, after much cursing, agreed to let me take him home where I left him and, with relief, headed back to my place.

Of course, I never heard from the young lady, which was just as well since I learned later that she was in and out of re-hab and often got onto a drug kick. And, having learned something of such "bar etiquette," if I run into her again, nothing will be said of the whole incident. And, as I have assured a number of people, what I hear in a bar, I leave in the bar. I never betray a confidence, not even one given in a state of inebriation, I might say, especially one given in such circumstances.

Much of the writing I do about such things is a "composite," stories that mix the characters and the stories in order to give a fuller picture of the things I see and hear and to protect people by keeping them from being identified. Further, I seldom name the place in such writing and never if the events are unflattering.

For example, last night I was in one of the better bars, friendly, relaxed atmosphere with many "regulars." A young, attractive woman was obviously in distress. She had been crying and talking to one of the older men who was a regular. After some time, she left and I wandered over to the old man who had come to know me as "Bodfish."

He shared the tragedy with me. The young lady had a little girl. The child had been born a "drug baby" because of the young mother's addiction. CPS had just recently removed the child because of the mother's "falling off the wagon." The woman loved the child dearly and was broken up over the loss of her little girl. She didn't know if she would be able to get her back.

As is too often the case, there was no man in the picture except the drunken bums who leech off such women and contribute to their "fallen" condition. I haven't met one in a bar yet who wasn't on the make. Such men don't frequent a bar to have friendly, civilized conversation with pretty women. The genuine loneliness of many of the men and women is of course, a too-often, legitimate reason for "cruising" and drinking. But, let's face it, the entertainment and attraction of the bars isn't in watching the interminable games of pool and stimulating conversation about the latest book read.

Another part of the tragedy is the large amount of money spent by those who can't really afford it on the California Lottery. The machines are kept busy and there are few winners. Between the constant flow of liquor and the gambling, many are bust by the time they leave.

Well, as I said, this night I was in one of the more relaxed bars; many regulars and the music was good, mellow Western mixed with soft Rock and an occasional early 60s tune. I reflected on the fact that as more liquor is consumed, the women get prettier and the men get handsomer. As a result, one woman confided that it wasn't so bad when she got a man home with her; she hated waking up and having the problem of getting rid of him in the morning. I suppose it works both ways but, as usual, women have the greater trouble.

Sitting there, sober as a judge (can't understand the origin of that oxymoron), has its drawbacks. Observing, stone sober, has its difficulties. Certainly a clear mind is necessary in order to recall, later, the conversations, the atmosphere, the action, and be able to write about it all. Getting drunk or even a buzz is not conducive to remembering essential detail. And, let's face it folks, getting falling down drunk is in very poor taste to say the least.

But sobriety under such circumstances does, I believe, cheat one of the total experience of the bars. Also, there is the inclination to be a "joiner" rather than sitting apart. I am, by proclivity, a loner, a man for whom a large degree of solitude is essential. But there is the, at times, overweening loneliness with which one, even someone with as solitary disposition as myself, has to contend. I freely admit to many of the common frailties of the human condition among which I suffer loneliness like any normal person.

Still, I consider it better that I don't drink and risk, perhaps, to that extent, defrauding myself of the total experience in the hope that the results will be of better and more lasting value to others. But it's still hard to be the round peg in a square hole. Oh, well.

My openly declaring my intentions, of writing about life in the bars, has led, understandably, to having to overcome some of the normal suspicions of bartenders. I'm not always successful, again, understandably, in doing so. But, in most of the cases, I have found the bartenders to be interested and friendly and willing to take me at face value; far more so, in fact, than in many of my dealings with more "proper," conservative individuals such as preachers and politicians.

The bartender this night was a particularly attractive and personable young woman. And what a worker! She was constantly on the move, mixing drinks, putting tickets into the infernal gambling machine, collecting money and making change, answering the telephone, cleaning, all this while maintaining the proper degree of attentive listening to the more loquacious patrons, the give-and-take of the business. It made me tired just watching her work. And, I understand, some of these folks put in twelve-hour shifts!

Since the early morning hours are the best time for me to write, it is important to get a night's rest. As a consequence, I don't stay out late. This night was the exception; I "closed" the bar, staying until 2 a.m. This did provide essential information in what was involved with closing up shop. Also, it gave me a view of the changing atmosphere among the patrons as the hour grew later and later.

The lady bartender was extraordinarily kind in taking the time to talk with me, the number of people in the bar being few this late and the pace somewhat slackened. I tried to be careful of not intruding into her time from her duties and was grateful for the chance to hear some of the human elements of the business from the other side of the bar.

A great deal has been written about bars, taverns and those that patronize them and work in them. It isn't my purpose to attempt anything original in adding to the body of knowledge in this respect. The "originality" of my reporting lay in the Christian view of such. This, in itself, is unique since most Christians, naturally, aren't going to be visiting the gin mills, and for good reason I add. Admittedly, most Christians will be aghast, understandably, at my doing so. My only defense of my actions is the same that led me to be the houseguest of the Imperial Wizard of the KKK and a guest at the Main Compound of the Aryan Nations in Idaho and other such adventures.

The work I am doing in building a database in my academic specialty, "The Psychological Basis of Human Behavior," demands as much factual input as possible. The search for truth in the human condition admits of no restrictive boundaries. And, in spite of media distortions, popular misconceptions, even ignorance and prejudice among those who should certainly know better, i.e., my "educated and erudite colleagues" etc., people are people regardless their personal belief systems or mode of lifestyle. As such, they have their side of the story and deserve, in some cases, need, to be heard; especially by an objective, academically and professionally qualified, Christian observer.

As a Christian, and one with nothing to lose, it is a self-imposed responsibility to give a voice of understanding to those who too often are ignored and even, tragically, despised, by the Christian Community and churches in general. Such an attitude does nothing for them in extending their own "data base" of understanding or compassion.

Having a pretty fair degree of knowing what I am doing (after all, I'm a big boy now) I take criticism with as much equanimity as possible. I know that I will suffer many slings and arrows for my actions. But it is well known that I don't play to the applause of the crowd. I am, as a consequence, very surprised that out of the thousands of people who read my writings in one form or another that I don't get more hate mail, especially from "conservatives!"

I know that in most cases, the lack of such response is due to my patently transparent views, to the fact that I have nothing to hide, my life is an "open book," and avoid attacking people simply because they disagree with my opinions or conclusions. Because of this, many powerful people in various organizations, in government, business and education depend on me for, at least, an open and honest discussion of subjects in which they have a vested interest.

Many of these will never have the experience of gaining insights from the "Rosies," certainly preachers can't afford to be seen entering gin mills, a state Governor can't be seen with Richard Butler. But the "movers and shakers" still need reliable information and insight rather than media distortion or paid pimps in order to act with all due humanity toward others. If this were being done as it should, there wouldn't be the murders of innocent people like Vicki and Sam Weaver, the necessity of Ellie Nesler having to do what elected representation and the courts are responsible for or the mindless, cruel insanity of Waco.

Leaders in our nation are not likely to give voice to things like the Ann Frank or holocaust hoax; the secret machinations of Freemasonry, but John Baumgardner can and does. Are leaders even aware of the massive amount of patriotic literature that is addressing the evils of Empire Beyond Reason? Do leaders need the input from people like John and me? Indeed they do!

I have just finished filling out the most recent survey from American Conservative Union headed by Senator Bob Dole. Now I know that neither Bob nor those he represents are as naive as the survey questions would suggest. But they are the typical questions of those who think (or pretend so) the situation in our nation can be solved by conducting "business as usual" and "What you don't say, you don't have to explain," the unique purview of preachers and politicians.

Another "survey" arrived from The Heritage Foundation; equally disappointing in evading the real problems and hard choices. And while Felten's book, "The Ruling Class," serves a useful purpose, the real problems, again, go begging and Felten's "Eleven Points" don't come close to addressing them. Yet they want me to be a part of The Republican Commission on the American Agenda. I don't think so. Gary North comes closer to the problem by pointing out George Washington's Masonic worship.

For example, politics as usual doesn't distinguish, doesn't discriminate when it comes to the really vital issues that they, liberal and conservative, Republican and Democrat, continue to avoid. Franklin, Adams, Jefferson were "Elitists" and "Racists!" They were also men of uncommon valor and integrity, Statesmen! Who in the political arena today would have the unabashed ego to compare themselves to such men? Who would even dare to do so? Not without a great deal of "qualifying" the comparison!

Now, Senators "debate" homosexuality. Real leaders, Statesmen, would never do this; there would be no need. Strom Thurmond and Jesse Helms are derided for speaking out against perversion. At the same time, a paroled pervert, one Conrad Jeffery in New Jersey, while out on parole, is caught in the very act, bloody-handed, of having tortured and murdered a little seven-year-old girl. If Caesar and his minions had done their job instead of debating the "rights" of satanic creatures like Jeffery, this little girl would never have met such a mutilated and tortured death at the hands of such a creature! Is there a "real man" out there within the judicial framework who will do to this monster what Ellie Nesler was forced to do to the one who attacked her and her son? Both of these monsters were on "probation" at the time of their depredations. What does this tell all normal, thinking people about the "system?" Where is the protection for the innocent children like this little girl from such monsters? Why of course! In our perverted Congress and perverted courts!

Clinton wants the pervert and pervert loving Roberta Achtenberg, as a deputy at the Department of Housing and Urban Development. He wants perverts in the military and as leaders in government. At the same time his allies in Congress, idiots like John Kerry, thinks sodomy is perfectly all right in the military, especially, as he says, some Congressmen engage in this bestial practice anyhow! And he is right in the accusation. There are perverts in the highest offices of the land. And God isn't going to judge this nation for this? That little girl's blood, along with that of countless others, cries out for God's judgment against such vile wickedness! Before I am taken to task by the reader for my "Jeremiad" against Caesar and his agents, I want you to bear with me while I lead you in a somewhat convoluted path in attempting to give a rationale for such.

My readers of long-standing know of my fascination for the hard sciences, mathematics, physics, astronomy, and biology. They understand the poet may also be a scientist. As a consequence, I often use the same spirit of inquiry in attempting to reach conclusions that have scientific merit, even in my philosophical writings.

Wisdom should, in fact, does, lead to understanding. The latest studies in Chaos and Randomness, which I have written about, offer a great deal of hope in building my database in Human Behavior. For example, and to make it plain: If A = a red marble, B = a blue and C = a green and they are all of the same size and composition we can say, within the parameter of "Marbles" that they are "equal" to one another. Thus, if A = B and B = C then C is equal to A. In sum, they are equal to one another. Any differentiation would be in the color. In the case of color, they are not equal except on the basis that each has the quality of "color."

But, regardless of the appearance of "sameness" in size, should their absolute size and weight be carried to molecular extremes in weight and measurement, differences would exist. In short, "equality" is defined within very limited parameters and your definition of such equality would have to have explicit criteria of definition.

Another point, if the red marble is cut into quarter portions, the four parts would still be equal to the blue and the green by one definition. But, obviously, it would lose its "equality" as a marble. Seldom if ever do we find such ruthless honesty of criteria in those that purport to speak to those issues that dominate our lives. So it is that so-called "Conservativism" refuses to define the actual criteria and the result is an unworkable equation: much like that which attempts to define the proper roles and relationships of men and women.

In the spiritual realm, portraying Jesus Christ as "religious," an icon of superstitious nonsense rather than his true humanity which answers to our needs, the churches have failed in their primary function to reach out to those to whom he is supposed to be The Answer.

(I know I make demands on my readers due to the length of my essays and, in some cases, their requiring that stream of consciousness without which complex material appears to lose direction and cohesiveness. I don't apologize for this as I want the reader to practice some degree of self-discipline in acquiring information beyond the usual format of "mindlessness" i.e. TV. Just recently, in Roubaix, France, police found a fully dressed skeleton of a man in front of his TV that was still on. I leave the reader to any conclusions that might be drawn, my own mind reels. In other words, it's good for people to have to pay attention to what they are reading once in a while.

I have witnessed another part of the "equation." Many of the young men who come by my place have no car. You'll remember my "brokering" transportation for the ex-Utah Highway Patrolman in my last essay; a typical case. The kid gets to drinking and destroys his car. He lacks a job that will pay for transportation. His "girlfriend" got the car. He had a car but... fill in the blank with every conceivable story imaginable. The bottom line: He doesn't have a car.

Another part of the equation: The girl has a car and allows these bums, leeches, deadbeats, use her for transportation. Typical case of a young girl: The parents helped her to buy or provided her a car. Dads, especially, are vulnerable to providing cars for their "little angels." However, it was never the intention of Dad that providing for his little girl would also make it possible for these deadbeats to sponge off his largess and his daughter's vulnerability to these snot-nosed kids who, typically, are only out for fun, drinking or taking advantage of the girl. And why don't the girls learn to discriminate?

It is, therefore, no wonder that the Jennifer Syndrome is in full flower in our generation, the seeking of older men by younger and younger women. I've had girls as young as seventeen "hit" on me and those in their twenties are commonplace.

Now rather than cave in to the flattering of the male ego (See, the old man hasn't lost it!) that feeds on such attention, I observe the tragedy in such cases. Naturally older men want to believe, ever as much or more than women, that they still "Have It!" But there is an old saying: There's no fool like an old fool! And I would rather eat dirt than ever fall heir to such foolishness. If I have any degree of fleshly pride to contend with, this more than any attention I get from a young woman, outweighs such. And what man in his right mind wants an Amy Fisher in the equation?

This does not, however, blind me to that part of the equation which has led to younger women, even girls, seeking the stability and responsibility which is, more and more, the purview of older men as opposed to those which lead young women such as my own daughter to saying they can't find worthwhile men in their own age group. At least, in this instance, the native cunning and pragmatic mind-set of the female psyche serves them well.

Speaking for the "older men," Mitchell Parish is dead at 92. If you have to ask: "Who was he?" you have the gist of the problem. As I sat next to a really interesting guy in one of the bars the other night, I was delighted to learn he had played trumpet with many of the Big Bands. We bemoaned the loss of "Artists" with the advent of mechanically, canned "music" through synthesizers, mixers, etc. This reminded me of the loss of teaching spelling and arithmetic in our schools; but these, as with true artistry require a high degree of self-discipline; something becoming ever scarcer in our modern culture.

As our ears were assaulted, our senses blasted by the noise from the jukebox, we agreed the younger generation had lost a lot with the disappearance of the music with which we grew up, and I could weep for the loss. Parish, by the way, was the lyricist for such songs as Star Dust, Sweet Lorraine, Deep Purple, Moonlight Serenade and many others.

I made the point that our society had become callous to real love and romance therefore the noise that passes, in too many cases, for "music" today is just that; noise. Young people have had to accept this counterfeit since they truly did not understand, could not conceive of, the era which this fellow and I had experienced. I don't have to match the age of the fellow at the bar; I have my mother to thank for my knowledge and appreciation of such music as she had those popular tunes like those of Parish's playing constantly when I was a child. As a professional musician myself (clarinet and tenor sax), "Ballroom" music was my especial forte.

In other words, a young woman who might catch my fancy would have to contend with the difference in our tastes in music and many other things. I often add this sequitur: *Schonheit vergeht, Tugend besteht*! (Beauty fades; virtue remains). As I have said, women may love poetry but I haven't found one yet who could abide living with the poet. I know, in my bones, she is out there somewhere; I just haven't found her yet; incurably romantic.

The lyrics of bar-talk concerning men and women play familiarly: Women/ Men are no damned good! The lyrics are, of course, supplied the necessary gender-related coefficient.

"93% of the people in here are stone losers! They all think they're having fun but it's just a bunch of losers sharing their misery."

"A man would have to be out of his mind dating one of them!" A reference to women bartenders; this may be more a comment on the men making such statements than the object of their scorn. Did the lady turn them down for a date or otherwise injure the male ego? And, as I have observed, women bartenders can't help but have a jaundiced opinion of most of the men they have to deal with in such an environment.

There are men and women who come to the bar to escape. They may be escaping from a husband/wife, boyfriend/girlfriend, they may be escaping the loneliness of a drear existence for a time, they may be "on the make" and hoping to "get lucky," they may simply be looking for some friendliness in a too-often unfriendly world. Alcohol does, at least, lower the barriers of inhibition where people are more likely to be open and honest about their inner thoughts and behavior. This doesn't make them "losers" in my opinion.

As to the loss of inhibitions brought on by alcohol, this is a two-edged sword. It's good to "let go" on occasion as long as it can be kept within somewhat reasonable bounds. There is the problem of the hugging and kissing, the touching that goes with the abandoning of sensibility. Too much of this evidences a lack of the person's own self-esteem, a sense of their personal value as a human being. Men, most certainly, try to take advantage under these circumstances. Women, on the other hand, learn early to "Promise them anything and give them nothing," to use their sex to lead men on to their own predisposed foolishness and naiveté and consequent disgust with women.

But we have to face the fact that there is too little hugging in our lives. Everyone needs a hug now and then and if it takes a couple of drinks to get that hug then, so be it. I certainly won't find fault on that score. It's when the hug becomes an inebriated embrace and kiss that too often leads to trouble. It is part of the human tragedy that many people can only find such a need met through a glass or bottle.

I'm sure there will be more on this theme but with summer coming on apace there is much to do and my schedule will preclude frequenting the taverns. I can't say I'm sorry. It has been a necessary effort but in most cases it has been depressing and a labor for which there is little reward in such effort.

I apologize to my readers for digressing a moment before I go on. The foregoing subject matter makes this personal digression necessary. And while the following will be enigmatic to most, the person addressed and I both feel there is something of value in its being shared:

Dear P.M.

As a result of the "research" in the bars, the "Rosies" and her daughters and so many others, a life lived too long already and too long in proximity with such others, I'm not sleeping well lately. There lurks in the shadowed corners of all of our minds those "things" which tear at the fabric of sleep and keep us, at times, mindful of the fact that there are legitimate fears that carry over from the childhood monsters, that, then, could often be dispelled by the soothing and comforting words of assurance of those who could be counted on in their love and faithfulness to secure us from every imaginable evil; if we were fortunate as children.

Now the man who has surely lived too long turns in his lonely and narrow bed, fighting, what? Most assuredly the monsters are there. He doesn't fear them because his life is already forfeit to a cause and no one like you belongs in that arena. No future for you in that. He grieves for what they are doing to the sheep. And to paraphrase you, dear heart, dear little one: "Where's the Shepherd!" A real man can't let that challenge pass. I plead your understanding and compassion in that. You know the music is still alive and well in my own heart and soul and I have not yet betrayed the best of the child within myself nor is it likely I will ever in spite of those who bid ever higher for my doing so.

And where will this final act for which you expressed fear for me find itself playing; in Romeo and Juliet, in the purest, blood-burst ocean sunset of you and that tragic boy or in The Killers and the foul, dirt trenches of anarchy and betrayal? Besides, to anticipate you, my thoughts are not your thoughts and my ways are not your ways. And that is not to be distorted or twisted in a vain attempt by our enemies to make it demean, patronize or condescend. I know you must know me well enough to not give that a passing thought. You know I could never entertain such thoughts toward you. Don't let our enemies get away with this evil construction. I am what I am just as you are what you are. No more, no less, and that is sufficient for both of us. So much depends on how you see me in this light and whether the melody of "Yesterdays" still haunts you as me. Whether or not, I depend on your prayers and you surely know you are in mine. Ever; to each his one and only you with all my love that belongs to you and can be given without harm to you, Don.

Pity poor Dr. Heath, he's "lost it." Much learning doth make thee mad! On the contrary, gentle reader, such a fine madness is something that all of us "madmen" cherish, it's a "gift!" The snakes that hazard our path through life are often only seen through the eyes of such madmen. And, too, such "sight" brings into proper focus the value of others and the promise of the stars.

The encouragement of the more poetic of my readers sometimes leads me to a license of seeming whimsy (my thoroughly impractical bent) but I enjoy a large degree of forgiveness of such among the more pragmatic brethren. They acknowledge the fact that I am capable of making sense now and then. And even those given to empirical excesses in their own lives need to engage their imaginations on occasion.

You see a lot of misery in the taverns, you see a lot to pity as well. But in my wanderings in bars, in the inner city ghettos and barrios, in all those places where grief and tragedy, hopelessness, find their proper harbors, none of this matches the pity I have for those who can't hear the music, for those to whom the poetry of life and living has passed them by. I pity those who have no knowledge or concern for the scribes of heaven and those treasures, new and old, which make it all worth while. And, tragically, many of such people are in the churches and the pulpits of America.

My pity for the wealthy and powerful that haven't any idea of what I am talking about, of what they are missing by not entering into the suffering of common humanity is just that, pity, never scorn. I scorn those who choose to be ignorant of what life is all about and sell their souls for the shabby and tawdry brass of counterfeit love and often at such a bargain price it isn't even a question of having the fare for the ride to perdition. I especially have scorn and loathing for those in positions of leadership, those false shepherds, who assume the mantle of "caring" and betray the trust of the sheep. If there is to be a new "Lexington" in the future of people like myself, it will be in confrontation to such betrayers of our nation and our children.

While I agree with my old friend who recently wrote about the need to go on the offensive in charitable works, I know he misses the point when he minimizes the impact of the verbal offensive, particularly the impact of the written offensive; particularly so since he publishes so many books himself. Without the Tom Paines, without the literature of confrontation with Caesar, a successful campaign cannot be waged. I think he should accept the criticism of others and me to avoid verbosity and engage the enemy with the needed candor and resources that I know he possesses.

If my own message is to penetrate skepticism, if it is to give hope to the hopeless, it will only do so with the utmost honesty and integrity. So it is that, many times, I wind up offending the sensibilities of many groups, many individuals, who would rather I confine my writing to strictly political philosophy rather than the issues of the ordinary, everyday lives of the masses who do, indeed, live lives of quiet desperation. And I remind my critics, in the words: "Even a tailor deserves a little happiness!"

If, in the process, I don't seem, to some of my friends, to pay enough attention to Ray Sutton's work in Covenant Renewal, his new responsibilities at Philadelphia Theological Seminary and his studies at Oxford, I can only plead the difference in our peculiar ministries. But I will order that 1993 U.S. Senate Calendar, the one featuring the prominent date of September 18, 1793 when George Washington deposited the plate and laid the cornerstone, replete with Corn, Wine and Oil, of the United States Capitol in a Masonic ceremony.

I recommend "Biblical Horizons," P.O. Box 1096, Niceville, FA 32588-1096, to my readers. You can order for a donation in any amount. I especially enjoyed Dr. Bruce Edwards' (Associate Professor of English at Bowling Green State University) account of the writings of Flannery O'Connor and Walker Percy. These writers are too-little known and Dr. Edwards renders a valuable service in critiquing such.

You probably don't know that if you leave your pet goldfish unattended in England, you can be fined and go to jail! N.R. 5/10/93. We in this country don't have a corner on the insanity of our laws.

In the near future, if my old friend, V.B. follows through, I hope to have manuscript in hand for a fascinating, first person narrative concerning events that led to the arrest of Manson and his followers. He was there and the story deserves to be told. The part of a "Fish Cop" being in on the bust is particularly fascinating.

The warm weather has finally arrived. It broke 100 in Bakersfield yesterday. The Desert Rat in me responds favorably to such temperatures.

To those friends who have asked if I will I be able to mount a campaign for State Superintendent of Instruction in California the answer is: Doubtful.

Will the state find someone capable of addressing the needs of our children and young people; equally doubtful. Too many snakes need killing; too many sacred cows need slaughtering for this to happen. Will the answers come through the elective process? As my good friend the Senator said: "Not in 200 years!" But we don't have 200 years for answers.

But I don't agree with my friend in Tyler that the answer is in abolishing the schools. Old buddy, you didn't think that one through.

Till next time.

Christian Perspective

June: Part 2

Proverbs 23:29-35

POETRY

Well, it seems I have been hitting some nerves lately in my last couple of issues of CP that leads me to some further explanation of my activities of the past month or so, particularly in regards to "pub-crawling" and the subject of poetry. I will attempt to relate the two and, in the process, hopefully give the reader something new to think about.

After the printing of publications like CP and before the mailing to subscribers, I always grab a few for personal distribution. In my travels, I am always meeting new people and, occasionally, I give them a copy in the hope that I will make new friends and get additional feedback from the subjects covered. This has resulted in some very sensitive and valuable input from virtual strangers.

In making the rounds of the bars, I have distributed some of the essays to a few of the bartenders with interesting results. These people, being in a profession where they often encounter the human condition in some of its rawest aspects, have insights that preachers could do well in possessing. I also feel an obligation to share my thoughts with those I write about. In the case of life in the bars, the bartenders are the experts, not me.

I thoroughly enjoy wandering through a volume of some of the esoterica of theoretical physics or astronomy; Stephen Hawking is more my meat than Stephen King. At some future date (warning you in advance) I'm sure to take off on a journey into Werner Heisenberg's Uncertainty Principle, taking it from its application to atomic structure and making application to Human Behavior. Fascinating stuff!

This statement to open the subject of poetry is sure to reinforce the opinion of some that I am simply weird or, at worst, dangerous and should be kept away from sharp instruments. In my defense I would call your attention to the fact that life itself has its own "Uncertainty Principle" and in nothing else is this expressed so well as in poetry. The problem is defining "poetry" to a society and culture that has little time or inclination for it. It is my hope that the following attempt at definition will shed new light on the subject and make it, once more, relevant.

First, I want to make it clear that I do not perceive myself as the O'Henry or Eugene O'Neill of bar nightlife. There is, indeed, a broken heart for every light on Broadway but until The Lord provides the inspiration for the healing words I seek, I don't flatter myself that I can give much voice to such. Further, much as I admire his genius, do not try to paint me with F. Scott Fitzgerald's brush; I'm not seeking Daisy but that one, special "bird with the broken wing," and one that won't fly away once healed.

I want to cover some sensitive material in this issue of CP. Before I do, I need to acquaint you with something that may be apparent concerning the last, few issues.

Several people have called my writing "poetry," especially when I treat of subjects like Fathers and Daughters and my view of God's Creation. Rather than disabuse those who make this comment, I have attempted an explanation of what poetry really is. Some of you are aware that the earliest historians were, in fact, what we commonly call poets. This is the reason that so much of ancient, historical writing reads like poetry: poets wrote it. Much of the Bible falls into this category. The lyrical cadences of ancient languages, of Old English, were produced by poet/historians.

The word Poet means "Maker." Those ancient raconteurs and scribes "made" the stories, the histories, of their peoples. Much as the Indian in this country who would recount exploits by "theater," the poets of ancient times would embellish, not to lie, but to make something, some event or person or persons memorable. As a result, much of such history is "interpretive."

As I made my way through my undergraduate years as a Litt. Major I was entranced by the mechanisms of poetry, the cadent language, the emotional, and, yes, the intellectual, imagery and the thoughts expressed so vividly through the magic of words. Perhaps most young men are poets at heart, I certainly was. There is something in the young man that wants to glorify the ideals of love and romance, of the beauty of nature in expressive language. Not the least of such motivation has, historically, been to convey the message of love to the object of that affection. Much of it has been with the intent of making ordinary things extraordinary.

But what of women poets; most of them, understandably, express these heart's longings and ideals in a somewhat different manner. There is the same longing for love and understanding, to communicate, but the language and sentiment takes a somewhat different route in arriving at a similar conclusion; and the difference is fascinating to a man like me.

I remind my readers of the comment that the magic age of the great musicals of the theater like Showboat and Oklahoma was that time "When Poets last worked" in our nation. And I would remind the reader that the "poets," the lyricists involved were virtually all men. I will pursue this incongruity later.

But I will say at this time, I believe the distinction involves the fact that God made the woman to be the inspiration, the poetry of the man and this leads to those softer and gentler elements in the man that a woman responds to. However, adultery, easy divorces and "sleeping around," passing themselves from one man to another, hardly commends any woman to those finer sensibilities. And those men who enter this same arena are hardly to be expected to "hear the music or the lyrics." Such men betray the best of the child within themselves; they do not become "poets."

Recently, I was visiting some friends in So-Cal and got into this discussion with them. When I began to speak of what a woman should be to a man, my friend's wife turned to him and said: "Are you listening to what Don is saying?" Turning to me she said: "Tell him more!" Now I have known these folks for almost twenty years. But I never expected my old buddy to find himself on the hot seat because of my sharing my thoughts about the inspiration and poetry a woman should be to a man. He was actually squirming. He had, in fact, taken a good and faithful wife much for granted and he knew it! Fortunately, we're still friends. My old buddy is a good man and knew my words were for his benefit as much as for his wife's.

When a lady bartender recently asked me why I was writing about the bars I told her: "I write about things that interest me. If something interests me, I know it will be of interest to others as well." Also, as with legitimate history, my writing has to be of primary source material, not secondary, to have the needed relevance wherever and whenever possible.

But what I didn't tell the lady was that I am in the process of re-defining Poetry! That sounds pompous on the very face of it. It would be, perhaps, more accurate to say that I am in the process of taking poetry back to its essential purpose of "making" by telling stories in a way that interests people, that makes the events and persons, nature itself, memorable.

A friend of many years wrote me some time back: "I am the leader of a theological movement." The Lord knows he is publishing enough material and books to substantiate his claim! I would not, though, like my old friend, ever want to give the impression that I am attempting to be a "leader" in the sense of bringing poetry, once more, into its honored, historical position of prominence by what I am doing. I do want to give my readers and others a chance to evaluate my claim for the need to do so and to explain the course my own writing has taken over the past couple of years. It will be the readers of my own writings who will either vindicate or condemn my position in this regard.

In my defense I need to point out what one young friend recently said of one of my recent essays: "My total impression was one of love for people." I couldn't ask for more humbling or higher commendation and justification for my argument.

Prose, long ago, became the accepted form of transition between what poetry had become and writing. But people have always, in spite of academic distinctions, seemed to sense that poetry was the mechanism of the heart and mind, the emotions and the intellect. Realizing this, there is often earned resentment toward those strictly enforced, formal, academic definitions of "proper" poetic expression.

In general, ordinary people, as opposed to the academics, seem to have the better sense of what the structure of poetry should be. This may be a part of primeval memory, I don't know. I know this, for centuries too many of those who became known as poets hid behind their verse, even, in some cases, purposely becoming abstruse in order to display their cleverness and, as a consequence, betrayed the purpose of their genius and calling (Not unlike theologians: "Found in a biography of St. Teresa of Avila: 'She tried to convert the theologians to prayer, but with little success.'" N.R. 5/24/93).

This is not a blanket condemnation of the use of verse to hide its author while giving vent to his feelings. The anonymity of the writer is often a valid point. It is, in fact, one of the reasons for the evolution of poetry to a more mechanical form.

In trying to bring back the more ancient form of Poet/Historian/Storyteller, I run the same risk that caused such a change; the risk of exposing the writer to the ridicule of the critics and those who would belittle romance, sentimentality and altruism. This is not to ignore the fact that most readers of poetry would agree that, too often, cadenced or rhyming verse fails of its purpose and degenerates into mere doggerel or syrupy nonsense. But in its legitimate form and subject matter, the great poets of recent history did much to justify what later degenerated into a deadly, merely academic form where "approved" structure took precedence over the subject matter and the sentiments expressed.

"The Face On The Barroom Floor" would not be considered good poetry. However, it is enjoyable reading and I think that is its justification; but "Richard Cory"? When this man who has everything (he even "glittered when he walked") that we consider essential to the "good life," Went home and put a bullet through his head, the verse gives import to the whole theme which would most certainly be lost in the mere recounting of the person and events.

So it is that I try to make people and things, events, memorable, even enjoyable to read about whenever possible. And, when I become somewhat lyrical, even rhapsodize or engage in whimsy or emotion, and that peculiar bent departs from mere narrative, I hope the reader is moved in his or her heart and singing or weeping along with me. That, my friends, should be the definition of poetry.

Last night I was in one of the bars and, being "coffeed out," asked for a glass of soda on the rocks with a twist of lime. As I sipped this a young lady I have become acquainted with came in. Seeing me drinking what appeared to be "the real thing," she said: "Hey, Don, I see you're getting into the bar scene!" I was somewhat chagrined even though the apparent deception was done in all innocence. But I couldn't let her believe a lie; so somewhat hat-in-hand I sheepishly acknowledged the fact that it was only soda. Now on rare occasions, beside the draft, I have actually had one of my old stand-bys, a scotch and soda, gin and tonic or the rare martini (The martini is usually reserved for business or formal functions where appropriate). Not to prove anything but simply because even I can only drink so much coffee (heresy!) and I still enjoy the occasional "real thing."

Having confessed and humbly apologized for the deceptive ruse, the girl seemed actually disappointed. Perhaps, as with so many others, she felt I was missing out and wanted me to have a little fun by "letting go." If so, I am duly appreciative of her concern; in any event, my having 'fessed up, she then asked me how my writing on the subject of tavern life was going. I gave her an update that included the tragedies I was witnessing. She immediately became reflective and repeated something I pointed out in an earlier essay, the fact that many come to the bars to escape, to find some friendliness in an unfriendly world. Then she said:

"In a way, I think you are trying to escape a little too!" She couldn't have been more right though, of course, she couldn't know of the things I attempt to escape. But I feel she would understand.

She also told me she could certainly write a book about her own experiences in the bars. I agreed with her. And, while all thinking people live, to a large degree, in their heads, she realized that I was fortunate to be able to put the thoughts that often rampage through our minds into words on paper, that catharsis which most people would do well to practice whether for others to read or not.

But that cautionary word still bears repeating: be careful of what you write and with whom you share it! For example, many religious readers of the previous essays took offense at my frequenting the bars and the whole, general subject. But the more sensitive (spiritual?) have been at least forgiving if not, in fact, encouraging, respecting both my motives and the results.

I hasten to point out the fact that I have heard nothing in the bars that I haven't heard in the churches or more "respectable" environments. The only real difference is the descriptive language that often accompanies the speaker's topic (And, of course, the churches lack the ambience of tobacco and alcohol fumes). Whether it be politics, religion, philosophy, men/women relationships, the subject matter, regardless the environment in which it is discussed, has a general sameness. People are disgusted, angry and frustrated with the same things, i.e., the political leadership, the way men and women treat each other, with the failure of our courts and schools, etc.

There is a primary difference, apart from the language used, in the, for lack of a better word, honesty of the discussions in the bars as opposed to those more "respectable" environs inhabited by religious people. People in the bars are far more transparent in their feelings about things and not as guarded in trying to be something they are not (otherwise known as hypocrisy).

Granted, many, while "in their cups," are not exactly paragons of wisdom or erudition. Still, there is something to be gained in listening to even the most ignorant of such people. Granted, as well, you can't listen to a drunk try to make sense for very long, particularly if you are sober.

I have a strong tolerance for such people simply because, at heart, I am one with those whose lives may very well be described as "failures" (And, let's face it, many of these do appear in the bars). I have made the statement in the past, and I mean it: How could one man (me) have made so many mistakes in just one lifetime? It boggles my mind and, if I go "chasing rabbits," it could throw me into the deepest depression to think about it. So, sensibly, I usually don't and chase butterflies instead. Like most of you, I try to just keep on keeping on. And, like most of you, without "answers" a lot of the time.

For example, I seldom know, until I face the computer, what my general essays are going to cover. I sit down and, following that Stream of Consciousness, begin to type and one thing leads to another. Yes, there is material from my other publications that is often a subject of discussion in my general essays like CP. But, for the most part, when I begin these essays, I go with my feelings about people and events and my experiences in the everyday world with which we all have to contend, the human condition of which I am a part. It is for this reason that I refer to Thoreau as my soul brother.

A most important factor in the content of the general essays such as CP is my night-notes. No matter how tired I am when I lie down at night, I can't seem to switch off my mind. I tossed and turned the other night until 3 a.m. Perversely, some of the most essential material of a sensitive nature comes to me just when I lie down and try to go to sleep. Whether the demons or angels with which I'm surrounded at such a time, my mind is relentless in its demand that I make a note, especially when I have met another bird with a broken wing. Sometimes I'm so tired that I can't believe I'm staying awake. And I have never been able to take naps; so much for trying to sleep during the day. And when the sun comes up, I'm up; whether I got three hours sleep or eight, it doesn't matter.

In spite of the fact that I have some of my best conversations (some confuse this with "praying") with The Lord when my head hits the pillow, I am still left, too many times, chasing the elusive butterfly of sleep after particularly strenuous, emotional "blood-letting" in dealing with people and their problems.

Writers, more than other artists, live in their heads; hence my predisposition for solitude and the curse of too many sleepless nights. Writing, being such a solitary occupation, the "loner" is a most natural state for us. Not necessarily an enjoyable one, however. And I don't necessarily enjoy being known as the "quiet type" true as that is. But there really isn't anything I can do about it. I was sitting at a bar, lost in one of my usual thousand-yard stares, when the lady bartender came over and said: "Staring into space?" And I had to explain; sometimes embarrassing.

These past, few weeks have been especially brutal. With my hitting the bars at night and the usual business of the day together with the young people coming by, I feel in sympathy with those suffering CFS. The fatigue, at least in my case, certainly isn't imaginary. I get a little angry with myself because I know I do my best writing with rest and a clear mind.

Fathers and Daughters was one of the rare exceptions. That was not only severely, emotionally draining, all that led up to it, the actual writing of it, left me physically ill for over two weeks. I had, in fact, not been feeling well when I caught that segment of Life Goes On which is why I was lying down, resting and watching TV, that normally never-failing, mindless and mind-numbing analgesic of the masses.

My condition worsened considerably as the thoughts tormented and churned feverishly in my mind, the things I felt compelled to write in regard to that particular essay. I am seldom ever sick. It had been years since I had even had a cold. But this essay, written under the conditions I suffered, physically and emotionally, really depleted my strength, the re-living of some of it I wouldn't wish on an enemy! It was the one, exceptional time when I had to confront the deepest possible emotions of love in its most profound and relentlessly demanding form. It is no wonder, as I pointed out later, that the essay was "unfinished." It took all I had to give to carry it as far as I did. And, as I also pointed out later, for the first time I had to meet the putting of words on paper with real courage. Did Diana and Karen approve? That was the real, haunting, omnipresent question.

The fact is that when someone you love deeply, with all your strength, heart and soul is taken from you, a part of you dies with them. There is a part of your own heart that dies a torn and bloody death even compelling some to embrace death themselves as that dark, close friend. But, curiously, another part of your heart is enlarged as though to compensate. Call it, if you will; a greater compassion for others, a more thorough understanding and empathy with those that suffer whatever might occasion their own loss and grief in life. The ability to enter into the suffering of others grows according to your own loss and how you react to it.

I am fortunate to have the belief and assurance that I will see Diana again as well as those other loved ones who have gone on before me. This, more than any other factor dispels any dread of death. Yes, as a Christian, I also believe in the joy of being with our Lord, when every tear will be wiped away. But the sting of death is removed in the anticipation of seeing Diana and those others who love me as I love them. And I credit The Lord with that hope.

I still have Karrie, my other Little Angel, so much like her sister in so many ways. That part of sharing the love of a father and daughter, the inspiration for writing of those softer and gentler things remains. And for that I am inexpressibly grateful.

But also essential, however, though certainly not of the same magnitude to the "character" of such writing, is, as my readers know, the walks in the forest and among the rocks and pines, along the trout stream, my stargazing, reading, my travels and listening to so many people from a wide diversity of backgrounds and lifestyles; and, the memories and the music. I continue to renew my strength and cleanse my mind and soul with these things. But even in solitary activities, in my mind, my sons and daughters, those others and many more, share in this with me so it is not always as solitary as it may seem. I'm sure many of you will relate to what I am saying.

Having said all that, I hope you will forgive me if I often lead you in unexpected paths. The Pioneer and Explorer in my own personality and interests leave me no other choice at times. Like most of you, I enjoy "surprises" as long as they are of a positive nature. I like to think most of you enjoy the sense of discovery when traveling new paths where we often meet the unexpected. In most cases, I hope such things will delight, will be of interest and excite curiosity and lead to further exploration.

Thus, I don't always "plan" my excursions. The delight of discovery is in meeting unexpected things and people who add to the dimension of living. Tragically, life being the often-arbitrary thing it seems, "delight" isn't always in the cards. Sinclair Lewis and Studs Turkle would understand. As do, I'm sure, many of you.

For example, I met another lady the other night in one of the bars that said she wrote poetry and wanted me to read some of it. I told her I would be glad to and gave her my card. And, like the girl I mentioned in a previous essay, I haven't heard from her, probably for the same reason; her "lifestyle." A sheer coincidence; it wasn't long after that I met another young woman of the same name in another bar who said she wrote poetry as well.

I never give false encouragement to any writer. It is a brutally difficult field to break into, particularly in the area of poetry. We are no longer a literate nation and poetry, more than any other artistic work, is the most difficult of all in which to actually earn recognition or money. But human nature, the need to express ourselves in a form beyond the mere putting of words on paper, continues in spite of the restraining influences of materialism, hedonism, etc.

And, too, notwithstanding my earlier remarks on this theme, most people who say they write poetry don't actually know what "poetry" really is. They, too often, lack the actual, academic and disciplined skills of the craft and confuse their intentions and feelings with the art. Even given the true "gift of the muse," nothing, as I have said repeatedly, is more common than the failure of genius when faced with the necessary accommodations of the realities of hard work, self-discipline and the absolute necessity of perseverance. I have had to disabuse too many people of the notion that their work has any real, literary or commercial merit. For that reason, I am usually very cautious about agreeing to review such efforts. More than most, I am far too sensitive myself to take on the task of hurting the feelings of other, sensitive people.

I do, however, encourage everyone to keep a journal, to put his or her thoughts in writing. If they think they can write poetry, I encourage them to keep at it. But I always temper my encouragement with the brutal reality that such things are best done for the private welfare of the individual, not with a view to easy fame and fortune and I will always be utterly candid in my remarks on the merits of the person's work. I've lost, understandably, a few "friends" because of this. In the final analysis, if the person is persistent in seeking material reward for literary effort, I can't improve on the advice of Sam Clemens: "Write without pay until someone offers pay!" Now, back to the subject of the women I have been meeting who write poetry.

There is another factor. If I perceive that sensitivity in another to which I so readily respond, I can, at least, give a professional analysis of their work. I am in contact with publishers who will give them a reading and in that regard, offer them something of value to encourage them. And, at times, as my readers know, if the work has real merit, I may debut it in one in my own publications.

I have come to the conclusion that many of these women write such things as I have seen because of their own dreams and hopes for the ideals I share with them, a reaching out for understanding, some compassion in the midst of cruel circumstances and people who have treated them cruelly. These women and I have much in common. Like them, I too am looking for that "spark" which will ignite and put meaning in our lives. I definitely encourage these women to keep writing regardless any lack of literary or commercial merits of their work. We can all profit by putting our thoughts and hopes in writing. But, I always give this word of caution; be careful with whom you share your innermost feelings, hopes and dreams. "Tigers" still lurk in the shadows to devour the unwary and the admonition of not casting your pearls before swine remains a constant.

The young lady I just mentioned, while somewhat intoxicated, had caught my eye. There was a sensitivity about her to which I always seem to respond, like the moth to the flame. And, while being singed a few times, I would rather take the risk than lose that "something" that causes me, often, to tread where angels fear.

Father Flannagan said: "There is no such thing as a truly bad boy!" I take exception with the good priest. However, I say: "There is no such thing as a truly bad girl!" Now I don't think we can both be right but I would rather he was the one wrong. Fathers and Daughters, remember? In defense of my position, I hasten to add that the good priest didn't have daughters or, I'm sure, he would have revised his opinion of boys.

For example, the young lady who caught my attention, while she was "having a few," was, to me, another "bird with a broken wing," not, as one man in the bar said of her, a "tramp." That one word directed at this girl sickened me regardless of what she may or may not have done to deserve such a cruel comment.

My heart goes out to the "birds with broken wings." And I knew this girl was one of those in this category. They need someone of understanding who is willing to take the risk in attempting to help their wing heal. I'd rather continue to play the fool in the attempt than sacrifice or betray that best of the child within me. There is a cry, a pleading for help in such young women (and, even, in some young men) that comes from the child within themselves. The best of the child within me recognizes that cry and responds to it. I had to face so much of this in teaching adolescents that it has become second nature to me.

My constant hope in such cases is that the wing can be healed before the grief and tragedies of life, the alcohol and abuse accomplish their task of making the heart so callous that hope and trust are destroyed. My searching for a heart not so calloused; not turned adamantine through betraying or betrayal that it cannot be marked by the poet's pen has taken me through a lot of suffering humanity. It is a hard area in which to do the work of a poet; as Jesus pointed out: "The words that I speak unto you, they are spirit and they are life!" We, as Christians, have neglected to mark the poet's task in this sublime Truth along with the obligation that he has in making Faith the substance of things hoped for, the evidence of things not seen!

Sadly, it wasn't long before the drink had its way and the young lady was involved with another patron in the bar and, the hour being late, I made my exit wondering, again, what was to become of another victim of alcohol and loneliness, of abuse and lack of self-worth, the demeaning activities that go with excessive drinking or other forms of drug abuse. What real gift of sensitivity might be in the process of being lost in exchange for...what? And I had to overcome, once more, the attraction of joining in the "total experience" by drinking myself.

I have made many enemies in the educational, religious and political spectrum because of my ruthless candidness in attacking the wicked people, problems and abuses in these systems. It requires some degree of courage to attack the problems I witness in the bars because of the fact that people so much like myself frequent them. The difference is that I am not a drinker. Because of this, I meet the same distrust and suspicion with which I have to contend in any environment where they view me as someone who is "different," someone to "keep an eye on."

It would be a simple matter to join in the drinking. In my youth I put away more than my share of alcohol, the so-called "rite of passage" of young adulthood. Knowing it was foolish at the time, how much more so now? But, knowing the end of such things, I can't relinquish the one thing for which I am too responsible to let go: a clear mind. I cherish that. It isn't a question of the "sin" of drunkenness. I don't credit myself for that distinction. I'm far too human in that respect among others.

The "curse" of that clear mind and Hawthorne's admitted "curse of solitude" is not being able to join in the abandoning of the "sensible" and bowing to the greater compulsion of speaking and thinking, clearly, for the sake of even those who condemn me for not being "with it!" I am not always properly grateful for the distinction. I would enjoy being hugged once in a while myself.

And it isn't that I am "too good" to make a fool of myself. The other night I met a couple I have come to know well. This was in one of the more "rowdy" establishments, frequented by the younger set. The lady insisted I dance with her. Now my readers know of the wires in my bones from my motorcycle accident that prevent me from the kinds of frantic and frenetic gymnastics required of the so-called "dancing" in such an environment where guitars are used as lethal, loaded weapons producing noise that has been reliably reported to sterilize frogs at 300 yards and scramble the brains of amoebas and salamanders.

But, the lady being thoroughly intoxicated, ignored my plea grabbed me and we "wrestled" through the, mercifully short, remainder of whatever the band thought they were playing. Did I look foolish? You bet! Did I feel foolish? Again: You bet! But it didn't prevent me from refraining hurting the lady's feelings in spite of the circumstances. I was grateful for the fact that I had not partaken of the pickled eggs and Jalapenos at the bar, this combination of foods tending to make one "socially insecure," particularly during strenuous exercise. I did, however, make my escape as soon as possible before the band "reloaded."

But, in respect to being hugged and kissed in the bars, those "wells and windows of the soul," my eyes, invariably betray me. Many people have commented on this over the years. Apparently it is the one feature about me, together with my weight, which has never changed. My eyes do have a penetrating characteristic over which I have no control. Partly, I'm sure, because of my inquisitive mind. I also, characteristically, look people directly in the face when I talk to them. As a consequence, they are either attracted or scared depending on the individual. On the positive side, they play a large part in my never being perceived as a "phony" in any regard. No one can pretend to be more honest than what we read in their eyes. But such honesty isn't always appreciated or, for that matter, even wanted!

All that to explain why even in the bars, women sense that I am not a man who is to be touched, hugged or kissed lightly or in "fun." My eyes warn even the occasional, phony-macho drunk away from me. The very seriousness with which I deal with people and events, the soberness with which I view the human condition and people's too-often cruelty to one another, seems to come through my eyes and hang a "caution" sign around my neck like the infamous Albatross, coming full force in the "curse" of my eyes; nothing to be done about that even if I wanted. Oh, well. I'm reminded of my old mentor, Walt Kelley's statement: "Don't take life so serious son, it ain't no-wise permanent." Sorry Walt, my eyes can sparkle and laugh when and if joy and happiness are mine once more. Till then?

In my last essay, I neglected to mention the correlation between bartenders and the "confessional." It is common knowledge that the bartender often becomes a "priest" in his relationship with his patrons. What is not so commonly known is the attitude I picked up from an ex-bartender. I have seldom met anyone with such a disgust for women.

He became positively lyrical on the theme of "Women are no damned good!" Some of my own detractors in this respect should have heard him. His rationale seemed to be based on his listening to women condemn their husbands and men in general and confide in him the most intimate details of their relationships with both their husbands and other men. But he confessed to having relationships with married women himself. I have always held to the belief that it is a poor excuse of a man who has to sneak in the back door to another man's wife. The willingness and easy seduction of the women has never excused this in men as far as I am concerned.

As long as I am mentioning bartenders, I can't fail to mention the fact that if the owner of the bar is a man, it isn't unusual to find them taking advantage of their position by preying on female employees. And, of course, this is true of any business and among politicians. I know of one bar where the women have a large turnover on just this basis. Why do they put up with it in this supposed "age of enlightenment" concerning sexual harassment? Because, at least in our area with little opportunity for employment, it is one of the better paying jobs.

Women do, of course, trade on their sex in order to make a better living for themselves. One older lady, an ex-bartender herself, when I asked about the difficulties peculiar to women tending bar told me she had discovered that her tips increased by at least ten per cent when she wore a blouse which exposed a better view of her physical endowments. Being a normal man still in possession of an active libido, good eyesight and plumbing in good working order, I haven't failed to notice the enhancement of a bar's "atmosphere" and income by attractive, women bartenders using their own equipment to encourage the predisposed foolishness of us men in this regard; as the old gal said: "If you've got it, flaunt it!" Or, to paraphrase: "Use It!" And, as I've said many times, this doesn't do much to promote respect for men on the part of women. But that's a sword that cuts both ways.

As an aside, I'm cognizant of the fact that my religious brethren, while consigning me to the outer reaches for my candidness and other breaches of "proper" Christian behavior and views, do derive a vicarious deliciousness in reading my writings about such subjects. I titillate their often-parched senses, and, hopefully, they come to realize their own humanity in the process. This, at least, is good for them. If my writing of such things as the bars will help remove them from "religiosity" and into the real world, the actual work of "the harvest field" in which Jesus commanded we "get grease under our fingernails," it serves a noble purpose.

I was sharing the comment by Sam Clemens that "Men and Women are natural born enemies" with a lovely, woman bartender the other night. She laughed and agreed. I wonder what the ex-bartender would have said to such? I know this; it doesn't help when the fair sex uses their most dangerous weapon, their mouth, to cut a man up. I'll never forget the riposte of a young lady, when asked for a date by, admittedly, a fellow lacking some of the necessary social graces: "I never date outside my own species!" Now that will really tear a guy up. Bad enough when the lovely object of your affection treats you like road-kill and this is done effectively with just the right look, let alone aided by words that cut like a surgeon's scalpel.

On the other hand (seems there is always an *On the other hand*), I have never envied the position of girls and women the immense problem of having to deal with the approach of a boy or man whom they really view as road-kill or outside their species. And particularly, when the goof is immune to a polite, civilized refusal and presses on. It has to be a really stressful situation for them. My readers may recall some of my essays about girls and women as "prey" and "victims" where I go on at some length about the situation. However, I don't credit Jews or Moslems with such pure motive in their prayer: "Thank You God I wasn't born a woman!" They have something quite different in mind.

If poetry is to ever again become relevant to our nation it will only become so when it deals with realities as well as the hopes and dreams of all of us in a form that is expressive of the heart's longings in a way that reaches hearts. Hopefully, some of you will respond with comment that will help provide such direction as I pursue the subject wherever it may lead.

I've received a couple of really thoughtful letters from a friend in Idaho. I wish I could acknowledge all such correspondence in print but the writers understand the constraints I'm under. Like the personal notes I sometimes attach to my essays. I wish I could write more of them.

Having just recently located to Idaho from California, she described the pure, clean, clear mountain air and blue sky and driving in a blizzard with snowflakes two inches across and "absolutely beautiful." I was most gratified, however, to hear that she has shared my writing with her Bible Study Group, especially the essay on Fathers and Daughters and "...all who read it were touched by what you wrote." Many people have responded to this essay in particular and, of course, several were not as sensitive to the subject. But many were. And, for this, I am most grateful. I was also grateful for her comment on the necessity of re-reading the essays several times to get their full meaning.

She asked the question, which several others have asked: "What do you mean by 'It's hard for a woman to live with a poet?' If they want a romantic they would have found one in a poet, at least that is what I would think anyway."

I have explained this statement in other essays at some length. However, it is appropriate in this context to address the issue. If you were to compare

Bacon, Wordsworth, Thoreau, T.S. Eliot, Ezra Pound and Dylan Thomas, for example, you would have the answer.

Given that Eliot dug himself a hole he couldn't get out of and, as a result, sought the answer in the traditions and structure of the church, that Wordsworth never wavered in his faith in Jesus Christ, that Bacon, correctly, named Jesus the greatest poet that ever lived and that Pound and Thomas gave vent to deeply held prejudices, stir it all together and you have the understanding for my statement. It was Thoreau, more than the others, however, that made his life a statement of poetry.

Thoreau's attempt at "classic" poetry never has held any charm for me; his tractate on Civil Disobedience; that is something else. The life of Thoreau, as poetry, is what has moved men's hearts and he being dead, yet speaks through the ability he had to make ordinary things extraordinary. But he was a thoroughly "impractical" man, a dreamer and wanderer. Granted the fact that he, as with me, was blessed with the ability to work with tools as well as words, and that he bowed to the necessity of "earning bread," he never betrayed the best of the child within himself.

Do women want a poet, a romantic? Yes and no. The human condition includes the ordinary tasks of earning a living, of washing dishes, soiled socks and underwear, paying the bills, disposing of garbage, cleaning house, illnesses etc. Little of romance in these things unless...?

We no longer live in a society where the poet can thrive. He has to go against the common herd, the common and vulgar lives given to the mere acquisition of "things," choosing to wrest time away from the demands of "getting" to spend some of it wandering along a trout stream, among the hills, trees and rocks, socializing with the "critters" and friends he has made through a great amount of reading, gazing at the stars and watching the myriad, changing colors of the sky at morning and evening. In short, as I have already said, he "lives in his head" and the living comes out in poetic expression of the things he holds of greater value than the accumulation of worldly possessions.

That a woman should be the greatest inspiration of the poet and in any man's life is no idle conjecture with me; it is God's Truth. Friends have said that my problem has been bad choices in women. Possibly so. I don't know. But the relationships have always begun in what seemed the mutual heart's longings for romance, trust, fidelity and commitment to the sharing of lives. That they have always ended in betrayal may be the proof of the opinion of my friends. As I said, I don't know.

But it is also true that I haven't given up hope of finding that woman who is willing to forego the definition of "success" by this world, in this thoroughgoing, materialistic and hedonistic society, for what I consider of far greater value; commitment and fidelity that unites two people in love for each other and for others.

I have known women who felt "ignored" by my need of the solitude that would encourage the very poetry and romance they say they want, who were slighted by not seeming to get their full measure of "attention" all the while I showed my genuine care for them by fixing the car or washing machine. Not exactly "romantic" endeavors by their interpretation. But I was never a man who could eat chocolates in the closet. If there wasn't enough to share, I gave it to the wife or the children; not very "romantic."

In a thousand different ways, our calloused society has misled women to believe that romance can thrive in an environment of selfishness, of some kind of ephemeral "equality," where competition, not faithfulness to dreams and ideals is the coin of the realm. The ugly fact is that poetry and romance are no longer the cherished things they once were, that our girls and women have been betrayed of these things, have become victims of the thorough emasculation of the gentle sentiments of chivalry and the obliteration of the most sensitive distinctives of what a real man is all about.

In the "quaint old days," I enjoyed standing up and taking off my hat for a lady, of opening the door for her and letting her go first, of the writing of notes expressive of my appreciation for her. And there were the flowers; I delight in giving a lady flowers. Are the feminists alone to blame that our young girls have no idea of what is their due as young ladies from young gentlemen? No, it took a whole society, corrupt leaders in the schools, the churches, and the government to cheat us, betray us of a generation of young ladies and gentlemen.

In the light of contemporary living, I thus become a "moral dinosaur," an anachronism, a very "impractical" man lacking "common sense." These are some of the kinder comments made by the women I have known. In spite of the current expression: Quality of life, few seem to be able to distinguish between "wasting" a few hours looking at a sunset and the stars coming out and the "need" for a newer car or bigger house. And, to my own damnation by so many women, I remain a man who subscribes to Thoreau's dictums: "If you don't want much, you don't need much," and: "A wise man lives simply."

By force of circumstances not of my own choosing, I have known many women well enough to have a good idea of what is working in the female psyche. But it is a rare woman who can go against the common herd in order to find the ultimate fulfillment in a man for which she was made of God. Hence, Solomon's own jaundiced statement: "A virtuous woman who can find, for her price is far above rubies!"

I would far rather give a woman the best of the child within myself, that gentle part of me which still finds wonder in God's creation, that promotes the desire to cherish the object of my love and that cherishing showing itself in the countless little tasks of everyday living and still find time for the stars and the hills and trees, most hopefully, together.

The Christian community itself fails to understand Jesus' statement: "Unless you become as little children, you shall in no wise enter into the Kingdom of Heaven!" My "brethren" would do well to try to understand the "Soul" in the light of my phrase, "The best of the child within us." They might, then, have a chance of comprehending the Truth they pretend knowledge of.

Do women, themselves, understand what it is they are seeking in a man; in most cases, in my considerable experience, No. And this isn't all their fault. Selfish and evil leaders have as I have said, sold them a bill of goods in a selfish and evil society that is the antithesis of love and romance.

To bring it down to the lowest level, I won't play pool with a woman. The other night, I was in one of the bars. I have come to take a special interest in one of the woman bartenders; she is a very beautiful and exceptional woman; in fact, I have invited her to dinner and she has accepted the invitation.

This lady plays a good game of pool. How's that for a "romantic lead-in?" Now if we should play against each other, it is a no-win situation. If I were to beat her, I would feel badly; if she were to beat me? I'm not so sure how she would feel, as I know little about her. But would it be just a "game?" I somehow doubt it. There would still be the unavoidable element of "competition." I don't want to compete against her, I want her and I to get to know each other as a man and a woman, as persons, individuals with our unique personalities, hopes, dreams and desires for lives with meaning.

Could a simple game of pool undermine any chance of this happening; probably not, but...? I won't compete with a woman. I'll treat any woman as a lady and I don't compete with ladies. Now that is really old-fashioned, Chauvinistic or the attitude of a poet who believes a real lady doesn't need, doesn't want to find a man who is trying to "beat" her or compete with her at anything!

At another bar, I am sitting next to a man who is well educated. His last job paid over $60,000 a year. But he is an admitted alcoholic. He doesn't have that job anymore. He wants us to get together soon and continue a discussion we were having when he is sober. But, as he shares with me, he will probably have the "shakes" for a couple of days and he wants the conversation to be a sober one. I agree.

The discussion we were involved in had to do, in part, with the things I have just written. What does this man and his problem have to do with these things? A great deal; what do people betray for the chance of true love and happiness? Invariably, the betrayal will be for things of no real value, for things that, often, destroy the real person and create a facade in their place, Elliot's "Hollow Man," if you will.

To put it as simply as possible, I am not in competition with any woman and won't be brought into competition with any. Yet, we face a society where the distinctives between men and women have been disastrously blurred, where the proper roles of each are no longer defined in any gentle or romantic, poetic way. Because of this and so many other things, where does a man like myself hope to find a woman who really knows what she wants, particularly in the role of a real man, a poet, one who has no doubt in his own mind of what the roles should be between himself and the object of his love and inspiration? Admittedly, it's a question without an answer at present. And only The Lord knows if it will be answered.

In a lighter vein, my friend also mentioned the "barter system" a friend of hers is involved with. This called to mind my own "salad days" where my skills as a builder and mechanic stood me in good stead. I still continue to exercise these most valuable skills. They are the reason for my present independence. I still fix the occasional "junker" and drive it, I still, occasionally, pick up a distressed house and convert it to a rental. I remain someone who has to use both his hands and mind to be fully functional. That it makes me money, I'm compelled in honesty to admit, is a modest incentive as well.

My recent "pub crawling" did bring up a problem in regard to my "Okie" proclivity in regard to modes of transportation. Folks do, indeed, judge by appearances. Now I can put on a nice sports outfit, comb my hair and shave and, in general, do what is required to make myself presentable. But when they see what I drive! Ah, that is something else.

It is a peculiar world in many respects. By one definition, I am a wealthy man. I am self-supporting, own a home and other real estate and am free of debt, I have the necessary means and am free of any detaining obstacles which would hinder me if I should suddenly have the impulse, at any time, to "just pick up and go;" the old song: "My heart knows what the wild goose knows."

But by another definition derived from the kind of cars I drive and the shanty house I live in, people would have me in the line at the soup kitchen or collecting food stamps. My "problem" is the same as that which Thoreau had with his fellow citizens. Not wanting much for myself, I don't need much and live a corresponding lifestyle; very simply.

The '69 Dodge Wagon is, admittedly, a really bad looking vehicle. Were I not mechanically adept, it would have been in the bone yard a long while back. But I can get in that old, disreputable heap and take off for New York, if necessary, without a concern for the vehicle being up to the trip. You'll remember my trips to North Carolina and up into Canada through Idaho last summer in the wreck.

But I can hardly blame a lady for not wanting to be seen in the old junker or wondering, understandably, about the financial welfare of its owner. Consequently, women are not attracted to me by my means of transportation, a not entirely bad thing. After all, you don't want someone to like you because of your 'Benz or dislike you because of your wreck.

However, I am working on an upgrade. Due to the circumstances of "barter," and trying to help a young fellow to move to Minnesota to be with his mother, I acquired an '80 Plymouth wagon. Now I didn't want the thing and even doing my own work I'll still be out a thousand dollars to make it roadworthy. But, at least, the paint is all one color and it lacks the distinctive sheet metal work (dents) of the Dodge. Also, the back springs are not flat promoting a more comfortable vehicle on the road. And, it has cruise control, a much-desired feature.

Now I wouldn't want to detract from my hard-earned image as a proper Okie but I'm more than a little ready to have a more comfortable vehicle and, hopefully, the Plymouth will advance me a notch above the kind of person people expect to find on the corner with a sign "Will Work For Food!" the image the old Dodge projects. But will the "new wheels" get the chicks? Hardly. Fortunately, I still have my Okie persona to protect and attracting women is not an overriding consideration. But when I was younger? That was then, this is now. And it is one of the methods that I have used successfully to remain free of debt, a not inconsiderable motivation. The thinking woman will be more attracted to this than the kind of car I drive.

And, in my defense, I am endowed with the requisite social skills and graces, protocols and knowledge to discriminate at formal functions and dinners, able to sort through the array of silver to select the appropriate forks and spoons. In other words, I'm civilized in polite society. The Poet, however, is another matter. That part of me refuses "captivity," refuses to be "tamed." More than one woman has failed in this attempt though it seems their nature to try, hence, I don't hold it against them.

I got off on this track, in part, because of something I have written much about: the lack of practical skills on the part of our young people. It doesn't say much for a young man who thinks he knows something about auto repair when he doesn't know the difference between a valve adjustment and a valve job, let alone being unable to do the actual work.

As a consequence, many of these young people lack transportation simply because they can't do the work themselves and certainly can't afford shop rates to get the work done by a qualified mechanic. I recently pulled the front brakes off a car to discover the "noise" the friend complained of being caused by someone having put a brake pad in backwards! The metal-to-metal contact had actually carved away fully one half of the rotor! Thankfully the owner had not had a "panic braking" situation before I found the problem.

I had to wonder, as I have done many times, about the number of vehicles on the road in need of repair because people are in such desperate financial straits that they can't afford to even get their brakes done by a competent mechanic. This has to be an increasingly dangerous proposition. And we all know about the vast number of uninsured drivers in this situation.

This makes me think of another thing I am witnessing, there are just too many people collecting aluminum cans around here. There are too many people looking for yards to clean and weeds to cut. Most of these are young people with no opportunity for meaningful work. Since this is an area with many retired people, the "Greedy Geezers" profit very well from destitute young people who will clean, weed and paint for a pittance.

I find the geezers sitting in bars and in Burger King. They are all over. Typical of such is "K---." 83 years old and contributing nothing productive, just a drain on the taxpayers and the future of the children, spending tax dollars on prohibitively expensive medical procedures that keep him alive, keep him seeing well and ambulatory enough to hobble into a bar or fast food joint. He's dead and they just haven't gotten around to burying him yet. He's one of the Walking Dead, but he can keep receiving his government checks, i.e., taxpayer money, and go on taking up space, eating, sleeping and breathing; nothing more. Unless, God forbid, the idiot still drives: a case for euthanasia.

It may be that I, surprisingly, may be old myself someday. But I have told my children that if I ever wind up driving like some of these geriatric fools, and we now know they are a leading cause of accidents, "please shoot me and put me out of my misery." Further, while senior citizens should receive a degree of respect, we now have a culture where they have little to contribute as deserving of such. Therefore, my sympathies lay, more and more, with younger people who are the victims of an older generation that created and allowed the betrayal of our nation and, as such, deserve the approbation of the younger generation. The bumper sticker: "I'm spending my children's inheritance" on the back of a $50,000 motor home is no longer a laughing matter; it's greed, pure and simple. Hence: Greedy Geezers!

The churches, being spiritually paralyzed for centuries, and particularly in the last throes of atrophication in the last 100 years, can do nothing about the situation. Not even Kant, Kierkegaard, etc. have anything to offer in this respect; James Joyce and Ulysses, not really.

I live a bachelor life. The grungy everyday things of living still require attention. There is laundry to do, dishes and vacuuming, general cleaning chores that any house requires. The needs in this respect are minimal but they still have to be done. I even have the life-long habit of making my bed in the morning. If I do any cooking (which is seldom), I still can't stand to have dirty dishes in the sink so I keep up on this. The occasional "breakfast" will, invariably, leave a stove to clean as well, especially if I cook bacon and eggs.

Don't get me wrong; I'm not really complaining so much as giving the reader a chance to interpret some of my writing in the context of personal lifestyle. This house in the Lake area is only a somewhere to hang my hat when I'm not on the road. I have no "certain dwelling place" and, much as I would like to have some place to call "home," it hasn't been in the cards for these past, few years.

I keep most of the essentials for my writing here. The laptop and portable printer go with me on my travels. When writing on the road, it is a simple matter to keep things on disk and transfer to a mainframe later. There are a large number of tapes and albums as well. I haven't transitioned to disk player yet. Culturally deprived?

I enjoy the old "Torch" songs and singers. Songs like My Man, Where or When, I can fantasize with the best when listening to such music. The "Old World Values" are still alive in my own heart. I'll die a "gentleman." No hope of changing to meet contemporary demands.

A seventeen-year-old girl has come by and, tragically, tells me she is pregnant. Who's the father? She's not sure. What should she do? Another girl shares the tragedy of being told by the local clinic that she has a particularly virulent sexual disease. The boy who infected her is probably infecting other girls as well. Where is the "romance" in the lives of these young people? No one taught these girls about "ladies and gentlemen." They got their "education" from perversion like MTV, broken homes and a perverted society.

This comes from my being the confidant of so many young people. They trust me to tell them the things that should come from family, from their church leaders, but too many of these young people have no family, have no church. Lacking these myself I am "one of them," and can relate to them in a way others cannot. There really is a lot of respect for my age among these youngsters; I have never lied to them. And I don't always have an answer for them; they know I will tell them the truth about this as well. The wicked freely strut about when what is vile is honored among men! (Psalm 12:8) This is the ultimate Truth with which we presently live in America!

We are drowning in a sea of lies. Government at all levels lies to us. Men and women lie to each other. The schools and universities lie. Is the truth too awful in most cases? Many of my essays have established the truth of this. I've known a handful of people who would lie when the truth would serve them better, pathological liars who couldn't even distinguish the truth. For them, a lie was the truth.

"All liars will have their part in the Lake of Fire...The Devil was a liar from the beginning and is the father of liars." God defines a lie as something that is told to both deceive and to harm, to gain an unjust advantage over another. We aren't talking about childhood fibs here. We're talking about the practice of intentional deceit to gain advantage at another's expense, to hurt, to cause grief and tragedy, maim or cripple because of deception. Many divorces are grounded and granted in a sea of lies. The Devil is right at home in the courts of men.

In the current conflict over abortion, why haven't women been told of the greatly increased risk of breast cancer as a result of abortion? Joel Brind, professor of biology at Baruch College asks this question of the media and publications like that of The New England Journal of Medicine. The evidence of this causal link to this deadly cancer has been available for a dozen years. Why isn't it being told women? Not "politically correct?"

I'm looking at a blurb for a publication of The Heritage Foundation called "Policy Review." Nowhere in the advertisement do I find any hint of this publication promising to address the real issues that are hurting and dividing our nation. "... an indispensable journal of serious thought" according to William F. Buckley Jr. I seriously doubt that Bill! You, as well as other such "conservatives," would still, intentionally or otherwise, have us "stomping ants while the elephants are rampaging through the village."

I was heading toward Wofford Heights from Isabella. A really scroungy fellow, dirty clothes and scraggly beard, was trying to hitch a ride. I stopped and picked him up. He was just coming out of a "seizure" and needed to get back to his "camp" along the river. He had been into town to see if his welfare check had come. These people only need a P.O. Box to get their checks. He was profusely glad I stopped and for the couple of cigarettes I gave him.

The area has a Burger King, the only fast food joint in town. I visit occasionally to watch the passing parade. I suppose if you sat in this establishment long enough, you would eventually see everyone who lives around the Lake. It attracts the young people and is a place for them to meet. But there are many old people who frequent it as well; quite a contrast. Then, there are the welfare people and the "hoboes," at least that is what they were called when I was a boy.

Some of these come in for a 59 cent hamburger, stuff their pockets with napkins, ketchup, sugar, salt and pepper in order to survive a little better. I know one guy, though, who owns a local business and does the same thing. He's either a simple thief or just plain too cheap for words. Naturally, the cost of such thievery is passed on to the legitimate customers.

Sitting in Burger King with a couple of old friends, we see a guy with a backpack, a good quality Daiwa rig, seated across from us. He appears to be in his 50s. He isn't dirty and his clothes, some kind of camouflage outfit, are clean. Good shoes. A collapsible fishing pole protrudes from the pack. One of my friends goes over and strikes up a conversation with the fellow.

Coming back to our table my friend shares with us that the guy isn't one of the usual welfare campers; seems he gets three, small "government," i.e. taxpayer, checks. They add up to enough to keep him fed and clothed. He says he chooses to live out under the stars rather than in town.

This small area doesn't have much in the way of violent crime. The lack of minorities has a lot to do with this. There aren't the racial and cultural characteristics that lead to conflict to deal with. Yes, there are drugs but we lack the big city environment and racial warfare that leads to gangs fighting for turf.

So it is that the area is attractive to those that choose or are forced to live out under the stars. The worse that usually happens is getting your gear stolen. But, as with the subject of poetry in an unfriendly environment, it will take a book to follow through on these topics. And they all have to do with the betrayal of our children, our nation, and real love and romance.

If "women in general" really want love and romance, let them start acting like it instead of being "suckered" by evil men and women who are only seeking an advantage over others. You would think the obvious fallaciousness of "equality" would be a double-starred, red flag. As with so-called "multiculturalism," such things are only used of unscrupulous people to gain their own selfish desires and promote their own agendas.

I have written much on the insoluble problems we face as a nation, insoluble when people will not do what is right and the force of law is the only alternative. Then, as in our present case, when the laws become as voluminous as to be incomprehensible, unworkable, chaos reigns. This results in what I have come to call the insanity of our laws, laws that have come to actually pervert the cause of justice.

Columnist Joe Murray takes up my point in regard to euthanasia; when suicide becomes socially and financially acceptable, when people are given the choice of a "designer death," those "Hitlerian Solutions" become attractive, the "unthinkable" become "thinkable." Having made the point myself that suicide is sometimes the only choice to a person whose grief is so profound that such an escape literally becomes the only alternative. And faced with a bankrupting, terminal illness; as Joe says: "Profit will make euthanasia OK!" From there the unborn, the unsightly, the retarded, the elderly, and the unproductive? We have already made great strides in killing the unborn; the others? Think "economics."

Tom Teepen recently wrote a column entitled: "Cynicism and dissent poisoning America." His point, one I have, again, written much about, is the failure of Americans to be able to define American! This, as he and I would agree, cannot be done in the face of cultures and ideologies in conflict. "Collapse of shared values?" Most certainly. But in the face of the utter greed and hypocrisy of our political and religious leadership, what else can we expect? But the curse of the liberal media inevitably rears its ugly head. Mr. Teepen can't resist hoisting the flag of a supposed multicultural answer to the problems. As if such a thing ever did, or could, exist in this nation or any other.

Peter Schrag addresses my point about "cumulative voting" in confronting the insanity of race-based districts thus enhancing the economic suicide of allowing the *Unearned Bread Masses* vote the mounting theft of the wages of the workers who supply the taxes that feed this insanity. With the further insanity of "minority" including everything from perverts to left-handed, mulatto typists, we have now bred a hundred different "minorities" clamoring for special attention at the cost of our children's future, at the cost of our future as a nation. And as Schrag, echoing my own writing on the subject, says, racial division and conflict is the unavoidable result of making race a "special interest," catered to by the sorry, hypocritical, betraying likes of the Willie Clintons, Browns, Rangels, Dinkins, etc. And California continues its slide to perdition aided by our Senators, Boxer and Feinstein approving of the pervert, Anita Achtenberg, as a top federal housing official, making her the first openly pervert nominee of Clinton to win confirmation by an equally perverted Congress.

My friend in Idaho did sound a sober note in regard to gang activity and graffiti, even a drive-by shooting there in "God's Country." She also enclosed the Blumenfeld Education Letter. I am acquainted with Blumenfeld's efforts on the part of our children and the schools and accord it good marks.

The issue of March, 1993 which she enclosed addresses the latest Trojan Horse in the "leadership elite" which goes by the acronym: OBE (Outcome Based Education). In short, OBE would do away with grades and input the entire family into a governmental system that would do away with the need of parents to have anything to do or say about their children's education. Not that they have much to do or say about it now.

OBE, in general, is a major step in accomplishing the total enslavement of all Americans and propagandizing them through the schools in accepting Caesar "taking care" of all of us. For a full expose of OBE, I suggest you contact: The Blumenfeld Education Letter, P.O. Box 45161, Boise, Idaho 83711.

My old friend Byron, the Episcopal Priest, has just been by. I can count on him for truthful and sensitive criticism of my work. We went together to visit another friend and minister, J.L., who, like Byron, is a very sensitive man. I count on such men to be truthful with me. There are a couple of other ministers, a Baptist and a Presbyterian, who also are counted in this "close circle." Having these men as dear friends encourages me. This, I'm sure, surprises not a few of the "brethren." But it helps to explain why I'm not "hopeless." We all agree that Jesus summed up the problem we face most succinctly when He said: "And because iniquity shall abound, the love of many will grow cold." Matt. 24:12.

In conversation with a lady the other night, she told me that she appreciated the way I did not separate so-called "spiritual" things from the real world but treated life as a whole, not "compartmentalized." Frankly, as I told her, I don't know of any other way to do so. It certainly isn't a conscious thing on my part. I know this; most of the sensitive input I have gotten from recent essays has been from women. This gives me a great deal of hope that a man like myself might be a spokesman for what the ladies wish men would say on their behalf. Let me know what you think.

In the meantime, I'll continue to travel that "less traveled way," refusing to give in to the demands of an iniquitous society that knows nothing of the love of God and has no interest in His plans for His children. I'll continue to seek out birds with broken wings and do all I can to articulate the things to which evil men and women pay lip service and deny with their lives. I will, with sadness, even anger, continue to do the work of confronting the evil of this world system that has betrayed our children.

Hopefully, and I live in hope, it will not continue as such a lonely task to the end. But better that than betray the best I find in people and forsake the responsibility to offer the little I can to help them live in hope as well.

Chapter seven

Christian Perspective

July

Ephesians 5:22-31 Titus 2:3-6 Colossians 3:18,19

Most conservative, political writing fails of its purpose in not capturing the interest and imagination of people. Much of it, like The New American, leaves people glassy-eyed and numbingly bored in spite of the much-needed, factual information contained in such publications. As a high school teacher of many years experience, I know how vital it is to have the interest of those you are trying to teach. Unhappily, most writers don't have this practicum as part of their experience.

Many of my readers have already made the connection between my political writing and the recent essays in CP. In sum, the problems we face in this nation, and the world, for all practical purposes, involves two groups of people: men and women. Not an especially profound observation, you might conclude. But let's carry this simple fact to its logical conclusion. The way in which the two sexes treat each other has, indeed, profound ramifications on the entire geopolitical sphere. No matter the subject, the problems and their solutions require the two genders working together in harmony. It is a major thrust of CP to encourage that harmony.

Last summer while visiting the folks in Fort Smith, I asked my mother why she didn't listen to the music any more. She replied: "Because it makes me sad!" I knew what she meant. I have mentioned several times the fact that my mother's great love for music had much to do with making it so important in my own life (so much so that I was to eventually play clarinet and tenor saxophone professionally). Whenever I lived with her and the current stepfather (she married six times) she always had the radio or phonograph going with those wonderful songs of the 30s and 40s. I'm listening as I type to Blue Champaign. There Goes That Song Again just finished playing. Poetry set to music, of a time when love and romance were still possible.

From earliest memory of childhood, I was exposed to the destructiveness of the selfishness of divorce, of a father who ran away from his responsibility for his own children and never hearing from him again. My mother found it convenient to leave my brother and me with our grandparents whenever we were in the way of her own "lifestyle," of her numerous "relationships" to use the current euphemism.

So it finally, in her last years, came down to the music making her sad. Too many memories of what might have been, of lost loves, of the betrayals of the romance and poetry of life, a failure to commit to a life partner. My own experiences in this "way too hard" has cheated me of much of the music and memories as well; large chunks of life too painful to recall, gone forever along with those whose own selfishness betrayed the ideals of faithfulness and commitment to marriage and family.

But when you are young with all of life before you, and especially if you haven't the support of a culture which values things like marriage and family, the actual love, romance and poetry of life, it is too easy to fall into the selfish trap of "There's always tomorrow and someone else!" without making a life commitment to such things. Divorced older women, especially, have to live with the tragedy of such thinking. Men pay the price of their own betrayal of the ideals of youth by becoming calloused to the gentleness with which they were to cherish the "wife of their youth." Proverbs 5:18. For such men, the poetry and romance of life are gone, the perversions of their own selfish lust having destroyed them.

I was visiting with a man yesterday who is trying to start a "singles" ministry in his church. The discussion involved the pain and grief of divorce, of how people are to be healed of this common tragedy and go on with their lives. It may seem that there is little room for my growing database in human behavior in such a philosophical context, of trying to make some sense of the human condition by some mathematical construct. Nevertheless, bear with me and I'll explain as I did with this man.

It is obvious that Clinton, like Robert Redford in "The Candidate," having won the election was left with the question: "What do I do now?" Clinton was on an ego trip. Now he faces the reality that ego won't run a country or answer the hard questions he faces and for which he is responsible. Hillary, Haircuts and Hollywood only acerbate an already disastrous presidency.

The adultery of Clinton, his failure as a husband, gives me at least some measure of sympathy for his wife. Clinton isn't known for much beyond his overweening ego and inability to make a commitment to much of anything but saving his own hide. His wife's demands for "payback" can hardly lead to much in the way of romantic pillow talk. And what bearing does this have on the president's decisions for the nation? I shudder to think!

Perot and Limbaugh? Not hardly. Neither of these people seems to be aware that engaging in rhetoric that glows with generalities and avoids specifics is going nowhere fast. Like the man with whom I was chatting, there is a desperate need for a database that will narrow the parameters to the point of viable definition. Only when that is done can the problems be addressed with any hope of real solutions.

The mathematical model is the one, reliable possibility. The challenge is to move the scientific method into the realm of the psychological basis of human behavior and remove the cant and prejudice, the bigotry and common frailties of opinion in lieu of fact. It is interesting at last, to see the media paying so much attention to what I have been saying for years about the quackery involved with so much that calls itself "psychological therapy." I have often pointed out the fact that a good friend can be of more help. Few are so sick that they can convince themselves that they can "buy" a friend as per expensive "counseling" by a "professional friend."

I used the example, some time back, that if sufficient data were inputted, I could tell the precise point at which a bullet would fall from a rifle shot into the air. Now if the degree of precision only required an answer of an impact point within ten square miles, it wouldn't require much of a database for prediction. But if the predictive parameter required the precision of an impact point within five centimeters, the required data would be of a truly astronomical amount.

Human Behavior is the most complex of studies. So complex, in fact, that rather than try to deal with it in empirical terms, it has been relegated to the quackery of "psychology." When discussed in philosophical terms, answers are few and far between. Of course philosophy doesn't answer questions; it only asks them.

When facing the issues of life, people, generally, do not use facts but generalities in lieu; they attempt to answer questions of life with pre-conceived "definitions" which are, largely, opinions and prejudices. The fields of theology, education, of psychiatry and psychoanalysis are based on such pre-conceived definitions rather than much in the way of any empirical data. The proof of this, apart from the abysmal record of "successes," a record of failures, rather, is the thousands of books and articles that abound on the "Theories" of these institutions. Folks; a theory is not a fact. Once a hypothesis is formulated, the theory is subjected to experimentation. The "Fact" of the results is based on Replication and Workability. Can the same results be anticipated in every case where the criteria, as a constant, remains?

Obviously, if the experimentation is based on false assumptions, inaccurate criteria, the theory will not hold up. But, false assumptions that are correlated with pre-conceived conclusions, which lead to unscientific experimentation, can "prove" a lie. The dishonest or mistaken criteria of polls and statistics are cases in point.

Thomas Huxley notwithstanding, some statements require repetition. Many a beautiful hypothesis has been destroyed by a stubborn fact. Fact; and one among many others that must be repeated: A nation that does not cherish its young has no future as a nation. So much for the predictable end, for example, of a nation that refuses to deal with this fact.

Generalizations are essential to fact-finding, however. For example, if I were to generalize that every person to whom I offered a million dollars would accept the money, the generalization would be correct. But it would have a precise flaw. There would be, in fact, a minuscule number of people who would refuse to accept the money. As a theory, the generalization would be "workable" within a broad parameter and this is necessary as a "place to start." But an ultimate degree of mathematical precision would only be possible with enough information, a large enough database, to predict who would refuse the money.

Fortunately, we are not plagued with a flawed mathematical system in building such a database for Human Behavior. For example, the inability of our mathematics to deal with the infinitudes of .3, .6 and .9 does not impinge on our ability to predict behavioral choices within specified parameters. And just think of what pollsters and politicians would be willing to give for mathematical precision in predicting voter results? It would hardly be gainsaid that many would sacrifice their first-born and not a few would cut a deal with the Devil himself (not that a great many haven't done so unwittingly and unbelievingly already)! But not even Ross Perot could afford such a study.

We choose generalities because specific, factual data is too much trouble to acquire; it interferes with a deeply held prejudice or some area of our lives with which we don't wish to tamper, etc. But the narrowing of parameters is essential to the refining of definitions. In the case of the impact point of the bullet, there would have to be an intense "need to know" in order to make the five centimeter prediction economically feasible. Why; because of the expense of gathering the information and building the necessary database. The "pay-off" in such a case would not justify the enormous expense of making such a prediction.

But the Stock Market; ah, that is something else, as I mentioned in a previous essay. Those Los Alamos boys knew what they were doing. Since the World Bank and the IMF got involved, I don't wonder we aren't hearing anything else about this. But what about predicting the choices and their consequences of human behavior?

For example, it doesn't require but the barest modicum of intelligence to understand the principle of "Tolerance," i.e. "Liberalism." In sum, it doesn't cost anything in time, money or effort to subscribe to such things. It doesn't even require any exercise of the mind. In short, you don't even have to think.

Why; because so-called "Liberalism" doesn't deal with specifics, only the broadest, most nebulous generalities. Even most of so-called "Conservatism" is generally guilty of the same mind-set (ignorance and prejudice) and meaningless rhetoric.

When the liberal cant says: "We must take care of the poor and elderly, educate and provide medical care for illegal aliens" what is actually being said? The specifics are: Steal from the workers who pay the taxes in order to give to these others! Another specific, the empirical fact that this only leads to the failure of an entire society by eliminating the hope of providing for families who are productive by bankrupting them to care for those who can't or won't produce is swept aside. Ignored is the historical and empirical fact that such "social programs" inevitably lead to anarchy or slavery. There has never been any middle ground excepting the course our founding fathers pursued.

Perhaps some of you will understand the combined enchantment and fascination of the poet/philosopher/scientist like Thoreau and others who did not fit into the mold of either/or. I find myself in good company in this respect. For example, when a woman combines beauty, sensitivity and intelligence, it is a most uncommon thing. Each of these gifts of birth carries its own responsibility to others. In combination, there is an even greater responsibility.

As an aside, one of the reasons for my not drinking is the fact that alcohol destroys inhibitions. In my case, that could lead to incalculable harm to others. My readers of some time know that I have many confidences and secrets that I hold in trust for those who confide in me; this, together with my cherishing that clear mind which enables me to perceive things about me and retain them with clarity, makes intoxication a definite taboo in my case; the responsibility factor.

The ability to perceive things in un-ordinary ways, to be able to ask questions beyond the most common speculations and most importantly, beyond the pre-conceived prejudices so common to ignorance and indolence, requires the functions of intelligence and sensitivity. Since the vast majority of people are not interested in Truth but, rather, a much broader parameter and interpretation which allows indolence and prejudice, which enables them to live with easier consciences by allowing and excusing others on this same basis, the Truth, the facts and empirical data, suffers accordingly.

Another of the many "How To" books on the market, this one written by a woman, Marianne Williamson, includes this statement: "Some men know that a light touch of the tongue, running from a woman's toes to her ears, lingering in the softest way possible in various places in between, given often enough and sincerely enough, would add immeasurably to world peace."

Two things: This may not, in fact, be overdrawn; and, removed from erotica to the purpose of God in men cherishing their wives, it is a valid statement. It is at least a shade ironic to find a woman making my point for me in this respect. The point being that if men and women would give attention to those things which bring out the best in each, undoubtedly the world would be a lovelier and safer place, especially in the cherishing of children and family. How could it be otherwise when, in fact, a man and woman cherish each other? Compatibility, as God intended, not Competition, is the antidote to the plagues of divorce, adultery and the destruction of family and family values.

Unfortunately, men and women are too busy in "tongue lashing" each other rather than lovemaking. It is an evil system, led of evil men and women that has betrayed the poetic connection between men and women.

I made the point in my very first book that the basic question of human behavior concerns what happened in the Garden with Adam and Eve, the purpose of God in their creation, the Fall and its consequences together with God's judgment and commands that resulted. I made the further point that once Adam tried to hide behind his wife, blaming both God and Eve for his own miserable performance, his abject failure as a man, it has made it tough going ever since. The betrayal of compatibility as well as the responsibility of leadership of God's intended "Oneness" and the resulting "Competition" begins here.

We can hardly go back further in history than this tragic failure of human behavior in order to begin an appropriate database. But it is essential to start here to avoid false assumptions. No matter how many "facts" are marshaled for your hypothesis or theory, if the basic assumptions are wrong, the entire fact structure will, eventually, fail. But it will take an army of scholars to input the necessary information for a database that will have mathematical precision.

I am having lunch with an exceptionally beautiful, sensitive and intelligent, young woman tomorrow. I will present her a single, red rose in appreciation of her accepting the invitation. What does this gesture convey to the young lady?

When a gentleman presented a single, red rose to a lady, in a softer, gentler time of manners and civil behavior, it meant the lady was special to the gentleman. That "specialness" might mean several different things. But, to begin with, it meant she was just that: "special" to him.

It is always an honor to a man to be seen in company with a beautiful woman (and, to anticipate you, a "beautiful woman" is not just one with that physical attribute). She bestows that honor on him by accepting the invitation to be in his company. The "specialness" might be anything from the incipient beginnings of a courtship or a mutual friendship. It might have been an acknowledgement of the lady's particular gifts that does honor to the man by her giving him of her time and company and the sharing of these things. It was not an invitation to sleep with him and it certainly wasn't an invitation to "arm-wrestle" in either an intellectual or physical dual!

Sam Clemens was against women having the franchise because: "It would reduce women to the level of men and Negroes!" Keeping his statement in its historical context, he was absolutely correct! Bringing it into its contemporary context, men, like Adam of old, can now blame women, equally, for the miserable failures of law and government! And with the Janet Renos and Achtenbergs, Boxers and Feinsteins, the shame of men, like Adam, who would not be responsible and lead is complete.

Because of the sensitive issues raised in my last, few essays in CP, I have been getting a lot of comments from women. Men are not as responsive. This, of course, is one of the legitimate complaints of women. Yet, the great poets and lyricists, primarily men, would seem to credit them with the capability of the sensitivity for which women yearn. The ugly fact is that we live in an age that seems to be moving in the opposite direction of such sensitivity. It thus becomes increasingly difficult for any man to express himself in tenderness, in terms of endearment.

I was chatting with a lovely woman the other night that expressed pleasant surprise at the personal aspect of my writing in CP. It was most uncommon, as she said, for a man to expose such feelings in a public way. She was not the first woman who commented on this, several others have also.

My explanation was the fact that unless men take the initiative to lead in this area, it does little good for them to try to make up for the failure to do so by engaging in "posturing" in other areas. For example, it doesn't matter if the man can bench press 300 pounds if he lacks the strength, the confidence of his real manhood in gentleness and sensitivity, of consideration for others.

I have mentioned the number of women I have met who write poetry. At the risk of further misunderstanding by those for whom the poetry of life has passed them by, to whom romance is only a word in the dictionary, I am going to share a most sensitive, recent exchange between a beautiful, young lady and myself. It will be of benefit to those who care and understand. All others will be busy picking up stones to cast. I pity such people because they have missed the best part of being human.

I'll begin with sharing a part of the young lady's writing:

There are times when I believe

Those people who say "The right one will come along."

The question is when this happens will I be so hardened with pain I won't recognize him?

Maybe I have already passed him by

I wish there was some magical, mystical formula to help me find him.

If he's out there what's taking so long.

How long must I wait for him the perfect one?

Maybe I should settle for the mediocre one, settle down leave this bohemian lifestyle behind

There have been so many with offers to take care of me
To love me dearly
To treat me as if I was the Queen herself

And yet I choose to crawl into this empty bed every night.
Knowing I cannot settle for second
Knowing that someday he will come

Until then I am learning to care for me
Sometimes it scares me
Lately I am noticing I care less and less

I will be ready this time when the "one" comes along
I will know myself

I won't engage in any critical comment on the literary merit of the young lady's writing. That would, obviously, be completely out of place if not, in fact, cruel. The sentiment is the important thing, the heart's cry for love in the face of a loveless existence and an uncaring world and the continued betrayal of those ideals of love and romance. The young lady speaks for countless thousands of others who have the same heart's cry.

As a result of meetings with this young lady and her sharing so much of her writing with me, I was led to write the following to her:

I knew from the very first moment I saw you that you were very special. You might have even caught me staring at you. For that I must apologize; I simply couldn't help myself. Poor excuse, that. I also recognized the fact that you were out of place and wondered about that. Your writing and the things you have shared with me only confirm that impression; no, not impression, that certainty! I'm sure The Lord has an answer to that problem along with a host of others in your life.

Like you, I keep asking The Lord why I face a lonely life each day and a lonely bed each night, choosing to do so rather than settle for someone who would, at least, answer to the basic needs of that loneliness.

But, like you, I'm sure, there has to be more to The Lord's best in our lives than "settling" for what would only, in all probability, be more betrayal and grief. This doesn't keep me from pleading with Him to give me a speedy answer to my prayers for that "One." It has been a hard task, as with you, waiting out His answer to that prayer.

Yet, one of the advantages of years is the learning of patience; of enough of life's experiences with its numerous betrayals, tragedies and grief's to teach me that God's best is well worth the wait. Love does, indeed, as The Lord says, suffer long and is kind, suffers all things, endures all things, hopes all things and never fails.

In a world that suffers so much pain from the loss of love, of real romance, gentleness and softness, it is a huge responsibility for those with the hearts of lovers to maintain that absolute standard in order to give hope to others. It still remains the Christian's duty, above all else, to be known as His children by the standard of that love.

Granted, people such as you and I are too often misunderstood by those in the churches, even condemned because we don't "fit the mold" of the preconceptions and prejudices of those who haven't been created of God to walk to a different beat. But ours is the responsibility to remain faithful to the gifts He has given us for the sake of others in spite of such gifts often being counted of little value by so many.

My own heart weeps at what you have evidently suffered. I wish with all my might that I could reach into your own heart and heal all the pain you have suffered and still suffer, to take your face ever so gently in my hands and softly kiss it all away. These things should never have happened to you and, in that perfect world where real lovers dwell, they never would have happened. We both know that.

Maybe, I pray, it will help you to know that there is one man who God has taught to listen to what women like yourself have to say, has been called of God to stand up against the kind of evil that has victimized so many like you and my own daughters, has cheated and betrayed the hopes and dreams you have of decent men in your lives.

I know I need the help of women like you to deal with the problems knowledgeably. In seeking such help, I often appear foolish and do, indeed, walk where angels fear. But, as I have said, I would rather take the risk as a man with nothing to lose than miss any opportunities to equip myself to better help others.

I'm just a die-hard Southern Gentleman of the Old School, that anachronistic dinosaur of an age where ladies and gentlemen knew what the rules were. It was a kinder age. I'll simply never fit into this one. D. H.

I share the ending statement of a young lady's notes:

"I will learn to accept the loneliness and pain."

My reply to her:

"NO! You weren't made for such a thing; you were made to be the music, the poetry and inspiration in the right man's life. He, in turn, will be the strength to which your softness will gladly yield."

Obviously, in sharing such things openly with my readers several things come to mind. Not the least of which is the question of what it has to do with the pragmatic, empirical building of that mathematical construct, that database I have referred to? I think the more sensitive reader will make the connection.

Empirical fact: Not all women are beautiful, not all men are handsome. But it takes the ideal to set the standard. True as it is that Beauty is within the eye of the beholder, standards still exist. The standard of Romeo and Juliet remains, for example. It is the standard that makes sense of Beauty and the Beast. Most people retain an awareness of the fact that a beautiful woman can be cold and cruel; a handsome man can be a ruthless user of others. It becomes a critical issue that definitions of "beauty" go beyond the merely physical.

In all personal relationships certain parameters of definition remain while others are given enough latitude to allow of a person seeing qualities in another that are not discernible to others, Beauty in the eye of the beholder, if you will.

While I have women friends whom I esteem and value highly who are overweight, for example, such women hold no romantic attractiveness to me; they never have and never will. It has nothing to do with their worth, their value as persons. Some women may have skinny men friends but such men will never appeal to them romantically. And so it goes. But there is a "romance of the soul" that binds people who may well lack physical attractiveness to one another. Let me give you an excellent example of just what I'm speaking of:

When I think of "beauty" and "romance" I can't help but recall Margaret Fuller. Often described as Transcendentalism's victim and heroine, her work in the feminist and humanist movements is nothing short of remarkable. But she had to have been one of the homeliest women who ever lived. Gifted with one of the brightest intellects of her time, she was the friend and confidant of the likes of Emerson, Thoreau, Channing, Freeman and Clark. Hawthorne, among such luminaries, remained aloof and withdrawn; his admitted "curse of solitude."

Being, in the coarsest language, "ugly," by any definition including her own, hers was the curse of a beautiful woman trapped in an ugly body. As she grew up, she made friends and causes the means of sublimating her tragedy of birth. It wasn't so much that she believed in these causes so much as the fact that, denied any degree of feminine attractiveness and gifted with such a brilliant mind, she had to find alternatives, compensating devices which enabled her to cope with her physical disadvantages.

Women like Margaret have peopled the causes of "Feminism" and "Humanism" from the early suffragettes on in our own nation for the same reasons that drew her. Lacking any physical appeal, they turn their energies to causes that do not require female attractiveness and make too much, as a consequence, of their "personhood." Their more appealing "sisters" are too often made to feel guilty and often join them more out of this guilt than any degree of conviction. That this brings them, as women, into competitive conflict and confrontation with men is of no consequence to those who, like Margaret, have no attractiveness to men. The "causes" take the place of a man in their lives. Unfortunately, they make the same unreasonable demands on all of their gender to join them in this "man-bashing." Sadly, such things even lead to perversions such as lesbianism.

Margaret did eventually marry a man described as "simple-minded," a man, though of noble birth, she could easily dominate, and had a child by him. Tragically, returning to the U.S. from Italy, their ship hit a sand bar outside New York and Margaret, her husband and infant son were drowned. Such was the high regard for Margaret that Thoreau, in fact, was sent to New York in an attempt to salvage any personal items.

It is, to me, a further tragedy that Margaret, after her marriage and bearing a child, had begun to ameliorate her own, strident views concerning so-called "feminism," and her death cheated us of her opportunity to fully recant and use her genius to further the softer causes of women. In due course, finding her fulfillment as a wife and mother, "saved" as she saw it from spinsterhood, it was natural for her to soften in her militant, anti-man views. Not very surprising from a strictly human behavior perspective; it would have been one of the saving graces of fate for the "Ugly Duckling" to have given way, at last, to the "Crying, Captive Swan."

My somewhat labored point is that it is the most natural thing in the world, given human nature, to make a virtue of a vice when, by accident of birth, people feel cheated of beauty, wealth, opportunity, etc. Such views and prejudices give rise to every kind of evil such as envy and greed, bigotry and narrow-mindedness even in those possessed of genius. It is up to others to see through such devices and apply Reason to these charades no matter how gloriously costumed in glittering phraseology. To deceive one's self is one thing; to crusade in the cause of deceiving others is quite something else.

I have a very dear and close friend of many years who raises and races Thoroughbreds. He is, by his own admission, "Horse Crazy." My daughters were afflicted with the same malady and kept me "horse poor" as a consequence. My rationale, at the time: "Better horses than boys!"

Now it would never occur to Bill to make me a convert to his own affliction. It is one area in which we lack common ground. But our friendship is based on mutual trust and respect for one another, we genuinely care for each other and in too many other ways, we share many of the same likes and dislikes such as our love of nature and philosophical viewpoints to allow something like the subject of horses to divide us.

Unhappily, most people seem to make unreasonable demands in the name of "friendship." I know too many people, for example, who demand of others what they do not expect of themselves. This, of course, is selfish, egocentric. One of the extremes of this selfishness is the boy or man who tells a girl or woman, strictly out of lust: "If you really loved me you would go to bed with me!" Sorry ladies, if you believe this one outside of the marriage bed, you are being very foolish and selling yourselves too cheap.

It is, however, a homely truism that "Misery loves company." The old adage: "If I can't be happy, I'll make others miserable." Too often, failure to come to terms with those disadvantages of the accident of birth makes people try to tear down those things of real beauty, to lower the standards to the point where the ugly can equate itself with the lovely.

We live in a very self-destructive and schizophrenic society that seems dedicated to bringing everything down to the lowest, common denominator, the old LCD of arithmetic. Standards of honesty, morality, integrity and beauty suffer as a consequence.

When a beautiful woman's speech is punctuated with the vulgarities of four-letter words, her beauty is damaged. It suffers further from the deception of using such language in the name of "equality." Equal to what? To vulgar men? Surely this isn't what she wants, is it? She thus becomes a further victim to the false and base demands of using and abusing men and women who relish the demeaning of beauty, the betrayal of Beauty's responsibility and integrity of its own standards.

Ugliness, as Beauty, takes many forms. It is understandable that the one should be the enemy, the antithesis of the other. But without standards, absolutes, it is too easy to drag Beauty down to the common mud of ugliness.

I have never been given to the ugliness of sex-jokes. These are too often given to the demeaning of women and, most certainly, to the demeaning of something that God, if not men and women, holds sacred. Talk about Old Fashioned!

Yet, it has become commonplace for girls and women to engage in this same kind of base "humor," as with vulgar language, seeming not to realize that this plays directly into the hands of evil and ugly men and women who use and encourage this, as with pornography, for their own predatory and evil, lustful ends. In this sense women betray, victimize, themselves.

Wordsworth said: "The child is the father of the man." I have often wondered if Wordsworth really understood the real implication of his statement or whether, as a poet of genius, he was playing with an entrancing idea. Much of his writing would lead one to believe the latter.

When I use the phrase: The best of the child within us, it isn't with Wordsworth's concept, as I understand him except in part. That part, with which I am confident the great poet would agree, is the innocence and trust, the easy faith of the child which should never be lost to a man or woman. Granted the obvious need of the growth of maturity in order to deal with duplicitous, evil men and women in an often harsh world, those elements of trust and wonder, of faith and innocent love should still be the guardians of the ideal, of those absolutes of Truth and Beauty, the God-given capacity to imagine and the ability to look with wonder at the stars.

It is a wonderful thing to be called a "special man," a "gentle, kind and loving man" by so many women. I do not think so ill of these women that I would accuse them of flattery, that would be an accusation of a lack of sincerity and I know these ladies well enough, and they know me well enough, not to give credence to such a thing. There are some others, equally sincere, who have used other, somewhat harsher, less kind, descriptive adjectives of me. But for those who choose to see me in a more favorable light, I can only say "Thank you" and do all I can to justify your estimate of me.

As I have told so many, it took another "accident of life," the fact that I have daughters, Little Angels, whom I love far more and hold far more dear than my own life, to give me the softness that led to my salvation from becoming the "worst of the lot," a thorough-going hater and despiser of the fair sex. You ladies who think of me as a gentleman of the Old School have my Little Angels to thank for that most humbling impression of me.

Is it naiveté to think and write that women want to respond to the strength of gentleness and kindness in a man, even to the strength with which he accepts the full responsibility of leadership and those decisions of life which impact on his family? Perhaps, but I don't think so. If it were naive, I can't believe God would have made such a relationship mandatory. Short of such an explanation, it would be a cosmic joke of immensely tragic proportions for men to attempt to "rule" in the face of such, often, intractable opposition.

But it hardly needs to be said that if such "rulership" is nothing but despotic, tyrannical, it must, in all justice, be opposed! And speaking of politics and Caesar, our need for a new Continental Congress.... No, not yet and not now in this essay although you can hardly blame me for calling it to mind. But I will leave such a thing to those other publications where the "gentle and kind" man becomes adamantly, confrontationally granite-like in the face of the despotic tyranny of Caesar and his minions in their betraying perversions of our liberties, their betrayal of our children's hopes of a future. No, at this time and in this space I want to devote myself to the antidotes of such evil, to the Love of I Corinthians 13 and all that God intended men and women be to one another.

The relationship between a man and a woman in so many ways remains the mystery it has always been. Think of the immense commitment, the meaning of marriage, of two people agreeing in union to make their entire world around each other in that unity (The two shall become one)! The wonder of it, you might say, is that any succeed in doing so. Enter "Chaos!" Not the seeming confusion and disorder which the dictionary defines as such, but the scientific, mathematical model I have been writing about for some time.

An article in U.S. News and World Report entitled: "The mathematics of human life" is a pretty good description. In studying things such as the seemingly chaotic patterns of cells and fractals (unusual geometric patterning), and particularly the fractal-like order of DNA, the seemingly chaotic firing of neurons in thought processes in the brain and especially during concentration, the body itself, with the brain in particular, would appear to be utterly chaotic; but it works! Rather than chaos, I would call it a symphony of indescribable (at present) patterns of order, even beauty! Seeming confusion, as is more and more being discovered, in the physical universe has an underlying pattern. The philosophical questions of life may, then, in spite of the huge complexity of mental processes that lead to so much disharmony in all human relationships, personal and between nations, have the potential of order.

For example, one very beautiful woman I know (you have gathered by now that it is my very great privilege to know quite a number of such ladies), a bartender, is given by the necessity of the profession to making light of the sexual interplay between herself and her male patrons. She knows the ribald language, the coarse jokes, the touching and kissing as part of her job. But she doesn't seem to know what to make of a man treating her as a lady.

Having come to know her well, and as a gesture of my gratitude for her as a woman and her contribution to my writing about life in the bars, I presented her a rose one evening. She was actually embarrassed! Not knowing what to do when confronted with the fact that I was not the kind of man she was so used to dealing with, her face became a study in conflicting emotions. This was a woman who could easily deal with the roughest and rawest kind of male behavior but didn't know how to react to a genuine gesture of appreciation and respect for her as a woman!

She finally leaned over the bar and gave me a feathery kiss above my left temple, turned away quickly without looking at me and murmured a quiet "Thank you." Her eyes, which had been so hard and brittle, took on a softness that should be in any woman's eyes when they are treated with due regard. That rose remained in the bar for over a week.

I was in one of the rowdier bars one night and I met a very lovely young woman who, in conversation, knowing through the "grapevine" that I was a writer and something of my writing requested a copy of my essay, Fathers and Daughters. I usually carry extra copies of my essays with me in my travels and went out to my car and got her a copy of this one.

She began to read it and, suddenly, at one point in the first part of the essay, she stopped, looked at me intently, her eyes moist, her delicate chin trembling. She laid the paper carefully on the bar, now crying softly and, bowing her head, grabbed my left hand and pressed it to her lips and kissed it saying, "God bless you!"

No one can possibly imagine how humbled I felt at this honestly raw response of a young woman who must have needed, desperately, the understanding of a man and father who wasn't too embarrassed to say the things I said in that essay. How priceless, those tears and soft, tender lips on this coarse and weathered hand, gracing it, laving it with that warm, precious moisture far beyond the value of mere, shabby gold and could never be purchased with any amount of it! For this to be bestowed by this young lady on a man who has already turned the pages of his book of life past youth and is reading the final chapters, who is living his own September Song! The humbling of such a thing, its very sacredness is so obviously far beyond my powers of description, may even be profaned in the attempt. But what an awesome responsibility to touch hearts in such a manner! No man, of himself, is sufficient for such a thing.

How much healing of ancient wounds might be accomplished if men would, once more, take the leadership position in honest sensitivity to women and their needs! And how desperately I wish I could finish that essay in particular! For that young lady if no other! God grant me that "One" who will help me finish it, who will break down that barrier that prevents me from carrying it through to completion for the sake of so many who are filled with such pain and hopelessness!

And speaking of humbling experiences, the other night I experienced a young lady with a marvelous voice singing to me! She sings with one of the bands and, due to some of the things I have written, she came over to where

I was sitting, sat down and while the band played, looked directly at me and began singing to me. At first, as you can well imagine, I had visions of old, classic movies in which such things happened; but for this to be actually happening to me? I'm no Knight in shining armor; the way of all flesh is too much a part of my own weaknesses and failures nor have I always spared my own desires for worldly pleasure. In short, I'm "damaged goods" and, in that respect, have no right to expect such miracles.

She said later that it was the only way she knew to express her appreciation for what I have been writing and saying about women and daughters. No, folks, I now know that such things don't just happen on the Silver Screen. They happen in real life when you expose your own feelings for others and take up the causes of those who lack a voice in expressing such things for themselves, especially the children and young people. Risky? You bet! But the rewards are more than worth such risk. However, the work requires people who see the stars as the glory and promises of God, not still, cold and lifeless.

Henry James had his "Admirable Nightmare" from his "gaping" while visiting, as a child, the Galerie d'Apollon of the Louvre. To be immersed in such glory, the sheer immensity of it all is more than any sensitive person can endure without a commitment. Ah, but the nightmare of trying to do what the soul and spirit demands in meeting such an awesome challenge!

As a boy living the wilderness experience in the Sequoia National Forest, I had a keen hunting instinct. My fishing rod, rifle and shotgun supplied much to the family pot. While opting for the sanitized abattoirs which provide meat so neatly packaged in the local shops, my hunting instinct, like that of James', remains not only intact, but finely attuned to larger game than deer. The larger hunt, the Safari of the Soul to meet the enemy or be his prey, the pain of life with all its betrayals of the ideals of Truth and Beauty, of felicity, demands the keenest of all hunting instincts. No small part of the hunt is finding yourself a Stranger in a Strange Land, looking at your own weapons and wondering, a part of the nightmare, if they will be sufficient to meet the challenge!

I have a few "readers," people who I depend on to give me the necessary input from my writing to keep me on track. Recently, I enlisted the aid of a young woman who, when I first approached her said: "But I'm not smart!" My reply to this hurtful, self-criticism of the young lady:

"I'm not looking for academic 'smart,' I'm looking for honest and sensitive smart, things of far greater value!" Pity the poor disciple whose master "knows it all," who has "nothing further to learn!" I have known far too many such "masters." God forbid I ever become such! How then, to read "new sign" while tracking the Beast! And to write so intensely that you forget to live? Never! It needn't be Henry's father's concern that if a man lives fully enough he hasn't time to write. Nothing could be further from the truth, as Henry discovered for himself.

The successful "hunter" will not, as a friend recently complained, "invest 17 years of his life on a project that resulted in a one-year payoff of $8.28." Now a person really has to be dedicated to failure to accomplish such a task! But I was never successful, during all this time, in getting his eyes off himself and onto others and their hurt and pain. He was too busy speaking and writing *ex cathedra* to heed the pain and suffering in others. He never became a successful "hunter," never could "read the sign" on the trail. His nightmare, as a result, has nothing admirable about it.

My old friend has been quite free in his denunciation of my own efforts in this respect. He doesn't have the necessary humility to appreciate, for example, Bar Families; that mix of people who, lacking the essentials of family in other ways, find what solace and friendship they can with mixing with others in the same circumstances. If my old friend could enter into the spirit of what is working in the loneliness and needs of common humanity, he wouldn't have "invested" 17 years to such an insignificant return on his labors.

It would serve such people well to have joined my "Safari" in frequenting the gin mills and listening, observing the attempts at some meaning, some relevance to putting in one day at a time while shuffling through this mortal coil. I have to wonder what thoughts go into the making of such hardness of heart that the softer and gentler things that are of such great and real value go begging; and, in men, who but women and children can teach such things of such great value? Must women, especially, continue to resort to so-called Romance Novels to find some degree of sustenance for their impoverished souls, for some assuaging of their own legitimate needs of real romance, gentleness, tenderness and love in their lives? The explosive success of such "novels" is a dire commentary on the failure of men in this regard!

I'm reminded of the song, "If You Could Read My Mind." You men, it doesn't take much to read women's minds in this respect. And, you ladies, you need to take stock of your own contribution to the mess we are in as to the part you take in denying yourselves the realization of your dreams of a caring and tenderhearted man in your lives.

But, in terms of the immensely complex thought processes that go into human relationships, we, as men, must respond in kindness and gentleness to those needs of the fair sex. Not in the phony, liberal mold of the wimp who would "understand" so-called "women's rights," not the destructive illusion of so-called "equality," but that strength of leadership where God gave men the responsibility to lead in understanding, love and compassion, not just the physical attributes that distinguish between men and women.

Imagine if you can the immense complexity of a database that would account for human emotions alone! And one hugely complex area, the antithesis of love, would be the area of betrayal, the Judas Complex, if you will. I have said that the problem of humanity is "heart trouble," the fact that so many have betraying hearts.

In talking with so many men about the problem, I have found men ever so willing to damn women, and, in too many cases, rightly so, but not so willing to accept their own part, their own just condemnation in the trouble. For example, I find too many married men who envy my single status. Why? Because if they would only be honest with themselves they would admit their own failure to cherish their own wives! They actually envy my freedom to still be able to find what they think they have missed! These men have betraying hearts but would never admit of the fact!

Judas knew he had betrayed innocence. In betraying Jesus, he had betrayed his own heart, had betrayed the ability and capacity to love. So profound was the knowledge of that betrayal, that utter, irredeemable loss, he knew he couldn't live with it and hanged himself. Not a few men I know should be, on this basis, out buying rope.

Listen up, you men out there who "envy" me! You better re-examine the reasons you married your wives. If the romance and poetry have gone out of the marriage, you better try to get a handle on the problem. You ladies had better look to yourselves and see what part you are playing in the loss of these things as well. It takes two, obviously, to make it work.

Granting the fact that it is much easier to "make love on paper," and a lot of poetry by whatever definition is just that, than in the actual arena of life, some things still need to be said, some need constant repetition. If, after watching the steamy scenes on some trashy TV soap or some video where all the men are Adonis and the women Aphrodite, you are unhappy with your mate, you had better examine your own betraying heart and get a grip on the root cause of your unhappy lot. Few will honestly examine their heart's motives in this light.

There is a definite mental process at work that causes men and women to view their mates as somewhat south of the phony standards of Playboy and Hunk! We have a culture and society; an "entertainment" media that would have us believe that sex and sexual attraction are the sum of all of life!

If, when you decide on that life together, you cannot say: "Come, grow old with me, the best, by far, is yet to be!" you better continue looking! Notwithstanding the harsh criticism I receive from some men that "Life is not all moonlight and roses," what is not said, what is not understood in our selfish and hedonistic society is the fact that the moonlight and roses are still essential! Fellow, if you missed them you had better look to your own heart and choices for the reason! You ladies better not try to spare yourselves the same examination.

I'm reminded of the child sitting in Santa's lap, who, when asked what he wanted for Christmas replied: "I want a mother." The Santa visibly upset at the child's request blurted: "You want a what?" "A mother," the child repeated, "A mother who will love me and care for me, who will buy me things and take me places I want to go, who won't shout at me when I do something wrong and will let me do the things I want to do. But you'll have to get rid of the one I have now, of course" (My thanks to Berke Breathed).

Most of the married people I know fall into the category of this "child." They have an itch they can't scratch and just "know" someone else is what they want to satisfy that itch. But first, they have to get rid of the one they have now. And they do so, in droves. The Price of such wholesale betrayal; beyond calculation!

But "Hillary Babble" aside, it takes more than the liberal cant and rhetoric of We have to be caring, we have to do something about society's ethical and spiritual malaise, we have to ... etc. What is lacking, as I have mentioned repeatedly, are the specifics that would be necessary to define the problems and their solutions. And no one in a position of leadership seems to have the courage to address the specifics. Franklin, Paine, and Jefferson had no such difficulties.

Lacking the courage of definitions, we are headed for, in the most honest language possible, things like putting the poor and incapables, those who are a drain on our resources, in their place! We must, of course, stop the insanity of the poor voting themselves what they haven't earned, stop them from taking, by the vote, from those who produce to give to those who can't or won't.

As to the Greedy Geezers who live in comparative luxury to what the young know they will never be able to afford because of the betrayal of those so-called Senior Citizens, why shouldn't that generation be held accountable for the betrayal? They did the betraying, why shouldn't they be called on to pay the Piper? Ignorance is a cruel and inexcusable excuse!

The lesser of two evils remains evil. The question in Newsweek: "Is Riordan only a bridge to L.A.'s Latino future?" Most voter response, whether for L.A.'s mayor or any other politician, is the same: "I voted for the lesser of the two evils." Folks when the choices as I have said many times comes down to between bad and worse, not between good and bad, the end is upon us as a nation!

Take Miss Achtenberg. Please! As noted in National Review: "She presented a target that only Republicans could have missed." One comment by Dole and she would have been history. But where was he? Jesse Helms has been such a target of media vehemence his remarks were made to be anti-Semitic which, of course, they were not. As Charles Taylor, professor of Philosophy and Political Science at McGill says so eloquently in his books: "The Ethics of Authenticity and Sources of the Self, there is an ethic of recognizing differences without dishonoring the facts of cultures and ethnicity." Dr. Taylor, as me, argues poignantly, the necessity of recognizing the complementary aspects of men and women to each other instead of focusing on the disparities, real and imagined. It should, as he and I both say, not be a complement of sameness, but the complement of differences! Just as the aspects of culture and ethnicity must be both acceptable and unacceptable depending on the parameters of definition and where such definitions lead to conflict rather than understanding without force of ill-conceived fiat of laws.

Gary North and James Jordan "duke it out" over the esoterica of Covenant Theology. Jordan calls some of the writing of Gary's father-in-law, Rousas Rushdoony "nonsense" and accuses Gary of an "Ah hah!" experience. Mr. Jordan wouldn't make a nit on Rushdoony's face, so great an intellect is Rushdoony's in the area of theology. I vote him Christendom's greatest living English scholar of the Bible.

My reason for picking on Jordan, besides his bad writing and accusations is the following quote from Jordan: "The law reflects the Word, the Son; while love reflects the Spirit...the Spirit is the love-agent of the Father to the Son, then the Spirit is the Agent of the begetting of the Son. The Father eternally begets the Son through the Spirit. The Spirit connects the Father and the Son...."

And so, you see, women are more "spiritual" than men. This sounds funny if we mean by it the kinds of things that "spiritual" often means today, but Biblically speaking I think there is truth in it. The things the Bible says about the Spirit connect more closely with the feminine side of life (both in men and women), while the things the Bible says about the Son connect more closely with the masculine side of life (both in men and women)."

Mr. Jordan then goes on to "explain" what all this has to do with the "Seven-Point Covenant Model" using the "Hittite Treaty" as a basis. This part, especially, would leave most readers glassy-eyed. The choice between Jordan and Taylor should be an easy one, provided you weren't into how many angels can dance on the head of a pin. In his generalized, philosophized, totally without empirical-basis-in-fact- theorizing, Mr. Jordan exemplifies the worst of what is wrong with both theology and the simpering accommodations to so-called "feminism." This is an insult to both God and women! Apart from the Scriptures themselves, such "glittering generalities" have promoted the mess we now live with. What damnable error but what some sober brow will approve it and bless it with a text!

The infamous Thor Power Tool decision did make the publishing of good books, even great ones, unprofitable, leaving a dismal paucity of such works on bookseller's shelves. But to do such writing as Jordan (and, in fairness, much of Gary's as well) leaves no doubt as to why such books as his should be "remaindered" to wholesalers and the 50% off table. We need such "scholarship" like a drowning man needs more water.

Ed Feulner of the Heritage Foundation continues to tell me that unless people like me respond to the cry of making Congress "accountable" we are doomed. But he lacks specifics and definitions of real action concerning the real problems, much like Mr. Perot. It is easy, as professional politicians and religionists discover, to refrain from saying anything in spite of their much speaking.

An example: The cover of Newsweek, June 21, '93 displays two lesbians (the word made prominent on the cover as well) hugging each other. The story in the periodical actually glorifies this perversion. Now how does the "leadership" respond? Most certainly not in the specifics that would call this perversion for what it is and the incalculable damage it is doing to our children and our nation!

I seek in vain through my California Political Review Update, through National Review, The New American, The New Republic, Republican National Committee Confidential Report, etc. without any sign of honestly addressing the specifics. It is no wonder that Boxer and Feinstein are, among others, trying to cover themselves by getting on the illegal alien bandwagon. But will anything substantive be accomplished in curing this long-term cancer in America? NO! Not until that other "alternative imperative" of history, anarchy, reaches epidemic proportions and spills over into Rodeo Drive and Beverly Hills.

But, I digress; I'll leave the vitriol and invective, including the sorry sagas of Randy Weaver and Waco and so many other insanities of Caesar for my "other" publications. Suffice it to say that God did not divorce me from common sense and pit that against intellectualism in my believing in God. I'm even a passable housekeeper, for a bachelor, to the point of vacuuming the windowsills occasionally.

Now Ben Franklin, Tom Paine, Tom Jefferson, Sam Clemens never had the "benefit" of "consciousness-raising seminars." But I strongly suspect they had a pretty fair idea of what was sensible and what was not. I'm sure they knew that people are different in respect to what they say and do in different modes of life and the audience they address.

When a young man is trying, desperately, to impress some lovely lady, he is wont to be somewhat unreal. In reality, how does the young man expect to be otherwise? The lady may very well find herself in the same situation. It is only natural for us to want others to see us in our best perceptions of ourselves and most especially in those "affairs of the heart." But eventually, they will come to know one another well enough to deal with those everyday, practical affairs of life with which we must all contend. The question will be whether they will do so on the basis of the compatibility of differences or whether it will as usually happens, become a contest of wills and selfishness?

Last night I find myself at Arlie's Club, the friendliest bar in the whole valley. I've gotten to know the people well and there is a trio that performs Friday and Saturday nights. Oscar, who plays a marvelous fiddle, leads the group in some of the best music around. I go in and sip coffee and just enjoy the music. I was invited to sit in at tenor sax but am too out of practice and had to, sadly, decline. I barely play the clarinet anymore and my embouchure is mostly a memory. But I still love the music and the memories.

I couldn't help but think at such a time of the people who I have known who thought they were musicians because they could read music and play an instrument but had no soul for it. The difference, to those with a soul and ear for such things, is grating. The sound becomes wooden, mechanical unless it comes from the heart and soul. More, the best of the music comes from those who have dedicated their lives to it, those who literally live for the music. I confronted that choice years ago and while I had the heart and soul for music, I knew writing was the art for which I would have to, eventually, dedicate myself and live.

But the "mechanical" musician will never be able to meet the needs of those whose ears and souls demand Truth. Such discernment demands a "calling" of those who would play to such an audience. Tragically, too many teachers, government officials, preachers have no such calling.

I find myself wondering, in such an environment as Arlie's, why it is that people have so much difficulty getting along with one another? The basic causes of greed, envy, and lust are all pretty well defined and predictable. But, sitting in a friendly atmosphere with good music is most certainly conducive to world harmony if the extension could be made.

I've met another beautiful woman with a horror story that removes it far from any anecdotal consideration since her history sums up so much of what I have written about girls and women as prey and victims in our society, especially if they are attractive. This woman was a product and one of the victims of the rampant anti-establishment, youth rebellion of the 60s, the drug craze and its catastrophically tragic fall-out. How could those young people have known they were being betrayed, sold out by an evil and corrupt system which not only countenanced but encouraged their rebellion, led of the enemies of God and America in the schools, universities, churches and government? Where was the voice of Reason and Absolutes of morality with the backbone to confront the insanity back then?

She showed me the glaring scars on her arms, an early attempt at suicide. It was all I could do to keep from taking this grown woman in my arms like a child and try to comfort her, so child-like the uncomprehending pain of such abuse when all she had wanted was someone to love who would love her! She even confided her girlhood dream of a Knight in Shining Armor. You don't hear that phrase much anymore. It ripped at my own heart. A life like hers covers the gamut of all those young girls and women who have been so dreadfully used and abused by evil men and women. She has learned the truth of what I have said about the two classes of people who never know who their real friends are: Beautiful women and wealthy men. But the girls become women, learning too late, often in spite of what parents try to tell them, the truth of the reality of their "value" to a depraved society.

So many girls and women I have met have had to "rent" their bodies to evil men just to survive. These are not "prostitutes," they are girls and women who have learned what their "real value" is to an evil society and are forced to accommodate themselves to that evil reality! The tragedy is an entire society that has forced this on these women, the curse of the "equality" factor. The betrayal of innocence by countenancing, even approving the perversions of easy divorce, abortion as contraception, homosexuality, and pornography all take their toll in the destroyed lives of girls and women.

Such a young woman was one who told me she had been raped seven times. Granting the risks involved with drugs and alcohol and the people too often associated with such a life, when such a thing as rape finally calluses a heart to the point of "It's no big thing anymore," all you can do is weep for such victims.

And it took a society to make it thus. The best of parents while trying to teach their girls and boys about the things of real value were fighting a losing battle against the evil leadership surrounding them in the schools, churches, media and government. It takes the values of an entire society to have any hope of teaching and protecting, preparing the young. That betraying generation which refused to take a stand against the rampant lawlessness of that time, the betrayal of its posterity, must now give an account!

Even as I experience and write of those softer and gentler aspects of the relationships between men and women, doing what I can to draw them from the armed neutrality in which too many try to co-exist and into the compatibility of differences, I know the risk of embarrassing offensiveness with which such things can be construed. There is also the Jealousy Factor with which I have to confront and contend.

Jealousy is usually an ugly thing. If I invite two different women to dinner, regardless the purity of my own motives, there is the jealousy factor. This has proved to be a real hindrance to getting the viewpoints of different women, especially if they know one another. Another problem: when I recently invited a woman to have dinner with me for conversation she was incredulous. She said, "For conversation?" She repeated this three times. She couldn't believe a man could want to have dinner with her simply for civilized conversation without the subterranean motivation of getting her into bed with him, let alone thinking she had something to say which would be of value to a man. Yes, it has come down to this, a society in which there has to be such a sexual connection in men/women relationships. Anything else causes amazement and suspicion. And to believe any man would be interested in a woman's opinion and point of view?

Perhaps, as my daughter Karen so well pointed out, women can deal with the approach of men on the basis of lust, of wanting to use them, but they no longer know how to deal with a man like myself who still holds to those "quaint" manners of a gentler more civilized time. And how to go back? But if we don't, Ladies and Gentlemen will join the dinosaurs in extinction; too close to that already.

People write and, in conversation with others, the question is posed whether I get proposals of marriage from women. Yes. They are, in fact, the most difficult things with which I have to deal. There are simply too many women out there who are hurting and in pain from using and abusing men. In comparison to such evil men, I often look like a better prospect on the basis, if no other, of my willingness to listen to them and speak out against such evil; and so many of these women are the victims of abuse including the abuse of welfare slavery, diseases like Chlamydia, that it, at times, almost overwhelms me.

Sadly, I have learned the lesson of the difficulty women face in trying to accommodate himself or herself to a poet and as sensitive as I have become to the needs of girls and women, it remains the better part of discretion to heed that lesson painful as it is. But there remains the constant temptation to heal my own loneliness by attempting to heal that of another as well.

Oddly, at first glimpse, some of the women I meet in the bars are attracted to the fact that I am not a drinker. Imagine if you will, the lady with a drink being attracted to a man with a cup of coffee. No incongruity, really. She may be having a drink but she realizes a boozer is the last thing she needs in her own life. And how many of these women have been led into drinking by a boozing man? I see too much of this kind of tragedy.

We still face the hideousness of the AIDS epidemic; it remains a mystery to the experts. From the recent Berlin symposium: "Despite the high-powered arsenal of contemporary biology, there is nothing on the horizon remotely resembling a cure for AIDS!" Just recently an 11-year-old girl was diagnosed with the disease. At present, there are none of the supposed causitory links between her and the disease. And a betraying Supreme Court wants to make us take in known AIDS carriers from other countries in the name of... what? Certainly not in the name of either sanity or concern for Americans! And did the pervert, Dr. David J. Acer actually murder those people, including Kimbely Bergalis, his patients, with his own AIDS tainted blood? I think so.

Churchill's grandson has urged an end to all immigration if Britain is to maintain its "way of life." Some leaders in this country are beginning to speak in the same manner; hard facts, hard choices.

The FBI has been proven guilty of "doctoring" evidence against Randy Weaver. So what else is new in this part of the "shadow government?" Now Caesar is trying to take the heat off him by trying to prove Weaver shot first. As in Waco, why was Caesar there to begin with?

An opportunity has presented itself for me to run for Congress. As you know, I took myself out of the State Senate race in favor of Phil Wyman because of the pragmatic considerations of the case. I know I made the right decision.

But to enter the political arena whether for Congress or State Superintendent of Instruction or any other political office may not be the best I can do. The need for that new Continental Congress still looms and those worthies will not likely come from elected positions.

The writing is my gift and obligation, just as it was for Paine and Thoreau. It will be the primary factor in whatever decision I make. The pen remains mightier than the sword. So, I will continue the writing and do so in the hope that it will make a difference.

Chapter Eight

Christian Perspective

August

II Corinthians 6:14-18

This issue of CP is substantially different from others in a most important particular. I have written voluminously concerning the hard facts and choices we face as a nation. My political writings are well known to most of you. I have been quite free in my criticism of those who will not deal with the specifics that must be faced if there is to be any hope for our nation, our children and grandchildren.

Permit me to introduce the subject by calling your attention to something I have been writing about, particularly the growing and tragic problem of girls and women as prey and victims in our society. This has had no small part in my recent decision.

Parade Magazine of Sunday, June 27, 1993 featured a lengthy article about Alice Vachss' battle against rapists and the perverted legal system which, to paraphrase her, has totally failed to confront this crime for the bestial thing it is.

In her own words, echoing my own: "Rapists are single-minded sociopathic beasts that cannot be tamed with understanding ... We must stop permitting it to be socially and politically acceptable to give rapists aid and comfort." She might as well have included that other class of perverts, those who prey on children, in her uncommonly candid assessment of such animals.

To quote from the article: "Now, in an excerpt from her provocative new book, 'Sex Crimes', Vachss relates her experiences trying to bring sex offenders to justice - and she comes to a startling conclusion: 'We need to go to war!' " How very much like my own conclusions concerning so many things in the insanity of our so-called "Justice System" and the collaborators and lackeys in Caesar's pay!

Does Vachss make the necessary connection between her crusade against perverts and a lenient judicial system and the other social problems, tragedies, actually, that are eating us up like a giant cancer? No. She wouldn't dare.

Why? Because to do so would call attention to the fact that the vast majority of such "animals" are found among "Minorities!"

Many of you will recall, in time past, if a newspaper recounted a crime the ethnicity of the perpetrator would be included in the report. The problem was that a hugely, disproportionate amount of such crime reporting would list the criminal as Negro or Mexican. The media, as a result, began calling these perpetrators Black and Hispanic. But even the use of these terms was called "prejudicial, discriminatory" and the practice of such truthful reporting fell into disfavor with "minorities." Their liberal, lackey politician "friends," aided by the "enlightened" universities and "enlightened" media fell into line and began to discourage such honesty.

As a consequence, the truthful statistics of the abuse of children and women by such minorities is little known. The cruel, indisputable fact of the matter is that such crimes as rape and child abuse are, predominantly, by a huge margin, committed by such minorities.

75% of California's prison population consists of minorities. No small part of the reason for this is the state's inordinately large minority population, legal and illegal. In fact, it is now estimated that all minorities taken together are now the majority in the state. But the bills, the taxes, still fall on the largely Caucasian population. Thanks to the tax and spend philosophy of state government (not to mention, Federal), the largely Caucasian businesses and skilled workers which gave the state it's tax base and created the jobs and paid the bills has been fleeing the state in droves.

To acerbate an already insane policy of catering to the poor and incapables, disproportionately colored, just recently here in California, Cal State University Bakersfield actually approved a separate graduation ceremony for its Mexican graduates! They called it a Chicano Commencement. No Caucasians or Negroes allowed! You can well imagine the howl of the ACLU, etc. if such a thing were even mentioned for Whites Only! Another double standard in the name of "equality" and "fairness," and I repeat like a broken record: Equal to what? Fair to whom?

A friend of mine is opening a business in Nevada. She has found that state much more amenable to business than California. The business, being in a gaming state, will have slot machines. As we discussed the move, she pointed out the obvious that in games of chance, The House always wins!

It doesn't matter if the machines only operate on a one-half percent margin, that small, certain advantage means the players can never beat the house. In California, the birth rates for Negroes and Mexicans are far ahead of Caucasians. This means, in simple terms, that they are bound to "win." And, as Caucasians leave the state in droves, it can't be long before Negroes and Mexicans will "own" the state! Will we, then, face the situation South Africa has been forced to deal with after it's too late?

We are told that the Black Caucus in congress now has enough clout to influence the laws of the land. That these "laws" will be of the very same character as those forced on California by the liberals headed by a Negro, Willie Brown, laws which have bankrupted the state is of no consequence to those who want a free ride on the backs of those responsible, hard-working and predominantly Caucasian, taxpayers.

With such obviously insane, systematic destruction of its tax base, California's "leadership" exemplifies the utter, willful ignorance and irresponsibility that George Will, echoing myself, recently wrote of NAFTA. He says, among other things, that such insanity rightly labels government as anarchy! It's about time George caught up to me in this assessment of Gore Vidal's and my estimate of Caesar as "Empire out of control and beyond Reason!"

There may well be a huge conspiracy to destroy this nation and enslave its inhabitants. The JBS, among others, beat this drum and, rightly, call our attention to the use of the UN to accomplish the goal of that "elite" who are attempting a new world order and "control." It wouldn't surprise me. But this can be accomplished just as easily through sheer greed, indolence and ignorance.

Among the irrefutable lessons of history is the axiom that all evil needs to conquer is for good people to do nothing. And they will do nothing as long as they remain ignorant and prejudiced, filled with "assumed knowledge" and too lazy to discover the facts for themselves. The cares of this world and the deceitfulness of riches still take an enormous toll in the battle against ignorance, prejudice and all unrighteousness.

The story of Mary and Martha is familiar to all Bible readers. Like some of you, I have often thought Jesus was somewhat unreasonable with Martha, chiding her in respect to her complaint, a seemingly justified complaint, about her sister, Mary, just sitting there listening to him while she was busy trying to cook, wash dishes, wait on people and, in general, do the necessary things attendant to the guests in their home.

I have read a lot of commentaries and heard a lot of sermons in justification of Jesus' remarks to Martha that she had her priorities mixed, that Mary had chosen that better part which would never be taken from her. To that I had to agree but there was still, to me, the nettlesome problem of the fact that with a houseful of people, it seems someone would have to be occupied with entertaining the guests.

The past few years, however, I have come around to Jesus' point of view on the subject because of several things I have learned in respect to "entertaining" and teaching. One family in particular, close friends of many years have given me real insight into the problem.

I seldom get together with these folks but what I confront the situation Jesus faced. My friend's wife is usually preoccupied with the "much serving" of Martha; in fact, she represents Martha in every respect in this manner. My old friend and I often get into serious discussions regarding many of the things of which we share common concerns only to have the discussions interrupted by his wife's constantly intruding some inane comment about housekeeping, or she will "have to share" some housekeeping hint or quip from one of the numerous Women's magazines to which she subscribes, or the latest from her children's families and what the latest grandchild has done, etc.

Unquestionably she is terribly bored by her husband's and my discussions and, in order to focus attention on herself, she incessantly intrudes to guide our attention back to herself. It has never occurred to her that her husband seeks relief from the mundane everyday concerns which totally occupy her mind and time, and needs, desperately, the discussions he and I are engaged in to feed his own mind and soul with things of more relevance than another hint on how to keep linoleum clean or the latest "cute" thing one of the numerous grandchildren has done.

It is painfully obvious that my friend's wife is very jealous of the time her husband spends with me in such discussions. But rather than take pleasure in the fact of his need of such things being fulfilled, she is too self-centered to seek his benefit unless it includes her. But is she willing to set her own egotistical selfishness aside and try to learn about those things which actually threaten her "comfortable, ignorant, little world?" No.

Yes, I know many men of the same type. It is equally ugly in them as well, the adult version of the spoiled child who insists that all attention be given them, who, in that self-centeredness, have no concept that the childish chatter, the empty, vacuous, "concerns" of shallow thinking have no place in mature relationships or discussion.

Like Mary, when I am involved with things of significance such as profound discussion with someone, when I am writing things about which I am intensely concerned and involved, I actually forget to eat! Somehow, when I am thus involved, whether the dusting gets done or the breakfast consists of a cup of milk and a piece of bread or is a full-blown "country feast" seems of no consequence. It is, obviously, a case of priorities. Of course "things" have to get done. But "being with Jesus" is of far more consequence and value than vacuuming or cooking! Martha's complaint, as a consequence, becomes that of a vacuous, spoiled child demanding attention to childish, in the legitimate and worst meaning of the word, concerns of little or no value.

There is an essential and necessary time and place to listen to children, to give them the attention they so desperately need. But not when Jesus is talking! They need, equally desperately, to learn the lessons of being children and listening and learning when adults are speaking. This is not unlike the Apostle Paul's admonition that wives should learn from their husbands; but where, now, the husbands who cherish their wives (and children) in such fashion to encourage such a thing?

I wrote some time ago of the dreadful experience of sitting with five other adults and having a five-year-old intrude into the conversation at will. It was apparent that this poor child would grow up to face cruel realities with which she would never be able to cope, never be able to comprehend, doomed by the very selfishness she was learning with the encouragement of parents who didn't care enough to teach her the proper role of a child with adults.

I see and listen to the adult versions of this poor child almost every day, those people who expect you to attend on them in spite of the fact that the only thing they want is the attention of others to focus entirely on themselves. And regardless of whether they have anything of substantive value to offer or not.

The "Martha's" and their male counterparts are everywhere. They started out like that five-year-old, never learning to listen to adults, never learning that sage dictum, the invaluable wisdom of what earlier generations had learned and attempted to pass on, that "Children were to be seen and not heard." As a consequence, as adults, they become easily "hurt" to learn that their peers are not interested in what they have to say, will not abide their childish, selfish behavior.

Much of the pain I witness in others has its roots in the fact that parents didn't take the time and trouble to teach their children the real facts of life, didn't take the time and trouble, didn't care enough to teach them to pay attention when adults were talking, to observe, listen and learn. The loss of proper manners, of civilized behavior as adults, of consideration for others is easily seen in the product of such a lack of good breeding, of truly loving and concerned child rearing. The schools, as a consequence, have had to deal with this on a hugely escalating, wholesale basis. Of course, the schools, with their liberal mind-set, have largely brought this condition on themselves and deserve little sympathy because of the essential role they have played in this national disaster.

A part of this national tragedy has brought about one of the ugliest and most destructive things I have witnessed over the years in the treatment of children by parents and our entire society, the double standard that boys can treat girls as lesser beings. Certainly it isn't a "new thing." But its ignoble, destructive history and its perpetrators must be confronted as the evil it actually is. As a consequence of this evil and destructive thing, the boys grow up to be predators and the girls as prey, professional victims to be abused and used by so-called "men." If you are one of those "fathers" who, because of your own perverted lack of morality, actually encourage your son in such treatment of girls, you are beneath the contempt of civilized men!

This thing of "Boys will be boys," the evil double standard, used as an excuse to treat girls as prey and victims of lust has to be confronted for the evil, ugly thing it really is! Insane as it seems, many girls actually think they were meant to be used in such a fashion! We have pornography and the "entertainment" industry to thank for this evil insanity.

This condition has resulted in the insanity of voluminous and incomprehensible laws that try to legislate morality, an impossible task. No amount of laws concerning rape, child support, divorce, spousal abuse can succeed in overcoming this double standard of the actual practices an entire society condones in the face of, and despite, the laws. The growing result of this hypocrisy is an increase in the violence and vindictiveness we are witnessing between men and women. Even many good men fight impossible odds in trying to hold a family together in the face of the insanity of such laws. And not a few women I know have faced the brutality of an evil system of such laws. The children, however, are the worst victims of such selfishness as is typically the root cause in divorce.

The Reader's Digest of July has a lengthy article concerning children as the victims of divorce. What God has said all along, men and women are finally facing in an entire generation that reflects the wisdom of perverted, selfish men and women in a perverted society as opposed to the wisdom of God! God had good reason for saying: "I hate divorce!" (Malachi 2:16, NIV), and Jesus had equally good reason for denying divorce on any grounds but that of adultery!

We are being inundated with stories of sexual abuse on every hand. Now we are forced to acknowledge the hideous phenomena of such abuse taking place at unimaginably early ages. Just recently eight 9 to 13-year-old elementary school children in Yonkers, New York were charged with sexual assault against a 12-year-old girl. The "children" were, according to school officials, "playing a rape game!"

Yet, this was beginning to occur in the 60s. But no one would believe me concerning the seriousness of the situation. The time would fail me if I got anecdotal about what I was witnessing in the schools way back then. Now, we face it daily. The "experts" will try to excuse even this heinous behavior as "good," unbelievably, by "explaining" to us simpletons that it is good for children to remove themselves from denial of their sexuality to expression of it, even if it means "playing rape games." Such is the thinking of the leaders of our universities, aided and abetted by homosexuals, in so-called "child psychology." And, yes, we can thank the proponents of adultery, abortion and "easy divorces" for this tragic abuse of children as well.

God says the lake of fire is reserved for the Devil, his angels, all liars and adulterers. I have to suppose that God will simply have to present the divorce charges made by betraying men and women as evidence of lying on a monumental scale. Few pieces of paper are so filled with the vile lies of vile men and women seeking their own selfish gratification in spite of the innocent victims of such abomination, the children.

In respect to the problems and their solutions, it is a "man's world." That was God's decision in His creation. Men continue to wield the power of nations. The abuse of that power doesn't lessen the reality of the situation. When good men rule, it is a happy condition. When, as the situation presently exists, evil and corrupt men have the rule, everyone suffers. And, like Adam, they will often try to blame women, and God, for the resulting disaster. Since men will have nothing of God's law, they will substitute their own to their destruction. Every time. A large part of the shame and ineffectualness, loss of relevance, power and authority of the churches has its roots in just this very thing.

Spousal rape; where can we hope to draw the legitimate line in such cases? It eludes a society that can't even define morality! When perversion in the forms of abortion as contraception, homosexuality, pornography, adultery and easy divorce is allowed legal sanction, when perverts can demand "special status" for their abominations, women and children pay a horrible price in devaluation, marriage and family become mock institutions when perverts are "partnered" by sanction, even encouraged by equally perverted, insane laws.

God has never, in spite of TV so-called "evangelists," placed a premium on ignorance. In other words, He did not require me to put my brains in a blind trust because of my belief and faith in Him.

Anyone with a factual knowledge of history, not the revisionist fables taught as such in the universities today, cannot fail to recognize the contributions of the Caucasian race, of Western Civilization, ideology and culture to the advancement of civilization in all the best meanings of that word. The greatest of art, music and literature are the products of the Caucasian race. The highest ideals of humankind are the product of Caucasian civilization. The Gospel itself has been, disproportionately, the custodial purview of the Caucasian race. It has been the Caucasian race that has sent the missionaries, studied the Bible and promoted God's message of Redemption to the world. Pride of Caucasian culture and Caucasian achievement is, in every way, fully justified notwithstanding man's inhumanity to man that has plagued all races.

I will never, for the sake of "political correctness," cave in to the enemies of America who persist in vainly attempting to make me "racist" because of my personal pride and gratitude of being a Caucasian, American Male! I thank God for this "accident of birth" and, with that justifiable pride and gratitude, acknowledge the immense responsibility of my circumstances. Bear in mind that my battle against Caesar and his cohorts, including the BATF, FBI, CIA, IRS, the liberal media, the universities and schools etc. *ad nauseum*, has accomplished a dual task: It has made me many enemies and many friends.

The readers of CP know me as a, predominantly, gentle man. I would like to continue to write of those softer and gentler things, the music and poetry of life and keep other publications as the means of expressing the hard things that must be said. But it seems you cannot always do as you wish. I have an obligation for honesty in all of my writing. So it is that I willingly risk friendships and misunderstanding by being honest with my readers in the following:

My readers of the past, few years, particularly those who receive my periodical, Christian Perspective, know me as an honorable man who has never engaged in any form of hate-rhetoric or mongering. Such things have always been, to my mind, reprehensible, particularly as a Christian.

My vitriol and invective has been reserved, primarily, for those who use and abuse others, those, particularly, who abuse their power and authority in government as per the recent tragedies surrounding Randy Weaver and Waco, Texas. When "Caesar" and his agents start murdering innocent women and children, no man worthy of the name can sit idly by.

But life often seems dominated by Heisenberg's Uncertainty Principle. I never in my wildest dreams ever thought I would be writing the following article because of the betraying of our nation and our children, because of my stand against those who have betrayed the hopes and ideals of those who gave everything they had to give, even to their lives, for that precious thing we call Liberty.

Some years ago, I started doing research corollary to another study on those groups called "White Supremacists." I confess a startlingly naive ignorance when I started this project. I, like many others, had a mind-set that was due, in a major part, to the media distortions and ignorance of the subject. At that time I had only the haziest notion of the distinction between "Supremacist" and "Separatist." However, I was certainly not ignorant of the history of the distinction which men like Franklin, Jefferson, Lincoln and so many others had made clear.

But I was abysmally ignorant of the distinction as it applied to groups such as the Ku Klux Klan. As a product of WW II, I was thoroughly propagandized as a child to hate the "rotten Japs" and "stinking Nazis." So, as an educated adult, I was aware when I started my research to be chary of any material that tried to encourage racial hatred. But, as a well-educated man, I was also trained to look for more subtle messages which would, with "enlightened rhetoric," try to encourage such things by the use of sophisticated phraseology, erudite, "scholarly" tomes, maps, graphs, etc.

Having had the further advantage of being well trained in research and knowing how systems such as statistical analysis can often lead to false conclusions if the criterion is slanted, purposely or otherwise I was able to sift through mountains of material to get the grains of truth; which were essential for legitimate conclusions.

The historical imperative that separation of races was essential to the building of any civilization and distinctive culture was clear to me. No nation in history has been able to survive what we have come to call "Balkanization," the failed social experiment at a "multicultural answer" to our problems. History is adamant in this regard; one, and only one, culture, ideology can survive within any geographical boundary. And, invariably, such cultures and ideologies survive and thrive by two essential things: a common language and a common ethnicity. The common values, goals and objectives of any nation are inextricably woven into these two things. The constant warfare throughout the world both in history and today proves the point. The imperative of history, hard fact devoid of any hint of racial prejudice or hatred, opposes, confronts the enemies of America who would have us believe in any so-called "melting pot answer" such as the obvious absurdity of "multiculturalism." Most civilized nations like England, France and Germany are forcing themselves to close their borders in an attempt to save their own identities from this utterly failed "social experiment."

The ideology of a nation is all-important. For example, today, Arabs kill Arabs, Muslims kill Muslims, Negroes kill Negroes in Africa and the U.S., Whites kill Whites as per Ireland, Indians kill Indians. When those of the same race are killing each other, as we did in our Civil War, an ideological war, not a racial war by the way, it becomes very clear that the ideology of a nation is the single, most crucial factor it faces if it has any hope of thriving as a distinct civilization.

My academic preparations have been remarkably well suited to confront the devastation of our Christian culture and its values by what have become, predominantly, Marxist/Leftist doctrines preached in the universities, trumpeted by the media (particularly the entertainment media) the churches and government. The latter, I have come to designate by the opprobrium: "Caesar." I have also come to realize that the U.S., due to the evil, betraying leadership in government and institutions like the universities and the chaotic dissension in the churches, has, in the words of Gore Vidal, become "Empire beyond reason!" As such, it reminds me of a wounded animal which will tear and rend all about it in order to relieve it's own pain, anger and frustration, killing and imprisoning all who attempt to stand in the way of it's goal of bringing all others into subjection to it's own sway and will, that will being the abject slavery of all Americans.

I am the product of Christian values, a Christian work ethic that teaches if any not work, neither should he eat! It is obvious that the poor, the indigent, the selfish and incapables, given the franchise (which our founding fathers never would have countenanced) will continue to vote themselves the fruit of the labor of others, to continue to live at the expense of those who work and pay the taxes to support the huge population, largely minorities, legal and illegal, who have been given this license to steal by a betraying government which, itself, lives in luxury on the backs of the, largely White producers, taxpayers.

These "drones" otherwise known as politicians, continue to make their appeal to the non-productive classes, buying votes, as though the money will never run out. But we face the present economic crisis in America because of such betraying, utterly obscene irresponsibility (or conspiracy?).

It is most interesting to see a Negro leader like Louis Farrakhan trying to win over the Jews. It is also most interesting to find periodicals like Newsweek equating his overtures to the Jews as an accommodation to "Whites!" Being trained to "read between the lines," I'm not surprised by the attempts of the media to try to lump the Jews into this category in an attempt to dupe Caucasians into accepting them as such, a distinctively fifth-column approach at infiltration. Nor am I surprised to find Farrakhan finally realizing that in order to make a successful appeal to political respectability, he must win Jews and homosexuals to the Negro (in his words: "His people") cause in order to succeed in the areas of politics, business and the media. Farrakhan is far more knowledgeable and pragmatic than most Caucasians. He knows who has the real clout in congress, business and the media.

But the Jewish agenda, aided by the ignorant churches which still think fondly that the Jews are somehow special to God and betray the Gospel by their simpering "love" for those that crucified Christ is totally alien to the America and its values which our founding fathers delivered us. One only needs to look at the Gestapo, totalitarian, despotic and purely racist nation of Israel to get a clear picture of the real character and agenda of these people. It takes a very determined effort at self-deception to consider such a race "friendly" in any way, shape or form, especially "friendly" to the purposes and ideals of our founding fathers and the Republican form of government they delivered us.

Anti-Semitic; not at all if one is able to deal with Fact, Truth and Reason, those three pillars of Justice and Liberty as our founding fathers did to a large degree, the largest, in fact, in history. Was Franklin, acknowledged the wisest man in America at the time, anti-Semitic in attempting to exclude the Jew from America by the Constitution? No, he had seen what Jews had done in France and England and his was a pragmatic opposition, not tainted in any way by prejudice. It was a further tragedy that his and Jefferson's appeal to abolish slavery by the Constitution was voted down and resulted in Franklin's imminently practical observation of the Constitution, as a result, being a flawed document but the best that could be hoped for at that time and under those conditions.

In the vernacular of *That was then, this is now*, it should seem obvious to even the most obtuse that in order to deal with the problems we now face as a nation, there are some extremely hard choices we must face if there is to be any hope of solutions. Let me begin by prefacing my remarks by the statement: Any nation that does not cherish its young has no future as a nation! Whatever course of action that is taken must have, as its goal, the provision for the posterity of our nation. Of what use is any action otherwise except those actions that are for the immediate benefit of the selfish?

I have noted a curious thing lately. More and more leaders are beginning to talk like actual racists. For example, when a leader in education says we have abandoned the best and the brightest (primarily Caucasian) in favor of the lowest, what is he actually saying? He doesn't dare explain what the real problem is, he most certainly doesn't dare tell the truth in so many words that the "lowest" are vastly, disproportionately Negroes and Mexicans. This falls into the same category of discussions concerning crime, drugs and prison populations that are also predominantly "minority" problems. The party line remains: Keep it general; don't deal with specifics. What you don't say you don't have to explain. But he has told a partial truth in an attempt to escape the appellation of "Racist!" And why do such leaders fear telling the whole truth? They know the media will pillory them!

The battle that looms before us for the Soul of America must, as a result, be fought by those who count themselves with those who put it all on the line in the cause of liberty in confronting the tyranny of the Crown those many years past. Life, Property and Sacred Honor are still the conditions of a successful confrontation with Caesar now as then.

It brooks no discussion that without the pen of Tom Paine as Washington said, there would have been no War for Independence. The power of words is well established for both good and evil whether Common Sense, Uncle Tom's Cabin, Das Kapital or Mein Kampf.

Therefore, it is of utmost importance that any writing and speaking done in the name of that freedom and liberty for which our forefathers and mothers fought, that America which they delivered us by their lives, property and sacred honor not be betrayed by hate mongering regardless the lofty ideals of the proponents of hatred. By all means hate and oppose the evil and those who would try to bring free people into slavery! But Fact, Truth and Reason are more than sufficient to confront and confound the enemies of Justice and Liberty. Any thinking person truly concerned with winning our country back from its betrayers must surely agree that "propagandizing hatred" has to be, ultimately, counterproductive.

True as it is that our founding fathers had to eventually resort to force of arms in the cause of our liberty, no one of any sensibility wants such a thing any more than they did. When bullets are flying, people die- the guilty and the innocent, the righteous and the unrighteous. Those who support anarchy are my enemies. My writing and my call over these past years are to the voice of Reason, not anarchy.

But if the voice of Reason fails, if confrontation with Caesar becomes unavoidable as it did in the case of our worthy ancestors, it must be done in the same manner in which our noble forebears asserted their own righteous grievances against the tyranny of despotic government. It begins with that same pledge of life, property and sacred honor. That last requirement is of paramount importance in the name of righteousness in any cause. When good men come together, as they did, to constitute duly appointed authority in opposition to another authority, then, and only then, is there a legitimate "call to arms."

Education is the key element. Most certainly not that "politically correct" education of the mass of people who are deluded by Caesar's brain-washing institutions and the mass media, but that form of historically honorable education in which actual learning is the goal in the dispelling of ignorance and prejudice.

For those of you who have had the joy of the music and poetry of life made real in the courting and winning of the girl of your dreams, you know what went into the effort. But the prize made it all worthwhile. No sacrifice was too great, no effort too hard in reaching the goal of that fair one's hand. Not a little of our effort in winning the confidence of the people of America will be like such a courtship.

There is that element of love which "... suffers all things, endures all things, hopes all things and never fails." There is also that characteristic of love that responds to Reason, Justice and Liberty. It is that characteristic which led Jesus to tell us that such love is liberating. It is a love that has both the gentleness and strength of accepting responsibility and taking whatever action is required to protect and care for those, like children, who have no voice or choice concerning their future and welfare and are forced to depend on others for such care.

But genuine love requires absolute Truth. A lie will damn all efforts for good. However, if you love enough, you will do the hard things as well, or better than the softer and gentler things. In genuine love, a mother or father may well cut off the arm of a child in order to save that small one's life. That is sacrificial love, when you do the hard things for the sake of others as epitomized by Christ's death on the cross.

Make no mistake. I firmly believe in the tenets of our founding fathers. This nation was founded on Biblical principles of Christianity. The franchise was to be given to, and exercised by, responsible people only, not "free-loaders." America was founded a Caucasian, Christian nation and its Constitution and Bill of Rights were written with those absolutes firmly in mind. They would be scandalized to see what the betrayers of America have made of those noble documents in twisting and distorting them to our destruction as a nation! This is an evil that must be confronted though it may well take a New Continental Congress to do so!

I know you are all, doubtless, familiar with the hoary tale of the gentleman on a sea voyage who was found leaning over the ship's rail, obviously in great distress, by another passenger who, touching the wretch on the shoulder cheerily told him: "Don't worry friend, no one has ever died from seasickness," to which the other replied: "Please don't tell me that, it's only my hope of dying that's keeping me alive!" A good story always bears repeating.

Like that poor fellow, too many of the "answers" to our distress seem to fall into the category of such a paradox. A Roman Senator, at a time near the collapse of the Roman Empire, stood up and made this pronouncement: "We have come to the place where we can no longer endure our problems nor survive their solutions!" If that is not to be the epitaph of America, we had better get on with facing the hard facts of our problems and the hard choices of their solutions without further delay!

My sincere hope is that good men and women of good character will rally to the call for confronting Caesar and his minions regardless of their present associations. Bear in mind that solutions will not likely come from those who hold elected office any more than they did at the time of our own War for Independence. In conversation with one of the senators I know well I asked him about his opinion concerning the problems and solutions. His reply was that if enough good men were elected to office he would have hope. Then he said: "But that isn't going to happen in 200 years!" And, folks, we don't have 200 years! Not long ago, I was a candidate for State Senator in California. Try as they might, those in the media could find nothing to use against me.

I have kept my life an open book in large part because of my battle against the betrayers of our America and have done nothing to sully my name in that cause. My conservative political views are well documented from my writing and publishing and are supported by sound scholarship, not rhetoric.

It has been urged that I run for congress. There are many who support me for State Superintendent of Instruction in an effort to win back our schools. But I realize that elected office is not going to be the answer unless my senator friend proves wrong in his dour pronouncement. Not to mention the advice of a trusted advisor that it is unlikely that one good apple is going to solve the problem; there are good men in politics, men like Jesse Helms, who would seem to prove this point. Further, if it comes to a New Continental Congress, I would hope to be in the forefront of that effort and elected office might well prohibit that undertaking.

Like most of you, no one gave me anything due to race, gender or special privilege of birth. As a Caucasian male, I earned my living and my academic degrees and credentials through dent of perseverance, ability, competence without the "benefit" of "compensatory" advantages such as the lowering of standards or money thrust upon me by government because of my being "disadvantaged."

As a businessman I discovered, first hand, the encroaching, incentive-stifling laws and regulations with which California and our nation has committed economic suicide. I experienced the truth of that warning of Jefferson's where the laws have become so voluminous as to be incomprehensible, the insanity of laws having come to actually pervert the cause of justice, where lawyers, as politicians, too often, as with a betraying Supreme Court, serve the enemies of America rather than its citizens.

I wrote some time ago about the strangling regulations which actually prevent a man from buying a piece of property and, by his own effort, building on it in order to escape "renting" from the bank through an oppressive mortgage. Building for themselves and their families, that noble "sweat equity," enabled men to be the providers for their wives and children, enabled men and women to build for a better future for their children. What do we face now? Permits and regulations that stifle all efforts at becoming independent, of providing better for our children. In the name of what; safety? Safer for who?

I ask, in the name of fairness and personal responsibility: Wouldn't most people rather live in a one room cabin and have hope of a better future for their children, of building by their own labor and hoping to actually own their own home than live in a relatively luxurious "prison" for which they have no hope of ever paying the mortgage? But Caesar and his bankers say

NO! We won't allow it! And, by oppressive taxation, laws and regulations, Caesar has it his way!

As a teacher and administrator I witnessed, personally, the decimation of our educational system in the name of "equality" and the "equity of fairness" insanity which robbed the best and the brightest of being the hope and future leaders of America and all the while parents were being betrayed by those who feathered their own nests, both in the schools and government, in the name of "Americans" by the use of high-sounding rhetorical phrases which promised much and delivered worse than nothing.

Folks, as I said for years of education, I now say in regard to all those betraying institutions of government: You don't solve problems by asking those who created them for the solutions! That is, obviously, insanity! Or is it a systematic betraying and gutting of those values, that heritage which made America the greatest nation, under God, in the world?

In view of the obvious, further insanity of countenancing, even encouraging homosexuality, abortion as contraception, easy divorces (even the liberals are now forced to my point of view on this hideous and destructive "murder of a family", this indiscriminate killing of a mini-civilization), pornography, making light of such things as adultery, how can one not entertain some idea of an evil conspiracy? What nation in history has ever been able to survive in the face of such rampant immorality? NONE! And for a nation to do such evil in the name of "equality" and "fairness," equal to what, fair to whom?

Hard fact: Negroes were better off, as Thoreau pointed out, under a Southern overseer than a Northern one! That not only hasn't changed, the truth of Thoreau's observation can be found in any inner city of America only now it is rightly called Welfare Slavery, worse even than that of those Northern overseers of the great poet's time!

Hard fact: It is difficult, really, impossible, to safely walk any street in major cities if you are Caucasian. But a Negro, Mexican, Puerto Rican, etc. can walk the streets of the majority of predominantly Caucasian environments with impunity. Why?

Hard fact: So-called "minorities" can have their own print media, radio and TV stations dedicated to the advancement of their cause but who dares to do so in defense of Caucasian, Christian culture and values without being attacked as "Racist?" I say "Enough of the evil conspiracy which tries its best to make me ashamed of my birthright as a Caucasian American Male, of attempting to make me ashamed of my noble heritage of what used to be a noble nation because of that Caucasia, Christian Culture which caused to come into being a nation unparalleled in history in freedom, in culture and civilized, humane treatment of others and other nations, a beacon of hope to oppressed people everywhere!" And, thanks to this nation's betrayers of those early hopes and ideals, of those far better men and women who delivered us this Republic, of all those who have died defending it, where are we now? NO! I won't have it so! It's well past time for you and I to take a stand for OUR KIND, for OUR PEOPLE and for OUR CHILDREN! It is, in fact, the only hope America has!

And how dare anyone or any organization allow Farrakhan or Jessy Jackson call Negroes "Their people," Jews, the ADL, the JDL, B'nai B'rith to call Jews "Their people," the Mexican politicos to call Mexicans "Their people" and at the same time condemn and heap calumny on me for calling Caucasians "My people!" The stench of such hypocrisy must reach the very nostrils of God Himself! Just who is orchestrating this destructive abomination of evil propagandizing against pride of Caucasian culture and Caucasian achievement?

Hard fact: 62% of the births in L.A. County last year were to illegal aliens, preponderantly Mexican! That's right, 62%! That meant 32,000 "instant citizens" born to criminals, law-breakers at the expense of predominantly Caucasian taxpayers! The initial cost of such flagrant abuse of Americans by the insanity of Caesar's callous disregard of U.S. citizens pales next to the on-going costs of such insanity in welfare and prisons for these "instant citizens." L.A., as with most major cities in America, is a War Zone, given over to the hoards of Vandals who have, for all intent and purpose, Balkanized these cities to reflect and promote their own evil agendas. L.A. is "lost!"

The fanaticism with which terrorists from countries like Iran and Iraq are now targeting America would lead to the conclusion that such things are sure to escalate. But the enemies within our nation are far more dangerous. They are, primarily, the ruling elite, the powerful in authority, allied with the bankers who have us by the throat, plunging us into such monstrous debt that it has pauperized even our grandchildren and no end in sight! And who is expected to pay this monstrous debt? The "middle class" made up primarily of Caucasians. But who speaks for us in the face of such outright treason by the leadership?

Are we expected to simply cave in to such "legalized terrorism," this "legalized blackmail" sanctioned and enforced by our Federal Caesar and his Gestapo thus forfeiting all our rights and freedoms in the high-sounding rhetoric of "Equality?" Our founding fathers didn't! L.A. and other such major cities have already been forfeit to the hoards of Vandals and Barbarians, can we sit idly by and allow the rest of our nation and the future of our children be forfeit by default of non-action as well? I pray not!

Are you aware for example that Social Services doesn't even dare send investigators for welfare claims or fraud into most parts of L.A.? Why; because that would put the investigators "at risk!" Blackmail by the inner city terrorists to whom taxpayers pay off like a slot machine, no questions asked! As a result, welfare fraud is pandemic to such cities. And such successful blackmail, terrorism, has succeeded enormously, so much so that it is a major reason together with its handmaiden, illegal aliens, for California's economic suicide, aided and encouraged by a state legislature led of a Negro, one Willie Brown and a host of other traitors to California, to America! Small wonder the debt, state and nation, has escalated out of control with no end in sight!

I have to admit to supporting those like Ellie Nesler, that mother who recently executed the pervert who molested her son. That she did so right in the courtroom is an ironic comment on the failure of our legal system to truly protect the innocent.

But faced with the mounting attack on our Caucasian, Christian values and morality, one cannot, in all fairness, abuse the actions of those who retaliate against this without looking at the whole picture including the lawlessness and murders resulting from the callous disregard of Caesar for those rights and liberties given us by those Founding Fathers; the most recent case of Caesar's murder of those women and children in Waco, Texas being a case in point. And who dares call the S&L and BCCI scandals and so many other things the murderous treason against Americans such things really represent?

If we want to get into the sheer magnitude of lawlessness, let's put the shoe on the right foot, let's go after the real law-breakers in the halls of power who have betrayed us, our children and our grand-children of a future, especially a future that used to promise better for the children of America than what their parents had! For the first time in American history, children have less to look forward to than their parents. As a consequence, teen suicide is epidemic as young people lose hope in mounting numbers.

Despicable and reprehensible as any act of violence is against anyone on the basis of sex, race or creed, let's not let the propaganda of the destroyers and enemies of America get away with trying to scapegoat organizations that stand in their way. And without reading Professor Claude Bowers' definitive work "The Tragic Era" no one has a right to pontificate about the original K.K.K. that was the only hope at that point in our history against a North determined to plunder and rape a defenseless South after the war. Our real enemies, the real "racists and bigots" will be found in places like the Congress of the United States, its Supreme Court and Executive Branch, in those lesser institutions of government which have robbed us, cheated and betrayed us by rewarding incompetence and sloth in the name of "fairness" and "equality," a media which twists and distorts to its own evil purpose and agenda, especially in the so-called "entertainment" field! The sheer enormity of such treason boggles the mind!

Just as those early Carpetbaggers and Scoundrels set out on punishing, plundering and destroying a defenseless South could only be met by the force of that early and honorable Ku Klux Klan, so it may take such resistance to the evil we, as Caucasians, confront at every turn today. The Carpetbaggers and Scoundrels are more numerous than ever and are intent on plunder, of selling us all into slavery to Caesar, and this in the noble rhetoric of "fair and equal!" I repeat: Fair to whom, Equal to what? Of course, to that Lowest Common Denominator where what is best and beautiful of real liberty and justice, of civilized behavior and manners, personal responsibility, is destroyed in order to drag everyone down into the common mud of the ugliness of abject slavery! Then indeed, the term "mud people" will have an absolute value, the value of the serf to his lord, to Caesar!

The "mongrelization of America," the plan of its enemies and betrayers will continue until Caucasians have the backbone to say: "Enough is enough" and confront this evil betrayal of America by going back to those "Ancient Landmarks," those noble ideals of the founding fathers that led them to deliver us the freest nation in history!

The Social Work Department at Minnesota's St. Cloud State University sums up fairly neatly the attitude of the universities in regard to perverts; seems you can't succeed in the program as a Social Worker if you display a "negative" attitude toward homosexuality. The University declares that its graduates must show "compassion" and "acceptance" for perverts- or else! The universities have their own religion of course; it is called Humanism, that anti-Christ philosophy, including multiculturalism that has wreaked such devastation on the morality of our entire nation.

Unquestionably there is widespread anti-Christian bigotry rampant from top to bottom in the schools and universities and the media. No small part of this is the "Jewish Intellectualism," read "Anti-Christ Socialism," that prevails in these institutions.

In California this has become so disastrous to real values (and property values), the incentive for personal ability and responsibility, that it has resulted in a mass exodus of Caucasian people and businesses from the state. Most distinctively Christian organizations have (or are in the process) moved to places like Colorado. Citing things like illegal immigration, crime, liberal social policies, defeating rules and regulations, failed educational system, a self-serving legislature; the list goes on; it is a wonder there are any responsible people left in the state! But the voice of Reason is lost in the shout of the voices of the unearned bread masses that cry to Caesar, his Gestapo and lackeys to care for them at the expense of those who work and produce.

As I talk, daily, with those who have lost hope, I point to things like the recent victory of us little people against Caesar in the case of Randy Weaver and Kevin Harris. It was because of us little people who would not roll over and cave in to Caesar and his Gestapo that these men were found not guilty in spite of all Caesar, the real criminal in the case, tried to do. And so I tell people: Yes! There is hope if good men and women will come together and fight for those rights delivered us by our noble forebears.

Amnesty International tells us that torture, massacres and state-sponsored murder, were documented on an unprecedented scale in 1992. I'm sure '93 will escalate beyond that of '92. In other words, it isn't getting any better. The indictment of AI that governments continue to put politics before people's lives, though, is a half-truth, not unusual for the organization. For example, the condition that is causing such widespread abuse is ideological; something the organization doesn't want to talk about.

It is that ideology of a nation that sets the values, the "truths and taboos," the morality with which the citizens of a nation have to live and defines their national character. Our nation was founded on Christian, Biblical principles. The Gospel alone separated us from most other nations just as it does between individuals. But the missionary command of the Gospel caused England, America and other Caucasian nations to send people, people like Livingston, with our culture and values into the most remote corners of the world. Along with the message of hope, such men also gave enlightenment to cultures steeped in cruelty and the darkest superstitions.

When we bring God's law down to its purpose in men's affairs, it is clear that the Gospel of God's love should, in fact, motivate to do for others, to care for the weak and the helpless, to provide a moral climate in which families are encouraged and helped to teach children and provide for them. Further, no religion in the world gives such value to women and establishes, honors their proper role in life, as the Gospel of Jesus Christ.

We are being warned that the U.S. is entering into a new era of isolationism because of the worldwide, economic depression. Unquestionably, in such times, nations begin to look to their own welfare and, reasonably so. We read the headlines: As Europe's political walls tumble down; immigration barriers threaten to go up. In South Africa:

"White extremists disrupt talks." In this nation, a TV station photographer is cited for kicking in the door of a Courts and Administration building to gain access for the media. What power these people wield when they express such an attitude in such a manner! Then Janet Reno finds fault with the media for having this same attitude toward this mass-murderer!

To confound the matter further, as I have continued to point out, in spite of all the howling by minorities, Caucasians keep power. But it is that Caucasian, power elite, by retaining economic power and the decisions that are made to retain that economic power that has betrayed and continues to betray us and sell us into slavery to Caesar!

Those laws, regulations and policies that stifle individual responsibility and integrity, that rob men of their manhood, women of their femininity, children of their childhood, that encourage perversion in every form, have only one goal: Slavery to Caesar and his minions!

We will continue to witness the insanity of law compound itself with such things as "Street Harassment" becoming a crime. Professor Cynthia Grant Bowman, in The Harvard Law Review, says the attention of men toward women on the street should be brought under control by more laws.

I used the example some time ago that women are not free to enjoy the wilderness unattended. In fact, they are at risk nearly everywhere they go because of the rampant immorality of our society. Girls and women are virtual prisoners already because of this and no amount of law and punishment will make it better until an entire society goes back to the moral Law of God! The NRA, the JBS and so many other organizations have their role to play in confronting Caesar as well. It is my fervent hope that all patriotic organizations will come together in common cause to confront our moral crisis, the continual betrayal by Caesar of our nation.

As Alice Vachss discovered, rattlesnakes cannot be reformed, it is their nature to hunt and devour innocent prey. In the natural environment of their world, they might well be left alone. But when such snakes stand up on two legs, don black robes, take elective offices and enter human society to hunt and devour the innocent with the abusive, highly selective laws they enact to betray our nation, when they rob, cheat, steal and murder for their own selfish benefit, when they are the ones guilty of treason, they need killing! God's Law provides for duly constituted government to execute "rattlesnakes." No individual has the right, under God's Law, to act as judge, jury and executioner. That is anarchy.

But, as in the case of Ellie Nesler for example, when the laws of men fail to execute justice for the innocent, it is far past time that a society takes the same course as that of our Founding Fathers to confront such tyranny of law!

I wrote some time ago about the prevalent insanity of trying to define "American." It is obvious that the Hyphenated American is no American; that such "hyphenation" only serves to separate people. I addressed this at some length on radio.

My visceral accuracy index may not be as infallible as Ann Landers claims hers to be but it remains fairly reliable. That "gut feeling" reacts, as I'm sure yours does as well, to things that fly in the face of common sense. It is with that Common Sense of Tom Paine, that Civil Disobedience of Thoreau, the humanity and wisdom of Franklin and Jefferson that Caucasian Americans must accept responsibility for confronting the insane betrayal of Caesar!

I have a Biblical morality that dictates my values and actions. Further, I have children that have every right to expect standards of behavior from their father that will encourage the same things in them. I have no right whatsoever to expect better from them than I do of myself. If I treat women with disrespect, my sons are given implicit approval to do the same and I encourage other men to treat my daughters so. NO! I will not give such approval by my own actions!

In just such a way I cannot be so hypocritical as to hide Truth, Fact and Reason in candied words that would betray these things for the sake of either political correctness or the appearance of phony "tolerance." It is just such hypocritical "tolerance" which has led to our present crisis.

It would be a puzzle were my worst nightmares not those of reality rather than some dread fantasy, were they not flesh and blood rather than some dread, dark steed of horror rousing me from slumber in sweat-drenched sheets, heart pounding from crashing waves of anguish that torment one's soul.

No, it is not a nightmare of fantasy, but one of realities, realities that form the midnight of the soul when the heavens are turned to brass and answers to such hugely complex problems, tragedies, seem too distant of hope of solution. It is in such sloughs of despond that the souls of men and women seem to be held captive in the oily, dark depths, the soul itself with broken wings, unable to fly away to safety, trapped in some nightmarish black hole which admits of no light and with siren voice beckons the soul to the curse of eternal forgetfulness.

Like many of you, I had my share of racing toward destruction with the swift-footedness of youth, eager to embrace that which would destroy. But, with the advance of age and maturity, being able to finally recognize the evil face of the destroyer, recognizing the danger, it seems my pace in confronting the evil is hampered with leaden step, weighted with the profound enormity, the sheer magnitude of the battle to be waged. I would, even hampered with such a burden, make my escape if there were anywhere of refuge to resort.

But this is my America, an America delivered to me in trust for my children by faithful men and women who paid an enormous price for the liberty which has been betrayed and whose betrayers it is my turn to confront. That it is a nightmare of stupendous proportion cannot dissuade us of the hope that what was done once can be done again. It can be done if men and women of the same integrity and ideals of those who paid such a price can come together in common cause, setting aside their own egos, special agendas and agree on the same principles that led our founding fathers to victory over tyrannical and despotic government!

One major difference which we must accept is the fact that the present system of Caesar is guilty itself of treason, is guilty itself of fomenting anarchy! Caesar has abandoned the major cities of America to the hands of terrorists with the attitude of "Let them kill each other as long as it doesn't spill over into our turf!" In a single example, that of drugs, it is obvious that Caesar and his lackeys are in the business for profit and have no intention of solving the tragedy. The drug business serves Caesar's agenda of enslaving all Americans just as the destruction of our homes and families, our churches and schools, of moral values works to the same end and agenda of evil.

I just had the joy of having my daughter, Karen, for a visit. My little girl is the strongest influence of my life in those softer and gentler things to which I would so much rather devote my life. Had I a wife, I would expect her to be the inspiration for the best I could do in the cause of advancing those things which would contribute to harmony between men and women, to an appreciation of that compatibility of differences which God intended between the two.

But until we have, once more, an ideology and culture which provides the fertile soil from which poets, artists and philosophers arise, there is no hope for the future, a kinder and gentler future which values those things of eternal significance, which cherishes family and children, where the ideals of beauty, romance, honesty and integrity have relevance once more.

Most people, especially women, no longer know how to deal with a poet. They don't know what makes him "tick." People now are guarded in the cynical attitude of "What does he want from me?" in meeting truth and honesty. This, more than anything else, defines the mind-set of a society that no longer has hope of anything better.

I mentioned Oscar and his marvelous gift of music in the last issue of CP. As we sat and chatted at Arlie's during an intermission the other night, I was struck once more with what possibilities exist for harmony among people if attention could, once more, focus on those things that make life truly worth living.

In the present cruel, dysfunctional society with which we have to contend, where the elements of love and romance, of fidelity and commitment, morality and integrity are victims of hyper-selfish barbarism, the necessary confrontation with evil looms as its own inescapable historical imperative.

I pray good men like James Dobson of Focus on the Family, good leaders of the character of Dr. Donald E. Wildmon of The American Family Association, good men and women in the schools and churches, organizations like The John Birch Society, The National Rifle Association and so many more will come together with that same Common Cause that was essential to our liberty as a nation. If this is done, victory would be assured. But will such leaders do as our founding fathers and put aside their special interests and egos in the battle for the Soul of America? That is the end to which I will direct my own energies in the hope that what was done once can be done again.

Chapter Nine

Christian Perspective

September

I Timothy 5:8 James 4:17

Thomas Jefferson warned, among other things: "I know of no nation in history that either enriched itself or advanced the course of liberty by increasing taxes and government spending...The best governed are the least governed."

Everywhere I go people are frustrated, angry and fed-up with government and elected officials at every level. Are they "Mad as hell?" Yes! Virtually everyone I speak with. And they have every right to be so.

I talk to people in the churches and the bars, businessmen and laborers, waitresses, truck drivers, doctors and lawyers (I keep my hand on my wallet when talking to most of the latter though I am privileged to know a couple of honorable ones). Drunk or sober, educated and uneducated, men and women are all talking about the insanity of our present system of government, that system I designate by the opprobrium of *Caesar*.

I am compelled, as a result to write the hard things of the confrontation of tyranny just as Paine and Thoreau did for their times. But I also realize, just as Thoreau, that a failure to address the needs of people in the areas of those softer and gentler things of the poetry and music of life is to fail in the single, most significant thing of all; that which promotes peace and harmony, love for one another.

For that reason, I am constrained to mention some of the things most conservative publications ignore; the very humanity that the warfare is all about. It is that human perspective that is too often ignored but people, human beings, are the proper subjects and far too many writers and politicians have lost sight of this human factor.

Those that read my essays are agreed on one thing: it is that very personal element of my writing that they find of most interest and causes them to read my essays while other publications and the work of other writers gather dust or go into the circular file. So, even at the risk of embarrassing myself, a not uncommon occurrence, I'll continue to intrude this personal element.

To those of you who count on my political analyses and those hard things I am compelled to write of for the sake of our children and our nation, I remind you that I am, first and foremost, a poet, constantly longing to write of those softer and gentler things, the music and poetry which I want to encourage and long to see in people's lives. As an honest poet, this includes, as well, the grief and tragedies that too often accompany the relationships between men and women.

I wish I could avoid this part of the human condition but cannot. I know this two-pronged effort, the hard and the soft, causes a shifting of gears in thinking but, in truth, the two are inextricably related, Thoreau being an excellent example of what I am talking about. The politics of a nation dictates the very environment in which love and romance, poets and philosophers thrive or perish. Conversely, those softer elements dictate the status of a nation's politics. In other words, you can't choose one without the other; you cannot address the issues honestly and consider courses of action in any other way but as a whole. I keep asking you to try to make the necessary connection, to treat life as a whole rather than trying to divorce the one from the other.

As a consequence of this empirical fact of human nature, I choose to mix the two and use the personal stories of my involvement with others as a vehicle to make the necessary points dressed in flesh and blood, not dry facts and figures as necessary as those are. People will read a story; they might not pay any attention to statistical analyses.

I will dedicate CP, more and more, to the human factor of ordinary people whose lives become extraordinary in their personal relationships, the joys and sorrows that become the stuff of poetry. This is working out well as I would far rather write of the softer and gentler things in people's lives, the things of great and eternal value such as the love between a faithful man and woman (increasingly rare but I encounter it occasionally). From the stories of people's lives, the political writing has the essential ingredient of humanity. The hard part of these stories will continue to be that of the betrayal of love and romance, the tragedies and grief's that result from such betrayal. But a poet has an obligation to see life in the raw, not as the ideal even though it is that ideal which motivates him to inspire others to honesty in their dealing with personal relationships and their treatment and appreciation of God's creation.

I ask your understanding and indulgence, therefore, for the so-very human stories that occupy the space in CP. It is this human factor of love and romance, of the grief and tragedies caused by selfish, using and abusing men and women that must be dealt with as well in order to make any sense of life by any definition and, in understanding and compassion, order our own lives accordingly.

Granted, as Thoreau also pointed out, if I knew anyone as well as myself, I would use them as the foil to tell the stories but I don't. Consequently, I have to use myself as the central character that mixes in the lives of others and tries to understand and convey the feelings of those others by giving them a voice in the printed page. Not a little of my own hopes and dreams, disappointments and even grief translate into that voice of others. But, of course, how could it be otherwise and still maintain the honesty and truth of poetry?

As it is, my forays into the bars and taverns have been providing more than enough material to keep me occupied as a poet for quite some time. It seems it will work itself out, of necessity, as a book, each of the essays of CP after editing being a chapter. If so, I'm sure it will be one of the more interesting I have written. In the meantime, I will appreciate the comments of all of you as to the stories and how you relate to them. Suffice it to say, life in the bars is becoming a major contributor to my database in human behavior and my mathematical model.

I'm sitting at the bar in the "Club" having the usual cup of coffee and listening to people. Seated to my left is a blonde woman quite obviously thoroughly intoxicated. I endure a few slurred attempts at conversation and she finally takes a staggering exit. The woman bartender comes over to me and says: "You know, Don, that's the first time I have ever seen you at a loss for words with a woman." She understood, of course, that people who are so heavily under the influence are poor candidates for profound discussion. But it made my laugh for the day and I really appreciated it. The tragedy of a life that the lady represented was the really sober element that weighed on my own soul.

A man whom I know well comes up to me and asks if he can pay for a subscription to CP in installments. This man and his wife have lost everything because of the insanity of California laws that heavily penalize those who try to operate a business legitimately. They now do odd jobs just to keep from going on welfare. They live in a tent at one of the campgrounds. They don't know what their situation will be when winter comes and the camps are closed. They have virtually nothing but willingly share the little they do have. And for such people in such circumstances to try to support my work in confronting the tyranny of Caesar and Caesar's laws? How very humbling such a thing is to me.

Some of these folks in similar straits will give me things like jars of peanut butter or canned goods, fresh fruit they have gleaned by doing odd jobs for others, some even offer to clean house for me or anything else they can do to help. One dear young woman, facing a really traumatic event (she may go to prison because of being set up by a disgruntled boyfriend, an all too common tragedy given the self-destructive lifestyles of so many young women) comes up to me and giving me a hug suggests that I may soon have a "harem" of such young women who I have tried to help.

Flattering as the idea is to the male ego, I don't think The Lord would approve. It only makes my own heart ache all the more that so many of these young women, so many my own daughter's age, seem to lack any hope of decent men in their lives. As an aside, this helps to explain the success of charlatans and abusers like Manson and Koresh in attracting women to themselves. It is a grievous tragedy that women seek out such men because of the failure of society to teach true morality and the proper roles and value of girls and women.

As you know, I have enjoyed the adult humor of Berkeley Breathed for some years. I have also, at times, taken him to task for some of his failures regarding political satire and the issues of the relationships between men and women. When he started his strip, "Outland," some time back, I wondered at it being suitable for the comic section of newspapers. I wonder no longer. His strip, which appeared July 25, 1993 in the Californian, was absolutely obscene and totally without regard to the children who should be able to enjoy the comics without exposure to such things.

The point he makes will seem valid enough to many men and women and, in another part of the paper, might even do some good. But in the comics! NO! Those should be for children. Most of you will remember that time past when the comics, the funny papers, were child-oriented and were, actually, funny. No longer. Too often, now, they make political comment, are actually mean or contribute to immorality.

It is altogether too true, as I have written myself, that most men find the sexual use, and abuse, of women the thing that gives "meaning" to their lives. But that is not the way it is supposed to be and we all know it!

When I am not traveling, I usually go to Arlie's on Friday and Saturday nights where I have come to know many friendly people and the music is good. Over time, I have come to appreciate Country music. Much of it has come to rival that of a by-gone era, the melodies coming closer to that, in many cases, than most other forms of today's music. Artists like Patsy Cline, Ann Murray and Tanya Tucker have had much to do with the transition from pushing 18-wheelers and Somebody Done Me Wrong songs to the present music. The lyrics, however, of much of the music requires some getting used to. While many of the songs deal with the immortal themes of the relationships between men and women, there is often a coarser element reflecting the present lack of morality as compared to the gentleness and sensitivity of that by-gone era.

Dancing. Some of the women I know have actually succeeded in getting me to dance with them. Granted the music has to be of the slower, mellower tunes for me to accommodate them. But I had forgotten how enjoyable dancing can be. I'm now glad they didn't settle for my polite protestations (these women can be quite insistent and persuasive); it has proven to be good for me. And while it will be some time before I am confident enough of my regaining my expertise with clarinet and saxophone, that too, I suspect, will come about as well if I remain much longer in this area.

I also freely admit to the charm of being able to take a warm, soft woman in my arms and move, rhythmically, in time to the music, letting it transport us from the ugly realities of day-to-day struggles into romantic escape where the music and that other person offer something of far greater value than "doing time" in an increasingly cruel society. And, to all you ladies who have shown such courage in teaching a guy with two left feet, I say Thank you. I'll be presenting a rose corsage to one lady in particular, one who has become my primary teacher, this Friday night. I'll let you know her response.

It is late and a couple I have come to know well, homeless, need a ride to their tent at one of the local campsites. When we arrive, as they are getting out of the car the man says: "Don, I almost hope you have some trouble sometime so I can help you." I haven't really done anything for these folks but their sincere appreciation for such a small favor touches me deeply; too many good people facing the tragedies of loss of jobs, homes, everything. I call out to The Lord, angry at the fact that I am unable to do more to help these folks: Why can't good people like these find hope in this supposed land of opportunity? Why is our leadership so intent on destroying the hopes of our citizens and children, too often seeming to be more concerned in helping others and other nations rather than our own?

I need to escape, occasionally, to places like Arlie's in spite of the fact that many of the hopeless folks I find in bars are going to engage me in conversation about their desperate conditions, their plight contributing to their drinking and the drinking, perversely, adding to their plight. Arlie's is an exceptionally friendly place, the owners and bartender's very kind in dealing with people. Slugger, at Slugger's Saloon, is also one of those rare people who help many, especially those young women who frequent her establishment; so much so, in fact, that many of these young women call her "Mom." I presented Slugger a rose one day in appreciation of her kindness to others.

It should be remembered that much of what was accomplished in prosecuting a successful rebellion against the Crown was done through meetings held in the pubs and taverns of that time. And it wasn't done by a bunch of drunks.

The jukebox is playing a very melodic tune by Tanya Tucker, "The Serenade They Played," one of my favorites. One very depressed young woman wants to dance. I lead her out onto the floor and, with her head on my shoulder, moving smoothly and swaying gently to the music, she is able to try, for a moment, to escape the ugly conditions of her life. But, with her cheek against mine, her soft hair brushing my face, I begin to feel the warm moisture of her tears. We share, silently, the aching wish that so many things were different. Lord, too many good people are hurting!

The bars represent humanity in many forms. Being often in Bakersfield, I have come to know a few of the better ones. One has an excellent country music band and, having come to know the people at this establishment pretty well, I can find dance partners here who are among the best dancers.

As an aside, those of you who have seen the picture of me on the cover of a couple of my books know I am, basically, a Westerner and often dress accordingly. Country Music taverns encourage this sort of attire. As a result, I am often out of my three-piece and tie and into Stetson, fashionable Levis and boots. Believe it or not I am real Cowboy material, at least in appearance, and I have learned to dance in the boots, a real challenge to me. But to my enormous relief, remarkably, I haven't stepped on a lady's toes as yet.

I mention this place in Bakersfield because of an unfolding tragedy with which I have become very well informed. In fact, I am literally watching it play itself out from start to finish. And, not being a drinker, I have taken it all in with a clear mind. Herein lies a tale of the human condition. You will understand, as you read it, why I cannot name the place or the people involved.

The band has some real degenerates who prey on women. One of them is 65-years-old and has had a couple of face-lifts in order to fool younger women. A few of them are into drugs and alcohol, not all that uncommon of course with musicians.

My readers will recall my comments on being able to appreciate talent while despising the character of some of those possessing talent, even genius. These men are prime examples of that fact. Good musicians but the moral equivalent of barnyard animals.

I often sit with the girl friend of one of the members of the band at her behest to keep unwanted patrons from hitting on her. This led to my close knowledge of the following events.

Some time back, a couple of very lovely, younger ladies began to frequent the bar the nights the band played. The younger of the two began to be a regular dance partner of mine.

Now the girl friend of the musician I mentioned doesn't dance with anyone because, as she put it: Her partner was up on the stage, playing the music. I admired her for this loyalty that makes what has transpired all the more poignant in the tragedy.

It is to be expected in the bars that men and women will become friendly and the prettier women get a lot of attention, much of it unwelcome. The younger lady of the pair I mentioned attracted the attention of someone I have come to know well, a decent and responsible man. He did get the lady to dance with him and became so smitten he confided to me later that he intended to court her with the object of matrimony. As he explained to me, he was looking for a decent woman to wed, not a "girlfriend" or a one-night-stand.

But this woman and the other were becoming the object of the attention of the degenerate musicians as well. It has to be admitted, of course, that the women did not have to cooperate, to their own hurt, with these men. Knowing all the players in this unfolding drama, and being concerned for the welfare of the women, I watched and listened with concentrated attention.

Those that know me well know I have never, and will never, approach a married woman or, for that matter, a woman who is involved with another man in any way. I am friendly with many but that is as far as it will ever go and none can ever accuse me of any impropriety in those friendly, strictly hands-off relationships. A real anachronism in this age, a moral dinosaur, I'm not much "fun" in this regard to many women I meet.

But because of my "outdated" morality, this left me the objective observer in the drama. Knowing all that was involved, I watched over the past month as this tragedy was coming on to its conclusion. And while I wish more preachers would visit the bars to get a taste of reality, I confess how hard it is to watch people let the abuse of booze and drugs destroy them. These things, tragically, have their evil place in the drama I am describing and I have to ask, logically, what the outcome might have been if the people involved simply had a couple of beers or a cup of coffee. Quite different, and happily so, I'm sure; the tragedies of drunkenness and drugs. How many otherwise good girls and women have paid a bitter price for the failure to keep their wits about them on this basis.

The older of the two, young women became the prey of the older musician. The younger one became the prey of another degenerate who actually had a wife and children. This "minor" responsibility had never kept him, however, from "playing the field" and using and abusing women for the sake of his own selfish lust.

I watched, over a period of time, as the one musician proceeded to trample the feelings and loyalty of his faithful girlfriend, the one to whom I had become "protector." I watched as the decent gentleman was rejected by the younger lady who opted for a man who persisted in the betrayal of his wife and children.

It will only be a short time, of course, before these two sorry excuses for men will dump their latest "conquests." The younger woman may have sacrificed her chance for a decent man in exchange for what; more self-destructive pain in her own life? I hope not.

I have been on that stage myself as a professional musician. As a poet and musician, I know all about falling in love with love, I know how attractive such personalities become to the ladies and how easy it is to take advantage of them in such circumstances having witnessed it too many times over the years. The accelerating drug abuse has only compounded the tragedy in many women's lives. Some are led into such a thing and, even, arrested with such "lovers." This has happened in many cases I know of personally to the hurt and pain of women who have foolishly thrown away rare chances of a decent man in their lives in exchange for faithless, using and abusing degenerates.

One of the bartenders at this establishment, a lovely woman I know well, has also been an observer of this story. It was late and few left in the bar when we began to chat about the whole affair. She knew what I did of it and then some. But she also confided the fact that she, at one time, had made the same mistake these young women had made. She fell into the trap because of the very same thing; a good-looking, talented man with a good voice who easily attracted foolish women only to use them and toss them aside.

I talk to all of the participants of this tragedy and they have come to know me fairly well. I don't, of course, try to interfere, knowing from sad experience how impossible it is to keep people from doing what they want to do, even those self-destructive things that brings pain for those like these young ladies into my own heart. It is hard to watch people hurting themselves and too many of these young women are easy victims to using and abusing men, particularly if they become intoxicated. Women need a clear head at all times when dealing with men in any environment.

I'll continue to visit this bar. I'll listen to the music, I'll dance with the women, and we'll take our grateful escape into the enchanted world where, in each other's arms in time to the music, the world is a kinder and gentler place. I'll thrill to the sweet-scented fragrance of the girl in my arms, the smooth softness of her cheek against mine, her hair gently brushing my face, the very warmth and softness of her body against mine creating its magically peculiar beauty, the stuff of the stars I so enjoy observing and wish I could share with others. If we are brave enough, we will even look into each other's eyes, searching for that something that tells us we have found someone who cares, someone who will be the inspiration and hope that cruelty and evil, using and abusing doesn't have to prevail. And I'll also watch and listen.

Once more I will wish that if God has a magic wand He would wave it and remove the hurt and pain in the lives of people like these and punish the wicked. I'll be angry, again, that such things have to happen and, like the Psalmist, I will, in that anger, cry out to Him; Why, Lord, don't you do something about it?

The decent man and the young ladies I mentioned will be sharing confidences with me of dashed hopes and shattered dreams as a result of betrayal and foolish, self-destructive decisions. The degenerates will be bragging about the two, new notches on their belts. If I'm around when it happens, the two young women may well be telling me how they were used and betrayed by these two, evil men. And what can I possibly hope to tell them that they won't have learned for themselves? But will they have truly learned anything of real value? Not as long as they think so little of themselves that they are eager to squander themselves on degenerate men.

I'm not sure, of course, what the conclusion of the whole thing will be. It is unlikely that I will be in the area much longer and may miss it. Perhaps my knowledge of the whole thing can best be put in perspective by recounting the feelings of the man who had fallen in love with the younger lady and had, in fact, proposed marriage to her.

If he could express himself to her he would have told her that no matter what she did, he would always love her; that a large part of the pain of his own broken heart involves the pain she has suffered. But an essential ingredient of love and marriage is trust. The young lady would never have any occasion of a problem involving trust on his part; however, what of the trust that he would have to have for her? Only time can answer that question.

"Why is it," he asked, "women can be so easily led astray of such obvious degenerates and good men are left alone at the last dance?"

I have no ready answer for him. There is an expression: Good guys finish last. I have added my own cynical addendum: "Nice" is too often a four-letter word spelled "Dumb!"

No, don't worry folks. I don't subscribe to that cynicism. I know, in too many cases, it works out that way but, as I explained to this fellow, I would far rather hold on to the dream and hope of a decent woman who will be attracted to Good and Nice than become hard and bitter over the many betrayals encountered by decency and true, faithful love.

If I do hear of the conclusion of this tragic story, I'll be writing of it. I can only hope the ending will be better than its present prospects. And, while such things lead to the expressions of Men/Women are no damned good, people need to look to their own choices in such matters to find the real fault in such things. Because of my daughters and, being a man myself, I most often find myself on the side of the women. God knows I have suffered enough betrayal by women to become a despiser of the fair sex. By the grace of God and the help of my daughters this hasn't happened. But it is men, in far larger numbers, who are the users and abusers, who prey on women and through their own unholy lust brings grief and tragedy into so many lives.

I've just read a letter from a very dear lady in Idaho, one of several good friends I have in that beautiful state. She has had to spend a week in a homeless shelter. Fortunately, she is involved in a good church and they are trying to do something for her. Included in her letter was a copy of a Christian publication "Berean Journal." It's good and filled with much useful information. The one flaw, as with all such religious publications, is that it doesn't dare become too specific about the problems facing our nation.

And, while I applaud and encourage the efforts of all those who try to confront evil in any way, someone has to be out there where the real tragedies are given a voice, that voice being more often heard in the bars and taverns than the churches. But I have to admit; I wish someone else had my job in this respect.

One of the nicest people I have met in the local bars is C---. He was in a bad accident some time ago and nearly died. He was in a wheelchair, then crutches. We are sitting together chatting when H--- suggests that he and I join her and her friend and go to Steve's Golden Palomino in Wofford Heights for dancing and drinks. Knowing I am a coffee drinker made me the natural, designated driver.

I agree, particularly since the place we are in has attracted a guy very deeply in his cups who is becoming a really objectionable nuisance to the women and to us. Also, it would give C--- a chance at exercising his bad leg in a most agreeable fashion.

One of the women is a strikingly beautiful, nearly full blood, Cherokee Indian with long, black hair and eyes you could drown in. She is also one of the most honest women it has ever been my distinct pleasure to know, a factor which adds greatly to her beauty in my estimation. I also know I'll be telling you more about her in the future. The other is a very pretty, pleasant woman and an excellent dancer but, as with so many women, has had mostly disagreeable experiences with most of the men with whom she has had to deal. Yes, there are a lot of womanizers in the bars. Fortunately, I have a reputation of not being among their ilk. But, because of the large number of women I know and with whom I associate, it is only natural that there would be "talk." Reminds me of the expression "I wish I were having half the fun people think I'm having."

People are continually surprised at the fact that I steadfastly refuse to take advantage of that kind of use and abuse of others by my own choices. In this small area, if I were doing such a thing, it would soon be common knowledge. Nevertheless, I walk a narrow line and, by such a life, give the lie to any gossip. Hurtful as it is to have to disappoint any woman's expectation of me, better that than join that crowd of using and abusing men even if it means more years of a decent man searching for a decent woman. I will have that to offer her if nothing more.

I have two, primary reasons for not falling into that degenerate crowd of using and abusing men; First, and most incomprehensible to the great majority of the people I meet, is the fact that I believe in God. That doesn't seem to mean much to people anymore and that lack of understanding has not a little to do with the destructive and rampant immorality of our nation. Secondly: My children. My children, as I've said many times, have a right to expect their father to maintain a standard of behavior toward others, particularly women. By God's grace, I will continue to maintain that standard in spite of its consequent loneliness and misunderstanding on the part of so many.

We pass a very pleasant evening at Steve's. The dancing is nice and it does my heart good to see C--- having such a good time. I remain steadfastly sober and the drive back is uneventful. Not so for some other friends.

One couple has been drinking heavily. The woman decides to go out to their car and rest. But, instead, getting into the car she thinks it would be a better idea to go home and water their dog and gets caught weaving on the highway by a local cop. She is taken into custody and spends the night in Lerdo Facility. Now she faces a hefty fine, Community Service, even possible jail time if they don't have money for the fine. Their car was impounded and that cost money to retrieve; the curse of drink and hopelessness.

But it is also a matter of cruel fact, as I have mentioned in a previous essay, that the police are having to write more citations and make more arrests simply on the basis of getting revenue for increasingly bankrupt cities and counties. As a consequence, they watch the bars like vultures ready to pounce on easy victims, though I have no sympathy whatsoever for drunk drivers and no one is more opposed to the drunk driver than I am. They are guilty of causing too many innocent deaths, too much tragedy on the highways. But I am opposed to making the bars the targets simply because of the fact that our government insists on an insane policy of taxing us into slavery.

A--- is a bartender. He should certainly know better. Nope. He takes his vehicle off the side of the road while in his cups. Now he has the notorious DUI hanging over him. He will do the time rather than pay the fine. Many people are doing this simply because they don't have the money for the hefty fines involved. Catch 22. Give more tickets to increase revenue. People are broke and can't pay fines. Take them to jail at taxpayer expense and increasingly contribute to the government deficit. Insane! It is equally insane to ruin a person's life, giving them a criminal record, with a DUI because of a single beer! But this is more and more commonplace. The cops know they can get a positive test on many people who have had, literally, one beer.

I thank God I haven't the "gene" of the alcoholic. I could always take the stuff or leave it. As I pointed out in another essay, I can't take any credit for being able to forego the stuff; I simply have no affinity for it as an "accident of birth." Having family who didn't drink helped as well. But no one of any compassion can help feeling deeply, the tragic consequences of the abuse of alcohol or any other drug. I do, however, freely confess my addiction to caffeine and Lady Nicotine if not John Barleycorn and Who Hit John. In regard to nicotine, all of us smokers are beginning to wonder when Caesar is going to start putting us in jail for our drug abuse?

Good news! A young, lady friend, M--- is celebrating a short sentence in County Jail instead of prison. She and another friend of ours wants to "do it right" and the three of us make the rounds. I can enter into the joy of the occasion because of my personal knowledge of the women and the events leading to the injustice of the one having to go to jail at all.

As we go from place to place, we meet a lot of mutual friends, all of whom share the joy of the event. We end up at Arlie's. While I have the usual coffee, the rest are enjoying a variety of beverages and everyone is feeling good. The girls and I are hungry and we order a pizza from the Pizza Factory down the block. When I arrive to pick it up, I discover they have burned it and I wait for them to bake another from scratch. Oh, well.

Finally getting back to the celebrants, we share the pizza around the bar. The jukebox is doing good service with a nice selection of tunes and all is well. One fellow, however, gets so drunk he can't remain. He actually thinks he will drive home. Fortunately, he is in such an inebriated condition he can't even find his truck. He falls down outside and a couple of the folks manage to get him into a car and take him home, another following in the drunk's truck. It is remarkable how these folks help one another in such circumstances.

M--- is telling me it would be a wonderful thing if I would choose her closest friend, a statuesque, beautiful, blonde young woman to be my girl. She says she knows I would treat her right and be good for her. I am touched by such an honest approach and humbled by her estimate of me as a decent man. That the suggestion is made in the name of genuine friendship for both of us is all the more touching. She has very little to share with others besides the warmth of her friendship but she takes a small crystal from her handbag and, placing it in my hands asks me to hold it tightly. Then she tells me she wants me to have it. I gratefully accept the precious gift. As to her hope for her friend and me, the curse of the poet still haunts all such relationships and, while maintaining continued hope, continued searching, I know the odds are definitely not in my favor; but out there somewhere...?

Drinking, conversation, music and shooting pool (As I explained in a previous essay, I don't compete against women and refrain from the pool table). The hours slip by. One of our friends, a very nice woman, wants the girls and I to go to her home and play cards and just enjoy being together in continued celebration of the good news concerning our friend. They have all read some of my essays and share their feelings with me. They tell me of the tears some of my writing has brought to their eyes. They also encourage me by telling me of their appreciation of my sticking up for them as women. I deeply appreciate their sincere, heartfelt comments.

The bar is closing and it is time to go. While very grateful for the invitation to join them, I have to decline and come back to the house alone to get a few hours of badly needed sleep. I'll be taking the girls to a celebration dinner tomorrow evening and from there to Road's End to meet another woman friend for drinks (a little misleading since I'll still be having coffee). Tomorrow's another day and I will, once more, face the Divine Comedy, the joy and grief of being human and, once more, prepare to enter into the joys and sorrows of my fellow humans.

Howard is a marvelous musician. He could have made it big but the circumstances of his life kept getting in the way. He married, had children and the roving life of the musician who would make it in that world was denied him.

I've written much about the demands any art makes on the artist. I made my choice between the music and writing many years ago. I think I made the right choice even though the music still remains, and always will, an essential part of my life. It is a monumental decision to live your life for something. And while the music lives in me, I knew early on that I couldn't meet its demand. So it was that writing became my life as an act of responsibility, consuming the time which Art demands for its own sake. But my heart and soul will always live in time to the music. Though clarinet and saxophone were my professional instruments, I love the guitar and still play it occasionally. So it was that Howard had me sit in as back up to his marvelous voice and pickin'. He plays for tips at one of the taverns where I met him.

The folks in the audience were stunned to find me on the stage with Howard, keeping time with him to some of the better Country Western songs. It was, admittedly, a lot of fun watching the expression of amazement on the faces of the folks who thought I was only a writer who loved music but never suspected I could make music as well. I admit it felt good to be a part of contributing, once more, to the happiness of others through the music. If you have ever been a performing musician, you'll readily understand my feelings. Like the dancing, there is a magic to producing music for the enjoyment of others. The poet in me finds license to practice in this arena as well and there is always the intrigue as to how far, and where, it will lead.

I also have to mention Brenda, the beautiful little woman with the marvelous voice and superb musical ability with her guitar. Thank you, Brenda, for the joy you bring others with your smile and music.

It's another evening. Two, new women to the club have come in, a mother and daughter. Both are quite lovely, but the daughter is especially striking in appearance, causing every head in the place to turn her direction. She is an instant magnet to every man in the place.

Without going into detail, I become her first dance partner. I also dance with her mother and, in conversation, come to know something of them. I go into the routine of warning about some of the men I know in the place, who is ok and who is not. They are grateful for the information.

I never pass up a chance to share some of my essays with women, they are the one's I depend on to give me the necessary and essential insights into their expectations of men, their views of what the relationships should be, their own hopes and dreams which go into my own poetry.

Learning that I am a writer, I offer to give them a sample copy of one of the essays that they kindly accept. Looking at my picture on the first page, the mother turns to me and says; "This picture doesn't do you justice!" I'm somewhat taken aback by the comment but manage to thank her for such a compliment. Others have inquired as to why I use that particular photo for CP since it so graphically portrays every line in my face, totally without re-touching. I explain that it is, to me, an honest picture and the things I write about in CP demand that kind of honesty.

The lady's comment might have had something to do with the fact that at the time I was dressed in Western hat, shirt, Levis and boots. Maybe I do look better in such garb, I don't know. But clothes don't take the lines from my face.

It wasn't long after this that a beautiful woman I know very well remarked on the long scar on my face that shows up so graphically in my photo. She said she and some of her friends had discussed it and concluded it was a stress line from caring too much about other people. I couldn't have more humbling confirmation of my own motive in using this photo. I don't know, of course, if she and her friends are right or if this has anything to do with the scar taking on the characteristic of a "care" line but, maybe so.

I'm in the club a couple of days later in the afternoon when, by chance, the two women come in. Seeing me, they come over to my table and we have a pleasant time chatting. It seems one of the men I had warned them of had followed them to a restaurant after they had left the previous evening. Being warned in advance of the man, they successfully resisted his efforts to entice them and wanted to thank me for my warning.

While we are chatting, the woman bartender comes over with drinks for the mother and daughter. Now I'm sitting there with my usual coffee and a water chaser. But after sitting the drinks before the ladies, she places a mug of draft in front of me. I'm somewhat nonplused to say the least. I look at the bartender and say; "What's this for?" Pointing to the end of the bar, she says; "She bought it for you." She is pointing to a beautiful woman friend of mine who is smiling at me in a most mischievous way. I have to say of this woman that she has the most beautiful, sparkling eyes and winning smile, making her attractive in a most unique way. No man in the Valley would call her anything but beautiful and that beauty is accentuated in her honest and straightforward manner in dealing with people.

Now this woman knows full well that I don't drink. But one evening, we did share a few because of somewhat extraordinary circumstances and she knew I would be able to handle it. The situation did, however demand some explanation to the other women as to why the beautiful woman at the bar was buying me, a coffee drinker, a beer. It was, to underemphasize the moment, an interesting conundrum compounded by the fact that I had no suitable explanation.

I managed, somehow, to fumble my way through and, having an appointment to keep, took my leave of the mother and daughter and, on my way out, stopped to thank my friend at the bar for her "thoughtfulness." Then ensued one of life's embarrassing moments; in my discombobulated state of mind, I call her by the bartender's name. She has since forgiven me this mental lapse but the story is now current: "Give Don one beer and he forgets your name!"

It was some time later that I got an explanation of her mischievous prank. Seems she interpreted the situation with the two women and me as a situation that required my fortifying myself with something a little more stout than coffee. I'll always be touched by the actual kindness she showed in such a gesture notwithstanding the awkwardness that ensued. It is just such kindness and thoughtfulness that endears her to me.

It reminds me, too, of the fact that some relationships I have with various women are dangerous. By that interesting statement I mean there are a few women who know, because of the kind of man I am, that we don't dare get too close or look too closely into each other's eyes. It limits our dancing together as well. We love one another in a somewhat unique way that discourages physical intimacy and leaves us with the actual poetry of a transcendental relationship. Sadly, most men wouldn't have the foggiest notion of what I am talking about; but the women have a finer intuition of such things.

Speaking of which, women, the attractive ones particularly, do run some risk of some man following them when they leave a bar. The following Friday evening the younger woman I was with during the beer incident comes in and joins me at the bar. It is early and the band hasn't arrived. We have time to get better acquainted and thoroughly enjoy visiting and chatting. The time passes quickly and the band is ready to play. It is Magic Time.

I've introduced her to several friends and, of course, since she is young and strikingly attractive, all the men want to dance with her and I'm able to run interference against some of the more undesirable one's. A woman, especially if she is attractive, needs a "helper" at such times.

I'm reminded of the time I go into Slugger's to find a lovely woman I know well the only woman in the place. I manage to get a seat next to her and we have a delightful time together just "visiting." Later, she says to me; "I was so happy to see you come in. Until you got here, there were only men in the place!" Now I'm sure she didn't know how that sounded. Faced with the choice of being offended or complimented and knowing the woman so well, I choose the compliment. No matter my detractors, I know I'm not chopped liver. Oh well, back to the story.

With the music and dancing, the evening passes all too quickly. It is 2 a.m. and the tavern is closing. There are a couple of anxious moments, a couple of men who get drunk and obnoxious to the women. One, in fact, might be capable of trying to follow my young woman home. I suggest, in view of her legitimate concern, that I follow her in my car and see her safely into her house. She readily agrees and so it was that I become the "protector" once more.

Arriving at her home, she offers to make coffee. The hour is quite late but in spite of my concern for that, I finally agree. I'm glad I did as it gave us a chance to become better acquainted and we are able to share some things of common concern. We all need friends, people who we can talk to and find the caring we all need from others.

I take my leave, regretfully, about 4 a.m. I'm really getting too old for such things but am grateful for being able to find people like this young woman who so readily give me the insights I need for those softer and gentler things I love to write of.

Since I believe in God, I have a somewhat different view of the stars. I have tried to explain this to various people. When Karrie once asked me what we were made of as a result of a Sunday school lesson I told her: Sweetheart, we are made of the stuff of the stars. Now I know the passage in Genesis but it is misleading. We are not made of "dirt," but of the stuff of the stars. This is why the heart's longing as we gaze out at that inexpressible, vast array of incomprehensible beauty and promise of eternity. We are made of the stuff of the stars and our hearts respond in kind to that eternal promise of immortality.

But, while I did not mention it to Karrie of course there are indeed, "dirt people." These are those with the morals of animals who use and abuse others without conscience, the so-called "people" who harm children and treat others as though they were there for nothing but the lustful pleasure of these dirt people. God has a hotter place in hell for such.

Whenever I think of people I know who are so busy using and abusing others as well as themselves, I have to wonder if they have ever had a thought of the consequences. To observe them, you would have to think not. For example, what woman in her right mind would pass herself off from man to man with no thought of the consequences? Granting the fact that such women are giving up any chance of a decent man in their lives, that other fact of that dread death sentence of AIDS would give them, you would think, considerable pause to be more careful. No. I know too many women who think, like children, it will happen to someone else, not them.

A man came by to visit the other day and shared a personal nightmare. He is afraid he has the disease but is afraid to go to a doctor for confirmation; as he put it; "If I have it, I don't want to know."

You would think, as I pointed out to him, he better find out before he passes it on to someone else. His response stunned me. He said: "Don, you know the women I go out with and sleep with. One came to my door at 6 a.m. the other morning just for sex. You have been wise to avoid contact with them. But as far as I'm concerned, they deserve what they get from me. It's just such women that gave me the disease if I have it!"

I know the woman he had named as his 6 a.m. caller. Given his knowledge of the woman and her sexual habits and attitude I didn't wonder at his concern. The insanity of the whole thing is obvious to rational people.

But when people behave in insane and self-destructive ways, it isn't any wonder that they engage in psychotic thinking. And some of them actually describe such behavior as having fun! But God has warned: Be sure your sins will find you out and *The wages of sin is death.* I retain the conviction that God means business regardless the attempts by men and women to ignore Him.

I'm sure to have a follow-up on this situation in the future. As with the young women and the musicians, I hope it has a happier ending than the events seem to portend.

I met a lovely young woman the other night and, getting up my courage, asked her to dance. To my delight, she accepted. As I got to know her, I knew I had met another bird with a broken wing. As you know, I'm a real softy when it comes to such girls and women.

As time went by, we danced often and, as her story unfolded, a tragic life with a drunken bum of a husband, the abuse and hopelessness of the situation led her to seek another life. I hoped, as usual, that I could be of some help to her and her children.

She was a child in the affairs of men and easily taken advantage of. It was that child-likeness that led me to hold her closely as we would dance. Like an abused and hurting child, she needed the comfort of caring arms about her and would escape to the protection of those arms, the music and the dancing. People will talk. It was noticed that I didn't dance with anyone else in the manner in which I would dance with her. I had also taken to sitting with her when we were not dancing.

I tried to explain, as I have in previous essays, the reasons for my genuine caring for this young woman and for holding her so closely while we danced. Of course, I would never divulge the innermost secrets of her pain, many of which she, herself, is unaware and it would take many hours of in-depth counseling to bring her to such awareness. Tragically, given her circumstances, this isn't likely to happen.

Sadly, as the song goes, she went looking for love in all the wrong places. The question, as usual, is how many men will have to hurt her before, and if, she learns the tragic lessons I keep trying to prevent people from having to learn the hard way. How many of us fit that same description.

As with my own daughters, I would do anything to try to spare the pain in such people's lives. But it isn't, I sadly realize, likely to happen in this case. As with so many others who think being "equal" with degenerate men means lowering themselves to that level, such young women can only reap more heartache and abuse. But people continue to do what they want to do regardless the consequences. As for revenge against those that have abused us, such a thing has always resulted in bitterness and cynicism. Too many lonely people have come to the end of their lives by such a sad and tragic way.

It was in a discussion with a close friend who, in sincere regard for my welfare, was trying to warn me against any involvement with this young woman that the topic came up concerning that Family of pain and loneliness one often finds in the taverns. As with so many others, I tried to assure him that while I might make mistakes in trying to help others, I would far rather that than develop the callous and uncaring attitude so prevalent among other men, especially because of the continued betrayal so common to such concern. But it is comforting to know I have so many friends so genuinely concerned for my welfare. I am a most fortunate man in this regard and I thank those friends from the bottom of my heart.

It was early and not many people had come into the tavern yet. The band was playing one of those lovely melodies that I love to dance to. The only problem was that I didn't see anyone except for one young woman that I particularly wanted to dance with and she seemed preoccupied with a friend.

So I listened to the music and let my mind do its usual thing of absorbing the music and atmosphere while I stared out the window to the hills in the distance.

Suddenly, there she was in front of me, asking why I was staring out the window. I was a little embarrassed since I had wanted to dance with her but didn't want to intrude. Now it seemed she felt I had ignored her. I tried to explain that I was simply lost in thought as so often happens. I hope she understood. Many people don't.

For example, as one woman explained it to me, when someone seems lost in thought in the bars, the assumption is usually made that the person is lost in loneliness and depression, thinking of the latest broken romance, some family tragedy or like thing. Few would consider a man simply lost in thought to the music and letting the vignettes of the surroundings write stories in his mind.

It is true, of course, that many men and women resort to the bars in search of someone to heal their loneliness, not just a one-night stand. Admittedly, it does me a lot of good to meet new people, to make new friends in just such an environment. But I remain choosy about the kind of music played. This determines, in most cases, the kinds of establishments I frequent.

In respect to the music, Oscar kindly invited me to do some clarinet work the other night. It was good to share in the music and I thank him for the invitation. It will be some time before I can play as I used to but the folks were kind and friendly and I really appreciated the chance, once more, to make music instead of just being a listener. As with the guitar playing, it is interesting to think about where this part of my life will lead.

I do have to leave you folks with some political comment. You might not receive any of the other publications where I devote my energies to confronting the tyranny of Caesar. Also, if you only receive CP, you might get the impression that I have gotten my eye off the ball. Nope, I'll keep fighting in that political arena until Caesar is dethroned or... well, you know.

It is a hard thing to have to confront Caesar, as did our founding fathers. The government is now the nation's prime employer. But its employees live on the backs of the largely Caucasian middle class. And how much longer can We the People continue to support such a betraying and all-consuming behemoth of such a devouring appetite of More and More! Slavery!

The present, titular head and betrayer of our nation, President Clinton, is claiming a "victory" for his so-called deficit reduction plan. If this is a victory for taxpayers, I shudder to think of his definition of a disaster! Can anyone with an ounce of sense see this "plan" as anything but plunging us even deeper in an already impossible debt? This betrayer, with the help of his fellow betrayers, Congress, has done nothing but promised to enslave working people to pay for bigger government and that tyranny of law which will take from those that produce to give to those that don't.

Israel is the gun our national betrayers use as the weapon pointed at the Middle East. It serves our "master's" plan to use Israel in such a fashion. Why does Israel accept this role? That nation has no choice. But the deal that is cut by our betrayers gives such people a vastly disproportionate influence in the destruction of America's Christian ideals and morality. Anti-Christ? In every way possible; such is America's "leadership."

I have had many people respond enthusiastically to my last essay. Folks who had given up hope of anything being done on their behalf in the face of such evil as we face are now getting an idea of what can be done if we will work together in the same cause as our founding fathers.

Concerning the tyranny of law which has done so much to bankrupt the nation and at the risk of being accused of "simplicity" I would ask: What is wrong with an employer insisting on his right to hire the best qualified person for the job? But, thanks to quotas, Affirmative Action, so-called "Civil Rights," etc., businesses in America have been gutted of the best and brightest and, because of Caesar's intervention and the tyranny of his courts, business in America can no longer compete successfully with foreign producers.

Added to this devastating "concern" of Caesar for ignorance and incompetence, for lack of responsibility and integrity in the workplace, his forcing businesses to hire unqualified personnel, particularly Caesar's own suicidal practice of such hiring in government positions, state and federal, it is no wonder the wheels of industry and government grind so inefficiently to our own destruction as a nation. Caesar, as a consequence, does his best to provide full employment to lawyers and judges, to those whose incompetence and betraying larceny, as with that of Congress, is actually rewarded at the cost of taxpayers and the destruction of the, largely Caucasian middle class.

Ralph Reed Jr., director of the Christian Coalition, has finally caught up with me in his belated assessment of the fact that the religious right had better start swallowing a large dose of "gospel pragmatism" if there is to be any hope of The Gospel having any influence in our society. But, as so many others, he continues to exhibit an extreme naiveté about things such as school vouchers (imagine any sane person thinking Caesar is going to "give" something for nothing?). However he is on target, finally, about the need for Christians to move out of their comfortable pews and get some grease under their fingernails in the actual work God expects of his people. I would strongly suggest Mr. Reed and others examine what I have written about Caesar's successful emasculation of the churches by the ruse of Tax-exempt status among other things for starters.

The two Scripture references at the head of this essay should be in the minds of all Christians. First, most Christians are blind to the fact that caring for their children and families means far more than simply seeing to their material and spiritual needs. We, as Christians, are responsible for the future of our children as well. That means taking an active part in the duty of citizens to see to it that the society in which we live is not immoral or tyrannical, despotic. The churches have failed, miserably, to lead in this most important area; and, as James points out: *To him who knows to do good and does it not, to him it is sin*! Brothers and sisters, that means active good, not pew-warming!

The American people are subjected to the escalating abuse by government on every hand. I think the greatest insult, personally, is that those like Dan Rostenkowski sell themselves so cheaply. For stamps? This powerful man sells out for a few thousand dollars worth of stamps? It boggles my mind! Of course if he kept his larceny within bounds it wouldn't be so bad. But this powerful politician, chairman of the Ways and Means Committee (he certainly provides new definition to that roll) has been guilty of treason; the S&L and BCCI scandals, his continued brokering more and more tax and spend programs which have bankrupted the nation. No real piker here. Maybe stealing, betrayal and treason have become so ingrained for him that he thought it his "right" to steal a few thousand dollars worth of stamps for pocket change?

It is to be expected that the thief and traitor is protected by his crony, House Speaker Tom Foley together with that body, Congress, called a "bunch of crooks" by another, proven crook, our California ex-senator Alan Cranston. Mark Russel: "Rosty knew he was in trouble when he went to the post office and his picture was on the wall." Well, Mark, it isn't but it certainly ought to be. But, then again, the crooks and traitors, if all should be displayed, would require much larger walls than most post offices have.

Now, to add insult on top of insult, we are told by this bunch that the files of the investigation are to be closed and not allowed to be seen by the very people, us, who have been preyed upon by these thieves! When Rep. Bill Thomas tried to rally support to make them public, his fellow crooks cheer Mr. Foley when he insists that they remain secret and that he be treated with "courtesy." Do I believe Thomas' charge that Foley requested that mass murderer and, shamefully, our Attorney General, Janet Reno, send a letter to the House requesting that the investigation be handled secretly and kept from the American people? You bet I do!

Let's face it folks, the American people are just a bunch of dumb sheep and sheep are for shearing! That is the pragmatic truth of the view our "leadership" has of us. And, until we are "Mad as hell" and take action and assume the responsibility of our own lives and the lives of the future of our children, the "shearing" is going to get a lot worse!

Several people have asked me if I think those who were arrested for an alleged plot to kill Rodney King and blow up the First AME church were set up by the Feds ala Randy Weaver. In a word: Yes! I am convinced the FBI infiltrators spawned the whole idea in order to trap these people. For those "innocents" out there, the usual procedure is to have an agent, usually one who is older and experienced who is able to gain the trust of his victims by his broad background and expertise in leading young people, especially, in the direction he wants them to go. Such an agent will begin by "suggesting" certain illegal actions. He will also have "sources" for illegal weapons and explosives. It isn't difficult, faced with the extreme times we live in, for such an agent to lead people into entrapment.

Shortly after I wrote this section of the essay, the accused in the case verified my own thoughts about the situation stating that the FBI did, indeed, cook up the whole racist plot and did the leading throughout. A clear case of the kind of entrapment procedures common to the Feds whether true in this case or not.

As I have written previously, the Feds became involved in the fiascoes of Randy Weaver and Waco, Texas because they lack reliable information. They cannot depend on their thousands of paid pimps for such data and often wind up making ridiculous, even tragic, mistakes. Such things as the So Cal fiasco are evidence of the fact that they are hunting for larger game. They know there are many patriotic groups that do, indeed, pose a danger to Caesar and his Gestapo system that will fight to the death against his escalating attempt to betray all Americans into slavery and worship of the state. I speak to such people and groups on a daily basis.

As to the mess in So Cal, it also serves to help them to gull the public into believing they are "doing their job" and "are on top of things." It should be recalled by my readers that I have warned people about those they meet at gun shows to not trust those smiling faces that offer illegal items to them. That smiling face often belongs to a Treasury Agent. This is one of the reasons I got out of the business. As a consequence, Caesar and his agents know I can't be set-up in this regard.

I also believe it was Caesar's agents who made the guns and explosives available to those folks in So Cal. At this point in time, I have seen enough of such chicanery through, and by, Caesar's agents that I wouldn't put anything past them. They have most certainly made such things available on a huge scale whenever it has suited their purpose in other cases. And when it has suited the purpose of the shadow government to meddle in the affairs of other nations? You know the lurid, scandalous answer to that.

The organizations with which I have personal contact are together in this respect; entrapment is the name of the game. Few of those with whom I speak and correspond would be so foolish as to think a race war could be started as simply as the media and Feds try to contend; and the stupidity of starting such a war in a third world nation like L. A.? Preposterous! They are already at war, Negroes, Mexicans and Asians are already killing one another and Caucasians have left the war zone or are in the process of doing so!

The whole thing does, of course, substantiate that historical imperative that only one ideology can be supreme in any nation. And, in either ignorance or conspiracy, the media and minority leaders continue to try to make this a "racial" incident. It isn't. It is strictly ideological and no one wants to talk about that.

Yet, these minority leaders, aided by the media and the crooks and traitors in government feel free to continue their own bigoted and prejudiced attacks on Caucasians and Caucasian culture, most particularly our Caucasian Christian Culture. It hardly helps when Louis Farrakhan, Jessy Jackson, Pete Knight, Kathleen Honeycutt and Marge Schott muddy the waters. But all of this is only more evidence that America, far from being a "melting pot," is a nation at war within itself and only one ideology can possibly survive this constant conflict, a conflict which will resolve itself whether led by enlightened men and women or by anarchy. The inescapable imperatives of the history of nations and human nature will not be changed or denied. Hard facts and hard choices face us. But the decisions of history and human nature are made with, or without, the cooperation of men and women. The question that confronts us is whether these decisions will be made by enlightened men and women of good will or...?

Only a middle class, working to better its own future through personal effort, integrity and responsibility has enabled the standard of living all other nations envy. But when that largely Caucasian middle class has, in fact, vanished? There never has, and never will be, a free lunch. Slavery, anarchy or the course our founding fathers followed, these are the only "solutions" history allows. And how many are willing to be branded traitors and rebels, willing to make the necessary sacrifices, to join that honorable host which delivered us our liberty and freedom, our Republic? It is my considered opinion that all patriotic organizations will have to cooperate in this effort; but if we don't?

While minority leaders recognize the historical imperative that only one culture, one ideology can possibly have dominion, they will continue to insist on the destruction of the only ideology that has enabled them to survive and be treated humanely; a Caucasian Christian one and not that silly, destructive oxymoronic so-called Judeo/Christian one that silly, deceived and deceiving so-called "churches" keep trumpeting.

A word to my "brethren:" I am meeting too many good people who are hurting and without hope. It has never been enough to say to these folks: Be warmed and filled notwithstanding you give them those things necessary for hope (James 2:16).

Carefully read Parade Magazine's lengthy article of July 25, 1993 by Daniel J. Boorstein. He borrows my argument that the hyphenated American is no American. Good enough. But, as a researcher trained in reading between the lines, I notice a few jarring details which gives the lie to his seeming "Americanism."

If you, as me, see yourself as an American with the traditional American values, values that are predominantly, Biblically Christian in orientation, you find yourself being made an enemy to Boorstein's definition of such. This Pulitzer Prize-winning "historian" says the colonists of this nation "... transcended the boundaries of European religion, race and tradition. At the same time they established a new tradition that welcomed the stranger."

Read between the lines and you find another message. Not only does Boorstein make a mockery of the actual history involved, he tries to get away, successfully I might add, with an outright lie! No half-way reader of the actual history can fail to see that far from "welcoming strangers," the first settlers of America were thoroughly opposed to those who were not Caucasian and Christian; and quite understandably so given the historical context.

Like all good Marxists, he says the U.S. has never had a religious war. What he fails, on purpose, to disclose is the fact that both the War for Independence and the Civil War were, by the broadest definition, religious wars. He claims: "We don't have a dogmatic ideology, which is a prison, but, instead, the great institution of our Constitution." The "we" he uses makes me want to vomit! He is no "we" as an American by any stretch of the imagination! He is an enemy and betrayer of that Constitution delivered us by our founding fathers.

As to the betraying collaboration between alien ideologies and our "leadership," I would invite my readers to discover how Boorstein became Librarian of Congress, the highest intellectual honor the U.S. can bestow. Yet his voluminous, revisionist "histories" used in our universities are an absolute, betraying treason against the facts of the actual history of our nation and have been hugely successful in helping his fellow betrayers in solidly implanting the Anti-Christ philosophy of Humanism in all of our schools. It doesn't take much of an in-depth study of things of this nature to explain the mounting antagonism of Caesar and his cohorts towards those who hold to the Biblical, Christian principles of our Founding Fathers, toward those of us who are working for solutions based on those principles.

The recent bombing of the NAACP headquarters was blamed on neo-Nazis but there are a whole lot of people in this country who are so angry they, like Thoreau and me, are walking about with "Murder of the State in their heart!" Many of us are growing more and more willing to throw the necessary sand into the destructive machinery of a tyrannical government that is set on destroying every vestige of personal liberty and responsibility, which has destroyed our hopes for our children and grandchildren.

For those that may not have heard, a doctor is calling for MASH units to be set up in the war zone of South Central L.A. A Vietnam Vet, the doctor says: "There's as much a war in the streets here right now as in Vietnam. I'm a soldier in a war, and it's a war we're losing." He asks for $20 to $50 million to set up the units. Apart from the obvious truth of his assessment of the War Zone, one I have made as well, one has to ask: Who is to pay for this? Of course! The taxpayers.

California's Governor Wilson is asking for the elimination of mandated government services for illegal aliens. Why do such "leaders" wait until the state is bankrupt before addressing the obvious insanity of such laws? As to the governor finally addressing an issue I have written much about, the further insanity of "instant citizenship" which pregnant illegals come in droves to acquire at enormous expense to American taxpayers, we can expect the ACLU and every other anti-Christ, anti-American group in the country to set up a howl; this in spite of the fact that we are the only nation to have such a stupid and self-destructive law.

Given the insanity of Caesar's tyranny of laws, it is no wonder Brokaw's "Lost Generation" got such large play. Multiplied millions of young people have no hope of a future. I have pounded this drum repeatedly but none of the "leadership" has been listening. And, to repeat: No nation that does not cherish its young has a future as a nation!

There is, indeed, a social epidemic of violent death stalking the youth of America. What no one is saying is the fact that this has it's roots in the major cities of America, major cities like L.A. that have become war-torn, third-world nations within the nation where the participants are Negroes, Mexicans, Cubans, Puerto Ricans, Asians, etc.

A homosexual Brazilian has been granted "asylum" in this country by our betraying courts solely on the basis of his perversion. Seems Brazil has a much more common sense attitude toward perversion than this nation. How many of these perverts in other nations are now going to use this mechanism to gain entry to the U.S.? Many of them, of course, will be AIDS or TB carriers. This is a major victory for perverts and can only hasten our own demise as a nation.

Chapter Ten

Christian Perspective

October

John 5:24

It was about 3 a.m. when the call came. I had been expecting it eventually but didn't know when it would come. She was nearly incoherent because of the pain and grief. She said she shouldn't have called but whom else could she call? I encouraged her to keep talking and finally asked her if she would like me to come and get her. She said yes.

I dressed hurriedly and got to her place within ten minutes of the call. She was standing outside waiting. I opened the car door for her and asked if she would like to go to the local coffee shop and have a cup of coffee. She couldn't speak but nodded her head.

Arriving at that hour of the morning, there was no one but the waitress, an old friend of mine. She took the situation in at a glance and had two cups of coffee in front of us immediately.

All I could do was put my arm around the young woman as she trembled all over, eyes red and puffy with spent tears and try to say the things she needed to hear under the circumstances. She continued to remain mute, unable to verbalize her own pain, the pain of the betrayal of her love for an unworthy and abusing man wracking her mind and body.

I wondered once more as I have so many times at the cruelty people inflict upon one another. If that man could see her now, tormented, hurting so badly, presently beyond the ability to force anymore of the needed tears that might bring some relief, grieved beyond the ability to speak, would he even care? I doubted it.

My Ph. D. in Human Behavior, my diplomas, certificates and credentials may help in some degree of objectivity in dealing with people's problems but the human factor, the actual pain and grief of the human condition in such circumstances goes far beyond any professional training. And none of these things can make a person care for others.

I remind myself that I have been there at the hands of cold-blooded women in my own life. No, it isn't just men who are abusers, I've known more than my share of such women as well. But, as I've pointed out many times, my daughters and the decent women I have known have saved me from being the kind of man who would ever be guilty of the kind of pain in a woman's life such as that which I was now confronting in this poor girl.

Because of my reputation in this regard, she knew of one man who would not take advantage, who she could trust to help and understand. It is a humbling reputation, gained at great cost in my own emotional life and the practice of never using anyone. That good name is, as the Bible says, to be prized above all riches.

Tremblingly, she managed to get the cup of coffee down. I quickly realized she was totally exhausted and should be in bed if she could only sleep. I asked if she would like to return home. She nodded "yes," still unable to speak.

Getting back to her house, I walked her to the door. There was no outside light and I had to use my cigarette lighter in order for us to see to get her key in the lock. Stepping into the house, she immediately headed for her bedroom. Going in, she collapsed across the bed.

She had been smoking but was unaware she had a lit cigarette in her hand. I took it from her fingers and extinguished it. Removing her boots and getting her properly situated on the bed, her head on the pillow, I covered her up with the blanket. She was still unable to say anything but allowed me, in fact, needed me, as would a child, to put her to bed.

I sat on the edge of the bed, holding her in my arms and stroking her soft, beautiful, waist-long hair. If it had been possible, I would have wept openly for her but my eyes have remained dry for too many years, that well of precious moisture drenching my heart from similar grief but unable to ever again find the channels of relief and release through my eyes.

She reminds me of a small, wounded animal that doesn't understand why it has been so grievously hurt and can only struggle against the pain, hoping for someone, something to put an end to its suffering. I know that kind of pain all too well.

In a very short time I could tell from her breathing that she was sound asleep in my arms. As gently as I could, I removed my arms from around her, lightly kissed her tear-washed cheek and with a prayer for her safety, hoping the mercifulness of sleep and the bright sun of morning will lift her spirits and thinking of my own daughters all the while, slipped quietly out of the house. I have done the best I can for her for now. And I know it isn't enough. But what will be?

In the past few months, I had helplessly witnessed the self-destructive choices the young woman had made which led to this event. But, I have been the witness of too many similar tragedies to do much but let myself be the comforter, the listener and understander when such things reach their inevitable, destructive conclusion, too often wrecking the lives of the innocents in such affairs. But people, as I often point out, will do as they please, even to their own hurt, in spite of the advice of those that genuinely and honestly care for them.

It was fortunate that she knew of one man she could call for help. Too many such young women don't and pay a heavy price for life-styles that promote such pain and grief. The little woman was a favorite dance partner of mine on many occasions, had, in fact, been one of my teachers. It was magic to hold her in my arms and dance to the slower, more romantic melodies. She had a warmth, softness and sensitivity that strongly attracted me. But her eyes were what first caught my attention, light blue with the honest pain reflecting the hard life she had had and was still having. Yes, another bird with a broken wing.

But this young woman had made the self-destructive choice of "sleeping around" to ease her own loneliness and other needs and I knew some of the men personally she had allowed to use her. Tragically she made the mistake of falling in love with one of them, not seeming to realize that her reputation preceded her, that it was extremely unlikely that any decent, self-respecting and responsible man would become intimate with her, let alone marry her.

Some time later, as we discuss her call and my treatment of her, she will express surprise that I didn't take advantage of her under the circumstances. This in spite of the fact that she trusted me not to do so and had called me more out of instinct than any conscious motive. At the time, I don't think she could have called me out of a reasonable and conscious choice, she was past thinking rationally. There was even an underlying, unstated disappointment on her part that such a thing did not take place. Not because she especially wanted me, perhaps any man who showed her any consideration or kindness would have done as well under the circumstances. She couldn't understand either her trust or my response to that trust.

Her disgust with herself, her loathing of her own lifestyle and her inability to see herself of any value to a good man and others dooms her to the self-destructive pattern of behavior I warn about. She can't realize or understand that the young woman I put to bed like a hurting child allows me an expression of love that is of such preciousness I wonder that more men don't relate to it. Perhaps only men like me who have daughters who taught them about the purest love in the universe can relate to such a thing. It is tragic that she doesn't understand it.

Will she be calling again? Probably. Along with others.

Lacking men in their lives who treat them with kindness and consideration women are left with the "other kind" to use and abuse them, particularly when they have come through a marriage or "relationship" where a man has abused them emotionally and physically. Such women often come out of such situations beaten down; often feeling they actually deserve such treatment at the hands of their abusers.

Perversely, they will often seek men who will continue the cycle of such abuse in their lives. They have actually been "taught" that they are "stupid, ugly, of no value." Tragically, drugs and alcohol play a key role in many such cases.

Strange as it seems, some people only feel comfortable in such an atmosphere of use and abuse. It's a little like the "institutional" men who are only comfortable in a prison environment. Unable to function in the outside world of work and responsibility, they choose institutions where they will be cared for, fed, clothed, housed, never having to make the decisions and choices life would demand of them otherwise. Naturally, the self-worth of such people is of the lowest kind imaginable. Like the women in a cycle of abuse, they see themselves of no real value to themselves or others.

But women, as I have pointed out, in our society, come to that point of their lives when they face certain, inescapable facts in their mirrors. They lose their youth and attractiveness and, as a consequence, lose any value in a society that has given itself to a sexual definition of "value" in regard to women. That women betray themselves by allowing such exploitation is of little comfort to those that pay the price of selling themselves so cheaply and, with the inevitable encroachment of age and wrinkles, are left with the loneliness and despair which are the wages they have earned for their own selfish, sinful choices. God never allows Himself to be mocked by our willful behavior. And, it doesn't matter what a culture or society says or does in denial of God's Law, He takes sin seriously whether we choose to or not.

The Honky Tonk life has its genuine fun and friendliness but it easily leads to tragedy as well. Human behavior runs the gamut in such an environment. You enjoy the CW music, drink, dance, fall in love, betray or get betrayed and start over again; so very human.

The trick, I tell people, is learning to not mind the pain (Emotional pain). I can easily deal with physical pain). Perhaps this is easier for me as a poet, I don't know. In talking this over with a very beautiful and close friend of mine, she said: "You know Don, if you ever meet the right woman you will have to learn to trust all over again." She was right, of course, but it is always a roll of the dice; the very dichotomy of beauty and the beast, wanting to trust and fearful to trust, knowing too intimately that monster that turns and rends those whose trust is misplaced and betrayed.

I had shared with her my own fear, the wall I had built up over the past, few years in order to escape the very grief of the young woman to whom I had ministered. I've already had more than my share of such grief and am not always properly grateful for having survived it. Will I ever meet such a "right" woman who will so capture my heart as to be oblivious to such a threat? Probably. But it remains a specter, the stuff of nightmares as long as that wall is up and that objective part of my brain functions at full power. As I tell others, it is far easier and safer to, as a poet, make love on paper rather than take such a risk in the actual arena of life itself.

I'm at the Club when a beautiful, blonde woman comes up and asks if she can take the stool next to me. I recognize her but have never spoken much with her; the few times I had seen her, her manner seemed aloof and she gave the impression that she preferred to be left alone. I saw her when I walked in but didn't know her well enough to stop and simply chat with her. Whatever the reason, she decided she wanted to become better acquainted and I had to give her credit for taking the initiative.

She was drinking beer and I had the usual cup of coffee in front of me. This is always intriguing to people who don't know me and don't know I'm not a drinker.

As we chatted, she noticed the coffee. I went into my usual explanation but she was insistent and called Joyce, the lady bartender, and told her she wanted to buy me a drink. I protested politely whereupon the lady said that if she couldn't buy me a drink she wanted to buy me a cup of coffee. Now Joyce, a really great gal as are Lois, Marlee and Piney, the other bartenders at the Club, is getting a real kick out of the situation. I seldom ever have a drink and you don't pay for anything but the first cup of coffee, if that, in the bars. Seeing the situation getting a little sticky and not wanting to offend the lady, I opted for a light draft and that took care of things.

Having successfully avoided a "situation," the visit continued in a warm and friendly vein, the two of us getting to know each other and enjoying it. We agreed that if she made it Friday night, we would dance together, something we hadn't done and would now look forward to.

As we talked, a really obnoxious womanizer I know well (he was among those who bragged of the one night stand he had had with the young woman I had put to bed) began to give everyone a bad time with his vile language. He had to eventually be eighty-sixed and the ladies at the bar waxed eloquent in denunciation of the degenerate. Seems he had tried to hit on all of them at various times and they all had their stories to tell of the women he had taken advantage of. With such a well-earned and vile reputation, I wondered again that he still found women so gullible as to believe he would ever treat any of them right.

The blonde has to go to work. Just as she is getting ready to leave another friend of mine, the beautiful Cherokee woman I have mentioned before, comes in. The two of them know each other and began to chat leaving me to formulate my usual mental notes which find their way into my essays.

It does seem that most of the time the bread falls with the butter or jelly side down; but occasionally it falls right side up. In this case, I have to wonder which it is since there seems to be some coolness between the women once they realize I know them both.

I'm reminded of T.S. Elliot and his seeming need to make people reach and stretch to make sense of some of his verse. I do my reaching and stretching before I write. Once I have done that in my own mind, I reduce the conclusions to common words and use those in a way that people can understand. My word pictures, as a result, are those that ordinary people can see and understand. I choose to use the most common of canvas and the plainest of colors because I would much rather have a larger audience of readers than make a display of vocabulary or risk being abstruse.

The situation I find myself in with two, beautiful women parrying as only women can do certainly conjures up a number of possible scenarios which it might well serve me better in using abstruse language to convey the mental images forming in my mind at the time. While sometimes being accused of being gullible and naive by well-meaning women friends trying to protect me from those they consider unsuitable of my attention, and I do thank them for their concern, I am not so far out of it that I don't recognize and appreciate the art of the language women use in trying to dispose of those they consider the enemy of a man's attention to them.

Both women know my reputation of standing up for women against using and abusing men. They also know I always go home alone at night. This undoubtedly contributes somewhat to the intrigue most women find in a man who is unusual in any way.

If I could, I would explain it has nothing to do with any "character" or integrity on my part. It comes from the lessons I have learned from God's Word, life experiences of being betrayed and my daughters whom I could never betray of their expectations of their father to do right no matter what the allure of temptation to follow in the steps of those very men who I have learned to despise because of their abuse of girls and women.

The blonde leaves and the beautiful Cherokee and I are left to ourselves. I delight in knowing this woman, she is one of the most honest and forthright women I know and we have become fast friends, sharing many confidences and talking of many things in which we share interests. Life has been hard for her, her beauty and intelligence in too many cases working against her. She has had to suffer the pain of being the object of jealousy of many women because of her physical attributes. The thickly luxurious, waist-long, coal-black hair and striking blue eyes in a beautiful face contribute to the envy of other women.

In speaking with many men on the subject, it is commonly agreed that there is no satisfactory substitute for women. Profound Philosophy 101. I might as well point out the obverse in relationship to the fair sex; they are equally hard pressed to find a substitute for men.

So it is that many of the conversations I engage in ultimately lead to the relationships between men and women, an inexhaustible subject since time immemorial. Now for an example of the male ego at work:

The woman entered and immediately every head turned her direction; the poor fiddle player, nearly dropped a stroke with his bow and the dancers on the floor almost stopped, both men and women. She was dressed in a simple, mid-calf, red gown with sash that flowed on her body like the most regal finery of a queen and she carried herself like one. She was fully aware of the impression she made and was so comfortable with it that the impact was all the more profound.

Her ash blonde hair, hanging to her waist, was pulled back to accentuate a face of classic beauty in near-perfection. Well above average height, long legs and a figure of perfect proportion she provided a picture of poetic beauty. And she would only dance with me.

I was in full Western garb, including black hat and Levis (to match my black heart, I tell folks). While her dress and appearance would have graced the finest ballroom, because of her obvious confidence and ease, her natural beauty, it oddly didn't seem to be out of place in the CW environment and we made a strikingly rare, contrasting picture together on the dance floor. We were certainly the focus of attention of everyone in the place.

The fiddler would smile his lascivious best each time we passed the bandstand and we caught his eye. He was having difficulty playing and watching my lady at the same time, as were the others in the band.

It would have been impossible to ignore the sheer envy of every man in the place, not to mention the jealousy of not a few of the other women, as they watched me holding this perfection of beauty in my arms and moving with easy grace in time to the music. I was fully conscious of the impression of the event and have to admit to the male ego rising within myself.

As we danced, I looked into her bewitching, hazel eyes. Her eyes and a slight smile conveyed the secret we shared, a secret only she and I were a party to. That same look and smile might appear mocking to those who didn't understand our relationship.

We laughed and talked with easy familiarity but I realized, once more, the sadness that in spite of the appearance of things, in spite of the palpable envy of every man in the place, the lady and I would never be more than good friends. This was our shared secret. No one, of course, watching us, would ever believe that.

The Lady in Red and I have a history. Because of the circumstances of our meeting, it was early established that we would probably only remain friends regardless of our mutual wish that it might be different. I have met several women where that mutual wish is shared. But the curse of the poet raises its hindering head in each case. As a consequence, I have to let that deliberate part of my mind control my emotions and, thus far, sacrifice my heart to making love on paper.

Do I love the Lady in Red? Yes; but not in the sense that some people would be able to understand. It goes beyond the merely physical. I love many women in the same sense as the love I have for the young woman I put to bed, the Lady in Red and others and that love has built relationships with some that go beyond a simple definition of friendship. In that sense, I love these women. Perhaps, as I previously said, only daughters can teach such love in a man's life.

For example, there is another beautiful woman with whom I share a smile. In that smile we have for each other, there is a world of meaning and understanding beyond words or any physical contact. We actually "make love" to each other with a smile. We risked dancing together once. Only once. And I pity those who can't understand what I am talking about. Such a thing, just as with the young woman I put to bed like a child, borders on the sacred and is the stuff of poetry and the stars.

My old friend, Byron, has come by and we are sharing some of the views we have on the subject of love and romance, of poetry. He is a very sensitive man and I heed what he has to say in this regard. He knows, of course, my background as a Litt. Major and of my life-long involvement with the literature of the great writers of Europe and America throughout history. His comparison of my writing, in spite of my protestations, to F. Scott Fitzgerald cannot be ignored entirely. I could certainly fare worse than such a comparison.

There is a disturbing element in my conversations with friends like Byron. I am reasonably accused of being a "romantic" as though there were something wrong with being so. Most poets are construed as romantics. The disturbing element has to do with the stories I tell about the relationships between men and women. I have mentioned this point in the past but I keep being reminded of it when I discuss these things with friends like Byron.

It is a given that people, by and large, have little idea of the world I move in. Not that many don't travel in these circles, they just don't see things in their minds the way a poet does. This is mostly due to the circumstances in ordinary lives, not to mention the factors of greed and lust so prevalent in many people's lives, which preclude most of these experiences from which I weave my stories and paint my word pictures.

The dissatisfaction which so many couples have with their mates leads to envy of someone like myself who has the means and liberty to go out and experience life, to meet new people and enter into new experiences. My own youngest daughter says I have a better "social life" than she does at her age. My eldest son concurs in relationship with his own experiences. He is planning to visit me soon and expects me to introduce him to some of the people and places I mention in my essays. I look forward to it.

Strange that my own children would be surprised at their father's busy, and, admittedly interesting life since they should be so familiar with it. But children aren't the only one's full of surprises.

Getting back to the point I'm trying to make, many men are envious of my knowing so many beautiful women and even become angry that they feel "cheated" because of their own circumstances precluding their going out and doing what I do. That their primary motivation is usually the lust of the flesh only aggravates the anger I have toward such misplaced envy on their part. But I envy those who have a life-mate whom these same men ought to encourage in the music and poetry possible of their own lives.

Far too many couples think there is nothing wrong that someone else won't cure. You would think they would get the picture after a few bad choices that this isn't the case. They would do far better in encouraging those elements that drew them to that other person in their lives rather than chasing an elusive "something" they think they are missing out on.

It is useless, I have found, however, to talk of love and romance, the music and poetry of life with those who think they have missed it because of their dissatisfaction with their present mate. For this reason, I find it nearly impossible to discuss such things with many of the married people I know. They have blocked such things out of their minds and their relationships have become, in far too many cases, "business as usual," mundane and unfulfilling to them as individuals, let alone as partners in life with another. This is tragic.

Yes, I do write about the romance and tragedies I find in people's lives. This is the stuff of poetry and I'm a poet. But Byron shouldn't miss that element of the granite in my own character which confronts the evils of a society and its leadership which has done so much to destroy the music and poetry of our national life, the hopes and dreams of our children, that moves me to confront those things which cause bad things to happen to good people. But Byron and many others don't read much of my political writing and it may be just as well. Not every sensitive soul can deal with those hard things with which I must contend. I often wish someone else had my job in that regard.

Opposed to Fitzgerald are also the elements of Melville, Hawthorne, Thoreau, Poe and so many others to weigh as well, not to mention the literature of politics as per Paine and Jefferson, which colors much of my writing. The hard things of confrontation of evil and tyranny still need to be written; would that I could devote myself entirely to those softer and gentler things of the relationships between men and women, of the needs and hopes of our children.

There was a benefit dance for an old, country music star, Charles "Bobby" Moore, in Bakersfield. It was held at Maitia's on Union, a beautiful, tasteful establishment given to fine dining and fine music. Maitia's specializes in Basque cuisine, a favorite of mine. The food is excellent, the prices very reasonable and the portions exceptionally generous. The service is faultless in both the restaurant and the lounge.

I was asked to help out with the affair. There were some CW notables in attendance and the music and dancing were superb; thank you Shannon, Inez, and Cricket for your efforts in making the affair a success.

Bobby's daughter, Paula, a tall, dark-haired and very beautiful girl played violin. She is an exceptionally gifted violinist and especially gifted with the genius for the classics. But she has taken to playing CW and singing. Her delicate beauty, virtuosity, personality and lovely voice should take her far in this field. I sincerely hope so; the competition is fierce and unforgiving.

Bobby, as so many others, devoted his life to the music but, as with so many others, never made much money at it. As I have talked to several of those whose lives are the music, who live for making music, I am once more grateful for my decision to turn my efforts to writing rather than music. Not because of the difference in material reward, but because of the fact that more people can make music than can write and it is essential that the music and the writing work together. This can only be done by those gifted in both areas; a rare combination and the "responsibility factor" dictated the decision for my life's efforts.

I stayed at Maitia's till quite late, enjoying the music and dancing; so much talent given to the enjoyment of others for so little reward beyond simply making music. But if it is in your blood, you play. As with all forms of show business, it becomes more meaningful if you have a good audience. Nothing is as hard as playing to a near-empty house.

Inez asks if I would like to take a turn playing and singing before I have to leave. I tell her it is Paula and Bobby's close friend's night but I hope to come back at a later date and take her up on her offer. Perhaps I will.

Regretfully, I take my leave and head back up the canyon to Lake Isabella, thankful to have had the privilege of being a part of the affair for Bobby. He had a lot of good friends and I know his wife and daughter appreciated the efforts of all who were involved in appreciation of the joy he brought to others through his music and friendship.

Last night, I visited Ewings on the Kern River. This is a beautiful restaurant and lounge; I judge it the finest in the Valley. The dining area gives a magnificent view of the Kern and the decor is tasteful throughout. There is a CW band that is excellent. Steve, John, Jerry, and Paul are superb musicians. I also know the owner, Bill, and the bartender, Tom. They are friendly fellows and really know their business.

During some of the faster numbers, a group of the women treat us to some really fine line dancing. I dance with some of them to the slower melodies and have a good time socializing.

As I dance with one lovely young blonde I'm reminded of my son's and daughter's comments on their dad's social life. No, kids, it isn't all for the fun of it, it isn't all for the magic of holding a girl in my arms and moving to the enchantment of the music. It is a good deal more than that. It often leads to the involvement in the lives of other people who are often without hope and seek escape to a kinder and gentler place where, for a moment, they can escape the ugly realities that dominate too many lives.

And, in fact, you don't always escape in the environment of the music and dancing. The young blonde had come up to me and asked me to dance. The male ego surges once more. Now I know I'm a handsome man but I had noticed another man "hitting" on this young woman and wondered how she was going to handle him since it was obvious she didn't want his attention.

So she grabs me. As we are dancing, she says: "Please don't say anything embarrassing." Ah, ha! The other man had obviously been one of those who, getting a woman in their arms, use the direct, often obscene approach of asking for sex. This is one of the ugly facts of tavern life; the women are exposed to such risks. And it sometimes turns ugly.

One night at another place I was chatting with a friend and saw a young woman I know well stop in the middle of a number, push the man with whom she was dancing away from her and come up to me to finish the dance. If the guy hadn't known me and knew enough about me to keep his distance under the circumstances, some kind of altercation might have ensued. In this case, it was the way he was using his hands and the things that he was saying to her that caused her to get away from him. No, it isn't all magic and enchantment.

For those that envy me the life I lead, if you heard the stories of the tragedies in so many of these people's lives you wouldn't be so quick to want to trade places with me. A friend recently said to me: "Don, how do you manage to listen to so many people's troubles and try to help them without getting totally depressed?" I kind of shrugged his question off because I didn't want him worried about me. But in fact, I do get depressed. There are times when I wonder, myself, how I manage to get so involved with others that I forget I'm a person with the same needs of friendship and subject to the very same human trauma as those I try to help. The real depression comes from being able to do so little to help.

A good man and friend, B---, is concerned about me. He is a bourbon and water drinker and insists on buying me a drink. I have turned him down on a number of similar occasions but this night is different. The tenor of the conversation and the events of his own life have made us, at times, partners in loneliness. For any number of such reasons, I feel I must accept his offer this time or risk offending him that I am loath to do.

The bartender is surprised by my acceptance of a bourbon and water but there are times.... At such times, I think of my youth when getting drunk didn't seem to be such a bad idea. It still crosses my mind on occasion but, as I've said before if it was a foolish thing to do then, how much more so now?

As I drink the bourbon, I reflect on the things that drive many to drink. I can easily enter into the sorrows of the lives of others, I can write of their dreams and hopes, of the betrayals of love and romance. But, as I sip the drink, I remind myself that this is also a part of the whole thing. So it is that I accept the offer of a drink on occasion, being duly grateful that I lack the gene and profile of the alcoholic. And B--- is happy to have done something he thinks is good for his friend.

As with the music, most of the time the rewards are simply your love for others and trying to bring some light and hope into the lives of those others. When someone tells me that something I have written has struck a responsive chord in their own heart that is sufficient reward for my efforts; when a young lady calls me at 3 a.m. because she has learned to trust me that is reward enough. When I am the dance partner of the most beautiful girl in the place, the whole scene providing the material for a word picture of interest to others that is reward enough. When a woman can turn to me on the dance floor to get away from a man who is behaving in an ugly way to her, that is its own reward. Living life through these experiences with other people, giving me the material to pass on to my readers to teach or enrich their lives is reward enough.

Then too, when you have studied and trained for the ministry, when you have served in a pulpit, you develop the heart of a shepherd if you have a sincere calling to such work. You might wind up selling cars or running a milling machine (or becoming a writer) but the heart of the shepherd stays with you. Mix in the poetry and music, the dancing and all the human factors that go into the Divine Comedy and you have a most interesting combination.

Since I have been writing CP for nearly ten-years, my readers of a long time notice certain themes and statements which I repeat. When asked, I have to remind them that I am constantly picking up new readers. Also, I personally hand out copies to people I meet nearly everyday. As a consequence, I do repeat some things for the sake of these new readers and subscribers.

For example, the statement: No nation that does not cherish its young has any future as a nation bears constant repetition. Another one: The relationship between men and women was never intended to be one of competition but one of compatibility.

As to the theme of the romance, poetry and music I find in ordinary lives and circumstances (as well as the grief and tragedy), this has been on going since I first began to write. After all, what is of interest to a poet but people and God's creation?

I had asked the woman if she would like to accompany me to go dancing. This wasn't to be a "date" as such; it was simply a friendly thing (so I thought). We were good friends (so I thought). It seemed to be a good idea at the time. Wrong!

People often talk about how forthright they are; the old "What you see is what you get" concept. But seldom do people really tell you what they think... until they have a couple too many. Now I knew the woman liked to drink but had never seen her really loaded. Tonight would be the night.

We danced; she drank. Now she knew I always danced with several of the women and had never exhibited any concern about it before. But as the evening progressed, it became apparent that she was becoming increasingly agitated with my dancing with anyone but her. So it was that with the increased drinking, her manner changed from one of heretofore friendship to one of outright jealousy. Yet, I had never encouraged anything between us but friendship.

The fact that she was a beautiful woman and had a number of suitors who would have loved to have been in my shoes might have given her the idea that she could have any man she wanted. But I never considered myself to be on her "menu." We aren't on such friendly terms anymore. She apologized the next day for her behavior, blaming herself for drinking too much and saying things she didn't mean but the damage had been done and was not to be undone.

Had I known she had any such feelings about me, I would never have asked her to accompany me but would have left well enough alone, content to see her whenever our paths crossed. But I have learned that it isn't just men who "collect scalps." They just happen to be the main predators.

Speaking of which, A--- has a reputation as a Casanova, a Womanizer and has admittedly done things that encourage his reputation in this regard. I see him often and have witnessed an ironic twist of fate in his life. He is in love. But I know very well the woman he has fallen in love with. So do a lot of other men. We are all agreed that A--- has certain judgment in his future as none believe this woman is going to be faithful to him but will hand him his head on a platter when she is finished using him. What goes around comes around.

This is unfortunate as I really like this fellow and, in some ways, he is a most friendly and agreeable man. But his reputation for liking too many women at the same time and using them to flatter his own vanity and ego was bound to do him in eventually. This is a small community in many ways. Getting the women talking about you in a negative vein is certainly deadly. A--- and I visit occasionally and he is definitely lovesick. It is all he can talk about and most of his friends are finding him tiresome on the theme. It makes the undoubted conclusion all the harder to see coming. But no one will ever convince him of that and I don't try. Maybe it will be justice of a form.

It was my distinct privilege to be sitting with three, very lovely women who know me very well as they began to warm to a conversation about A--- and a few other men they class in the same phyla. They were all drinking and in their enthusiasm of cussin' and discussin' the various men they knew, seemed to forget all about the man (me) in their midst; A most interesting situation. Few men will likely ever have the opportunity to be privy to such a conversation among women.

Suddenly, as the petite redhead to my right was becoming really eloquent in denunciation of men in general, it seemed to dawn on all of them at once that I was there. She stopped mid-sentence and grabbing me in a tight hug, laughed and said: "Except for Don, here." They were all laughing at once and all I could think of to say was: "I'd sure hate to get on the bad side of you ladies." It was a rare moment and I meant, most sincerely, what I said. If more men could hear women talking together about them, it might do some good in correcting their behavior toward women.

I'm at the coffee shop and Moe comes in. Moe is one of the most interesting men I have met in the Valley and we became fast friends from the start having many discussions, often of an esoteric nature. He is given to a kind of Zen approach to life mixed with a lot of astrological beliefs. We simply agree to disagree on much of this but it does lend a zest to our discussions.

He is concerned for my welfare and that is deeply appreciated. His major concern is my going to the bars. I have assured him that I am not looking for anything but the material that lends authenticity to the stories of people whatever the environment I find myself in.

Being of a poetic nature himself, we share our ideas of the human condition and, of course, our views about women in general. His is substantially different largely because of the difference in backgrounds and experience.

"Don," he asks, "just what are you looking for in a woman?" Understand that Moe is given to a much wider view of the relationships between men and women than I am. In other words, he isn't "hampered" by my, he would put it, "narrow morality." Now I have given that question considerable attention and faced with the bald question from a friend I felt compelled to answer.

It isn't so much a physical thing with me as it is a search for that "spark" which will ignite. It most certainly will begin with what I see in that special woman's eyes and what she will see in mine. Yes, physical attractiveness is important to the extent that beauty is within the eye of the beholder and giving due credit to that maxim of love being blind.

In regard to special likes and dislikes, I prefer smaller women. I prefer a quiet woman to the more voluble, extroverted. I prefer a woman who enjoys walks in the forest and looking at the stars rather than "partying." Most importantly, children and people will be important to her and she will be able to relate to the things I write about.

But when all is said and done, there is no accounting for love and it will be the person, not her physical endowments or anything else that will capture my attention and it will be, as I said, her eyes that will tell me if I want to pursue the relationship. Being of sensitive nature, Moe could at least relate to my answer even if he found it short of satisfactory by his own lights.

It seems an ancient custom among both men and women to have several on the string. This, of course, is egotistical and encourages vanity in the person. One man I know openly brags he has three girlfriends and that they even know about it. Curiously, this man has little to offer any woman but one, ugly item: Drugs. But he would like to believe it is his charm to the ladies that they find attractive, not the drugs he makes available to them.

Drugs are all pervasive in the Valley. It is only the lack of minorities that keeps us from the violent crime so attendant to such a thing. It is tragic that so many young men and women are wrapped up in such a lifestyle but the lack of employment, the lack of hope in so many lives easily leads to alcoholism and drug abuse.

I returned to Maitia's last weekend to do some follow-up on Bobby and his daughter, Paula. I arrived early enough for the line-dancing instruction with which so many CW lounges are involved. Attendance throughout the whole county is down due to the fair going on here in Kern County. But there are about eighteen women and a few men going through the routine and it is fascinating to watch.

As I sip my coffee, I reflect on the curious fact that, having been born in Weedpatch and raised on the old "Hillbilly" kind of music indigenous to early days in Bakersfield, that CW would come into its own from such inauspicious beginnings as to make the city Nashville West. Because of my own involvement in those early days, I find the CW environment quite comfortable. The fact that the music is so natural to me has a lot to do with those early days. I easily pick up the music with my guitar and it flows naturally. Since I am a Westerner, I am equally comfortable in the kind of dress that goes with the music and the environment. But it sometimes results in some curious situations.

There are three ladies sitting at a table close to mine watching the line dancing as well. One of them, a pretty, petite blonde gets up and comes over to me. She says: "I'm the host to the two girls over there. One is from Spain and the other is from Finland. They want to know if you are an authentic Cowboy, you certainly look authentic."

Now folks, you all know my ambivalent attitude toward horses. I supported that habit for the sake of my daughters but my preference is still for transportation that has an engine and uses gas, not hay, for fuel. But, since I didn't want to disappoint them of going back to their native lands with a romantic encounter with an authentic cowboy, I told the lady: "I'm certainly authentic in being a Westerner and I sing and play guitar." That satisfied the ladies and gave them a story to tell.

The illusion is created by the fact that I have the look and the voice to accommodate the romantic concept of what a cowboy is supposed to look like. That together with the hat, boots, shirt, vest, fashion Levis, belt and buckle, bolo tie, etc. that go with the CW environment make a picture commensurate with what is happening in this whole phenomena of CW culture.

Unquestionably, CW, due to the music and lyrics having fled other fields to "Country" some time ago (I mentioned this some time back. Hence, the phrase: If it ain't Country, it ain't music, is proving to come to pass), is perceived by foreign nations in a somewhat distorted way. Videos and movies have given a false perception of the "West." Some foreign travelers still expect to see "Wild Indians" in our Western states.

There is no doubt in my mind that the CW phenomena is a harking back to simpler times, a search for "values," real love and romance, simple answers to hugely complex questions. One indisputable fact: Real dancing, which was suffering decline, has come back strongly due to the music and atmosphere provided by CW.

That the CW culture is a search for simplicity in a society which has become complex beyond the ability of many to cope, that it offers an escape from much of the increasingly bad news of war, crime, the corrupt, cold, callous antipathy of government leadership is a further attraction. Many I meet are "putting in their time" in the CW environment just to escape the helplessness and hopelessness, the anger and frustration they feel in an increasingly violent society and the alienation of our government from its own citizens.

And something else: In discussing this with a woman friend of mine at a club in Bakersfield, something clicks in my mind for the first time. This lady has suffered a great deal of abuse in her life from childhood on. She is very beautiful and has had the worst of what I have come to call the curse of beauty in our society. Lacking the guidance of a caring father and mother and left pretty well to her own devices, she became the victim of many men who used and abused her.

We were discussing music in general and it occurred to me that much of what I lost in this regard due to the betrayal of women I have loved has been regained in my returning to my childhood roots in CW. When I had asked my mother why she didn't listen to the music anymore and she had replied: "Because it makes me sad," I knew what she meant.

Much of the music I had enjoyed and played when I had a family was taken from me for the same reason, memories now too painful to recall. But it was the music of the 50s and 60s; it was the Big Bands and soft rock, etc. CW was a complete departure from that kind of music in spite of the same themes in regard to the relationships between men and women.

So it is that this woman and I are sharing together in the CW phenomena, in part, as an escape into an environment and among people who are not a part of the tragedies of the betrayals we have both suffered. Not that it isn't any less likely to happen in this new world, but it has been a new beginning for many of us who have been in that other world; as one song puts it so eloquently in its simplicity: "There Ain't No Future In The Past!"

Of course, as the woman and I dance, we both know the possibilities of betrayal of love and romance in our new environment as well. The song we are dancing to is, "I'm Holding Heaven In My Arms Tonight." We both smile at that and she is fully aware of the sentiment, of her own warmth and softness in my arms. And we are both reminded, both share, the same fears of falling in love, of having to try to trust all over again.

She is a very petite little woman, long, Raven-black hair and dark eyes, her beautiful, milk-white complexion a striking contrast to her hair and eyes. The top of her head barely reaches my chin as we dance and I have to bend my head down in order to feel the smooth softness of her cheek against mine, the brushing whisper of her soft, fragrant hair against my face as we hold each other closely and live in hope once more that there are caring people who are not given to betraying, to using and abusing others.

The other afternoon I happened to drop in at the Club in Isabella and Gabby was there. He has a marvelous voice and plays guitar exceptionally well. He wants to know if I would care to come over to his place and we would make some music. As we are chatting, Gino comes over and asks if I can give him a ride home. Since I have to get my guitar anyhow, I tell him ok. But before we leave, Brenda comes in. She and Gabby are a marvelous duet in singing and playing. I take off with Gino, go by my place and pick up my guitar.

When I get back to the club, Brenda and Gabby have their guitars out and I join them in a threesome. Then Bob Tanner, another really gifted singer and picker, comes in. Now we are four. The bar patrons are being treated to some marvelous, free entertainment and are duly appreciative, so much so that I wind up drinking two beers gratis the audience's appreciation of our impromptu performance. But I am grateful to return to my life's blood, coffee.

In the fraternity of musicians, such things happen and they are marvelous to be a part of. As I have said so many times, wouldn't it be a wonderful thing if people would pay more attention to the music and poetry of life, if we could come together around such things rather than fighting with one another. As Brenda, Gabby, Bob and I played and sang, the whole bar was with us and all the ugliness of our lives was held in abeyance for that magic, moment of time. I'm able to escape, temporarily, the hard things I have to write about and deal with in the political spectrum. The music takes the bad taste of such necessary work out of my mouth for that moment in time when I give myself over to music and dancing. I'm also away from that ubiquitous infernal machine, the telephone.

I'll be in the Club later today, Sunday, playing with Howard, Brenda, Gabby and Bob. It is a rare privilege for me to be a part of making music with such gifted people. I'm grateful for their allowing me to join with them. Brenda is a talented singer and musician. But her life has been a tragedy. We are sitting together at a lounge we both frequent and where we first met. She has been drinking too much and knows it. She has also been crying. She wants to know what she should do. She has been going with a man for a long time but he demands she do everything his way, demands that she accommodate his life and ego. She feels beaten down and is losing any sense of her own worth.

I know she realizes that real love is not selfish and seeks to please the object of that love. As so eloquently expressed in I Corinthians 13, real love keeps hope and faith living and vibrant in a person's life. She loves another man and he loves her. What to do?

She has tried to break away from the man who is using her on a number of occasions but, until R--- came along, she had no hope of making it on her own. I understand her fear, her indecision, the feeling that your life is out of control and you desperately need to do something but what?

We have known each other for some months now and have shared a lot, especially the music in our lives. She is a very sensitive woman and has a lot of understanding concerning the things I write about. She has the ability to read between the lines and it makes it easy for us to talk together about the sensitive things in each other's lives.

I'm hurting for her as she cries softly. She knows this and, turning to me, she puts her arms around me and, kissing me on the cheek, thanks me for being the friend she desperately needs right now. I hold her for a little while as she cries and I try to say the things she needs to hear from a real friend, trying to reassure her of her own value as a person with a lot of love to give the right man.

Perhaps R--- is that man. I know him as a very decent and sensitive man with deep feelings, especially for Brenda. But, as with many of us, having been betrayed, the fear of trusting, of hoping, of making another commitment is there to confront and overcome. Almost on cue, R--- comes into the lounge. Taking the seat on the other side of Brenda, he is immediately the comforter she needs and I am grateful for the role of friend to both of them.

But here comes the man she needs to break away from. He has been drinking heavily and the scene that meets his eyes inflames his own jealous rage. I have already been the object of his jealousy because of the close relationship I have with Brenda. In time, he came to accept the fact that we were only friends and he learns of my reputation for never trying to "hit" on any woman who is involved with another man, married or otherwise, but that jealousy was still a source of contention.

Now he sees both R--- and I with her and it all comes boiling out. He starts toward us with murder in his eyes, shouting expletives. I start to get up to confront him but another friend of ours is there, grabbing the man in a tight hold as I put my hand to his chest trying to use quiet words to defuse the situation. The bartender is getting ready to intercede if necessary.

It's an ugly scene, made all the uglier by the man's drunken condition. With several people ready to come to Brenda's aid and obviously opposed to the man's ugly behavior, he finally gives it up and leaves the lounge; but not for long.

In about half an hour he is back, quietly; too quietly. He takes a seat at the far end of the bar but something is sending a danger signal to my brain. He is sitting next to a friend of mine and I use this as an occasion to walk over. As I talk to my friend, I include this man in the conversation. I direct my attention to him. We have had enough familiar conversations in the past for me to be able to get him talking.

He finally divulges that he has a pistol in his waist and intends to shoot the little lady and the other man then shoot himself. Being an expert in both guns and psychology sometimes has its advantages. I can tell he does not have a gun. That's an immense relief though I know I could deal with it if it had been true.

The other item has to do with something he says: "I think I'll shoot her in the knees first." There are certain cues of language and behavior that clinicians can depend on. This, fortunately, was the case. The man posed no real threat for the moment and, with a few well-chosen words of warning and advice to him, which must have been sufficient since he left immediately and did not come back, I was able to return to Brenda and R---.

I took R--- aside and told him what had happened. My last words to him were: "No man really loves a woman and says he is going to shoot her in the knees." Silly? Not in the slightest. It took those exact words for the light of understanding to come on in R---'s eyes. As I leave the lounge a short while later, R--- and the little lady seemed to be doing the things they needed to do for each other, sorting things out and having the rational discussion they both needed about the possibility of a life together. The potential for real tragedy still exists. Will something really snap in the other man's mind, will he really get a gun and use it? It happens.

I had to warn a young woman once about leading one man on just because of this very thing. She might have been having "fun" toying with the man but didn't realize the threat this posed. I knew the man and I knew he was taking her "play" very seriously. The obvious fact, to everyone else that she might simply have felt kind of sorry for him and was trying to include him in the music and dancing didn't register with him. He was a very lonely man, had a disability and was ripe to fall for any woman who showed him any kindness, these things made him dangerous.

One night she was with another man when this fellow asked her to dance with him. Her polite refusal caused him to go to the bar, his face masked in cold fury. He slammed his glass on the bar and sat there in murderous silence. I know him well and I know he poses a real danger unless he can regain a rational balance and accept the reality of what was really going on in the young woman's attention to him.

I'm sharing the lyrics of a Rod McKuen song, "The World I Used To Know" (I used to play and sing a lot of Rod McKuen, Glenn Campbell, Johnny Cash), with a close friend. He is a sensitive man and it brings tears to his eyes. But, the poetry of the lyrics, we both agree, is largely lost to most women. I have explored the reasons for this at some length in previous essays and won't belabor it here.

To help make the point, he and I began to discuss the merits of various guitars. He knows my sorrow about having to sell my Gretch some years ago. My motorcycle accident prevented me from continuing to use this marvelous instrument to its full advantage. The loss of so many chords and riffs because of the mangling of my left hand cost me much of the music at that time. But I had held on to it for a long time, slowly regaining enough expertise to play melody and harmony. But it was still a waste, to me, to have such an instrument and not be able to take full advantage of it. He understands my feelings in this regard and why I had to turn it over to someone who could use it and appreciate it fully.

I tell my friend that I compare that Gretch to a beautiful woman in a silk, evening gown. To hold such an instrument and move your hands over it, caressing it in appreciation of it's beauty and craftsmanship, and, as with loving a woman, to bring out the best of it's tone in haunting melody in appreciation of that beauty is an unforgettable experience. My friend stares at me and says: "Don, you really are a poet!"

But I will share another story in partial explanation of my oft-repeated observation that while women may love poetry, I haven't found one yet who could live with a poet.

The guys and I had been playing. One very pretty young woman in the audience was obviously in some distress, crying softly and drinking too much. I've made the observation in the past that you often see the human drama at a greatly accelerated rate in the bars and lounges. In just a few hours, you can observe an entire cycle of an affair between two people that might take months in other circumstances such as the work place, the churches, etc. The environment, the music, the alcohol all play a part in the hastening process of people getting acquainted in less inhibiting circumstances than in most other areas of our lives.

As I write, I'm treated to a covey of quail in my backyard. A lookout flies to the top of the house while the covey feeds. They chuckle to each other and do the quail things that entrance and entertain me since childhood. I'm reminded, once more, of my affinity with God's creation and never fail to hearken to the warning that much of our lives is taken up with things of little meaning and significance unless we can keep a perspective of what is real and what is not, what is of lasting value and what is simply "plastic" and temporary.

And, so, when someone who is jaded by life tells me I should "grow up," should "get with the scene," when some man or woman tells me I'm "missing out" because I don't "run with the pack," I don't bother to try to explain that to do so would be a betrayal of the best of the child within the man, a betrayal of those who live in hope that "Nice" is preferable to vanity and ego.

I was dancing with an especially beautiful woman. She lays her head on my shoulder, pulls me close to herself and whispers: "You're a nice man Don." I took that as high praise, not a put-down. To that extent I have been accused of being naive, gullible, not "with it." Oddly, most of those that have used that accusatory tone to me have been women. If I were treating women as most men do, would I gain the approval of decent women? Not in my opinion. And I would never hear those whispered words that mean more to me than the approval of those that would demean real love.

Many women don't seem to realize that the real poetry of life regarding love and romance comes from those idealized standards of what is right and wrong and the loss of purity resulting from the failure of adhering to such standards underscores the meanness and loss of hope in many people's lives. So, even at the cost of ridicule from some, I will remain "gullible, naive, not with it." I'll refuse to "grow up" and continue to be able to enjoy the quail in the backyard, continue to thrill to whispered words of being a "Nice man."

But, if the hardness of this "Nice man" in confronting the evil tyranny of Caesar were known among those that think kindly of me, that think of me as unprepossessing and gentle, I might suffer as a consequence. For that reason, I try to keep that part separate from the music and dancing. Not that I have anything to be ashamed of in regard to my battle against the forces of evil in our nation; quite the contrary. But the time I spend with the music and poetry is essential to my own balance, to keeping a clear mind of what is important and what is not and what the battle is really all about.

Admittedly, I would far rather devote myself to music, philosophy and poetry. But the battle rages on in the political spectrum in which I play a key role. It is, however, a role that I don't want to talk about when the music is playing and I lose myself in the magic of that however temporarily.

For this reason I have devoted CP to those softer and gentler things that speak of love and romance, of the poetry and, yes, the tragedies in people's lives. I become even embarrassingly personal in laying bare some of the experiences that I hope will be of some benefit to those who have forgotten to dream, have forgotten what the priorities should be in living life.

If I have played a key role in Governor Wilson's recent attack on illegal aliens destroying our state and ruining our economy, I don't want that to be the focus of the conversation I have with a woman at dinner. If the Feds are taking well-deserved heat because of their stupid, idiotic and tragic blunder in Waco, I don't want my part in bringing that pressure to bear on them the subject of talk when I'm dancing with a woman. Proposed legislation that addresses the real problems of our state and nation that depends, in part, on my political analyses are not going to intrude when I am playing or listening to the music.

Yes, it is all a part of the whole and works together. But there is a proper time and place for all things. Tonight I am taking a lovely woman to dinner. I want to enjoy the time together, getting to know each other as persons. I want to enjoy the privilege of the honor she does me by being with me in such an environment. I do not want the evening to revolve around the part I played in the firing of some bureaucrat who shamelessly abused his power of office.

Last week, a very lovely woman invited me to dinner. Her concern was whether I was too chauvinistic to accept a dinner invitation from a woman. The question is a disturbing one. I remain a Southern gentleman of the "old school." But I also realize there is nothing wrong with a woman asserting her own wishes and I most certainly do not think any less of a lady who makes her thoughts known in such a manner. We live in a society that, in many ways, has brought enormous pressure to bear on women. I'm not about to add to it by adhering to some false standard of "propriety" in such things as a woman asking me out to dinner.

Like O'Henry and O'Neil, I want to write of real people, to tell the stories as I live them with these people. If, in the process of doing so, things get too personal, I hope the resulting embarrassment falls on me, not on someone else. I am never reluctant or hesitant in any way to call down the fire of Heaven on the heads of corrupt judges, senators, etc. But I hope never to embarrass anyone but myself in writing of real people and the real experiences of my involvement with these "ordinary" folks who, like myself, would rather live and let live without the tyrannical and despotic rule of Caesar intruding into every facet of our lives, betraying and stealing our liberty and the birthright of our children.

The "True Love Waits" movement among some churches deserves the support of all of us. That there are young people who can still be reached with the Biblical message of chastity and purity should be a most welcome breath of fresh air in the midst of the rampant, moral pollution in which our nation is drowning.

I just got a card from my old neighbors who walked away from their place (like so many others are doing) because of the failure of California's economy and the resulting inability to keep up mortgage payments. In this case, as in so many others, the falling values of California real estate play a key role. They are now in New Mexico, quote: "Great place and great people Don, wish you were here." I wish them the best. They are discovering, along with a host of other people, that there is life outside of California.

Race and gender cases dominate the U.S. Supreme Court's term. The battle of the sexes, the battle of the races continue to acerbate tensions in our nation and the fact that the insanity of trying to legislate morality fails of recognition by the leadership gives new meaning to the hoary precept of the *Blind leading the blind.* We can expect more of so-called "Law" which actually perverts the cause of justice.

Insiders are telling me that Vincent Foster who was CIA in Clinton's Arkansas days, who worked with Hilary on classified matters, who reportedly committed suicide actually had two bullet holes in the back of his head. Do I believe this? Yes. The "Federal Black-suits, Delta Force, Task Force 51," these are the prerogatives of power and are used where "necessary for national security and the public good."

The passage of time is no guarantee that Caesar and his agents won't reach out to punish those who they think pose a threat to the New World Order. The F.B.I. is presently trying to prosecute a case against the KKK because of possible "agent involvement" in a killing some 36 years ago. Was the agency "involved?" I have no doubt about it. The Shadow Government has, and does, commit murder when it suits its purpose. Then, when it suits its further agenda and purpose, sacrifices are made, even of its own people. Compare the Russian Revolution of 1917 and other such historical imperatives of "The end justifies the means." As with the government's cover up of suicides in the military, Caesar continues to blunder his way through despicable acts against We the People in the name of what is "best for us."

The betraying "leadership" of California led of the chief betrayer, Willie Brown, now wants to get on the bandwagon of "Illegal Aliens Bankrupting The State." But look at the laws, state and federal, which led the state and nation into bankruptcy in the name of the high-sounding rhetoric of "Fair and Equal" (I repeat: Fair to who, equal to what?) and, particularly, look at those like Brown who caused such insane laws to be passed.

It is no wonder that so-called "racists" are gaining such ground in countries like England, Germany and France. All one has to do is look to the factual history of nations, of human behavior and ideologies to acknowledge the insanity of America's betrayers trying to force "multiculturalism" down our throats. I, and history, repeat like the proverbial record: "One, and only one, ideology can survive within any nation!"

Why is the fact that Negroes in South Central L.A. and other cities are given over to virtual anarchy, lawlessness treated as "news?" *As long as they are killing each other, who gives a damn*? is the actual, political position of the "leadership." Negro leadership knows this but because of "leaders" like Willie Brown, they have to live with the monstrous situation they themselves created. I would find it amusing if it were not so tragic in its consequence that Newsweek would treat the whole subject as "news" in its August 30th edition. I could have written the same article 25 years ago when I was a high school teacher in Watts.

An interesting side note. Why haven't the advocates of the silly, oxymoronic doctrine of Judeo/Christian acknowledged the fact that the so-called "Fundamentalism" of this idiotic concept perpetrated by the likes of

Jerry Falwell and Pat Robertson actually advocates the slaughter of the Jews? Theologians like John Walvoord, spokesman for Falwell, et al., propagandize the idea that two-thirds of the Jews will perish during the Great Tribulation yet these same people advocate helping Israel as some kind of extension of Christian ethics.

If Falwell and others were really concerned for the Jews, if they really believed what they preach, they would be doing their utmost to get Jews out of Israel before the anticipated "Tribulation." The logic of their position dictates they advocate such slaughter of Jews. Maybe that is why Ronald Reagan had his address in BelAir changed from 666 to 668?

I might as well repeat my question of some time back, since so many are now asking the same question: What the hell are we doing in Somalia? Of course, that is rhetorical. My readers of a long while already know the answer to that question.

No wonder I would so much rather do the work of a simple poet and lose myself in the music. Someday, maybe. Right now I'm going to go get my guitar and get together with Rod McKuen.

CHAPTER ELEVEN

Christian Perspective

November

Psalm 41

I have a lot of ground to cover in this issue of CP. I have reserved political comment together with a sample of my work on the mathematical model of Human Behavior for the end of this essay. But I will start with some of the stories from my usually hectic but interesting involvement with my fellow travelers along life's highway.

In the course of those events that often leap out and change our lives, whether of joy or tragedy, it sometimes becomes such as deserving the sharing with others. That I haven't completely lost my sense of humor is due to my being able to enter into the lives of others on a level that maintains the equilibrium between what is of value and what is not, what is truly humorous and what is not.

With that thought in mind, I hope you will enjoy the following true story and reserve judgment until you get to the punch line:

We entered the lounge together and immediately had the attention of everyone. They all knew me but no one had seen the beautiful young woman with me. We were dressed in matching, black and white Western attire. It would almost be trite to describe her as the most beautiful woman in the world, but I would introduce her as such and no one could do anything but agree with me.

Long, soft, auburn hair and blue eyes reflecting such exceptional intelligence that most men would find it daunting in a hauntingly beautiful face provided an immediate impression of inapproachability. About five-feet, six inches tall, a perfectly proportioned figure and a face with perfect complexion so disturbingly beautiful you have to wonder if your own eyes aren't deceiving you; so striking in appearance that men are in awe of her.

Joe, my old, Irish friend comes up to us. He stands and stares at my young lady for a moment and says, almost reverentially: "God surely used you as the model for the angles in heaven!" He turns and walks slowly away without another word, just shaking his head at the vision. He pretty well summed up the impression of every man who sees her. And she was so very quiet, nearly impossible to engage in conversation. Her natural shyness, her utter lack of any vanity only makes the impression she makes on people, especially the men, all the more profound. To my friends, I did, in fact, introduce her as the most beautiful woman in the world and none accused me of exaggeration; on the contrary, they all agreed they had never met a more beautiful woman.

I had brought her here from up North, not because of her indescribably natural beauty, but because of her voice. She has the most beautiful singing voice that I have ever heard. There are no superlatives in the language to describe it. Once heard, it is never forgotten and you can't even think of anyone with whom you can make a comparison, such an attempt would even be demeaning.

Male vocalists are a dime-a-dozen. Not so female vocalists. And the combination of such exceedingly rare natural beauty in combination with such an incomparable voice was not lost on those in the music business to whom I was introducing her. They are all ready to kill to have her with them since they all know, without question she would be their ticket to unrealized fame and fortune.

Of the many groups and bands in the area, none has a female vocalist. The reasons for this are several; a man can be ugly as sin and if he has a good voice and can play a guitar he can get away with near-terminal ugly. Not so the lady. She not only has to be able to sing well, she has to be at the very least good-looking. Also, a woman has to contend with many things men don't have to confront on the "stability" side, tending to be somewhat more temperamental than men. Women often bring some attendant problems to music simply by virtue of their being women, especially if they are attractive and have a good voice. I'm talking about sex, in case you missed the point. It isn't fair but men get away with a lot more in this department than the women.

We're at this particular lounge to introduce her to another of the several groups I know locally. They all want her to sing with them instantly but I won't allow her to do so. Why? Because we are going to make the studio demos first and only the best-qualified group in the best environment will get the privilege of a debut. It is also vital that she feel comfortable with the group and place where she is to start her career.

I've known this little lady virtually all her life. As I watched her grow up, I became increasingly aware of the fact that she was an exceptional child in many ways. It was of intense interest to speculate on which of the several gifts she possessed would come into full flower; as it is, when she developed a mature voice that in combination with her beauty made the choice obvious to me. And she trusted my decision to bring her into the music business.

At the local level, I'm having, admittedly, a lot of fun taking her places and being a part of the drama we are creating as a couple. Every man who sees her wants her. Those that know me maintain a respectable distance however they all wonder where she comes from and just how serious the relationship is with me. I make it clear to all of them that this is "My Lady" and they keep their distance. But the men who don't know me, at least those with the courage, try to get her to dance or let them buy her a drink. She refuses them all, simply and politely hooking her arm through mine and the point is made painfully obvious to them. And she doesn't drink anything but coffee or soft drinks.

I wish I could share a picture of the two of us in our matching, black and white western wear, and even the black hats were matched. As I danced with her, I was, understandably, the intense envy of every man in the place. I wouldn't be human and not have relished every moment.

To make matters worse for the men there and to their consternation, I happened to be seated between the young lady and another exquisitely, beautiful young woman, the Lady in Red I mentioned in my last essay. That I could dance with both, that I was seated between the two of them was a rare stroke of good fortune and, frankly, quite surreal.

Such things are the stuff of dreams, they don't happen in real life do they? But, as I mentioned in the last essay as well, sometimes the bread falls butter or jelly side up and, just a word to you men, sometimes "nice" really does count for a lot. This is emphasized dramatically as the beautiful Lady in Red leans toward me at one point and kisses me fully on the lips in sight of everyone while my other little lady has her arm through mine at the bar (And, to anticipate you, the Lady in Red was not being "casual" in doing this. She knows I love her and she would never treat such a thing with me lightly).

The male ego could hardly have had more cause to rise with a vengeance in my breast but I have to admit that I did an admirable job in controlling it (well, as much as possible anyway). But, honestly, how many men wouldn't give a bundle to have the attention of two such beautiful ladies? Ah, vanity of vanities is not the sole purview of women.

But suspicion is aroused in many who, seeing my little lady and me together, cannot fail to see the family resemblance that is too striking to miss. Yes, this is Karen, my daughter, my little girl, my little angel, the light of my life and the only woman in my life.

So it was that I had the liberty to dance with the beautiful Lady in Red and pay attention to her at the same time I was with this other angelic lady. This did confound the other men (and the ladies also, I'm sure) who had to wonder just what the devil was going on. No man had any right to two such beautiful women; it just wasn't justifiable under any circumstances. I think I was working on earning the undying enmity of some of those present since I was so obviously opposed, with the ladies' cooperation, to "sharing."

We had our joke on many who deserved such a trick, like many of the men who felt they were God's gift to women getting shot down in flames when they couldn't get to first base with this so very beautiful little lady. Not a few of the women I know really appreciated this "pay-back" to barroom "Romeos."

Many were suspicious because they knew I would never "rob the cradle" when it comes to women. Seeing me with such a young girl really shook them until we made the relationship known. But you can well imagine the fatherly pride I took in being able to show off my beautiful, little lady not to mention the justifiable pleasure I had in being seen with her. As a father/daughter team, we made a rare combination, unbeatable.

As to the music, that is serious in every way. Having accomplished our purpose down South, we returned north where, with the cooperation of friends, she will make the studio demos and, when she is ready, she will make her debut. But while we were about it, we made a couple of tapes which I am sharing with a few friends just to whet their appetites and give them a preview of what my little girl has to offer. That took some doing, however.

Karen, as with so many of her generation, has been devoted to rock music. The transition to CW will be difficult for her. When we arrived, I asked her to pick out at least one song she could do as a sample of what I needed from her.

She didn't have any idea, so I did one for her as an example. She then chose the song: "Dreamin'." But she was so self-conscious about singing such a ballad type song that the only way I could get her to sing it was by accompanying her, making it a duet. I'm glad in a way that it worked out this way. You can't imagine the preciousness of the moment as I sang with my little girl.

There was a little humor involved as I kept trying to keep the mic in front of her and she kept trying to push it back to me. As a result, we had to make several attempts to get any kind of balance. That tape is one of my most prized possessions. I play it frequently. Professionally, it is remarkable as a father/daughter duet. I can hardly wait for us to do some music together on stage.

I've played the tape for several friends and they are all agreed on the beauty of her voice and the promise of an outstanding career awaiting her. Not a few were surprised that "dad" could sing so well also. I've pretty well kept that part of my life secret. But if that is what it takes to get Karen singing CW, another "singing cowboy" is in the offing.

Made the circuit from Bakersfield through Lancaster this weekend; while in Lancaster where I have many friends, I got together with one and we visited the Calico Saloon and The Buffalo Club. Both are fine CW establishments, the people really friendly and the music was good.

The evening at Calico was memorable especially. I have seldom been in a place where there were so many good-looking women; being a mere man that was bound to impress me. I danced with several and just enjoyed myself. Not being much of a drinker, one beer and cups of coffee sufficed for the evening. Wound up with one of the local TV personalities, an especially beautiful girl, nearly in my lap.

Of most interest was the lady from Nottingham, England. She was seated with a group of notable people dressed in fashionable eveningwear. She was a striking woman in appearance, long black hair and dark eyes. She wore a full-length, black velvet gown adding to her allure. She came over to me and after the proper introductions and dancing with her; I learned she was interested in the CW possibilities in Ireland, of all places. We exchanged cards and plan to get together in the near future to compare notes on this aspect of the CW phenomena abroad.

Just a quick note to the precious lady and friend who recently wrote me of her concern that I was going to get picked off by some floozy I meet in a bar. The places I go for the CW entertainment are the better establishments, many having a cover charge, where people dress in evening wear or very expensive, quality Western attire. No drunken rowdiness allowed; just good music, dancing and well-behaved, civilized folks. And I do meet many nice ladies in these places; not all of them are "hunting."

For a real "slice of life," I do visit some of the bars frequented by the type of people this dear lady expressed fear of but that pragmatic part of the poet's mind still functions quite well and I continue to go home alone. And, I seldom have a drink, a key factor in maintaining a proper perspective at all times.

I was in one of these places the other night where I was sure two women were going to come to blows and it was all I could do to keep the peace by escorting one of them outside. No, it isn't just the men by any means that provide this side of the "entertainment."

As to the poetry and music of life, such things as the incident described contribute to the dark side of such. There is a need to deal with this in such mediums even if the results are often jarring to our senses of what is right or wrong, sensible or unreasonable, what is melodic or only "noise." It is well known there is something going on in music, in language that the ear and brain is always trying to make sense of but the connections are often lost in the very cacophony of our lives, too many things demanding our attention to what is of little value while the things of real value go begging.

I'll call him Sam, a decent name for a decent man.

I've known Sam long enough to credit what he tells me as truthful. His reputation as a kind and loving man is well established and I've never heard anyone speak harshly of him. All in all the kind of man people readily trust their children to; the kind of man in whom many confide, and the kind of man parents hope their daughters will marry.

I was in the coffee shop when Sam came in that Saturday morning. Normally of a cheerful and outgoing disposition, it was very disconcerting to see him looking so dreadful. He obviously hadn't slept much if at all. Unshaven and haggard, he looked like death warmed over. I was so shocked at his totally uncharacteristic appearance and condition it took a couple of moments to even respond and call him over to my booth.

Wearily taking the seat opposite mine, he ordered a cup of coffee and sat silent and motionless. It didn't take much to see that my friend was in a great deal of pain. I was instantly reminded of the girl I put to bed that I wrote of in my last essay. And here we were in the same coffee shop where I had brought her at that time.

But now, instead of a young woman, a man I know seemed to be in the same condition. For the same reason I wondered? Sure enough.

As Sam began to sip the coffee, I waited patiently for him to start telling the story for which I knew he had instinctively sought me out to begin the healing of his tormented mind. After a few sips of coffee, his hands trembling and tears forming at the corners of his eyes, he reached across the table and grasped my hands in his. Lowering his head, his body shuddered and I wondered for a moment if he was going to break down completely. I needn't have worried, I knew Sam as a man who is as strong as they come with that inner strength of soul and character that doesn't allow emotional breakdowns for the sake of others. I felt confident of him being able to bring himself under control. And he did.

With a deep breath and a long sigh, he let go of my hands and sat back. He took out a handkerchief and wiped his grief-stricken eyes. A visible shudder went through his body and he clasped his arms about himself to bring it under control. Seldom have I seen a soul in such obvious torment and I knew I was in for a painful session with him. But I was his friend and I counted it a privilege and honor that he sought me out in the confidence of that friendship. We looked at each other with the understanding that comes from each of us helping others. He knew he could count on my patience and understanding. And he could. Picking up his cup in his now calmer hands, he took another sip of coffee and, with a long, ragged breath, began to speak.

"I had a date with a beautiful woman last night, Don. I'm in love with her. I don't have to tell you who she is; I know you already know her. I only ask for my own peace of mind that you don't judge her too harshly when I get through telling you what has happened. And, let me thank you for my knowing I can tell you."

Sam knew he had nothing to worry about. He knows my reputation for never betraying a confidence by naming names in my writing without permission. He just needed a way to start talking and his first concern was, characteristically, for someone else; in this case, the woman who was so obviously the cause of his tormented state.

"It has taken weeks for me to get her to go to dinner with me, Don. She has been so horribly abused by other men that I frankly believe she was actually afraid to go out with someone like myself. As you well know, I don't get drunk or do drugs; I'm a responsible, hard worker and have never been in trouble; probably on the boring side to most women.

"But Don, from the first moment I met this lady; she caught my heart in a way that I simply couldn't let go without trying. I knew her reputation but I sensed something of very great value in her that I knew others had missed.

"It didn't help that my friends were calling me a fool for even being interested in this lady. But after coming to know something of her as a person, I knew she was worth everything I could do to win her, I knew we could have something really wonderful together if she could only be made to understand how very special she actually is, if I could only get her to accept the truth that a man like myself could really and truly love her."

Sam had to stop at this point. What he had already said was done with such a quiet passion and with such an effort I knew he had to have time to gather his tortured thoughts before he could continue his story. He had such a tight grip on his cup; the tendons of his hands were bulging. I knew he wasn't even aware of the stress he was under and I hurt for my friend.

"It took a lot of courage, Don, for her to accept this date. I won't tell you how I know this, there is a lot to it that I don't think I will ever be able to talk about, not even to you. But she did and I thought that, at last, I was going to finally win. Don, this lady needs me, she needs everything I can do for her and her children, all the things she should have had from a man who really loves her. I knew I loved her enough to do anything in the world for her and the children if she would only give me a chance to prove how much she meant to me. Last night, I thought, was going to provide that chance.

"When I went to pick her up, her eldest son told me she hadn't been able to talk about anything but our date; that she was really looking forward to it. I can't tell you how happy I was to hear that. Her son is a really good kid and has had a rough time of it having to contend with the men who have abused his mother. He hasn't had much time to enjoy being a child, he had to grow up too fast under the circumstances and I'm really proud of the way he cares for his mother. I think he realized how much a man like me could mean to his mother as well.

"When she came out, she was a picture of poetic beauty. Here in front of me, at last, was my whole heart's desire fulfilled in this beautiful, sensitive and intelligent woman. I can't describe how lucky I felt that she really wanted to be with me. Any man in his right mind would have envied me.

"We went to dinner and then into the lounge where the band had started playing. I had looked forward to dancing with her, to hold her in my arms and let the magic of the music speak to our hearts. But she had started drinking. I had been afraid of that. I already knew the role that alcohol and drugs had played in much of the abuse this beautiful lady had suffered; but how to stop her without offending her? That I didn't know.

"As the hour approached midnight, I suggested we go to another place in the hope that that would help with the drinking. It didn't. She continued to drink. Then a strange thing happened. A man I didn't recognize came over and sat next to her. He seemed to know her quite well. I didn't think too much of it at first but she seemed to actually be far more interested in talking to him than in me. This made me begin to really feel uneasy.

"It was getting close to closing time when the guy finally left. The band was starting to play the last song and I had really been looking forward to having this last dance with her. But she got up and danced with another guy she knew. I was really hurt by this. Not only had she let another guy monopolize her time, taking her from me, now another man gets the last dance with her!

"We finally left as the place was closing. I thought to myself, well, at least I am getting to take her home. Maybe, I thought, we can get some coffee and at least have some time together before the night is over.

"As I pulled up in front of her house, there was a strange car in front. It was now just after 2 a.m. She said something to the effect that the car belonged to someone she had to talk to. I was dumbfounded! This was really bad. Then we walked into her house. The guy she had spent so much time talking to was stretched out on the floor in front of her fireplace. He had actually built a fire and obviously knew how to really make himself at home in her place.

"I didn't know what to make of all this. What I had counted on as a beautiful and special time for the two of us was ending in a nightmare for me. I asked her if she preferred that I leave her to her 'friend.' I was desperately hoping she would kick the bum out and ask me to stay. No. She wanted me to go.

"I couldn't believe it. I had tried, desperately, to show this lady how much I cared for her, I had taken her out to the finest restaurant and had been nothing but a perfect gentleman to her and now I was nothing but the 'delivery boy,' delivering her to another man to spend the rest of the night with her.

"I walked outside and started to get into my car. She followed me and grabbed me around the waist. I had told her earlier that I wanted to so something together with her Saturday.

"She seemed genuinely sorry about the turn of affairs. She even promised she would call me and we would get together the next day. She never did call, by the way.

"As I drove away, I was shaking with the pain. It wasn't that I had been taken as a fool, I genuinely love this little lady and there wasn't any way I could help her keep from the destructive things she was doing to herself. As I drove, it came to me that the conversation she had been having with this guy probably included making arrangements for his being at her place when I brought her home. They probably planned it this way knowing the kind of man I am, knowing they could easily get rid of me and get on with what they wanted to do.

"You can tell I haven't been to bed. There was no hope of sleeping. I just sat in the dark next to the telephone, hoping against hope that she would come to her senses and call me. She didn't, of course. You know my pain is as much for her, Don, as it is for me. She is destroying herself and, much as I love her, I know there is nothing I can do for her.

"You remember that essay where you quoted that guy who said: 'Why is it that nice guys never get the last dance?' Well, here is another one asking the same question. Did you ever figure out the answer to that? I sure would like to know. Not only didn't I get the last dance, I wind up delivering her to another man! Stick that in one of your essays!"

The pain, hurt and anger had come boiling out of Sam at last. And I knew, good a man as he was, that Sam wasn't angry at this lady, he was angry at the way she was allowing others to use her, he cared enough to grieve for her and, at the same time, have the righteous anger at the total unfairness, the injustice of it all, angry at the fact that there was nothing he could do to keep her from hurting herself and him, possibly destroying the one chance she had at a decent man in her and her children's lives.

As Sam let his grief and pain out, I couldn't help thinking of the many women and children I know personally who have let alcohol and drugs destroy them. And, too often, it has been using and abusing, degenerate men who have led them into such destructive, betraying lives. But it is the children, far more than the adults that make the anger rise in my own heart. When I witness them as the helpless victims of the corrupt and selfish choices of men and women, these children who are so betrayed by the selfishness of so-called "mothers and fathers," I want to scream out at the whole system that promotes such evil.

Sam hadn't said so in just those words but I strongly suspected that alcohol and/or drugs were the factors, among other things like lust that had turned his "date" with this lovely woman into a nightmare. He was right; what should have been a beautiful and special time for him and this lady, a time that might have led to a life for the two of them was betrayed for such utterly selfish and destructive reasons.

It makes no sense, of course, for Sam to continue to grieve over a woman who won't look into that mirror and, seeing the truth, confronting it and deciding to change, deciding to do something with her life, continues to refuse to give a decent man like Sam a chance to let his love be the healing thing she needs. People, as I continue to point out, will do what they want to do in spite of all the love others may have for them, even to their own destruction in too many cases I know of personally.

Another time, another place. She is one of the most beautiful and courageous women I have ever met. She was only a child when an accident left her terribly damaged. At first, the doctors gave her up. Then, having surprised them by living, she was told she would never walk or speak. When I met her, she not only spoke, haltingly, but could drive a car, had a baby and her own apartment.

Because of her damaged leg, she walks very slowly, but she walks and she does a lot of it. Her speech, while slow due to a damaged diaphragm, is clear and her mind works very well and intelligently.

But she is a child in some ways, another bird with a broken wing. I fell in love with her the moment I met her. That she had survived, that she had endured and overcome so much with such a winning smile and such courage in the face of such obstacles that would have left most others in, at the very least, the thrall of bitterness and resentment left me with no choice but to love her.

The tragedy in this young woman's life is not her physical disabilities. It is the vile and contemptible men who have used her because of her normal needs of companionship, of love, trust and understanding. Because of such degenerates, she has a child, the father of whom is long gone. She has picked up men in the bars out of sheer loneliness. That she is so very attractive with such a smile and personality; she does attract men, the kind of men who prey on such innocents.

When I met her, she was involved with a man who exemplified the very worst of all the vile characteristics of such predators of whom I have written so much. This man proved to have no job or even his own car, lived with his mother, sponging off of her for years, had a proven track record of never being responsible to anyone and serving nothing but his own lust and selfishness.

The girl paid for everything, the dinners out, the trips to the mountains, gifts for this degenerate. As it turned out, she told me he had never even bought her a flower. There wasn't even a simple card for her recent birthday.

Due to the circumstances of our meeting, I asked her to let me take her to lunch and she agreed. As we ate, she shared several other things with me that gave me some insights concerning the shambles of her life, of her own emotional turmoil which led to so much of the abuse she had suffered from men.

She had a request. She wanted me to be with her to confront this man as to his intentions toward her. I readily agreed. I had another appointment that afternoon but I arranged to meet her later in the evening at one of the nicer lounges in town.

When I arrived, I found her sitting at the bar, playing one of the numerous, trivia question games now so popular in some places. She had saved a stool for me and I joined her in helping to answer some of the questions. Her mood was subdued and I could tell she wasn't really having much fun. This was confirmed when she turned to me and said: "This is my life, Don." I knew what she meant and the statement pierced my own heart.

I have come to know so many for whom the bars and lounges have become their "life." That family of seekers who are looking for someone to heal their loneliness; nor am I immune from that same "seeking."

Leaving the lounge, we went to her apartment where she called the man she wanted my help with. She did not let him know I would be there. When he arrived a short time later, he was obviously in some distress at finding me there. But it didn't take me long to get to the point of my presence.

It was pathetic. During the whole exchange, she desperately wanted this vile excuse for a man to simply say he loved her. He wouldn't. It went on at some length, exhaustingly. I confronted him for the vile excuse for a man he was. Being utterly without any sense of shame, he simply sat there and took everything I threw at him.

He finally left without once saying any of the healing words that would have given the girl a chance to get on with her life, to get him out of her mind. He had chosen his victim carefully. She was only a source of easy and ready sex for him, a victim who would take him places and pay for his "companionship." To compound matters further, she has a disability income which provides a living if she is careful with her money. This degenerate knows this and yet he encourages her to spend money she can't afford on him!

She knows, now, that he is only using her for his own contemptible gratification; that he isn't going to change. In spite of this, in spite of her promise to me to never see him again, he was back the next night and she remains his victim, so much so, in fact, that she has actually called me and asked that I try to sooth his "hurt feelings" over some of the things I said to him.

Unbelievably, she has tried to defend him by claiming responsibility for allowing herself to be used. This after the session she herself requested which so clearly showed him to be utterly without any real love or concern for her! Psychologically, I know the pattern this follows where the victim convinces herself that she actually invited the rape, invited the mugging, invited the abuse, etc. Will this ever excuse the actions of degenerate men; never in the sight of God or decent men and women.

I know his type all too well. I know his methods thoroughly. He has pretended to be grievously wounded and actually has his ever so well-chosen victim pleading his case! Unbelievable? I wish it were so. Women who have succumbed to this type of predator follow the same cycle unless a decent man interposes and offers them a way out. But even this depends on the woman's ability to deal with the truth. And this doesn't happen very often.

She will actually become angry with me because of his successfully worming his way back into her bed, preying on her real decency of emotions in contrast to his utter deceitfulness. Satan himself has taught such creatures the tactics of seduction and this sorry excuse for a man has proven an adept pupil of his father, the Devil. So much so that this monster has his victim pleading for him with me!

Will he marry this girl and provide for her and her child? No! That was never his intention. Will he ever care for anyone but himself? No! This poor, grieving girl will still stand up for him even knowing it won't last, even knowing he is simply using her. Such is the nature of this demonic plague and the successful pattern of its perpetrators and their depredations.

Did I waste my time? I don't know, only time itself will answer this question. I have warned her that when he gets through with her, when something better comes along, he will dump her immediately as though she never existed. She knows this. But he was back the very next night in her bed, his oily way having been perfected by his use of several other such victims.

As a man, I recognize such degenerates for what they are. But even confronting the fact in their own lives does little good for those so desperate, like this poor girl who pay such a dreadful price out of the need to be loved. It seems there is a seemingly ceaseless supply for such vile creatures to continue to find willing victims for their depredations. I would weep for such "children" but, as I have said, I have had to deal with too much of it and the tears continue to drench my heart while my eyes remain dry.

It should come as no surprise, by the way, that this man who could take such advantage of this girl, claimed to be a good, Bible believing Christian. I couldn't help but be reminded of Esau and his "crocodile tears" and the story of Ananias and Saphira. This man hadn't only lied to people; he had lied to God Himself, shaming God and His Word by his phony religiosity. His condemnation, therefore, will be all the more severe when he goes to meet the Righteous Judge of all mankind. As with all religious charlatans, he uses religion as a mechanism to elicit respectability but his works deny any pretended faith.

In sharing this tragic story with a few people it didn't surprise me, though it still hurt, to have some of them condemning the girl for being "easy." She, in fact, condemns herself for allowing this man to take advantage of her. The reaction of most "good church people" was easily anticipated. To most of them, the girl is just another slut. Strange that they know so little of God's Word that they fail to recognize the fact that He places the responsibility of seduction on the man, not the woman.

But one dear friend and beautiful lady, after sharing the story with her, replied: "Again!" To explain this otherwise cryptic exclamation, this dear lady knew I was in love "Again!" Yes, the curse of the poet leads me very easily into falling in love with those birds with broken wings. In the case of this poor girl, as I said at the beginning of this tragedy, it was easy for someone like myself to love her, to respond to such rare courage in the face of such obstacles, not only physical, but overcoming bitterness and resentment and still have the capacity for loving in her own life. She has an abundance of rare qualities to offer the man who will love her for what she is as a person. I can only hope such a man will come into her life soon.

Is there, as my daughter and others tell me, such a small supply of good and decent men out there that women like this poor girl have to resort to such victimization to achieve even a small degree of escape from the loneliness and hopelessness? And at such a price? God help us if this is the case!

I was having dinner with friends in Bakersfield. I had another man with me, an ex-con who I had brought with me in hope of helping him find a job and a place to live. Our meeting and my involvement with him will make a story for a later essay. It was the after dinner conversation upon which I want to focus attention. I hope some of my readers will respond to the comments made and the conclusions I have drawn as a result.

Our host works in an environment where the employees are 85% women. As a man, he has commented on his observations of these women, one such being the attention paid him as one of the few males. This often proves inflating to the male ego in such an environment.

It occurred to me, since our host is married, that his interest in these women must be sexual. Why? Because he is married. I pointed out to him the fact that since married men have the advantages of constant female companionship in the structure of a home and family, the only other interest in looking at other women, even pursuing them, has to be sexual; all the other facets of "seeking" are, or should be, satisfied in the marriage relationship.

It hardly needs to be said that the sexual part of a marriage should preclude the need for a man or women to continue to pursue that part of our needs with others outside the marriage. But it happens- and too often.

An unmarried man such as me looks at women from a totally different perspective. None of those things, companionship, children, sharing the ordinary things of ordinary life, are available to me by association with that "significant other" in my life. Sex, then, is only one component among many others that is in mind when I look at women.

Married people will take immediate exception, in their defense, of their "looking" at others. But if there is an interest in doing so outside the marriage, I will stick to my opinion that it is solely sexual in orientation no matter the protestations of "innocence." If men and women have all their other needs satisfied in the marriage, sex can only be left as the cause of "roving eyes" and that itch so many who are married can't seem to scratch.

I have met with the beautiful English Lady from Nottingham. My mind reels with the possibilities. She is an extremely gifted composer, musician and singer. Her voice is lyrical magic, reminding me of a bubbling stream, of birds singing in the heather.

She is making an album of songs to take to Ireland and I am helping her with some of the lyrics. Being a "Wordsmith" has its advantages and we have had a marvelous time working together.

We had met for lunch at a Black Angus in Lancaster where, in conversation, we discovered we had some amazing things in common, not the least of which was our orientation around Christian principles of belief and behavior. Further, there was the common bond of the music and poetry, the things of real value in life and other people. Not at all sure where this may lead but the possibilities are exciting and intriguing.

Since I am in town (Isabella) this weekend, I'm at the Club Saturday night for the music and dancing. The band doesn't start playing until 9 p.m. and I arrive early enough to socialize with many of the folks I have come to know well. But I'm hoping to see a "special" lady who promised to be here.

It is 10 p.m. when she calls and tells me she isn't going to make it. Oh, well, if you're going to be "stood up," it might as well be by a beautiful woman and early enough to make the most of it. I do thank her for being thoughtful enough to call; many wouldn't have bothered. But I can't help thinking of that now familiar refrain: "Why is it that nice guys are left alone at the last dance?" Of course, in this case, there wasn't even the first dance or any other with her this night.

The following morning, we all awakened to the first snow of winter. The valley is covered with a white blanket and, while beautiful, the cold I dread has come upon us. I'm a "summer" person and don't take to the cold.

It's Sunday and in the afternoon the sun is shining, most of the snow has melted from the valley floor but the snow on the mountains promises a very cold night. Since I'm still in town, I go to the Club where Howard and I play our guitars and have a good time with the music until about 7 p.m. We then have a good time socializing until the hour grows late and we go our separate ways until next time. It is bitter cold when I go out to my car and drive home alone again, naturally.

As the turmoil and chaos continue to escalate in our nation and the world, it becomes increasingly important for me to do my part in the political arena where so many depend on me as a voice of reason. But the very things that create the need are those very things that easily lead to the same depression that inflicts so many people faced with the immensity and complexity of the job to be done.

This together with the fact of such monumental corruption, betrayal and sheer ineptitude on the part of government leadership, the mounting alienation between government and the governed, easily leads those of us involved with the active confrontation of Caesar into depression at times. To escape becoming so moribund as to lose sight of the priorities, the hopes and dreams of our young people, especially, I try to involve myself with some of the more ordinary aspects of life and the ordinary people who lack a voice in the affairs of the "Ruling Elite."

For those of you who have evidenced concern for me (which is deeply appreciated) by my forays into the saloons and dance halls, I can only say that the music and dancing, the poetry I find in the ordinary lives of ordinary people helps me to maintain that essential balance ever as much as my life-long reading of the great writers, walks in the forest and watching the stars at night.

Before going into any more of the stories of my research into the CW phenomena, I have to pay my dues as a political analyst even for the readers of CP, especially for those of you who don't receive any of my other publications which are primarily political. The hard facts, questions and choices, as I have often said, which confront all nations throughout history will not be denied. Answers and solutions will come about with, or without, the aid of enlightened leadership. To repeat, history only allows of three choices for any nation: Slavery, Anarchy or the course of our founding fathers.

The betrayal of those noble, Christian ideals of our forefathers has resulted in an ironic condition in our nation's capital. The mayor of D.C. wants the present, chief betrayer, Clinton, to call out the National Guard to police the place. To quote the mayor: "We've got a war on our hands." It hardly does any good to point out the obvious fact that this is due, primarily, to Caesar's successful efforts at making the Capital a Mecca for Negroes by the mechanisms of liberal welfare and the "minority hiring" practice of "Affirmative Action" making government offices a sea of black faces. Apart from the government itself, Congress, the White House and the Supreme Court, the purview of the most successful crooks, D.C. is awash in Black Crime due to the paucity of qualified and educated Caucasian professionals.

Racist? Not at all. The facts speak for themselves but "political correctness" forbids calling attention to such facts. However, not all the political correctness in the world can cover up the media necessity of bringing the issue to the forefront of the people simply by virtue of demographics if nothing else. For example, the great majority of high crime communities like Watts are virtually 100% Negro. That is not a racist comment- that is demographic. The problems of such rampant crime in "certain areas" of D.C. that prompts the mayor to ask Clinton to call out the National Guard to police the area cannot change the demographics of such violent areas being, primarily, Negro.

Devoid of emotion and name-calling, of political rhetoric, the hard facts and the concomitant hard choices remain and not all the wishful, so-called "liberal" thinking in the world is going to change this. But Thoreau was absolutely correct in his assessment of the situation when he called attention to the fact that life may have been hard under Southern overseers but life under Northern ones (the system that was destined to become Welfare Slavery) was eminently worse.

As to hard facts and hard choices who would have thought Boxer and Feinstein, with such oh, so very correct, liberal credentials would call for sealing our borders with Mexico? My own estimate of the cost of illegal aliens to California, about $5 billion, was right on target as per the recent study by San Diego State University researchers. But I assure you I didn't get paid as well as the university for being able to figure this out.

And who would have thought that the idea of surrounding our prisons with lethally charged electric fences would gain "liberal" support? Some of you should go back and review some of my political writing of some years ago when I warned that our nation would have to eventually confront those same "Hitlerian" conditions and "solutions" if the leadership didn't get down to the business of dealing with the incipient beginnings of just those same conditions Germany and so many other nations have faced.

I continue to watch what is happening in foreign nations with a great deal of interest. Speaking of Germany, it seems the government has halted a plan to distribute a comic book entitled "Hitler" to high school students because it "glorifies" the Nazi regime. Not your usual "comic" book since it is a glossy paperback about 200 pp. in length and sells for the equivalent of $15.

It may not be coincidental that a jury in Berlin acquitted two rightist militants of firebombing a Holocaust memorial, a verdict that the Jewish community called "incomprehensible." Perhaps to them, but not to many others like myself. Germany and France have the scandals of the cover-ups of their own politicians trying to hide their part in AIDS tainted blood finding itself into hospitals.

Among such "incidentals" is the growing tolerance of judges in this country to allow marches by white advocate groups and the judge who recently cleared David Duke of charges of misusing campaign funds. It was refreshing to hear a judge say he didn't think there was any evidence of knowingly or willfully breaking any law in respect to any political figure and be able to believe him.

Yeltsin is packing the "foreigners" up and shipping them out of Russia. Ethnic Cleansing? Of course; what else can he do in order to maintain a viable, national ideology and government? It's the only sensible alternative he has. I'm not sure about the move of Russian lawmakers banning foreign missionaries from Russian soil. Granted a lot of the charismatic kooks and quacks were taking advantage of the previous, open policy but I do have to wonder if they haven't thrown the baby out with the bath.

Too bad, in a way, that our leaders aren't of the same stuff as Shusuke Nomura. When his bid for power failed, he simply shot himself right in front of the Japanese media to make his point.

The recent trial in L.A. of the Negroes who tried to murder Reginald Denny was an obvious travesty. What is equally obvious is the fact that Caesar is not likely to equate the beating of Rodney King with this beating. The "Double Jeopardy" protection clause of our Constitution which Caesar totally disregarded in order to satisfy the blood lust of Negroes by sending the Caucasian cops to prison will not be used against Denny's attackers. The reason for this will not be lost on those of us who have been active in opposing Caesar's insane policy of punishing those of us who are proud of our Caucasian heritage and the policies of our founding fathers.

NAFTA is another insane policy of Caesar trying another gambit of forcing the great unwashed into slavery. The obvious intent of the treaty is to make the rich and powerful more rich and powerful at the cost of further lowering the standard of living for Americans and, as an added "benefit," more attempts at forcing the failed social experiment of multiculturalism down the throat of Americans.

For all you ill-informed folks about the status of Bakersfield, not only is the city properly called Nashville West, here's a list of some of the folks who will be speaking at Saturday's Business Conference: Gerald Ford, Jimmy Carter, George and Barbara Bush, Jack Kemp, Mario Cuomo, Donald Trump, Lee Iococca, T. Boone Pickens, Williard Scott, Lesley Stahl, Mark Russell, Burt Bacharach, Dionne Warwick, Glenn Yarborough and Phyllis Diller. No matter your opinion of some of the speakers, it makes for a pretty impressive lineup of high-powered personalities. Suppose these people know something about a city that prompts more jokes than serious discussion?

Of interest is a tidbit of which most people are unaware as well. Seems Henrye Margenau, co-editor of the prestigious "Cosmos Bois," Theos believes creation of the universe by God is the only convincing answer to the legitimate questions of science. 60 top scientists, 20 of who have received the Nobel Prize, wrote the publication. But our ignorant school leaders will continue to taut so-called "evolution" as a fact when most reputable scientists have long since abandoned the theory.

I have just been reading a recent addition to the growing list of publications dedicated to racism. The publication, oddly enough, is a large metropolitan newspaper, The Bakersfield Californian. "What," you say, "The Bakersfield Californian has turned into a racist publication?"

True. Just read the most recent editions that have been given over predominantly to racial issues. Now the fact of the coverage of the recent Denny trial together with so many other racial crises might have led the editors to pay an inordinate amount of attention to such matters and, as a consequence, might lead one to a false conclusion. But the fact of so much newsprint being given over to such a thing certainly makes the appearance of racism plausible. The resulting Letters to the Editor? Whew!

Much of the paper's attention has been given, for example, to the recent attempt of a group of Caucasian students attempting to start a White Pride club on a local Bakersfield high school (Stockdale) campus. Given the fact that the schools have Black Pride, Hispanic Pride, Asian Pride, even Gay Pride clubs, why disallow a White Pride club? Obvious. White Pride isn't politically correct. Gay, Black, Brown, Red, Yellow Pride? Yes! White? No! The irony of the thing can't be lost on even the most obtuse.

Then, the recent beating of a Caucasian student by three Negroes comes into play. In spite of the mother's appeal to the D.A., one Ed Jagels, the Negroes won't be prosecuted under the Hate Crimes law; the incident has been treated as a "school fight." The Negro attackers will do a couple of months in Camp Owen at the worst. But if a Negro had been attacked by three Caucasian students? Throw the book at them! This lesson isn't going unlearned either.

I think people of all color are beginning to realize the truth of what I have been trying to say for so many years; the war going on in our own nation is not a racial one, it is ideological. False leaders and a distorted media keep trying to make it a matter of races in conflict rather than cultures in conflict. But the truth is there for all to see. Until America gets back to the principles that made the nation the greatest the world has ever seen, bigotry, ignorant prejudice will be the things false leaders and the media will encourage rather than the truth.

But not all of the paper has been dedicated to racist propaganda. There is hope for its redemption. I'm referring specifically to an article concerning an issue of consuming interest to the whole nation and completely devoid of any hint of racism. It has to do with the possibility of a magic cream that will reduce fat in the thighs of women, a national plague of monumental proportion. Of course my old friend "Jerry" considers fat women a national catastrophe but he has a reputation for aberrations.

Hey! You "ordinary folks" out there; what do you think of the jury in Mobile Ala. acquitting the father and son who killed one teenager and shot out the eye of another because the juvenile criminals stole their truck? The media is decrying the act as "Vigilante Justice." Personally, I don't see any other kind of "justice" having a chance anymore. A breakdown of the criminal justice system? Of course. Especially since the insanity of laws protect the criminal and pervert the cause of justice and can do nothing to protect or recompense the victim. The father in this case put it very plainly and spoke for all of us who still possess a modicum of reason: "I'm tired of being a helpless victim of criminals!" Do the laws, then, force us into vigilantism? No wonder I call it the "insanity of law!"

While not overtly racial, the recent shooting of a motorist by an IRS agent still has my attention. Does this mean that the IRS has joined the Shadow Government's Black Suits? And when will my appeal for a New Continental Congress to confront such abuse by Caesar and his Empire Beyond Reason cause a nocturnal knock on my door by his Gestapo? It may only be a matter of time. But he still has the problem of my not wearing any "label" but that of the N.R.A. and believing in God. But when I consider the fact that the poets and intellectuals were the first that had to be disposed of in Stalin's and other dictator's regimes it does give me pause to wonder at times.

Abortion, School Vouchers, Racial Terrorism, rampant corruption in government; oh, yes, solutions and answers will follow national chaos and turmoil but will such solutions and answers come from the enlightened self-interest of Paine, Jefferson, Franklin and Emerson, and Thoreau or will they be those of Hitler and Stalin?

I'm almost amused at the recent missives I have received from Jack Kemp and Bob Dole. Jack and Bob can't, of course, call people like Clinton and Reno chief betrayers of America in so many words like I can. They can't say, "Rattlesnakes can't be reformed or rehabilitated, they can only be killed." But I can and do. My point? Unless people like Jack and Bob start calling a spade a spade, little is going to change in the view of us "ordinary Americans."

Jack, Bob, I have a few words of wisdom for you and all you so-called "conservatives": You cut government spending, you cut the size of the monolithic, devouring and betraying monster of which you are a part and a contributor, then, and only then, will I believe you are concerned for my America and the future of our nation and children!

And, by now, most people are aware that the causative agent (CS gas) for the explosions and fires that killed those women and children in Waco was ordered pumped into the complex for a full six hours with certain knowledge of the results. The murderers: Clinton, Reno, Sessions and Higgens can now be named to that infamous list of those who act according to "political expediency" as the excuse for "the end justifies the means."

I'm not sure why this reminds me of Kary Mullis, the quirky biological genius, but his procedure (polymerase chain reaction, PCR) to reproduce a single gene or DNA fragment a billion times in a few hours is now a standard tool in the most important laboratories in the world. The genetic possibilities are mind-boggling, bringing a host of potential evils as well as good things to the fore. This, together with the recent study showing a link to "chance" in the genetic codes, makes for an even more intriguing (frightening?) scenario.

Things like this make the needed research of my own mathematical model of Human Behavior even more important. For this reason, and because of the request by so many of my readers, I am including an example of this in this essay. Here it is:

Having piqued my reader's interest in my work on a mathematical model of human behavior for quite some time, I thought it best to give you some idea of its status and where it is going together with a more thorough understanding of what is involved in an attempt to make predictions of behavior based on scientific criteria. I'll do my utmost to make it, at least, interesting to you.

You don't necessarily have to be particularly adroit in the field of mathematics to appreciate what Stephen Hawking has to offer in the subject. His best selling book, "A Brief History of Time," proves this point. I am going to lead the reader into, what I hope will be, like Hawking's book, some understanding of the Mathematical Principles of Human Behavior, the program I have mentioned to which I am devoting so much of my own time and effort, utilizing some of his findings and speculations. But with a significant difference!

While I have taught high school and undergraduate classes in algebra, geometry and trigonometry, the fundamental theorem of calculus, integral (infinitesimal) and differential, is unique in its contribution to such a data base and is necessary to a degree of understanding the monumental complexities in human behavior. But I will try my best to keep it simple enough for the math-avoiders to get a grasp of the concept. As I used to tell my students, just keep in mind the fact that you can only do four things with any numbers or variables; you can add, subtract, divide or multiply them. As you will recall from your earliest days of basic arithmetic, these four procedures group into two in which the one provides the check on the other, the inverse operation if you will. No matter the complexity of the mathematical system, the complexity of the problem, this is all you can do in solving mathematical problems from the most elemental to the most esoteric.

In trying to assign a specific value that incorporates the use of both negative and positive factors, the number line is conceptualized with zero as a point where the one passes through an accepted value of infinity to the other. Whether the vectors of a chart where the rays intersect, the areas, positive and negative, or the assigned values of variables in an equation, the "philosophy" of something we do not understand or have the capacity or mathematics of even imagining, that point of infinitude, called absolute zero, serves as a practical point of transition, in other words, it is a workable concept.

Perhaps, as Hawking says, it is impossible to travel at the speed of light based on his supposition that at that speed one would be into the realm of time travel and no one has come back from the future to prove the reality of achieving such speed. Conversely, one would have to reach such a velocity, by our present mathematical concepts at least, to disprove Hawking; hence, at least for now, philosophical. But the practical limitation of a thing does not cheat us of the ability to imagine its possibilities and the philosophies that arise from such imaginings.

As a result, I take exception to the great mathematician's "closed system" of the universe, his "in-progress" theory of reality in which "... the universe would be completely self-contained, neither created nor destroyed - it would just be." As entrancing as I find the theory it not only fails to do justice to a Prime Cause, to believers this is God Himself, but it fails to do justice to the philosophical realities of imagination. It might be well to consider Heisenberg's Principle of Uncertainty in this context as well.

But I do understand the necessity of Hawking having to think in his own way of such things because, in his own words, "... asking what happened before creation is meaningless." Understood from his point of view, he has no other choice. That does not rob those like me of those philosophical realities that, if Hawking were able to intrude himself, would allow of a far larger universe than he pragmatically rejects as a part of his own philosophy.

I think Hawking cheats himself by seeing the stars as cold, still, lifeless, of not having the "poetic connection" of Creation to draw his mind into other worlds with a more "precise science" than the one in which he seeks ultimate answers. But I thank God for the genius of Hawking and his ability to seek answers beyond the realm of most common speculations at the same time granting him the sympathy of someone who would intrude such speculations into those other worlds. I do wonder if, with all his exceeding rare genius, he considers what possibilities exist in even having the capacity to entertain such questions as "Where and how did it all begin" as more than a rhetorical question or trying to enclose the "answer" in some neat, presumed mathematically precise (more likely imprecise) box? Such a presumption that excludes a Prime Cause is, in my opinion, likely to fail. If I can succeed in the mathematical model of human behavior it might well cause Hawking and others to take another look at their self-imposed limitations of philosophical data.

In seeking that Holy Grail of all physics, the Grand Unification Theory which would explain The All, it may very well be, to entertain any hope of such, that a much larger part will have to be played by philosophy than is usually the case. By that I mean that some degree of understanding of infinity would have to be at least conceptualized, and an understanding of what "Life" actually is must be included. That, of course, falls, at present, entirely into the field of the philosophy of physics apart from the fact of "something" animates at birth and departs at death. This is an area of mathematics that has not received its due attention. Yet who can deny the longing to fill that void of the soul's cry for understanding while looking at the stars, the only sensible measure of infinity which presents itself to us, that longing for a seemingly "intuited" immortality which the stars seem to betoken?

At present, the philosophical properties of space, matter and time are "workable." I assign the term "philosophical" because of the lack of the ability of our present mathematics to definitively discriminate. The infinitesimal calculus only assigns a "point," not an understanding of that point. Such a limitation forces us to assign "labels" in lieu of real understanding. Time, for example, by such "labeling," is easily "understood" as consisting of past, present and future. It is not essential for our present requirements of "workability" to actually understand the calculus of that exact point of transition where the present becomes the past or the future becomes the present. Nor does the need of workability suffer our not being able to precisely vector length, breadth and height in regards to matter or the space it occupies.

If there were an intense enough "need to know," we might well be spending billions on trying to discover the physics of differentiating the mind from the astronomical amount of seemingly, random, chaotic (actually, I believe, symphonic/fractal) patterns of its electro/chemical biology.

Now, rather than exhaust one's inventory of invective, maledicta and just plain, ordinary, everyday cuss words at such seeming esoterica, I'll do my best to speak good old plain American as Phil Harris would say.

All definitions require proscribed parameters. For example a cup; now if you go into a store and ask the clerk to sell you a cup he is going to ask you "What kind of cup?" This assumes you are not in the lingerie section in which case it would be a question of size, not kind. Little weak humor there.

No, I am not trying to be fiendishly clever; you will have to be somewhat precise in your description of just what kind of cup you are in need of, coffee, tea or milk, ceramic, glass, china, plastic, patterned, plain, large, small, etc. Reminds me of an old Jack Benny skit where he goes in to buy a pair of shoelaces. The most ordinary things can, indeed, become quite complex depending on the variables involved; and if the individual is practiced in making mountains of molehills.... But the use of the calculus methodology is not an exercise in either *reductio ad absurdam* or impossible. Nor will I resort to the Greek analog of the runner who never finishes the race, philosophically. It is a means of precision of definition, and like the concepts of *Weltschmerz* and *Weltanschauung*, must start with a corporate meaning and become ever more and more precise in the mathematical model of human behavior.

The intended use of an item is often sufficient for its definition. You go into a restaurant and order a cup of coffee; you have every reason to expect it to be served in a coffee cup, not on a saucer or plate. Further, while you may get a spoon in concert with the cup of coffee, you don't expect to receive it in attendance with a knife and fork.

Such things are "practiced definitions" and usually brook little need of elaboration. People know what you mean when you say "cup" within the context of the use of the word.

We use the words Love and Hate as definitive of certain emotions. But we do so in the knowledge that such words and their corresponding concepts often fail to convey precise meaning, precise definition. Now if we conceptualize a number line with -10 to +10 and assign the most extreme form of Hate the number -10 and the most extreme form of Love the value +10 with absolute 0, the transition point between the two, we could assign a numeric value to all those emotions which fall between the two extremes, 0 being, let's say, the point of ambivalence.

As you can readily see, a tremendous amount of data would have to be inputted in order to cover the vast possibilities, the most subtle shading of meanings and differences in order to obtain an absolute degree of precision in just this one instance.

I will look forward to sharing more of this with you as time and circumstances permit. Let me know your thoughts.

Chapter Twelve

Christian Perspective

December, 1994

Is God capable of error and has He made mistakes? "But we are not of those who shrink back and are destroyed, but of those who believe and are saved." Hebrews 10:39

"On the relation of man to God rests the relation of man to his fellow men; this is the sociological problem which forms one of the great tasks of the nineteenth century." Phillip Schaff: History of the Christian Church. 1853.

I can think of no other question that could so call down on my head the fire and anathemas of the churches. To think that such a question by a man like myself would be asked to purposely ex-communicate myself from the body of believers, to so alienate me from those I love and the church I love would be, obviously, an insane act.

Schaff, in the above quotation, could scarcely realize how naive his hope and how far removed we remain in the twentieth century, soon to move into the twenty-first, from an answer to his sociological problem. The task remains and continues of no ready solution, in the greatest part, because of the failure to address legitimate questions which would lead to greater understanding of those very elements of the natures of God and man and this failure has led to incalculable hatreds and inhuman acts of violence.

Too often, as in the time of Martin Luther, when the possibilities of Reformation and Illumination working together exist, it is the extreme ideologue that would destroy the potential harmony of the two. And, of course, these Pharisees always do so in the name of their god and their professed love of the Truth.

I have too often had to confront this thing of "The wisdom of this world is foolishness with God" among ignorant and self-righteous men who, in their own pride and foolishness, would decry any attempts at reasonable questions and answers concerning religion. Too often, like those despicable Pharisees of old, such people fail to recognize their own blindness and make every attempt to stifle an honest search for truth.

When I raised the questions that head this essay in my first book some time ago, I got an immediate response from a friend of many years, Gary North. Gary is the leader of a theological movement called Christian Reconstruction. He publishes widely and is the son-in-law of one of the most respected Bible scholars in our nation- Rousas Rushdoony.

I have great regard for the comments of those like Gary but, unfortunately, I had not sufficiently explained the question or my speculations concerning it in that first book. As a result, Gary wrote me a four page, single-spaced letter urging me to publicly recant my position and to write a newsletter and send it out to all my readers informing them of my recantation. The alternative, Gary said, was to suffer the fires of hell in eternity for my heresy.

The following is a much belated reply to my old friend's condemnation of me as a: "Self ex-communicated and lawless man!"

It was a beautiful, starry night that summer nearly four years ago when, looking up at the beauty of God's creation, the heavens that declare His glory, I came to the decision to start asking and seeking answers to those questions that the churches do not allow. That the questions even exist is a testimony to God's creation of man in His own image. Without that divinity of God Himself within men, a divinity that reaches out even beyond the stars in questioning wonder, the divinity that searches our own hearts for answers to these questions, that recognizes the conflict within our own hearts, our innermost thoughts; there would be little difference between men and the beasts of the field.

This thing called *conscience*, for example. Some have it in large degree while there are some who commit inhuman acts against others without any seeming vestige of such a thing. Why?

My own background, my extensive studies in theology and human behavior, the many churches in which I have served in both lay and pastoral positions, these have acquainted me with the problems I face in even trying to place these questions before the brethren. Further, the twists and turns of my own life which have alienated me from acceptance by those with whom I yearn to have fellowship have made me, in a unique way, the very person to ask such questions. Why? Because God has, in me, a solitary and badly flawed man without wife or family due to divorces, with nothing to lose and no empire but God's Kingdom to protect.

The situation I face is certainly not unique. There is a plethora of examples from the past including virtually every prophet of Biblical history. I cite only two, however: The Apostle Paul and Martin Luther.

My own claim to the office of Prophet consists only of the strictest definition as one who Proclaims, not the corrupted sense of one who foretells the future or pretends to be the voice of God. If, in fact, I speak for God in any fashion, it is strictly on the basis of His Word and strictly in accordance with His Word. And at that, I only speak as a man who thinks he knows something of the love and nature of God, of His love, understanding, compassion and forgiveness in my own life. As such a voice and being a believer in God irrespective of my many sins, weaknesses and failures I intend to confront facts and ask the hard but legitimate questions that deserve an answer.

The Apostle found himself, as did Jesus, vilified by the very people for whom he had suffered so much. In the end, he found himself, again like Jesus, alone. But his questions and directions for the Church live on in his epistles. One question stands out: Am I become your enemy because I tell you the truth?

Martin Luther sought to bring reforms to the institution of the Church only to find himself the enemy of those very ones he sought to help. His questions and directions however, like Paul's, remain.

In bringing my own questions to the attention of the brethren, I have found resistance, even being cursed, by those who had a duty before God of addressing those questions. There have been exceptions among some friends. But even the best of these have great difficulty with me because of what I have come to call Blind Orthodoxy together with the fact that they know too well my own sins and failures to credit me with much in the way of Spiritual insight. I give them full credit, however, with adhering to God's command to love and their forgiveness of me in all my imperfections and weaknesses.

It is in the practice of God's Royal Law, to love one another, that I have found in Christian friends the motivation and hope that has sustained me through many a midnight of the soul and have not given up the hope that my own labors are not always in vain. If these good people have not given up on me I simply cannot fail them in giving up on myself.

The primary difficulty I have faced as a teacher, both secular and religious, is the confusion that reigns in people's minds and hearts because of their inability to separate what they Know from what they Believe. The two, you would think reasonable people would recognize of course, are obviously not necessarily synonymous. In fact, those who confuse the two are rightly identified as bigoted, prejudiced and/or ignorant.

At the simplest level, we are all aware of some of the false conceptions (beliefs) throughout history that were held as nearly sacred knowledge that have been proven totally false. I won't bore the reader with the innumerable examples of which they must surely be aware. Socrates was said to have been condemned to death for asking reasonable, but hated, questions. It was the presentation of a belief system, that of Christianity, that condemned so many to death in the history of the Church.

It might be safely said that history is a record of the difficulty, even martyrdom, men and women have faced in holding to what they believe as truth. My own belief system leads me to present, as evidence of knowledge, that God *Is* and that His very creation of men and the universe declare this to be true. I present this as a fact even though it admits of no empirical proof unless one is disposed to accept it as such.

Therefore, I recognize such proof in my own belief system but have to realize that the apologetic for such proof is in the heart and mind of someone who is willing to accept such a belief as knowledge. To that extent, I accept the fact that I may well be called one that confuses what he knows with what he believes.

In this regard, we have a discipline of study called Philosophy, the King of Disciplines as a search for truth. The application of certain disciplines is essential to such study and its prosecution is, primarily, the formulating of questions and seeking answers.

Within this discipline the empirical proofs of the hard sciences are neither required nor, for the most part, possible. The questions raised by philosophical inquiry are those pertaining to the nature of man and God, of the world, the universe and things of relationships that are not subject to the testing mechanisms of the laboratory.

Mankind has always had the need of philosophy. In many cases the philosophies of men have led to monumental error, even heinous crimes against humanity. But it is really ideological differences that have led to things like the Spanish Inquisition, the Salem Witch Trials, wars between nations and hatred between races and, as per our own attempt at national suicide, our Civil War between people of the same race, brother against brother.

It is thus apparent that the study of Philosophy, while not subject to the empirical proofs of the other sciences, is one that leads into very dangerous areas that offer empirical results in the practice of philosophical beliefs. So it is that the Philosopher cannot be dismissed as a harmless entity nor can the issues addressed and the questions raised by the philosophical method of inquiry be lightly dismissed.

Any standard text on philosophy will show the reader how vastly complex the study is. The ideas of men have enormous complexity and the subtleties of thought are seemingly endless. Yet, in order for any society of men to function, certain specifics must be agreed on and put into practice. The founding of our own nation as a Republican form of government was an exercise in philosophical specifics and flexibility of thought resulting in a most unique configuration of freedoms and responsibilities never before seen in the history of the world.

While the scientist has to insist on the empirical method of proofs, his equivalent in philosophy seeks proofs that will explain the nature of man and God, the relationships that make use of scientific findings that benefit mankind and contribute to an understanding of our world and the universe. In the seeking methodologies of both the philosopher and the scientist, a search for order out of chaos is a primary goal.

This leads to my call for a New Systematic Theology, a coming together of Godly men and women of wisdom and good will to address the questions raised by honest inquiry into the nature of God and man, of the Creation and man's place, present and future, in the context of this relationship to meet contemporary demands for new knowledge and order in the face of mounting chaos.

The earliest Church Council; that of Jerusalem was called to examine the question of Gentile believers. We have the record of the conclusion of that early meeting of the Church. The striking thing, to me, has always been that it was a consensus of both the men involved and The Holy Spirit. We thus have a record of the Holy Spirit entering into the deliberations of men in order to reach a conclusion.

I know of no other meeting in the last, few centuries of the Church, where such a thing can be claimed. Yes, as churchmen, we recognize the Holy Spirit must have been involved in the directions the Church has taken on a number of occasions but because of the confusion of the last decades especially, the fracturing of the many parts of the Body, there has been only dissension and fighting to mark the condition of the churches today. And the world has taken note of this condition and has, rightly, like Balaam's Ass, condemned the false, even chaotic, directions of so many false leaders and prophets.

In my political work the questions most often asked of me by so many are: "What can I do and how can I do it?" The questions apply equally to the condition of the churches in the world today.

One old friend (ex?) has called me a self ex-communicated man because of the questions I have raised about The Lord, His Word and the churches. He may well be right. But, like Paul and Luther, I don't seem to be able to let go and fall back on some of the comfortable dogmas of my past church life.

But if there is any answer to the moral morass of our nation, if there is to be any hope in successfully prosecuting a battle against either the tyranny of Caesar or the evil of the present world system and our ancient enemy, Satan, it can only be done with honor and the hope of God's help on the basis of truthfully facing the hard questions both of the Faith and our political system.

I think many believers would agree that the churches are in deep trouble; that only repentance of sins will lead to revival. And just what are the sins of the churches? Certainly the loss of love and hardness of heart, the lack of true missionary zeal, the chaos and utter disharmony and dissension among the brethren can easily be seen all about. But where is the Council which would come together, under the blessing and auspices of God Himself, to address these ills in the churches; perhaps only in the written word.

I am a writer. I have been a professional writer for many years. So it is not surprising that I would think in terms of seeking a consensus among believers by use of the printed page. Among men and women people like Tom Paine, Harriet Beecher Stowe, Marx and Hitler changed world history by use of such a means. Luther could hardly have realized his 95 Theses would cause such world upheaval and change the course of history but such was the case.

While Luther's obvious intention was to call churchmen to discuss the issue of the sale of Indulgences, his questions went far beyond this. Whether wittingly or not, Luther had raised questions relating to some of the broadest dogmas of the Church and, in the end, the failure of Godly men to come together to honestly address these questions caused the schism that exists to this day.

But what might have been if honorable men of the Church had come together in honest inquiry and seeking of truth and discussion of these questions? Tragically, such was not the case and we live with the failure today.

If God's men in our nation had cooperated would we still have the Bible as a textbook in our schools today? Would prayer still be part of the beginning of each school day and the Ten Commandments still posted on classroom walls? Would we have honorable leaders in government and industry? Would families and family values still be the strength of our nation? These questions, for many such as me, are obviously rhetorical.

Taking the times of Martin Luther as a classic example, one cannot separate the political from the religious. As the one goes, so goes the other. The reasons for this are self-evident. Political leadership reflects the beliefs and the practices of those beliefs in every society.

Since chicanery and corruption are a hallmark of our present leadership, it can safely be said that our society has produced such leadership in government. If, as the churches claim and I believe, the Gospel is the salt which would preserve what is good and noble, what is honorable and true, what is of lasting value, it is the churches which must accept the responsibility of the failure to produce such a society.

Thomas Jefferson said: "Rebellion to tyrants is obedience to God." But churches, which feed at Caesar's table through tax-exempt status, have, as a consequence, become, as the proverb says, Caesar's dogs and can hardly be counted on to bite the hand that feeds them.

Thus an immediate question, a hard question, arises: Should the churches accept such a condition to exist which preempts them from prosecuting a battle against the tyranny of Caesar and his insistence on the worship of false gods (special consideration and protection for homosexuals and tax support for pornography for example) and continued bowing to his unjust laws which pervert the cause of justice?

It is an argument without foundation that any organization can fight a legitimate battle against an enemy while accepting aid and comfort from that very enemy! And if you have come to the sorry point as the churches now have, that your very existence as an institution depends on such aid and comfort?

Just one, single point has to be made in this regard: A church loses its tax-exempt status if it supports a candidate by name for public office. Now I ask, reasonably, if the ordinary citizen has such a right and an institution relinquishes such a fundamental freedom in exchange for the largess of Caesar, who has the most integrity and power? And to think that God Himself is blind to this distinction! Hardly.

It was a legitimate confrontation of wrongs within the Church that led Luther, and the Council in Jerusalem, to address the hard questions raised. From time to time, the churches have been called on to confront special problems of both dogma and politics.

It may well be, faced with the questions of today such as abortion as contraception, homosexuality, euthanasia, the tyranny of Caesar and Christian political activism, etc., the Lord's men and women are going to be forced to deal with such questions whether they want to or not.

The problem is that while the churches themselves are in such a chaotic state, no certain trumpet sound is possible which will have a consensus among those that call themselves Christian. As a result, I have elected the methodology of our Founding Fathers, particularly Tom Paine, to Pamphleteer; as with the questions of Paul and Luther's theses, I will raise the questions in a written format and enjoin men and women of good will to come together to discuss these questions.

We can safely assume that God has not been dictatorial in settling many of the questions I intend to raise. I suggest that the earliest question posed by men in the Church in Jerusalem would not have needed a council to settle it if God intended the Church to be the rubber stamp of a dictator; but that early council indicates the need of The Lord and His people cooperating together to arrive at a solution. I would further suggest that the question was a legitimate and serious one leading to serious discussion of the issues involved resulting in the first directive to the infant Church and was accepted as binding on all believers.

From this point on and from time to time, the canon of Scripture grew and finally resulted in the book we call the Bible. The various councils of early church history added further instructions and admonitions but, clearly, as Luther so well illustrated, the Bible was to be taken as the ultimate authority in matters of the Faith.

But while God has given us an essential Primer in His Word, He clearly expects us to continue to pursue knowledge and wisdom with His Word as the foundational guide. For example, a legitimate question concerning the Suicide is not clearly answered in Scripture along with a host of other questions. Councils are clearly still needed to address legitimate questions of the Faith.

It is equally clear that with the growing body of knowledge throughout history, some changes in earlier dogmas must allow of accommodation to more contemporary needs and challenges. We may no longer be overly concerned about meat offered to idols but the guiding principle, as so well illustrated by Paul, of that early decision in Jerusalem is still valid. And that principle upon which Paul became so eloquent is a Spiritual one; it is not one of the Letter of the Law.

For example, the use or not of actual wine in celebrating the Lord's sacrifice and the method of baptism continue to be a battleground among the brethren. Why? Even in Paul's time some could eat meat sacrificed to idols and some could not. Times have changed but the need to pursue knowledge and wisdom has not, the principle of acting in a spirit of charity toward others has not.

Paul certainly makes the position of women in the churches clear yet some churches seem to be able to completely ignore the very Word of God in this respect. Why? Obviously they don't accept Paul's words as the words of God.

If the Council of Jerusalem proved anything, it set the precedent that the individual is not expected to come to conclusions binding on others on such matters. Answers are to be found in the agreement and consensus of leaders and the Holy Spirit in harmony.

As a consequence, I do not place myself, as an individual, in a contradictory position by raising questions and suggesting possible answers *ex cathedra.* I know the answers to such questions must be found and accepted on the same basis as that early example.

Jesus did say that where two or three are gathered together in his name, he is in their midst. May I suggest that answers to these present questions I am raising might be initiated in just such a manner with such small numbers in agreement?

In science we have to confront anomalies, things that seem paradoxical to the present system of knowledge that cannot explain such things. We recognize, therefore, that more knowledge, more learning is needed for an explanation.

It is tragic that in the area of theology men fail to recognize this so very apparent fact. I would suggest that God, in His wisdom, left many legitimate questions unanswered so that we would study and search for answers. Just as any earthly parent delights in a child's earnest learning, so God must be with us as His children. To think that such a seeking of knowledge is limited to searching the Scriptures is indeed foolish.

God's Word, as I said, should be viewed as a Primer, a foundation of knowledge, not the answer to all questions but pointing the correct way to finding answers. There is a Spirit of the Word that God says transcends the literal written word. The Spirit of the Word therefore, as God says, gives life whereas the literal word kills. For example, if God's natural creation leaves men without excuse for not believing in Him, it well behooves men to seek knowledge in that very creation which declares the invisible attributes of God the Creator.

Because of the Hubble telescope, astronomers have discovered there are not enough Red Dwarves to account for gravity, a previously held theory. Theoretical Black matter or some other material has yet to be discovered, therefore, to account for gravity. Also, because of Hubble, astronomers now estimate the age of the universe at 8, not 16 billion years.

As a result of the Hubble telescope, more scientists than ever are speculating about the possibility that God Himself has some force or power undiscoverable to us that holds the universe together, a cosmic glue that is beyond our powers of discovery. Whether or no, the search for, and speculation about possible answers, is exciting.

The search for answers, for knowledge, should be exciting. Perhaps such an approach to the Lord and His Creation, His plans for our future, might encourage some of the very excitement so badly lacking in churches. Ted Turner was right about one thing when asked his view of religion and the churches: Boring! As I've often said myself, if the churches could make heaven as exciting as hell they would be packed!

Hebrews 6:1,2 is good advice in this regard. But when will the churches stop playing Sunday school and get down to the realities of life itself? The old stories of faith and ancient victories need to be taught to the young. But to rehash the dusty, musty tales every Sunday and pretend an application to the realities of today is a travesty easily seen by the worldliest individuals.

To try to substitute enthusiasm for knowledge and the excitement of true discovery won't work either. You might give the impression of having a good time but, like the results of drinking too much, tomorrow morning will come and with it the headache; the party's over and nothing of value to show for it.

When the pabulum of such teaching common to the contemporary churches is simply supplied a garnish and expected to sustain the adult something is missing: The Meat! As a result, the churches become a sad joke when it comes to real learning and real knowledge and people stay away in droves or go to the sects and cults which at least offer partial hope of explanations to the questions of life the churches ignore or are not capable or qualified to deal with.

It should be an easily recognized fact that the human race has made tremendous advances in knowledge throughout history. Sadly, it is admitted; we have not shown such an advance in wisdom or compassion. In fact, we seem to be retrogressing in these areas.

But my point is that God surely expects us to grow up in the acquisition and application of knowledge and wisdom; as Paul said, "When I was a child, I acted like a child. When I became a man, I put away childish things." The churches seem to have been intent on turning the vice of childishness into a virtue of prejudicial ignorance in too many cases like fighting over wine and modes of baptism while a suffering world goes to hell. To honestly formulate those questions of eternal import and find suitable answers to today's needs requires adult maturity, not childishness.

Make no mistake, there are many Biblical, theological questions with which churchmen and scholars still wrestle which are worthy of continued study. And I continue to revel in such questions and the seeking of answers. But the questions I raise are not answered in Scripture. For example, why the death of babies? That is a legitimate question. And while the vast majority of believers would say the question admits of no answer but conjecture based on some nebulous faith or hope of an answer beyond the grave, it is ignored that the question of Gentile believers could have been treated in just such a manner. But it was not! And men, in cooperation with the Holy Spirit, came up with an answer.

Perhaps this singular question about babies cannot be answered. But too many others go begging that I am convinced can be. And, of course, I supply some examples of such questions:

In the temptation, Eve saw that the fruit of the tree of the knowledge of good and evil was good for food, pleasing to the eye and desirable for gaining wisdom. Now what was it, exactly, that gave the fruit of this tree this last characteristic and how did Eve perceive such a thing?

Another Bible question: It would seem that man was a vegetarian prior to the Flood. But in Genesis the 9th chapter, man is given meat to eat as well (though prohibited from eating it raw). What changed? Why did God make such a change in the diet of men?

I find such questions intriguing. But they are not the kind of questions that call down the fire and ire of the brethren. The question of tax-exempt status for the churches, ah, that is another matter.

I was called by Gary North a Self ex-communicated heretic because of a most foundational question I raised in my first book: Is God capable of error? I carried it even further; I asked if God has admitted of making mistakes?

Even the non-religious world trembles at such a question being raised! But there it is. Small wonder Gary took such vehement exception and consigned me to the outer reaches and the fires of hell.

The question might be even considered frivolous except for its source: Me. I'm a studied academic with a Ph. D.; I'm a believer in God, of a hereafter, in a heaven to be gained and a hell to shun. Therefore the source (me) of the question is a serious one and the question to be taken seriously as Gary North quickly realized.

What qualifies the questioner is something that must distinguish how seriously we take the question. Has he enough knowledge and wisdom to take the question seriously and reasonably expect you to do so as well? Is he qualified enough to make it a legitimate question of honest inquiry as opposed to idle speculation or merely attempting to be argumentative and divisive?

The answer to such a question is, obviously, of the greatest and most enormous import. If God Himself is capable of error, we might very well tremble at the consequences of such a thing. But viewed as an honest question, it might well result in discussion of things that would lead to discovery in other areas as well. Simply dismissed, it results in nothing but continued ignorance of the very nature of God Himself and He may very well hold us accountable for this failure in seeking truth.

Before I pursue this question any further I must point out the single most disturbing element of the question: Is an act of love to be considered a mistake when the results are blasted by the betrayal of that love? If the motive is pure and the objective is to love sacrificially not knowing if the object of such love will prove worthy or reciprocate in returning that love or betraying it, can we rightly condemn the resulting failure and it's consequences as an error, a mistake on the part of the Lover?

The historicity of betrayal of love in regards to the human race begins in that Garden of both promise and infamy. What began as an act of love resulted in death; such is always the case when innocence is blasted by the intrusion of a third party whether Satan or a seducing adulterer. The consequences of the betrayal of God's love have been monstrous; the death sentence incurred by such betrayal, the host of miseries the natural creation itself suffers along with mankind, the ultimate need for those who believe of the sacrifice of the Son of God to redeem mankind.

The question is whether an act of love resulted in being a stupid mistake or does the guilt and the consequences of the betrayal of that love rest squarely on the betrayer? If so, the purity of the motive may absolve the Lover but the consequences of the act remain. The Lover can hardly take any pleasure in those consequences and, in fact, may be powerless to ameliorate them.

I may love someone with all my heart but I cannot always save them from the consequences of the betrayal of my love. Am I then, to be blamed for making a mistake in choosing an object of my love when betrayal leads to misery for both me and the object of my love? I have had multiple marriages resulting in multiple divorces. Did I make a mistake in marrying these women? The fact that the marriages were blasted by adultery carried heavy consequences of the betrayal that could not be prevented. But since love was the motive in marrying, was marriage itself a mistake, an error?

I could easily be blamed for errors in judgment in choosing women who would betray me. But who in their right mind would actually come forth and say to me at the time: This woman is going to betray you? No one has that necessary crystal ball. Love takes a risk every time it chooses an object of that love.

The marriage relationship is to be one of love and trust. When the marriage bed is defiled, all that love has tried to build comes crashing down and in many cases the innocent, such as children, suffer terribly. But who can ever tell whether their love and trust will be betrayed, whether the object of our love will prove worthy or not? Yet, to risk it all on love seems to be the inherent characteristic of God and those of us who, made in His image, take the same risk.

Error, mistake, or something else: thus the need to honestly address the question. Another point needs to be considered as well. I would suggest that even as we cannot tell whether our love will be betrayed, neither could God. Obviously no one would choose to love a betrayer. And, once betrayed, how to deal with the consequences? In some cases, since love keeps trying, we may be able to offer some help even to the betrayer. But our help is going to be limited due to many unforeseen and unanticipated consequences of the betrayal.

The ultimate betrayal of the love relationship such as adultery in marriage results in death, the death of the relationship. Something has been broken that cannot ever possibly be mended. Forgiveness will not undo the betraying act. It stands forever. For this reason adultery and death are the only two legitimate reasons given by God for the ending of the marriage relationship. Keeping these fundamental questions and facts in mind, I now plunge into that area which has caused me so much grief among the brethren. I can only hope that some will have an open mind to the honesty of the question.

For the Christian, the search for answers into the nature of God is a fundamental one. Yet, if the search is limited by Blind Orthodoxy, by ignorance and prejudice, we must live with the results just as we live with the failure in Luther's time to honestly seek answers to the questions he raised.

Yet, perhaps the answers to other questions might well be found in searching out an answer to this one, primary question. For example, the questions of pain and suffering, of sin and disease, of injustice and the prospering of the wicked, the death of babies, of suicide and the lack of conscience in some individuals, of some of the anomalies of science and history, of life itself might hinge on the answer to this singular question of such import.

It can hardly be accepted that God planned such misery in our lives and His natural creation; that he would do so intentionally would seem to make Him a monster beyond human comprehension. Yet, we are asked to believe that God is compassionate and loving. I don't find a satisfactory solution to this seeming paradox, this enigma, this anomaly apart from errors in the creative planning and work.

Speaking only for myself and because of the many mistakes I have made out of love and loneliness and the consequent tragedy, pain and grief of the betrayal of misplaced love and trust, I am more than willing to accord God the same errors from love and compassion; and as God Himself does, I will continue to risk it all on love rather than give in to a vile spirit of revenge and bitter callousness.

Does God admit of making an error in His creation of man? He was pained in His heart that he had done so. But, since love always risks it all, I'm prepared to accept the Biblical account that God, once more, risked it all again on Noah. And did Noah turn out to be perfect? Not by any definition short of the condition of his heart toward God.

David was called a man after God's own heart. Talk about imperfections! In how many instances did David fail of God's expectations for him? Yet, the love relationship remained intact throughout it all; and so with many other examples in Scripture.

God further admits of His Spirit in opposition to evil men, of striving against such men and warns that He will not always do so. Wherever we encounter strife, we encounter moves and countermoves not unlike a chess game. Obviously the possibilities of errors in such striving are extremely complex.

And mistakes will be made. It is said that wars are won primarily by those that make the fewer mistakes. My trust in God remains, irrespective of my heretical view that God and His people will win because we will make fewer mistakes with love as our guiding principle rather than hatred. The enemy, I believe, has an enormous, fatally terminal weak spot in not being able to comprehend sacrificial love as spelled out in I Corinthians 13.

I would further suggest that we might find answers to the questions of the creation of Satan and God's plans for us in eternity by pursuing this course of inquiry. Is God's creation a once for all thing or has He made the very stars our future domain, a future that includes us as gods (Psalm 82:6 and John 10:34) to enter into that very on-going creation?

According to the Bible, God took counsel when He created man. He said: "Let us create man in our image." In other words, there were others involved in this decision. A question naturally presents itself: With whom was God taking counsel? A council of the sons of God as described elsewhere in Scripture?

Dogmatic, systematic Christian theology has maintained this was a meeting of God the Father, God the Son and God the Holy Spirit. But other possibilities suggest themselves that are ignored or glossed by commentators. In the Creation itself, we read that God created the heavens and the earth. He further said Let there be light, etc. and these things came into being.

One idea certainly is suggested by Scripture and rational thought: that God, as the Master Builder, did not have to, of necessity, put His hands to the work. Just as a general contractor may say he built a bridge or building, it is the vast number of workman under his supervision who did the actual work. Michelangelo gets the credit in spite of the number of workmen under his supervision.

That an angelic world existed before the creation of man is a tenet of Scripture. We are told very little of this spiritual domain but enough is suggested to grant possibilities in a number of directions.

So, in spite of church dogma, the council held before man's creation may have been something other, or more, than that of Father, Son and Holy Spirit. One thing is held as a constant: That God is the giver of life, that He breathed life into Adam and all other creatures, that He, alone, has ultimate power and authority.

Christ, in turn, says that he will make us joint heirs with him in eternity of all that the Father has given him. An astounding future awaits us on the basis of this promise! How very restrictive the churches have been in not exploring the possibilities suggested in this respect in all the various dimensions that present themselves.

However the churches face the dilemma of addressing such possibilities by their too narrow view of so many other things which blind them to such an exciting adventure and exercise of the mind and God's marvelous gift of imagination. Heaven is not the boring place, in my opinion, that the churches would have Ted Turner believe.

Just before the flood, we read: "God's heart was pained because he had made man, because every inclination and thought of man had become evil continually."

I asked the question in another book whether God didn't risk it all on love. I asked whether in loneliness, in seeking someone to love Him and be loved by Him, Love always risks it all. The risk of betrayal of that love is a constant; no amount of years with another (as I well know from personal experience) is a guarantee at some point our love will not be betrayed.

God was going to destroy man from the face of the earth but He found one man, Noah, and He decided to risk it all, once more, on love. Was God Himself learning something about love and betrayal in all of this risking? Throughout the Biblical story, we find God loving men who betrayed His expectations of them. Risking by loving in the constant hope that One will be found who will not betray, who will prove worthy of that love.

The Biblical literalist has a real problem. God says in one place: "My ways are not your ways and my thoughts are not your thoughts." The literalist might conclude we have no hope of knowing the mind and heart of God. If we accept this passage of Scripture as a black and white sum cum all of God, it would automatically negate any attempt to seek answers to honest questions. Such, clearly, is not God's intent.

Much of Scripture becomes contradictory if we are forced to accept literalism in every case. We are called of God gods ourselves, we are to have the mind of Christ, we are told to be perfect even as God is perfect. A legitimate question comes immediately to mind. A question of what God means by perfect?

Certainly perfection is not monotony. On this all would agree. My own conclusion of many years is that God means something other then man's dictionary definition of perfection. God has called some men perfect who had obvious flaws of character. My own perception of this thing God calls perfect has to do with the heart and its motives, not an infallible character nor the inability to make mistakes.

God has called Himself perfect by this definition; not man's. Nowhere in Scripture does God claim infallibility, omniscience, to be omnipotent or omnipresent. These are man-made claims of attributes of God, not His. God is perfect by His definition of perfection; not man's.

It is in the nature of man, created in God's image, to create, to build, to dream, hope and love. And, yes, to hate. It seems foolish to me to deny that God as the Master Creator is ever satisfied that He has either finished with all that is in His mind to do or that He is ever completely satisfied that He has done His ultimate best.

It is natural for the artist to continue to strive for the best of which he is capable. That is a part of the divine nature. No matter the flaws in a masterpiece, it remains a masterpiece in spite of imperfections. A beautiful woman remains a masterpiece of God's creative heart and effort though this work of art may be terribly flawed by any number of factors such as foul language, ill manners, coldness and vanity.

As a mere man, I appreciate beautiful women. My own daughter, Karen, is indisputably the most beautiful woman in the world. But her beauty is enhanced tremendously by her utter lack of vanity and her natural quietness and shyness. Yes, she has flaws that her father recognizes. But the flaws in her case only accentuate her natural beauty.

Is she perfect? Yes, to me her father. Objectively only a fool would call any beautiful woman or other work of art perfect. But there is a perfection beyond the dictionary definition; it is that perfection of God that allows of the flaws of attempting, of trying and working and building on the knowledge of errors, mistakes made in the creative process.

So it is that I can call my own, beautiful daughter perfect. As with so many other beautiful women it has been both my privilege and, too often, heartbreak to know, there is a perfection of beauty that goes beyond the individual. I can easily appreciate the genius of some masters and their work while despising the character of the artist. But that standard of beauty, the genius of the creator of such beauty goes far beyond the human agency of its creation.

I can appreciate the beauty of God's natural creation while mourning nature red in tooth and claw, I can immerse myself in a truly great work of art irrespective of its flaws, whether a beautiful woman, a painting or masterpiece of literature remembering that it isn't always the heat and passion of the flame that draws the moth.

As a poet, a romantic, I have been drawn to many beautiful women only to be betrayed many times. I have written extensively on this theme and won't belabor it here except to provide a further example of the errors of love.

It was God Himself who said: "It is not good for the man to be alone." And so God created Eve and, as some wit said: It has been hell ever since! Be that as it may, men and women are hard pressed to find a satisfactory substitute for their love and affection and we may not like the rules but there is no changing them. Certainly there is nothing like the relationship between men and women that so calls forth both the best and the worst of each. The results of making a mistake in love; sometimes catastrophic, even leading to murder and suicide.

Obviously I would discount any motive but the purity of heart in God's love. Concerning men and women, on the other hand, we have the problem of lust to consider. The Bible says "when lust has conceived it brings forth sin and sin when it is finished brings forth death." Too true, and we aren't talking about just physical death. How many an empire has been toppled by such a thing, how many of the rich and powerful have been destroyed by just such a mechanism. Yet, the question remains of just how the mechanism of lust works in the whole scheme of things, in the natural creation and the controls instituted by God and a society in an attempt to contain the natural lust of men and women for the larger benefit of a society.

We usually come to such questions with a definite mindset that, unless we are very careful, is assured to predispose us to predetermined answers. Yet, any scholar of literature knows of the science of hermeneutics, that scientific discipline which teaches us to interpret (exegesis) writings on the basis of a number of empirical factors such as the times, the history, the mores, even the geography and other things which have to be taken into account when attempting an interpretation of anything we read. This is especially essential to the Bible as well as Shakespeare or the orations of Cicero and the histories of Tacitus.

Most come to writing such as the Bible with a predetermined mind set (prejudice) that colors their interpretation of what they read. It might be that of the Roman Catholic or Baptist, even an agnostic, but unless they are schooled in disciplined thought processes, in the necessary skills of scholarship, many hurtful ideas are set forth as personal, or organized, dogma that have no basis in fact.

For example, Paul says a woman is not to pray with her head covered. Do the churches follow this dictum? No. What changed? Granting that Paul, in this context, is talking about customs and practices among the churches, he seems pretty dogmatic about this particular thing.

Paul said Timothy should drink a little wine for his health. Many fundamental churches deny this advice and even make themselves appear foolish in their childish attempts to make this wine, like that of Jesus' miracle in Cana, into unfermented grape juice. An obvious prejudice against reason and the reality of Scripture opposed to the doctrines of men.

In the area of human behavior, all of us can easily set aside Reason from our hearts. And the heart is very deceptive. I have fallen in love with women who, objectively, were no good for me. Of course, they made the same mistake you might say. Men and women seem to be able to do this with amazing regularity. The recognition of the need to deal with this thing called falling in love has resulted in some societies utilizing things like the dowry or arranged marriages to circumvent the often foolish desires of the heart.

Follow your heart might make good romance and poetry but the results are often less than desirable. Many hurtful relationships result from such a thing. But, how to set it aside; you simply cannot; it is there and won't go away. The "I have to have him or her" syndrome is a reality and must be faced honestly. Since I have fallen heir to this same kind of thinking in too many instances, I have to recognize the part the lust of the flesh has played in some of my own hasty decisions. But the part that loneliness in our lives plays in such things cannot be overestimated.

Yet, it was God who created us with the desire for sex, for family and children, though sex I believe to be a part of the curse God pronounced upon Adam and Eve, falling most heavily upon Eve. As a man, I have the need to be the protector and provider as well. This certainly comes into conflict with contemporary thinking about some so-called and ephemeral thing called equality between the sexes. I have written reams on this subject and won't belabor it here (Ask for my book: Birds With Broken Wings for example). I simply call it to attention for the purpose of raising the point that such things as lust and loneliness make us prone to error in too many cases and must be taken into account when we consider love, and the corruption of love, in all its dimensions with the concomitant potential for mistakes.

I don't think we can believe God would divorce reason from the heart in His decisions. Yet, the best motives and planning even on God's part has resulted in dreadful betrayal and consequences of that betrayal of love and trust. There was a time when Satan was great in God's Kingdom. But we are told he fell heir to the sin of pride, betrayed God and was expelled from his high estate. Some things have never changed in this regard and our own human condition mirrors much of this even now. Certainly the battlefield of the World, the Flesh and the Devil has not changed; these remain a constant.

No one would be so foolish as to claim to have the long view of the future that God has. His planning and creations obviously are for the benefit of His children, those who will inherit eternal life. But, if eye has not seen nor ear heard, neither has entered into the heart of man, the things God has planned for His children, it most certainly invites the most avid speculation of what those things might consist of.

Here again, an investigation of the natural creation and the mind of men at least give us clues together with the things we find in our basic Primer, the Bible. If we are led to look with wonder, even longing, at the stars and we see them as much more than cold points of light in the vast darkness of space, couldn't it be that we intuit those worlds out there as the proper domain for us in eternity?

My own conjectures have led me to believe that God, in love, has a plan and design which will include our entering into His on-going creation which would incorporate our immortality with the work like His own of exploring, creating, building on a scope obviously beyond present human comprehension.

Does such a plan necessitate beings who, through sin and suffering, trials and tribulations, the mistakes made in simply trying different things, betrayal of love and trust with the concomitant forgiveness of such, learn the necessary skills, love and compassion which are essential to such plans that God has for us in the future?

It might be well at this point to address the question that long prevented me from undertaking the task of writing about these things: Just who is Don Heath to think he is the one to do so; granting the fact that I may be uniquely qualified to do so as I said at the beginning of this essay, I will provide the following elaboration.

The Apostle Paul gloried in his infirmities so that God alone would receive the glory for the work the Apostle did for the sake of The Gospel and others. In a sense, I suppose my recognition of myself as a badly flawed man might serve the same purpose in my own attempts to help others through the same mechanism of The Gospel in loving others and trying to harmonize those things which separate those that call themselves Christian. It may well be that Paul and I, as such notorious sinners (he called himself the chief of sinners; I'm not that humble) might be such like instruments in our unsuitability for the task in order that God might get the credit, not us.

So it is that I took courage, not pride, from those very unsuitable things in my own life which would disqualify me from any recognition by the brethren for the task at hand, turning cursing into blessing, and like Peter, that sinful and profane man, serve The Lord and others in all due humility knowing that in me is no good thing apart from The Lord.

Phony humility, false pride and false modesty? Hardly. The public record speaks for itself. In this respect my life is an open book and a pretty shabby book at that, filled with failure upon failure. I have said it in print a number of times: I don't know how one man, in one lifetime, could have made as many mistakes as I have. And this could well be just one more.

But, like Paul, I didn't come to this task, this thinking in heretical ways, in a moment of time. It took years of meditation, study, and life experiences to make this decision real in my life. Paul, after the Damascus experience, had to go into the desert of Arabia alone (Galatians 1:17) re-thinking, questioning and evaluating many things he had once accepted as truth. I found the desert and mountain wilderness areas very needful to myself in this respect as well as my habit of stargazing.

And, like Paul, once the hurdles of Blind Orthodoxy had been overcome in my own thinking, the real work presented itself. And it's been a hard-going and extremely lonely task ever since. Not a job anyone would apply for but, again like Paul, I happened to fit the job description apparently.

I have made the point in other books and writings that the relationships between men and women are of the utmost importance in attempting understanding and answers to both the human condition and the relationship we have with The Lord. I include one excerpt from my book on Birds to make my point:

It is easy to understand the frustration of both men and women when it comes to this thing called romance. They both know it is out there somewhere but seem to find it the most elusive thing in their lives. Like gold, it is hard to find.

I believe a lot of the frustration largely derives from the fact that women know men are capable of romance, creativity and great sensitivity. After all, the preponderance of the greatest artists, composers, writers, poets are men. And these men derive the greatest of their inspiration from the other half of humanity, women.

A great deal of the frustration on both sides is the further fact that we live in a very materialistic and hedonistic society which seems to place a very low value on virtue, a predominate characteristic of those men and women who seek real love and romance in their lives.

So apart from sex, I want a Lady and these are increasingly hard to find. More than that, I want a Lady without a betraying heart. The Romantic that delights in giving his lady flowers, delights in writing about his lady's charms and attributes, the Romantic that finds the inspiration his heart seeks in that special woman, that virtuous woman, that Lady, wants a great deal more than SEX. Because of this, I'm somewhat more difficult to seduce than most men. Not impossible, just more difficult. The reasons for this will become clear as you get into the book itself.

As a boy, I have had a pet skunk and a pet porcupine. Both were difficult pets to live with. Not impossible, but difficult. Certain accommodations had to be made of necessity because of the distinctive, peculiar natures of the little beasts. So it has been with my experience with all the different women in my life.

Unhappily, while I often found the accommodations to these beautiful and delightful creatures difficult at times, I never found it impossible. They, on the other hand, found me impossible. But I have a marvelous tenacity and am patient to a fault; I refuse to give up and bow to Clemens' judgment that men and women are natural born enemies. I do, somewhat, subscribe to my own finding that the relationship is more often that of armed neutrality...

I want to intrude a quote from one of the chapters of this book at this point:

"Another of the many How To books on the market, this one written by a woman, Marianne Williamson, includes this statement: Some men know that a light touch of the tongue, running from a woman's toes to her ears, lingering in the softest way possible in various places in between, given often enough and sincerely enough, would add immeasurably to world peace."

Two things: This may not, in fact, be overdrawn, and, removed from erotica to the purpose of God in men cherishing their wives, it is a valid statement. It is at least a shade ironic to find a woman making my point for me in this respect. The point being that if men and women would give attention to those things which bring out the best in each, undoubtedly the world would be a lovelier and safer place, especially in the cherishing of children and family. How could it be otherwise when, in fact, a man and woman cherish each other? Compatibility, as God intended, not Competition, is the antidote to the plagues of divorce, adultery and the destruction of family and family values.

Unfortunately, men and women are too busy in tongue lashing each other rather than love making. It is an evil system, led of evil men and women that has betrayed the poetic connection between men and women…"

As you can readily see from the above, not all my writing is of a distinctly religious nature and this has not had a little to do with my alienation from the brethren. But I steadfastly refuse to make my life in The Lord a religious life. I hold to what one lady told me: "I like the way you don't put God in a box and you insist that He is more human than the churches give Him credit." Amen; would that I could convince the brethren to be more human as well.

As an undergraduate Litt. Major I reveled in the great literature and art of the world. I was, and am, a poet and romantic. I always will be. I chose Human Behavior for my doctoral program because of my fascination with the mind of man, my intense interest in why people do the things they do. I even came up with a theory of a mathematical model of human behavior. I still work on this occasionally. It was most natural, as a result of my varied interests in the humanities and the hard sciences like physics and astronomy to try to make sense of so many chaotic things, to search for relationships that would contribute to understanding and answers to puzzling questions about people and our universe.

That the relationships between men and women would capture much of the interest of the poet and romantic is understandable. But, like Thoreau, I don't believe the search for understanding and answers can be left to those specialists like seminary professors or so-called *professional educators*. A much broader view of things is necessary than such people seem capable.

I'll conclude this initial essay concerning my call for a New Systematic Theology with a very human side of myself taken from the last chapter of Birds:

The chase is still a thrill and that Safari of the Soul still commands my interest and attention. I've made a few enemies along the way but more friends. Those that have taken a vehement exception to some of my opinions concerning what the relationship between men and women should be generally want the license to do business as usual. That is, they don't want anyone to condemn their part in the loss of virtue in our nation and in our society.

She was a very lovely, blonde woman. She had an interesting comment during an evening while we dined and talked about romance: "Don, I don't really believe there is anything such as a 'slut'. I think women have the same desires as men in the sexual department."

I wasn't sure how to respond to her statement. By the time we had gotten around to this dinner date I had come to know a few things about her. That she was opening the door to a sexual encounter was obvious. Was her statement simply a justification to get to bed as quickly as possible without any game playing? If so, I had to applaud her audacity.

But I also knew she was wrong in the sense that there are both men and women who would qualify for that ignoble appellation. I wasn't going to judge her opinion in the respect that a society should never condemn women for the same behavior that would be smiled about in regard to men, the double standard hypocrisy so rampant through the ages. I have recognized the same needs in a woman that a man has. But I have also recognized that in spite of the depraved mores of a society, there are those that hold out for the better way, the better standard of virtue. But I'm reminded of that Dark Side too often and this brings it's own kind of despair into my life.

I'm sitting with an extraordinarily beautiful, young woman. She is a prostitute. I've suspected as much in spite of the fact that she has tried to hide it from me. I have never let her know that I am aware of her business. To me, she is a marvelously sensitive and intelligent woman. We have shared so much of the matters of the heart, of romance and poetry that she has come to look forward to our meetings and has wondered why I haven't tried to reach her sexually.

But in the short time that we have been seeing each other, I am far more interested in discovering whether she can respond to the kindness and gentleness of a man who sees her as a beautiful, sensitive and intelligent woman, not a whore or an object of lust. It is at one point in a story that I am relating to her that the tears suddenly come to her eyes. She shakes her head in bewildered surprise, wiping at her eyes. She is genuinely astonished to find them there.

"Don, I can't remember the last time I have cried." And I believe her. And I'm reminded, once more, of the tremendous responsibility I carry when my words can move such a young woman's heart to tears.

She lowers her head and in a soft murmur says "How I wish I had met you a long time ago." I have given her my handkerchief and putting my arm around her I draw her close to me. What can I tell her? I wonder, sadly, at the truth of that in such a young life. Yet I know she has lived a lifetime of use and abuse in just her short span.

I'm not some older man with some young thing. I'm long past the point of feeling flattered that such a young woman could want a man my age. I'm too familiar with the reasons young women like this are willing to settle for such, are willing to trade their youth and beauty for genuine, responsible caring. NO! Dammit, I'm angry, not flattered. I'm angry at the system of evil that brings young women to such a point of despair in their lives.

I'm a man who doesn't think as other men. And I am in pain with her that I'm not twenty years younger, that we didn't meet when I was younger before she had given up hope of a decent man, I'm in pain for her because I know the thoughts that are going through her tormented mind, that psychosis of grief of a life lived for all the wrong reasons. They are the same thoughts that would torment me if our situations were reversed.

Thoughts of my own daughters come to mind as I sit there holding this beautiful, young woman. What if their choices had been the same? What if they had been cursed with a father who didn't care; worse, if they had had an abusive father or molesting step-father as was the case in this young woman's life?

I recall another lovely young woman in tears who simply wanted some one to love her. I had been playing guitar in one of the local clubs when we met. I couldn't miss seeing the despondent mood she was in. After the set I joined her and she poured out her story. She had just broken up with a drug addict who had finally tried to sell her into prostitution to support his habit. I know this story all too well. I've seen it happen too often.

In her pain she wanted me to take her somewhere and make love to her. She said she didn't care if I had a condom, just please, make her believe she was loved! She just wanted some human contact, some one to make her feel wanted for herself. It hadn't taken any sum of years to bring her to this point; she couldn't have been more than 23 years old. It doesn't take that many years to bring people to that point of grief and despair; of the kind of killing loneliness that would even risk AIDS just to feel loved even if you have to deceive yourself that someone cares!

The old song plays in my mind: "If that isn't love it will have to do, until the real thing comes along." And just what are the chances of the real thing in such young women's lives?

My Lady In Red carries my letter in her purse. She showed it to me and said she often looks at it when she gets depressed and despairs of things getting any better. She still suffers the curse of beauty but is learning to cope with it. My letter, she says, is often the one thing that she depends on when things are really too much for her. I can't think of more humbling praise for me, an ordinary man, to be of that kind of help to such a beautiful, wonderful, sensitive woman. Thank you, My Lady In Red.

This has been a tough book to write- harder to live. But there will be more as long as I stay above ground. I can still play and sing. I'm sitting on the porch of the home of a beautiful, young woman. I've been helping her by working on her car. But a friend comes by with a guitar he is thinking of selling and wants me to give him some idea of its value.

I tune it and start playing and singing an old Glenn Campbell song. The girl's little boy comes and sits beside me, enthralled with the music; a magic moment with grease under my fingernails and the thrill of making music for the boy. His mother comes out. She wasn't aware of my musical ability. She watches with the tenderest look and smile imaginable. It melts my heart. I can only guess at her thoughts of what might be possible. She knows we are in love though we have never been intimate; we have even said the words. But there's no future for us together. I'm too old for her and the boy. And I remain the poet with whom women fall in love but can't seem to abide or live with.

So the hunt goes on. I will hold out for that better way in the hope that I will find that One who will be the answer to my prayers, that rare woman who will be able to live with and abide the poet, the impractical man with no common sense who still sees more in the stars than cold points of light in the darkness.

I'll still love the flowers though most of the scent and color are missed with no one with whom to share them. I'll still enjoy a good thunderstorm and the freshness of the grass and trees washed clean by the rain. The birds and animals, the mountains, sea and desert, a pristine trout stream in the wilderness, all of God's beautiful if sometimes inconvenient creation will still hold its magical charm and stir the heart of the best of the man, the child within me, who will not yield to the vain philosophies of adults and their too often distorted realities.

And whoever you are, wherever you are, please come quickly. Neither of us has time to waste. That greater work still awaits the two of us and September is nearly past; winter fast approaches.

But if we should fail to find each other, if I, in fact, remain only the chronicler, the scribe of encounters with beautiful women and lost, betrayed loves, I will do it though without joy. As I have said; Who would choose to wear such a mantle? But if it fits?

Even at that I will have had the better part of real love and romance than those who have been the users and betrayers; that I know full well. But while the memories will be real enough, I'll never deceive myself that they will ever take the place of you in my arms and in my life.

And this, folks, is real life; not a religious exercise.

About the Author

Samuel D. G. Heath, Ph. D.

Other books in print by the author:

BIRDS WITH BROKEN WINGS
DONNIE AND JEAN, an angel's story
TO KILL A MOCKINGBIRD, a critique on behalf of children
HEY, GOD! What went wrong and when are You going to fix it?
THE AMERICAN POET WEEDPATCH GAZETTE for 2008
THE AMERICAN POET WEEDPATCH GAZETTE for 2007
THE AMERICAN POET WEEDPATCH GAZETTE for 2006
THE AMERICAN POET WEEDPATCH GAZETTE for 2005
THE AMERICAN POET WEEDPATCH GAZETTE for 2004
THE AMERICAN POET WEEDPATCH GAZETTE for 2003
THE AMERICAN POET WEEDPATCH GAZETTE for 2002
THE AMERICAN POET WEEDPATCH GAZETTE for 2001
THE AMERICAN POET WEEDPATCH GAZETTE for 2000
THE AMERICAN POET WEEDPATCH GAZETTE for 1999
THE AMERICAN POET WEEDPATCH GAZETTE for 1998
THE AMERICAN POET WEEDPATCH GAZETTE for 1997
THE AMERICAN POET WEEDPATCH GAZETTE for 1995-1996

Presently out of print:
IT SHOULDN'T HURT TO BE A CHILD!
WOMEN, BACHELORS, IGUANA RANCHING, AND RELIGION
THE MISSING HALF OF HUMANKIND: WOMEN!
THE MISSING HALF OF PHILOSOPHY: WOMEN!
THE LORD AND THE WEEDPATCHER
CONFESSIONS AND REFLECTIONS OF AN OKIE INTELLECTUAL or Where the heck is Weedpatch?
MORE CONFESSIONS AND REFLECTIONS OF AN OKIE INTELLECTUAL

Dr. Heath was born in Weedpatch, California. He has worked as a manual laborer, mechanic, machinist, peace officer, engineer, pastor, builder and developer, educator, social services practitioner (CPS), professional musician and singer. He is also a private pilot and a columnist.
Awarded American Legion Scholarship and is an award winning author.
He has two surviving children: Daniel and Michael. His daughters Diana and Karen have passed away.
Academic Degrees:
Ph. D. – U.S.I.U., San Diego, CA.
M. A. – Chapman University, Orange, CA.
M. S. (Eqv.) — U.C. Extension at UCLA. Los Angeles, CA.
B. V. E. – C.S. University. Long Beach, CA.
A. A. – Cerritos College. Cerritos, CA.

Other Colleges and Universities attended:
Santa Monica Technical College, Biola University, and C.S. University, Northridge.

Dr. Heath holds life credentials in the following areas:
Psychology, Professional Education, Library Science, English, German, History, Administration (K-12), Administration and Supervision of Vocational Education and Vocational Education-Trade and Industry.

In addition to his work in public education, Dr. Heath started three private schools, K-12, two in California and one in Colorado. His teaching and administrative experience covers every grade level and graduate school.

Comments by some who have read the author's works

Your writing is very important. You are having an impact on lives! Never lose your precious gift of humor. V. T.

You raise a number of issues in your material ... The Church has languished at times under leaders whose theology was more historically systematic than Biblical ... (But) The questions you raise serve as very dangerous doctrines. John MacArthur, a contemporary of the author at Biola/Talbot and pastor of Grace Community Church in Sun Valley.

You have my eternal gratitude for relieving me from the tyranny of religion. D. R.

Before reading your wonderful writings, I had given up hope. Now I believe and anticipate that just maybe things can change for the better. J. D.

I started reading your book, The Lord and the Weedpatcher, and found I couldn't put it down. Uproariously funny, I laughed the whole way through. Thank you so much for lighting up my life! M.G.

Doctor Heath, every man with daughters owes you a debt of gratitude! I have had all three of my girls read your Birds With Broken Wings book. D. W.

I am truly moved by your art! While reading your writing I found a true treasure: Clarity! I felt as if I was truly on fire with the inspiration you invoked! L. B.

You really love women! Thank you for the most precious gift of all, the gift of love. Keep on being you! D. B.

Your writing complements coffee-cup-and-music. I've gotten a sense of your values, as well as a provocativeness that suggests a man both distinguished and truly sensual. Do keep up such vibrant work! E. R.

Some men are merely handsome. You are a beautiful man! One of these days some wise, discerning, smart woman is going to snag you. Make sure she is truly worthy of you. Desirable men like you (very rare indeed) who write so sensitively, compellingly and beautifully are sitting ducks for every designing woman! M. G.

Now, poet, musician, teacher, philosopher, friend, counselor and whatever else you have done in your life, I am finally realizing all the things you say people don't understand about a poet. They see, feel, write and talk differently than the rest of the world. Their glasses seem to be rose colored at times and other times they are blue. There seems to be no black or white in the things they see only soft pastel hues. Others see things as darker colors, but these are not the romantic poets you speak of. C. M.

You are the only man I have ever met who truly understands women! B. J.

Dr. Heath;
You are one of the best writers I've had the privilege to run across. You have been specially gifted for putting your thoughts, ideas, and inspirations to paper (or keyboard), no matter the topic.
Even when in dire straits, your words are strong and true. I look forward to reading many more of your unique writings. T. S.